The Reformation of Ritual

The emergence of Protestantism in early modern Europe led to a re-examination of all liturgical acts. Ecclesiastical rituals were transformed to embody the new version of the Christian faith and to transmit it to the people. In *The Reformation of Ritual* Susan Karant-Nunn explores the function of ritual in early modern German society, and the extent to which it was modified by the Reformation.

Employing anthropological insights, and drawing on extensive archival research, Susan Karant-Nunn outlines the significance of the ceremonial changes. This comprehensive study includes an examination of all major rites of passage: birth, baptism, confirmation, engagement, marriage, the churching of women after childbirth, penance, the Eucharist, and dying. The author argues that the changes in ritual made over the course of the century reflect more than theological shifts; ritual was a means of imposing discipline and had the effect of making the divine less accessible. Church and state cooperated in using ritual as one means of gaining control of the populace.

Taking into account emerging Calvinism as well as the early Lutheran Church, and considering regional variations in religious practice, Susan Karant-Nunn compares the new Protestant observances to the wide-spread Catholic ones of the late Middle Ages. She also draws on primary sources to describe how far the official views were adopted by the laity and the people. *The Reformation of Ritual* provides insight into the politics of reforming religion and into the practices of the wider community in early modern Germany.

Susan C. Karant-Nunn is Professor of History, Portland State University, USA

Christianity and society in the modern world

General editors: Hugh McLeod and Bob Scribner

Also available:

The Jews in Christian Europe
John Edwards

Social discipline in the Reformation
R. Po-Chia Hsia

The Reformation and the visual arts: the Protestant image question in Western and Eastern Europe
Sergiusz Michalski

European religion in the age of great cities
Hugh McLeod

Women and religion in England: 1500–1720
Patricia Crawford

Forthcoming titles:

Calvinism and society
Philip Benedict

Popular evangelicalism 1730–1870
Louis Billington

The clergy in modern Europe
Gregory Freeze

Religion and social change in industrial Britain
David Hempton

Religion and revolution 1400–1650
Michael Baylor

The British missionary movement 1700–1950
Jeff Cox

Representing witchcraft
Charles Zika

Women and religion in early America
Marilyn J. Westerkamp

Christianity and sexuality 1450–1750
Merry E. Wiesner-Hanks

The reformation of ritual

An interpretation of early modern Germany

Susan C. Karant-Nunn

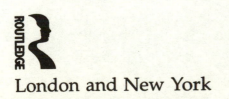

London and New York

First published 1997
by Routledge
11 New Fetter Lane, London EC4P 4EE

Simultaneously published in the USA and Canada
by Routledge
29 West 35th Street, New York, NY 10001

Typeset in Palatino by Routledge
Printed and bound in Great Britain by Mackays of Chatham PLC,
Chatham, Kent.

British Library Cataloguing in Publication Data
A catalogue record for this book is available from the British Library

Library of Congress Cataloguing in Publication Data
A catalogue record for this book is available from the Library of Congress

ISBN 0–415–11337–7

To Jessica and Marianna

Contents

Acknowledgments

Surely every author incurs more debts of gratitude than can ever be repaid. I owe much to the kind staff members of many German archives and libraries who immeasurably facilitated my research. A stay at the Herzog August Bibliothek in Wolfenbüttel, with its collections and accommodations, is always a scholarly idyll. The Fulbright Commission in Germany granted me a research fellowship in 1993–94; and through the good offices of Hans-Christoph Rublack, the University of Tübingen admitted me to its libraries during that year. My colleagues in the Department of History, Portland State University, gave me leave during autumn quarter 1995 to finish writing this book.

I want especially to thank Robert Scribner, who has generously lent his patronage to colleagues around the world, at no small cost to himself in time and energy. The stimulus of his ideas will be apparent. Others, too, read all or parts of the first draft and gave me the benefit of their rich erudition: Sharon A. Carstens, Craig M. Koslofsky, Edward Muir, Gerald Strauss, Lee Palmer Wandel, and Merry E. Wiesner-Hanks. Roderic C. Diman saved me from some egregious mistranslations of Latin. The staff of Routledge publishers have made my part in the publication of this book a happy experience.

As before, my primary debt is to Frederick M. Nunn. He has consistently provided a model of devotion to the active scholarly life.

Portland, Oregon
October 1996

Introduction

Some will think it strange that such an obvious research project has not already been undertaken. A full generation after pioneers like Keith Thomas, Natalie Zemon Davis, and John Bossy introduced historical anthropology to Anglophone specialists in early modern Europe, no study of ritual change in the German Reformation had been done. This begs the question of why not, particularly in view of the fact that the venerable anthropological interest in ritual had already shown itself in myriad essays and books.[1] Furthermore, German scholars have lately engaged in innovative research on the early modern period in their own country—but not on Reformation ritual—or not at length.[2] I think that one reason for this apparent neglect is that the German Reformation has retained its confessional coloring and its intellectual historical approach longer than the equivalent religious movements in other countries. German scholars inside evangelical circles have been reluctant to apply newer methodologies to their subject matter, perhaps fearful that the glare of non-denominational, interdisciplinary scrutiny would undermine their founders' authority; and academics less clearly affiliated by faith have given in to their universities' traditional preference for the study of elite thought and elite institutions. Some of their fellow countrypeople, innovative researchers on early modern social life who do not identify themselves as specialists in the Reformation per se have nibbled away at the edges of the field, unable to ignore the epoch-making and intriguing religious activities of the age. Especially members of this latter group are effecting change in the German university, that bastion of tradition. Karl Lamprecht is commanding respect.[3] In the meantime, non-German scholars, not as often subject to the same restraints, have been freer to concentrate on the social history of the Reformation and have assumed the leadership in applying literary and social scientific theories to early modern religious movements.[4]

The spread of theory from literature, philosophy, and linguistics—not to mention the obvious sociology and anthropology—made me uneasy at first because it presented a mind-boggling array of choices. Implicit, and sometimes explicit, in this array was the initially troubling assertion that the historian invents the past out of whole cloth. In the last ten years, along with numerous of my colleagues, I have gradually come to see theory not as the edge of the abyss but as a stimulus to think about subject matter and about evidence in new ways. I have felt liberated to experiment with interpretation. At the same time, as a frequenter of archives I must agree with the cogently presented position of Joyce Appleby, Lynn Hunt, and Margaret Jacob, who have not only digested but contributed to the historiographic changes of our day. They have called for "practical realism" in our approach to the past, affirming that despite our inability to be objective in some detached, scientifically verifiable way, because we humans share the medium of language, "we can reach out to the world and give a reasonably true description of its contents."[5]

I am content, then, not to arrive at a higher truth with which everyone else will be compelled to agree. I have striven for plausibility in my account of the shape and meaning of early modern rituals. But how does one achieve "plausibility"? When accused of using "an excess of invention" in reconstructing the relationship between Bertrande de Rols and Arnaud du Tilh in *The Return of Martin Guerre*,[6] Natalie Zemon Davis responded by explaining how she used her rich local knowledge of the times, the people, and their ways of looking at the world in filling in the documentary gaps. She "embedd[ed] this story in the values and habits of sixteenth-century French village life and law, to use them to help understand central elements in the story and to use the story to comment back on them..."[7] Just so. In the case of German ritual, no ceremonial "text," no parish visitors' account is either self-evident or penetrable apart from its multilayered context. As the Music Man said, "Ya gotta know the territory." I have used multiple kinds of sources in studying each ritual, including ecclesiastical ordinances, visitation protocols, ritual manuals, visual depictions, the lyrics of hymns, catechisms, sermons, letters, works of theology, and official creeds. I spent time in eleven archives distributed through much of Germany in an effort to balance my prior concentration on Saxony with sources on the West. I relied heavily, too, on printed and secondary sources, including indispensable (if otherwise intended) works of modern theologians and liturgists. I have tried to acquire "rich local knowledge." But knowledge is amoeboid, ever changing its shape. Each new "find" alters the image previously held. That is the historian's existential predicament. I have deliberately avoided the temptation to be drawn into the voluminous printed literature on the territorial politics of church and state, even as I acknowledge that each example I bring forward fits within such a context. My purpose has been to look across Germany at *patterns* of behavior, and in order to achieve this I have overlooked much specialized scholarship. German critics will detect this immediately, for their love of documentation is famous—and in many settings very helpful.

The value of reading anthropological works was that it provided a theoretical framework within which to comprehend better the now conscious, now latent meanings embedded in early modern ritual action. No such framework was by itself entirely relevant, of course, for, as Pierre Bourdieu has affirmed, we can only decode ritual practice "by relating it to the real conditions of its genesis, that is, to the conditions in which its functions, and the means it uses to attain them, are defined."[8] Every ritual, even every ritual instance—if that were possible—must be *located* within the setting that generates it. Even though I have drawn on them only in part, those conceptual schema that I have found particularly helpful are several. All of us have appropriated Arnold van Gennep's "rites of passage" and made them part of our vocabulary. Even the popular press tells us often that baptism, marriage, and funerals are such rites.[9] Victor Turner extends this concept, seeing in ritual a means of resolving conflict and achieving reconciliation (*communitas*), which enjoys certain exemptions from "the norm-governed, institution-alized, abstract nature of social structure."[10] He has explored liminality as an intermediate condition. He sees in rituals symbolic configurations that it is the anthropologist's role to decipher, but at the same time he perceives their embeddedness in a historical context, a dimension of his work that has doubtless rendered him more attractive to historians than he might otherwise have been.[11] Historians have repeatedly drawn on several of Clifford Geertz's essays, and I am no exception. Geertz has regarded religion as the symbolic encapsulation of a people's worldview, and that is doubtless one of my underlying assumptions.[12] Adopting Gilbert Ryle's idea of "thick description," he has insisted on the multiple layers of meaning within any transaction.[13] Most directly relevant to the subject of this book is his examination of ritual misunderstanding in the midst of social change, which explicitly includes the historical context.[14] Maurice Bloch has discussed ritual as a means by which those in authority ceremonially impose and maintain their will in relation to those who are subject to them.[15] I have found this useful as I examined the discipline-and-confessionalization-bent elites of church and state in sixteenth- and seventeenth-century Germany. James Fernandez has contended that symbols do not hold uniform meaning to all who behold them, but that the rituals in which they exist may nonetheless effectively bind people together.[16] I find this notion apt in regard to late medieval Catholic and post-Reformation Protestant ritual. Most recently, Catherine Bell's book has helped me to survey the field of ritual studies and to select from among a broad array of theorists. Above all I am persuaded by her argument that those in power may actually fail in their effort through ritual to achieve their hegemonic goals. Bell insists that lesser participants in what are intended to be rites of power exert themselves through consent, resistance, and misinterpretation; they appropriate rituals and make them their own.[17]

These and many other scholars have given me fruitful pause. They have altered my way of seeing. Still, I have adopted uncritically neither their ideas nor their descriptive categories, for as a historian, I must insist that the actors in and the backdrop of a particular ritual instance are decisive. Early modern Germany is uniquely itself, although it is crucial to know what was going on in other parts of Europe at the time.

Ritual parts can become archaic. It may well be that at the end of the Middle Ages, some people found that celebratory procedures, including their practitioners (priests) and their sacred artifacts, no longer embodied the outlook of those who were nonetheless still required to participate in the official cult. This may help to explain outbursts of iconoclasm as well as the inclination toward Martin Luther and other dissident preachers. Such ritual disjuncture was found most of all in the cities, those fulcra of social and economic change. Here traditional relationships gradually dissolved, and the burgher elites and their aspirants . sought to distance themselves from the rustic and the "natural" through an accumulation of material, cultural, and behavioral symbols of success. With few exceptions such as Zwickau, this was not the group from which radical change arose. It came initially more often from the ranks of the artisan middle, the group perhaps most threatened by a downward economic spiral, for their hold on financial security was not firm. Ritual outmodedness was surely not the crux of their matter, but ritual's power to *represent* was great. A recurring question here is what it did represent to them.

The Reformation provided the leaders of the religious movement with an opportunity to reorder cultic observances. In case the emblems of ritual, a jumbled inheritance reaching as far back as nearly a millennium and a half, no longer coincided with people's cosmic understanding, the break with the Catholic Church provided an unprecedented opportunity to set things right. This is one of the most enticing aspects of sixteenth-century ritual change. Few other events have permitted the invention of ritual anew. In the more usual settings, the problem of archaism threatens the historical ethnographer with complete misapprehension, for gestures and symbols tend to collect in a kind of cultural backwater, no longer laden with their original meanings but unable to be freed into the purging stream. Of course, even the elements so caught in the slough have been accorded new significance, but I would still maintain that the focal points of ritual can in an altered setting recede as others move into the center. The rise of the cult of the Virgin beginning in the twelfth century is one example of this phenomenon, while the emphasis from the thirteenth century upon the Host, the body of Christ, is another.

This book is about the ritual decisions that the Reformers and their successors made. In order to assess the qualities of these changes, I have found it necessary to depict late medieval Catholic practice. Only in relation to that standard is it possible to appreciate the kind and degree of Protestant continuity and innovation. I have pointedly examined Martin Luther's opinions on marriage, baptism, the churching of women after childbirth, auricular confession and the Mass, and death. I have then looked to see what he and those who adhered to his teachings actually undertook during the course of the century, up until the outbreak of the Thirty Years' War. In the beginning, contrary currents circled about the figure of Ulrich Zwingli in Zurich, but as it turned out, their influence within Germany proper was not prolonged. A serious challenge arose at mid-century in Geneva, and before 1618 most notably drew the Rhenish Palatinate and finally Brandenburg into its camp. I have looked in the direction of Reformed (Calvinist) ritual positions by way of comparison and because even those territories of Southwest Germany that remained under the Lutheran rubric derived certain influences from Calvinism. This book is, in the end, more about Lutheran than Calvinist ritual. To the degree that it can be, it is also about popular practices and perceptions. The former are easier to approach than the latter, but I have speculated about popular attitudes as well.

Some will reproach me for writing about elite and popular preferences, as though society were a clean dichotomy. Alas, language conveys such misapprehension. I share the view, as I shall say again, that every town and every village was made up of gradations and shades of identity, as well as many blends of lifestyle.[18] All too often these no doubt rich differences elude the historian's scrutiny, for the sources usually do not convey such distinctions. This is regrettable. There did come to be, however, a governmental program, carried out by a consortium of the leaders of church and state, for improving everybody else; and this agenda of religious and moral reform, because it was directed at the broad masses, also produces a sensation of "us" versus "them." I would situate this study within that body of literature that deals with the concepts of confessionalization and social discipline.[19]

Finally, I have sought the underlying meanings of the alterations that were made. Clearly I have taken the changes that were wrought as indications of the tenor of the day. While many have inspired me, in the end I must take full responsibility for the credibility of my interpretation.

1 Engagement and marriage ceremonies

Taming the beast within

Of all the worldly rituals that the churches, Catholic and Protestant, have attempted to influence and incorporate over the ages, engagement and marriage have been the most resistant to change. In this inseparable, sometimes almost indistinguishable, pair of rites are incorporated society's most personal interests—the economic and the sociosexual. The one is rooted in the fluctuating, ever uncertain, and threatening circumstances in which society finds itself and through the manipulation of which human beings attempt not only to survive the present dangers but to ensure their future wellbeing. The other entails family interest, to be sure, but in the northwestern European pattern also makes concessions to that erotic attraction between individuals that defies rational explanation. In early modern Germany, aside from the highest echelons, for which dynastic considerations were decisive, the selection of mates probably represented a combination of anticipated practical benefits to families and individual sexual – emotional gratification.[1]

The wisdom received by my generation was that Martin Luther radically altered the status of the marital condition. Representative of this position is Roland Bainton's famous line that "the Luther who got married in order to testify to his faith actually did more than any other person to determine the tone of German domestic relations for the next four centuries."[2] The confessionally oriented Protestant view has been that although technically a sacrament under canon law, marriage had been a condition (based on the writings of St. Jerome) treated as inferior to virginity, and that according to Catholic clerical teaching, it was preferable to take vows of celibacy, even though subsequently breaking the concomitant promise of sexual abstinence, than to marry. Marriage, then, as a sacrament was officially sacred but widely devalued by representatives of the Church.[3] Luther proceeded, according to this train of thought, to denigrate celibacy for all but the very few, all male, who, like Nicolaus Hausmann the Zwickau pastor, had a "gift" for it and to elevate the marital estate as the one desired by God at the Creation for virtually all of subsequent humanity, and certainly for all females.[4]

Feminist scholars have examined these assertions critically and tended to conclude that Luther, consonant with other forces at work in his day, did help in bringing about change, but that the nature of this innovation was not invariably of the elevating, liberating sort that the Reformer himself seems to have believed.[5] With the beginning of the Reformation, the middle-aged Augustinian friar and priest did not shed many of the prejudices of his clerical culture and of learned, including much humanist, opinion.[6] Nor, we now realize, could he have. During the sixteenth century, women's economic and legal standing deteriorated, and local courts carried out an unprecedentedly rigorous oversight over the domestic and private—that is, over women's—sphere.[7] This evolution cannot be laid at Luther's feet, although, it must be added, he was a man of his age.[8]

I shall maintain in this chapter that via the alterations they sought and that they made in engagement and nuptial rites, the Reformers, conscious of it or not, sought first of all better to tame and domesticate the wild beast of sexuality than Catholicism had, so that human beings might be adequately insulated against the lesser world of nature and fully introduced into a higher existence, a *civilized* existence, characterized by the channeling of base instincts. Both Carnival and unfettered sexuality, including unfettered marital sexuality, threatened the loftier humanity that they desired to create.[9] In their view, the Catholic Church had grounded its own unsuccessful effort in a false anthropology as much as in an unfulfillable theology of works. In theory the Church, faithful to Pauline admonition, had never failed to see the good in marriage nor attempted to persuade the laity to renounce their sexual drive. And this is true. But official Catholicism's ambivalence was of monumental proportions. The prelacy assented passively, even when not actively, to the projection upon women of their own repressed desires, ascribing to Eve and to womankind perpetual culpability (to be relieved only by the dawn of the millennium) for the arousal and seduction of men.[10]

The second major purpose of the reformed wedding ritual was to teach women and men their appropriate roles and behavior, in relation to one another and to the world. The clergy achieved this by means of selected Bible passages, descriptions of role definitions that were increasingly built into the ritual formulae, and wedding sermons widely given from about mid-century on. The second purpose is not unrelated to the first. Through the establishment of the "holy household," with the properly regulated marital bond at its core, women's temperamental disinclination toward order and subordinance would be held within limits and directed toward strictly constructive—that is toward domestic and maternal—ends.[11] On the other hand, if a man behaved in an unacceptable manner, a meek and pious wife might, by her example, persuade him to look after his soul's good. In both cases, misbehavior might or might not be sexual, but the advocated domestic arrangement was seen to lessen the likelihood that unfettered eroticism would "rage through the streets."[12]

Luther took up and disseminated the theme, which was already available in the late Middle Ages, of God's creation of and intentions for nature. Although he carried on the traditional scholarly view that Adam and Eve had not experienced lust before the Fall and only afterward "burned" for one another, he also wrote about sexual yearning as a divinely implanted nature that ensured the perpetuation of the human race.[13] His corrective of prevailing Catholic opinion was, then, that hardly anyone ever enjoyed—and *enjoyed* is still the right word—an exemption from the urges of the flesh.[14] This was so for a divinely condoned purpose: so that the species might not simply die out. Vows of celibacy were intolerable because they absolutely could not be kept. Without the remedy of marital intercourse, both men and women (not just women) would behave like the animals of the field and couple without restraint whenever desire came upon them.[15]

Yet, quite in keeping with late medieval confessors' manuals, Luther warned against excessive lust in the marital relation itself.[16] God would forgive faithful married people the sin of passionate physical love.[17] They had, however, an obligation ever to strive for *moderation*, a recurrent word, and never to try to excite one another more than was necessary to adequate performance, or they would make of the marriage bed "a manure heap and a sow bath."[18] Here, again, the bestial world is the antithesis of the proper human existence. For this reason, too, husbands were forbidden to enter their wives from behind, for this would have made them animals.[19] Nonetheless, Luther saw no reason to govern sexual activity by the ecclesiastical calendar, for human needs persisted throughout the liturgical year and did not render people more impure than they already were. The transactions of engagement and marriage constituted, then, not simply the threshold from one social state to another. Just as important, they were that nebulous, threatening zone within which the animal and the human encountered one another and sought an accommodation that still left distinct these perceivedly incompatible levels of creation. Negotiating this threatening liminality exercised leaders of church and state in the sixteenth and seventeenth centuries. Having turned the household into the building block of the Christian community, authorities now had to face the reality that at the core of that household was a highly charged and ongoing erotic tie that was like an unwatched candle alight in a half-timber-and-thatch cottage. Under less than strictly regulated conditions, a blaze might break out that destroyed one or more of society's constituent elements, possibly even the entire community.

LATE MEDIEVAL CATHOLIC LITURGY

Under Catholicism, couples' unions received the priest's blessing in a number of settings ranging from private to public and from plentifully witnessed to minimally observed.[20] Particularly society's well-to-do and higher ranking brought the priest to their homes for the religious ritual that constituted but a tiny fraction of their elaborate social wedding observances. But numerous connubial blessings were performed in churches, though seldom before the congregation. The evidence is, to be sure, anecdotal, but whereas some took place before the altar, the more usual location was either on the church porch or, in cities with larger churches, just inside the south entrance, above the outside of which Adam and Eve were often depicted.[21] Whether the pair then attended a bridal Mass was optional, and this had no bearing on the validity of their union.[22]

Both Lutheran and Reformed faiths ultimately brought couples in before the altar or the table that in "cleansed" Calvinist sanctuaries took the altar's place. In either instance, this location was the most sacred in the parish. This removal placed the bride and groom symbolically before the scrutinizing eye of God even as it conveyed divine approbation. It raised the couple's affirmations and exchange of rings psychologically to a new level of seriousness, for the pair now did not merely consent and affirm as they said, "Ja," but, even with no change in their simple language, they took oaths before the Deity. The translation to the altar or table was, then, emblematically part of the Reformers' effort to make the ecclesiastical ritual more important than private, secular ritual.

Other than the fact that Catholicism circumscribed the times of the religious year when one could marry—which is to say, when it was acceptable for one to engage in sex and to rejoice immoderately—the numerous priests in urban parishes were willing to accommodate most couples. Morning, even then, was the approved time for wedding blessings, but afternoon and evening ceremonies did occur. While the Church did not wish to desecrate the Sabbath by instituting a fleshly bond on that day, the requirements of the agrarian and the urban communities dictated the choice of a day when work was proscribed anyway. Under Catholicism and Protestantism, the two conflicting motives of avoiding desecration yet not taking away unduly from the work week are continually in evidence.[23] For Lutherans and Calvinists, desecration did not consist so much in sexual intercourse between husband and wife as in drinking to excess and giving way to immoderate, often lewd behavior. Nevertheless, they did generally continue to forbid weddings during Advent and from the beginning of Lent until after Whitsun.[24]

Like women to be churched, couples entering the church after receiving their blessing on the porch were led in by the priest. This *einleitung* might be seen as having a similar effect as the leading in of the post-parturient woman: the power of his office, his sacred vestments, his attendants' holy water, censer, candles, and crucifix protected the sanctuary from this intrusion of sexually inclined and preoccupied if not already sexually active bride and groom. As in other settings, the sacramentals mark a liminal state and facilitate by reducing the danger in the transition being made. The ritual handbook of the diocese of Breslau (early fourteenth century, but widely in use throughout the next century), in its "Ordo benedictionis super sponsum et sponsam," provides a good example of the official late medieval liturgy. Wherever the ceremony occurs, first of all comes the blessing of the ring.[25] The officiant prays for God's spirit to descend upon the ring, so that it might aid the couple in attaining eternal wellbeing (*salutem*). The priest then blesses the bride and the groom, referring to them as "young people" (*adolescentes*). He must then enquire of those present if they know of any obstacle to this union. If no reply is forthcoming, he asks the couple whether they wish to be joined. An affirmative answer is taken for granted. Psalms and prayers follow, including "Blessed are those who fear the Lord," "Kyrieleyson," and "The Lord's Prayer." He asks God to make whole His servant and His handmaid, and to send them divine help and keep watch over them.

> Bless, O Lord, these your servants so that in your name they may grow together, may preserve their purity [*pudiciciam*], and may serve You diligently all the days of their lives, and so that without stain they may come to you at the end of the world. May the Father Almighty bless you, may Jesus Christ care for you, may the Holy Spirit illuminate you, and may the Lord show His face to you, have mercy upon you and give you peace; may the Lord fill you with every spiritual blessing in remission of sins, and may you have life eternal. Amen.

They may kiss each other. This is, however, not the beginning of their intimate relationship but is rather based on the kiss—as in the assumption of lordship and vassalage—that seals a contract. This handbook then specifies that Mass shall be said. It begins with a reading from First Corinthians 6: 15–20:

> Do you not know that your bodies are limbs and organs of Christ? Shall I then take from Christ his bodily parts and make them over to a harlot? Never! You surely know that anyone who links himself with a harlot becomes physically one with her; but he who links himself with Christ is one with Him spiritually. Shun fornication. Every other sin that a man can commit is outside the body; but the fornicator sins against his own body. Do you not know that your body is a shrine of

the indwelling Holy Spirit, and the Spirit is God's gift to you? You do not belong to yourselves; you were bought at a price. Then honor God in your body.[26]

The priest was then to read from Mark 10: 1–9:

On leaving those parts he came into the regions of Judea and Transjordan; and when a crowd gathered round him once again, he followed his usual practice and taught them. The question was put to him: "Is it lawful for a man to divorce his wife?" This was to test him. He asked in return, "What did Moses command you?" They answered, "Moses permitted a man to divorce his wife by note of dismissal." Jesus said to them, "It was because your minds were closed that he made this rule for you; but in the beginning, at the creation, God made them male and female. For this reason a man shall leave his father and mother, and be made one with his wife; and the two shall become one flesh. It follows that they are no longer two individuals; they are one flesh. What God has joined together, man must not separate.

The couple then make their offering, perhaps by placing it on the altar or giving it to the priest. He then carries out the Mass, then places one pallium over the two individuals and speaks a final blessing:

God, who by the power of your virtue have made all things out of nothing, [and] who, the universe having been set in order in the beginning, bestowed an inseparable helper upon man—he being made in the image of God—in the form of woman, the first of whom You took from the body of the man, teaching that what it has pleased You to establish must never be put asunder; God, who in this excellent mystery have consecrated the nuptial union so as to prefigure in the marital joining the mystery of Christ and the Church; God, through whom the woman is joined to the man and her companionship, ordained [by You], is given [to man] by means of this blessing—[the woman's subservience] having been eliminated[?] neither by the penalty for original sin nor by the judgment because of the flood; look kindly upon this Your [woman] servant, who, to be joined in the marital union, asks to be strengthened by your protection. May the yoke of esteem and of peace endure in her; may she be faithful and chaste in Christ and the imitator of the woman saints; may she be as amiable toward her husband as Rachel, as wise as Rebecca, as long-lived and faithful as Sarah, and in none of her acts let her be the author of untruth; may she be bound to the commanded faith, joined to one man, may she flee illicit contacts; may she fortify her weakness with vigorous discipline; may she be modest, serious, reverently decent, learned in celestial doctrine; may she be fertile in producing children; in Your favor and innocent may she attain the rest of the blessed and the kingdom of heaven, and may she see her children's children even to the third and fourth generation; and may she reach the fullness of days.[27]

There are at least five salient lessons incorporated in this ceremony— which, in this case, does assume that the couple will attend the Mass. The first of these, taught via the blessing of the ring (only one ring: the bride's), is that the wedding ring is a sacramental that can actually aid the pair in making a success of their union.[28] This was not a unique or a surprising lesson, for, as we have seen, through his ministrations, the parish priest regularly converted numerous everyday objects into bearers of beneficence and through his authority ritually neutralized threatening things and conditions. Secondly, by inquiring whether bride and groom each has consented, the officiant reminds all participants that marriages without consent are no marriages at all.

Thirdly, this traditional ceremony emphasizes the dangers of sexuality. Even though the wedded life is respectable, because of its characteristic erotic bond, it is fraught with opportunities to sin. Bride and groom require this reminder that the body is the temple of God. Next, marriage is indissoluble.[29] This makes any painful consequences of this Christian contract inescapable, and it lends particular solemnity to the occasion, even though young and enamored couples might fail to grasp this.

Finally, the lengthy concluding blessing catches our eye today for its disproportionate attention to the bride, and specifically to her imputed negative qualities. God may have established marriage in the Garden of Eden, but clearly the daughters of Eve are the ones whose potential transgressions require enumeration. These lurk as the mirror images, the reversals, of every virtue the priest refers to: her subservience, peaceability, faithfulness, chastity, amiability, self-discipline, modesty, sobriety, decency, spirituality, fecundity, innocence. This liturgical prayer, while intended to instruct bride and groom and to lessen the dangers posed by the feminine partner—while intended, in other words, to be constructive—exposes the deep, underlying misogyny of the clerics who composed it.

We must observe that the Catholic rite need not have been a public one. It is hard to think of the brief ecclesiastical observances as designed to shape community. Members of the parish were not typically present even though the Bishop of Breslau envisioned every couple submitting to the performance of a Mass. So many late medieval Masses were private that we may imagine, supported by artistic evidence, as few participants as the priest and his acolyte, the bride and the groom, and a couple of witnesses. Of course, others may have attended, but this would have varied greatly with time, place, and preference. As the couple were bedded, the priest's words were brief:

"Bless, o Lord, this bed and all [*sic*] those who dwell in it, so that they may be steadfast in your peace, persist in your will, live in your love, and grow old and multiply in length of days." He made the sign of the cross.[30] The formulae in other ritual handbooks carry references to the moderate sexual behavior of the bed's occupants. Sometimes the priest or his helper swung a censer over the bed or sprinkled it with holy water. In part these acts were to guard the couple against witchcraft, widely seen among the people to interfere with sexual performance and fertility.[31]

MARTIN LUTHER'S ADVICE

No one was more aware of the practical (as opposed to the theological and legal) peripherality of the religious element than the shapers of the young Lutheran creed. From the mid-sixteenth and through much of the next century, they railed against the nonchalance of the populace about coming into the church—and this was now the accepted setting—and reciting their nuptial vows. It is ironic indeed that theologically and legally Luther and others insisted on the strictly temporal nature of the connubial tie at the same time that his followers struggled to extend the umbrella of religion not only over the wedding rite but over the entire marital relationship.[32] As in connection with other rituals, the Wittenberg Reformer initially envisioned a much humbler role for the church, one in keeping with, as he saw it, the civic nature of marriage. Luther wrote in his "Wedding Booklet for Simple Pastors," probably dating from 1534,[33] that the marriage rite was a worldly transaction that varied greatly from place to place: "All such and similar things I leave to the lords and councils to create and do as they wish; it has nothing to do with me." He added, "but if somebody desires of us that we bless them, either before or in the church, we are obligated to do that."[34] Theology aside, Luther would seem to depart little from past practice. The Catholic Church had been content with a legalistic conformity with its rules, including those governing forbidden days and ways of having sex. It appears not to have minded the smallness of its role. And Luther professes a comparable casualness. But he disparages both the lavish festivities that have accompanied monks' and nuns' taking of final vows, and the foolishness and mockery that are seen at weddings. The people need to recognize marriage as a very serious matter and by no means as heathen monkey business. In the end he sets out a brief ritual for those pairs who happen to perceive their need of God's help in entering this new estate. This is how the bond should be forged if bride and groom should desire and request a role for the church.

Banns having been proclaimed from the pulpit and no obstacle to the marriage having been brought forward, the clergyman unites them in front of the church (*für der kirchen*)[35] with "such words" as these:

Hans, do you wish to have Greta as your wedded spouse? (Let him say, "Yes.")
Greta, do you wish to have Hans as your wedded spouse? (Let her say, "Yes.")
(Here let them give the wedding rings to one another, and join their two right hands together and say,)
What God has joined together let no man put asunder.
Because Hans N. and Greta N. desire to marry each other and declare this here publicly before God and the world, after which they have joined hands and exchanged wedding rings, I pronounce that they are married, in the name of the Father, and of the Son, and of the Holy Ghost.
(Before the altar, let him read God's Word over the groom and bride.)
"And the Lord God said, 'It is not good for the man to be alone. I will make him a helper, to be his counterpart.'[36]
"And so the Lord God put the man into a trance, and while he slept, he took one of his ribs and closed the flesh over the place. The Lord God then built up the rib, which he had taken out of the man, into a woman. He brought her to the man, and the man said,

'Now this, at last—
bone from my bones,
flesh from my flesh!—
this shall be called woman,
for from man was this taken.'

That is why a man leaves his father and mother and is united to his wife, and the two become one flesh."[37]
(After that let him turn to them both and speak to them thus:)
Because both of you have entered into the marital estate, in the name of God, so hear first of all the commandment of God about this condition:
"Wives, be subject to your husbands as to the Lord; for the man is the head of the woman, just as Christ also is the head of the church. Christ is, indeed, the Saviour of the body; but just as the church is subject to Christ, so must women be to their husbands in everything.
"Husbands, love your wives, as Christ also loved the church and gave himself up for it, to consecrate it, cleansing it by water and word, so that he might present the church to himself all glorious, with no stain or wrinkle or anything of the sort, but holy and without blemish. In the same way men also are bound to love their wives, as they love their own bodies. In loving his wife a man loves himself. For no one ever hated his own body: on the contrary, he provides and cares for it . . ."[38]
Secondly, hear also the cross that God has laid upon this estate.
"And to the woman he said:

'I will increase your labour and your groaning,
and in labour you shall bear children.
You shall be eager for your husband,
and he shall be your master.' "[39]

And to the man God said,

" 'Because you have listened to your wife
and have eaten from the tree which I forbade you,
accursed shall be the ground on your account.
With labour you shall win your food from it
all the days of your life.
It will grow thorns and thistles for you,
none but wild plants for you to eat.
You shall gain your bread by the sweat of your brow
until you return to the ground;
for from it you were taken.
Dust you are, to dust you shall return.' "[40]

Thirdly, it is your consolation that you know and believe that your estate is pleasing and blessed before God, for it is also written,
"So God created man in his own image; in the image of God he created him; male and female he created them. God blessed them and said to them, 'Be fruitful and increase, fill the earth and subdue it, rule over the fish in the sea, the birds of heaven, and every living thing that moves upon the earth.'"
"So it was; and God saw all that he had made, and it was very good."[41]
For this reason, Solomon too says, "Find a wife, and you find a good thing; so you will earn the favour of the Lord."[42]
Here he stretches his hands over them and prays thus:
Lord God, who have created man and woman and ordained them for marriage, and also blessed them with offspring, and symbolized [thereby] the sacrament of Your dear Son Jesus Christ and his bride the church, we ask Your Limitless Goodness not to allow your business [*geschäft*], order, and blessing to be displaced or spoiled, but graciously to preserve them in us, through Jesus Christ, Your Son, our Lord, Amen.

The rite that Luther prescribes resembles the late medieval Catholic one even as it departs from it in other ways. Both are brief. Both refer to the creation of human beings and God's institution of marriage. Both retain the metaphor of Christ's being wedded to his bride the church. Both refer to the bearing of children, for this is the chief reason for the nuptial tie. Both express concern about the nature of womanhood. On this last point, though, the Catholic observance and Luther's early prescription differ. The medieval ritual reflects, as said, concern over women's sexuality— that it may not be held within bounds. Many of the virtues listed in the benedictional prayer from Breslau have sexual connotations: faithfulness, chastity, modesty, decency, fecundity, innocence. Luther, by contrast, stresses the relationship between husband and wife, including its sexual element, but setting forth an inclusive manner of behaving toward one another. As abbreviated as the early Lutheran formula is, and even though at this date it lacks the wedding homily, it nevertheless includes scriptural passages that *instruct* the couple on their respective roles. Because of the Fall, the wife must be subject to her husband in all things and bear her children in pain. At the same time, the husband must bear *his* penalty for Adam's disobedience in the Garden of Eden: despite every discouragement, he must gain the family's livelihood. Furthermore, he may not harbor resentment toward his wife for her inheritance from Eve. He must love his wife even as himself, for husband and wife are now and forevermore one flesh. Luther is not worried about women's alleged lustful predilections any more than he is about the men's. By 1534 Luther had redistributed the onus of responsibility for carnal desire, placing it as heavily upon men as upon women.[43] The Lutheran establishment continued officially to disparage sex acts that were not necessary for performance but that sought to heighten pleasure; it made concessions on days but not on ways.[44] But Luther's principal intent was at the wedding itself to establish husband and wife in right relation to one another: the husband as master and representing the household in public, the wife as subordinate and confined to the private sphere. Of course, the Catholic Church subscribed to this fundamental division, but I am writing here about shifting emphasis as revealed in wedding rituals. More than their predecessors, the Reformers saw a need to define and disseminate models of marital deportment. The couple themselves required God's help in resisting the inveiglements of the Devil, but the marriage bed was as an object invulnerable and required no "superstitious" words or any aspersion.

THE WEDDING CEREMONY AFTER LUTHER

Nevertheless, the young Lutheran church reflected the sense that the wedding ceremonies, religious and secular, with their barely latent sexual energy, could have the effect of desecrating holy seasons. It reached no consensus on permissible times of day and days of the week, in some territories fluctuating between the feelings that nuptial festivities were unsuitable for the Sabbath and that they should be concentrated on that part of the week when people would be free of their normal work. If people were obliged to marry on Sunday, the local ordinances often specified that they should do so before the congregation but only after the sermon—presumably on that occasion a wedding sermon, so that the entire gathering would benefit from the expatiation on the marital estate.[45] But numerous examples can be found of forbidding weddings on Sundays, too sacred a day for sex-laced frolicking, and this had the effect of eliminating part of the community.[46] This might mean that wedding sermons fell on fewer ears, frustrating authorities' efforts to use them as a vehicle of public moral instruction. Everyone would, however, in the regular course of life, have several opportunities to hear the pastor talk about the proper roles of husbands and wives. Sometimes the morning was preferred, in the hope that bride, groom, and guests would not yet be drunk, having already imbibed the wedding breakfast, the *frühsuppe*. Very often indeed this was a vain hope, alcohol consumption playing the prominent part in engagements and weddings that it did. In Magdeburg in 1583–1584, the clergy lamented to the visitors:

> They [wedding parties, including guests] don't come to church before they are wild and drunk [*toll und voll*] like pigs, they yell and call out in the church and carry on all sorts of foolishness such that a person can't even hear his own voice when he marries people.[47]

Night weddings, except for people of high rank, were widely prohibited. In Saxony, where they were permitted, the higher fees charged such couples for having the church bell rung suggest that here, too, only richer people availed themselves of the evening hours.[48] When monthly days of prayer (*Bettage*) were established, weddings could not be celebrated on them, nor in Nassau-Usingen during the entire following week.[49] Those in charge experimented first with one rule and then another, evidently never entirely satisfied with the result. That they thought weddings in some measure incompatible with the spiritual life is verified by the almost universal prohibition on marrying during Lent and Advent, a continuation of Catholic proscriptions.[50]

The ecclesiastical ordinances provide numerous scripts for joining women and men in wedlock. Even though these differ in a number of smaller ways, underlying patterns reveal a basic unity not just of form but of belief and purpose. As princes became ever more intimately involved in the details of ecclesiastical practice in their territories, the combined authorities of church and state made ever longer, more detailed scripts available to pastors. Increasingly, pastors had no choice as to whether to use them. Nor had couples any longer the option of entering upon matrimony inside the church or elsewhere. Duke August of Saxony was typical in proclaiming in 1557,

> And because some [people] get themselves married at home in their houses, courts [or courtyards: *Höfen*], even under the sky and not in the church, from which all manner of impropriety follows, from now on except when necessary the marriage and giving together or blessing of the bride and the groom shall take place nowhere other than in the church before the Christian community [*gemeine*], and with the prior knowledge of both parties' parents, guardians, or next of kin.[51]

The parish church became a qualitatively different environment than it had been before, particularly in those urban parishes with multiple endowers and in rural sanctuaries patronized by noble and monastic donor patrons. Whereas the Virgin Mary and her mother Anne had provided concrete images of the ideal wife and mother, after the Reformation these were largely removed from view. Mary became an ancillary figure (as women "ought" to be), and Anne nearly disappeared.[52] The clergy resorted more and more to words in molding their congregations. Some of those words were Luther's.

Heinrich of Saxony, August's father, had adopted Luther's ritual formula in his, Heinrich's, detailed prescriptions for pastors in 1539, and August drew heavily on these even in his great church ordinance of 1580.[53] Luther's *Traubüchlein* served as a model through much of Germany, but even before his death all the Reformer's tentativeness concerning the role of the church was ignored even though reprinted in his pamphlet. With rare exceptions—usually for the nobility—every couple had to be married in church and in front of a gathering (even if not before the entire congregation); weddings marked the establishment of the family and as such were fraught with significance for the entire Christian community. The private had become public. As the state inserted itself more and more vigorously into the previously private world, it instructed pastors not only scrupulously to adhere to three announcements of the pair's intent to wed, but also to keep careful written records of every wedding performed. In addition, clergymen were never to marry people from outside the parish, "in view of the fact that much and frequent error of all sorts follows from this."[54]

With regional variations, groom and bride were usually no longer led into the sanctuary. Many church leaders obviously perceived the "superstitious" aspects of *einleitung* and eliminated it. The couple either entered the church specifically in order to get married, or they sat (as was increasingly the position) or stood through the normal church service waiting to called before the congregation after the sermon. Structurally, the post-Reformation ritual of marriage is a combination of two elements. The first of these is very brief. It includes the inquiry about consent, the exchange of rings, the joining of the bride and groom's right hands, and the pronouncement that they are husband and wife. This remained from Catholicism, and it constituted a valid marriage. The second part constituted the "going to church" (*kirchgang* or *brautmesse*). This is the section that every Protestant denomination expanded during the sixteenth century, and within which it displayed its liturgical creativity. In some parts of Lutheran Germany, these two did not immediately merge but retained their separate identities, with the couple's summary initial consent and blessing followed by their subsequent return to church, even after the sexual consummation. The "Order of Ceremonies of the Church of Haldesleben" (near Magdeburg) of 1562–1564 provides that "marriages are to be contracted on Sundays at the fifth hour [in the afternoon], and on the following day at the tenth hour [in the morning] they [the couples] return to church," where they are read to from the Bible and from Martin Luther's "'Das Traw-buchlein'," at the end of which, after the prayer, they are blessed and dismissed.[55] But in most places, these parts now became part of one more elaborate event, their independent origins revealed only by the occasional curiosity that the pastor declared not once but twice that the pair were formally wed.[56]

The nuptial rite in "The Church Agenda for the Preachers of the County of Mansfeld. 1580" exemplifies some of the tendencies that we are observing in other ritual and temporal settings. The ritual itself is preceded by warnings to the clergy against marrying any of the numbers of vagrant folk about, such as gypsies, unspecified transgressors (*tattern*), and mercenary soldiers, whose qualifications to wed cannot be adequately examined. All of these are lumped together as frivolous knaves (*buben und bübin*) who baptize their children and marry anew "ten times over," wherever they happen to be.[57] Other people urgently seek to be married because they have had sex before wedlock and the woman is pregnant. Pastors may not comply, but must require the couple to undergo public penance before they can be joined.[58]

An interesting feature of this ritual itself is the repeated declaration that the officiant acts "in God's place" (*an gottes stat*) in uniting the bride and groom before him. This is but one more indication of the rising official status of the pastorate during the sixteenth and early seventeenth centuries. The length of the Mansfeld formula owes as much to the clerical admonitions of the couple and the congregation as it does to the verbatim reproduction of Bible passages. The pastor announces to the couple and to the gathering that the man and woman have come into the presence of God and of his holy Christian Church and asked to be married so that they might live together honorably before all the world. The congregation is urged in all seriousness to call upon God on their behalf. The people should pray for God's special blessing as they begin connubial life, that He might grant them children, that the pair might live in heartfelt love, unity, and good health and be protected from "poisonous Satan's" evil attacks.[59] The Lutheran conception of marriage as a communal act and a basic public institution is strongly in evidence here. Whereas the selection of life partners had always had pronounced social and economic meaning, after the Reformation this transaction takes on symbolic weight—at least in the eyes of the authorities—for society as a whole, representing more prominently and pronouncedly than before the promises binding God and His church. In some sense, the wellbeing of the earthly community depends on the moral rectitude even of individuals, and certainly of pairs of individuals.

After the clergyman pronounces that they are husband and wife, and before the reading of the customary scriptural verses, he must explicitly instruct them in their proper behavior toward one another; more than recitations from St. Paul's letters are thought necessary. The man must regard his wife as God's gift to him. He is to exercise reason (*vernunft*) in his dealings with her at the same time that he loves her from his heart. He may never be separated from her, except, finally, by death. "In God's stead" the officiant informs the woman that she must accept her husband as her ordained lord and head, and treat him as such; she must be submissive and obedient to him in every legitimate matter and care for and serve him. She may never leave him.[60] The male's signal capacity and restraint is to be reasonable, but the woman, lacking reason, can only be safe when the man shelters her with his rational gift.[61] Gradually brides and grooms had to swear to comply. While under Catholicism, and initially under Lutheranism, those about to marry had simply to state with the word *yes*, indicating that they freely consented to marry, increasingly the practice spread of vowing to accept the behavioral principles laid out by the cleric. The 1561 "A Wedding Booklet for the Simple Pastors in Mark Brandenburg" made the groom swear to the following:

> My son in Christ Jesus...you have heard what God has laid upon you, namely that you shall eat your bread in the sweat of your brow, which is to say that you shall faithfully attend to your vocation, with God['s help] and the honor of the work of your hands shall nourish yourself, without betraying your neighbor, so that you may feed your wife. Secondly, St. Paul says that man shall love his wife as his own body...If she is weak, fragile, and ill, this is how you should behave toward her, you should treat her in a friendly manner and [even] when in deep distress and misery show her the greatest loyalty. If you are willing to do that, confess it here openly before the countenance [*angesicht*] of the entire Holy Trinity...and in the presence of these pious Christians, who are listening too, and say in God's name, "Yes."

The bride was then told,

> N., my dear daughter in Christ Jesus...you too have heard what God has given you to do, namely, that your will should be subordinated to that of your husband, and he should be your lord; that is, you should do with a glad heart everything that he says, and everything that he forbids you to do you should leave alone and not undertake or do; you should do everything with his knowledge and consent and be obedient to him in all godly matters...If you will do this, confess it now publicly before the countenance of the Holy Trinity, that is God the Father, Son, and Holy Spirit, and in the presence of the dear angels of God who are with us, and in the hearing of these pious Christians, and say in God's name, "Yes."[62]

In a long prayer that follows, the pastor recites yet again what is expected of the pair before him, adding with respect to the bride the request that she be "a good mother" who, together with her husband, brings up her children to the honor of God and for the growth (*ausbreitung*) of the kingdom of heaven and the Christian Church.[63]

In other places, bride and groom were made to repeat a vow, usually a complex sentence, that referred in summary fashion to the behavior that had been described to them just before. In Calenberg-Göttingen (1542), the groom repeated after the pastor,

> I, N., in the presence of this Christian assembly, take you, N., to be my wedded wife, and I swear to be true to you in all matters, and never to leave you or separate from you, till death parts us.

The bride repeated these words in her turn. Interestingly, the benediction at the end of this ceremony is that of the Diocese of Breslau, focusing lengthy, fearful attention upon the sinful proclivities of the woman.[64] *Women saints* is now rendered as *saintly women*, and this sentence has been inserted in the original, "Grant, Lord, our God, that they love one another and get along well."

Unlike funeral sermons, wedding sermons have not yet found their patron-scholar, their Rudolf Lenz.[65] Yet these homilies were given, collected, and published, and though they were never as numerous as funeral sermons, they very likely abound in German libraries.[66] Their ritual location was in the now much-elaborated second element, the going-to-church.[67] From around mid-century, more and more pastors gave what were usually brief and undistinguished homilies—the printed ones were more often composed for elite weddings, and sometimes the preachers were paid a fee for preparing and delivering them. Several conscientious city pastors tapped their imagination and their extensive knowledge of Holy Writ in composing wedding sermons, lessons that took up multiple facets of the marital relation and that used the broad pertinent spectrum of biblical sources. Johannes Mathesius and Cyriakus Spangenberg were among these.[68] But the ordinary sermons by less gifted preachers simply reiterated those principles already contained in scriptural texts, ritual language, and certain hymns. In the humbler parishes, such homilies were printed and distributed to pastors for them to read aloud.[69] They constituted but one more means of conveying these to the bridal couple and, just as important, to the members of the community in attendance. The subsequent circulation of printed collections further inculcated the Protestant ideal of marriage upon the public.[70]

Either during or after the service, the new husband and wife made their offering. Whereas in the Catholic wedding this contribution had been made to the clergy, Lutheran practice often designated it for the poor. Many couples simply put a coin of suitable denomination into the alms chest. But this represented a financial loss to pastors and deacons whose incomes were often meager to begin with and who were suffering the ravages of inflation besides. For this reason, in other territories the ancient fees (*Stolgebühren*) charged for every priestly ministration were retained, and brides and grooms gave the requisite gifts to the officiant and to the sexton.[71]

THE PROFANE CEREMONIES: THE LONGER DURÉE

Lyndal Roper has superbly described and analyzed wedding practices in and around Augsburg after the Reformation.[72] I shall draw on evidence, nearly all of it corroborating, from northern Germany. At about the end of the sixteenth century, Pastor Johann Adolfi, called Neocorus, compiled his *Chronik des Landes Dithmarschen*, in which he described the history, land, and customs of the people among whom he lived at the mouth of the River Elbe.[73] Cyriakus Spangenberg, by contrast, was born in Nordhausen and flourished as a clergyman during the 1560s in the earldom of Mansfeld. He dedicated his huge volume of wedding sermons, *Ehespiegel*, of 1561 to the mayor and city council of Nordhausen.[74] Both of these men's depictions of betrothal and wedding practices, then, reflect a general Saxon background. At the same time, they share the purpose of prescribing very firmly what they regard as proper Christian procedure. Even so, features of folk custom untrammeled by reform are visible, sometimes earning these commentators' censure. These accounts are additionally valuable because they pertain to ordinary people and not just the rich. The Dithmarschen region was mainly rural. Nevertheless, we may be sure that the poor could have afforded only a foreshortened version of the display portrayed in Adolfi's *Chronicle*, and in any case the numerous sumptuary ordinances of the early modern period strove to enforce strict class distinctions.[75]

In every setting, men negotiated, men decided, men acted. It reflected upon their honor to be in charge. Women ostensibly played passive roles, with only two exceptions. The one is, insisted on by the medieval church, that the bride as well as the groom must freely give consent to the union. The second is that, where fathers and male relatives were lacking, mothers took part in negotiating premarital agreements for their children, but in consultation with authorities. Despite the more active informal part that we can be sure young women played as a rule in indicating to prospective husbands whether or not their wooing would meet with favor, preparing a trousseau, however great or humble, and executing other arrangements, it is significant that, on the face of things, women pretended passivity.[76] Passivity, hundreds of wedding sermons given from mid-century on reveal, was central to the definition of ideal womanhood, and even though (as the severity of the sermons on this point confirms) this was far from the daily reality, young women may have been willing to assume this persona for the duration of the nuptial observances. Their reward was, in a society that did not honor feminine aggressiveness, to be the center of attention during the wedding celebrations.[77] Female honor, as Roper has pointed out, was associated with sexual comportment.[78]

According to Adolfi, a young man (*Geselle*) looking for a wife ought diligently to look around, in regular consultation with friends and relatives, for honorable young women of praiseworthy origin, robust health, and domesticated habits, and similar to him in age, height, and strength.[79] Having come to a decision, he authorized two good friends[80] or his parents if they were still living to serve as suitors (*werber, freyer*) on his behalf. These went to the homes of even the less directly involved relatives of the desired woman in an effort to be sure that the groom was fully informed of her circumstances and her probable response. If there were resistance from any quarter, the would-be groom could extricate himself with his honor intact. But, if all were in general agreement that the match was a good one, the suitors went again to the home of the woman's representatives for confirmation. They asked the future bride's family to set the date of the public announcement (*Bekenntniße*). This might, in fact, for one reason or another, be some distance off. Adolfi comments that the whole business side of courtship might take a year or even two years from beginning to end.[81] On the occasion of announcing the provisional agreement to wed, the future bride's father or closest male relative filled a brand-new drinking bowl—it must never have been used before—with freshly made beer. The young man, or if he were not present, his proxy, drank a toast to the bride and consented to a future marriage provided financial negotiations were successful. Afterward those present ate and drank their fill, "often until dawn."[82] The women of the household presumably prepared and served this engagement meal and were thus very much present.

The next step was for both sides, including any "good people whom they wanted to have there," to draw up a contract specifying, among other details, what the bride would bring to her marriage as trousseau and dowry, and what disposal would be made of these if either party (or both) should die. Sometimes such business took place in a house and sometimes in the church or other customary place. Negotiating in the church was intended to keep the men honest—and to make any subsequent violation the more reprehensible. After reaching an agreement, the groom and his men thanked the relatives and other representatives of the bride "with friendly honor and offering of hands." Both parties then adjourned to a house, a profane setting, in case the transaction had been carried out in the sacred one. There they drank the famous *lövelbier*, in Lower Saxony called the *Lövede-Beker*. Adolfi tells how it was done:

The Father or the [male] cousin or the closest [male] relation fills to overflowing a bowl or goblet that has never been used before, with beer out of a fresh jug and a fresh cask, and from this the groom drinks to his daughter or related woman friend [as proxy] in the name of the Father, Son, and Holy Ghost... After this the same [drink] is poured for every person in turn who is present, and likewise each one must empty the bowl to its very bottom.[83]

After the vessel has gone completely around, the groom takes it to himself again and makes a mark upon it so that it will never be used again for any purpose. If the bride is not in the house where this ritual has transpired, the groom will take this cup to her in the evening, give her a coin of significant value [*mit einem stattlichen Ehren-Penning*], and drink to her.[84] But if the bride is in the same dwelling where the *lövelbier* has taken place, now for the first time she is led by her mother, (female) in-laws, and worthy women friends into the room where the drinking has been going on, receives the cup, and locks it very carefully in her trousseau chest.[85] When all this has been accomplished, the tables are laid, and the entire company is entertained at the bride and groom's expense, often until the morning star appears; "and in some places, in procession the groom and his men are honored with a lovely red banner, which with joy and song they take home with them and signify their triumph."[86]

Spangenberg's account is compressed and little detailed. He refers to the "old ceremonies" of wooing, by which is meant that the would-be groom named suitors, who sought the young woman's parents' reaction before approaching her herself. This was, he says, traditionally done in the morning, when people were still sober.[87] They should allow the woman and her family eight to fourteen days to consider the proposal, including seeking the advice of other relatives and friends. On the appointed day and in the presence of his closest relatives, the father gave the answer. If it were positive, the future bride presented the future groom with a wreath.

Among us it is the custom that the bride gives the groom a lovely wreath that has a golden or a silk cord on it, and that she sets it on his head herself in order to show that she intends to hold and regard him as her lord and king; and, since the wreath is a symbol of joy, that she will give him joy and happiness by her obedience, love, faithfulness, friendliness, and submission.[88]

Here, of course, the pastor interjects his ideals and those of his clerical colleagues. He continues with the fairly ludicrous statement that "the wreath is presented to the groom as to one who has triumphed over lewdness [*vnzucht*], has kept his body pure and chaste until the marriage bed, has not allowed bad company, [male and female] couplers, whores, and [female] knaves to conquer him."[89] Among the people the wreath symbolized a woman's virginity, her sexual honor; and via the wreath she now places this in the hands of her future husband. It was the custom in many parts of Germany for the bride to wear a wreath of her own on her wedding day.[90]

In Spangenberg's region it was the tradition to seal the engagement with a meal, the *löbde* (a linguistic variation on *lövelbier*) either on the same day or several days later. The father of the bride is the host and entertains the groom and his closest relatives. Spangenberg regrets very much the excessive imbibing that occurs, "for the Germans don't leave off their boozing...even though it's not right and brings them little [reputation for] piety." He wishes it were possible to change this custom. He says that material deliberations take place at this *lövelbier*, a marked difference from Dithmarschen custom.[91]

Before the wedding, Adolfi continues, the groom looked for suitable lodging for the couple; he had to take into account the wishes of the bride's family. The bride, meanwhile, gathered household provisions to load upon her bridal wagon—chests and what went in them, silver and gold objects, bed and bedding, clothing and jewelry, linen and wool. She had formally to display all these goods to the clothing-wife or wives (*Kleiderwiff*, *Kleiderfruwen*) and the bridesmen (*Brudeknechte*) selected by her husband-to-be, but she also invited her own relatives and friends to the viewing. During this period, the pastor proclaimed the banns on each of two successive Sundays in the parish to which the bride belonged. In the county of Mansfeld and most of Lutheran Germany, banns were read three times.[92]

A few days in advance of the wedding, official "bidders" went around and invited the guests.[93] On the day before the bride and groom officially began their sexual converse, in some places the "bridal bath" took place. Despite all the possibilities for vulgarity such an occasion entailed, not even Spangenberg objected, "as long as one doesn't make a disorderly drunken binge out of it and does it modestly and honorably."[94] A wedding ordinance from Saxony-Weimar in the early seventeenth century indicates that a meal was held afterward, but it strictly prohibits this practice in the name of economy.[95]

There having been no objection on the grounds of relatedness or morality, the pair came before the entire congregation of the bride on the appointed Sunday morning, and in accordance with God's Word, the pastor joined and blessed them. In Adolfi's account, this is the sum total of attention devoted to the religious service! Spangenberg, however, pays more attention to the "going to church" (*kirchgang*). The ancient practice of leading the bride to church with lighted torches (*brautliechter*) that were decorated with multicolored silks was still done in some places, the numbers and grandeur depending on the economic station of the families involved. And, indeed, mainly families of high rank continued this observance. But still in use across the social spectrum were fife and drum. To their sound, the suitors led "the groom, the closest relatives, father and brother, the bride to church." Men led the procession, and women, including the bride, followed. Spangenberg complains that most of the wedding guests do not bother to attend the church service and admonishes people to pay more attention to the religious rite than the wedding dinner (*mehr achtung haben auf Kirchgang dann auff Tischgang*).[96] Whoever is there, according to Spangenberg, the first part of the ceremony, including the wedding sermon, takes place someplace apart from the altar, for only after this is the pair led before the "high altar" to the pastor. There the rest of the ritual occurs: inquiring about their consent, reading about marriage from the Scripture, instructing bride and groom in their proper demeanor, the exchange of rings,[97] the pronouncement that they are husband and wife. They then kneel and the benediction is read over them. After the wedding, two men lead the bride home, and one of them carries before her a gold or silver drinking vessel. The bride wears or carries in her hand a wreath of maple leaves, or people strew grains of wheat on her head as she goes into the house, "as a sign of and wish for fertility."[98]

Adolfi, the pastoral folklorist, provides a particularly detailed description of the highly ritualized customs governing the transfer of the bride to her new home, though it is evident that such lavishness could not have been typical among the poorer ranks of the peasant and laboring population. According to him, on the following Thursday, the bridesmen, numbering "six, eight, even ten or more," rode on horseback with four wagons to get the bride. The first of these wagons hauled her bridal attire. On each wagon four or six people sat. In the second one was the bride herself with her two attendants (*Spriddeldocken*) and the musicians. Other women of the bridal circle filled the last two vehicles. At a set location the procession was honorably received by the oldest bridesman and his helpers with bared heads, bows, and all accordance of honor. These accompanied the bride's wagon to the bride's parental home, from which the women carried out the bridal loaf of bread, protected against damage by the bedclothes. This loaf was almost as long as a man and decorated with roses, hearts, the figures of little children, wreaths and other adornment. Also borne out now was the great bridal cheese, of "a splendid size."[99] The bridesmen brought out the bridal chest and any other containers of trousseau goods, and though Adolfi does not say so, the bridal bed, and other objects, loaded them into the (first) wagon and made them fast so that they would not be damaged in transit. When this wagon had departed, the oldest bridesman expressed gratitude in the name of and on behalf of the groom. The bride's father pressed the entire company to remain and entertained everyone, men and women alike, with food and drink. When the meal was over and the Holy Ghost goblet brought in, the table was cleared off and removed.

Every bridesman then danced with a woman, probably an attendant, representing the bride, but this preliminary dance (*Vordantz*) was brief and controlled in comparison with the abandon of the wedding dance proper.[100] The oldest bridesman asked for permission to speak, which was refused. He then bared his head and in all reverence asked to be heard. This time he was allowed to speak. He made a formal speech, thanking the bride's family—and using their titles—that all had transpired in such an orderly manner. He begged them now to permit the bride to proceed to her new hearth, for the bridegroom was asking for her; and even if the bride did not want to be with him, surely she wished to be reunited with the goods on her bridal wagon. He was refused in a friendly manner. He repeated his request several times, and each time was put off by the bride's relatives. This ritual often lasted till after midnight and sometimes through the whole night—unless the bride had a long way to travel.[101]

At last the company gave in to the senior bridesman and permitted the bride herself to be brought in, together with two of her appointed women attendants. Up till this time she had been with her matrons and some maidens in a separate room, and these had dressed her in her bridal attire. She wore her bridal headdress (*Hoike*), given her by the groom. Her face and head were covered completely by a white cloth, with just a sufficient opening that she could breathe and see, held in place by a headband. When she arrived, the women who were sitting by the stove (*in der Horne*) made room for her. Her two attendants sat by her "on both benches." When all was ready for travel, the bride's father, brother, or male relative gave her, with comforting words (*mit trostlichen Worden*), into the care of the senior bridesman to be conveyed to the groom. She was blessed (*gesegnet*) or wished happiness and health (*Geluck unde Heill*) by each person present. After the bride had departed, the rest of the company continued to frolic. Adolfi approves of these traditions and maintains that they have their foundation in Holy Scripture, for the chaste Rebecca also concealed herself. The bride should show herself only to her spouse. This covering of the bride's countenance and beauty stands, he says, for the secrets of marriage that are to be kept hidden from all the world and never revealed.[102]

Adolfi notes that in some places the bride's chief male relative takes her by the hand and leads her through the street to the groom. This is done, he says, so that everyone may see that she is not marrying on her own wish and whim, but that her family have given their consent. In the meantime, at the couple's new dwelling, the groom greeted the bridal wagon and had the bed itself taken in and set up.[103] He had the cushions placed by the oven in the place of honor and properly bedecked the best bench. The chests and other containers were stood in the chamber near the bed, so that the bride, when she arrived, would find everything in proper order. The bride herself came with riders, wagon, and musicians, in accordance with the groom's wishes. Those people who attended to the occasion entered the house, but the bride went up to the door but remained outside with her attendants. The groom came to the door with his head bare. Three times he asked, "May I in honor bring in my bride?" And three times he heard the reply—the text does not say who spoke— "Bring her in in God's name!" He took her by the hand and had her turn around (*herumme kamen*) three times, and the last time he swung (*schwenget*) her gently into the house and said, "In honor I bring my bride in." He led her to the bedchamber door, kissed her three times, and the third time swung her politely into the room, where he left her.

The bride now removed all the regalia of maidenhood and of the bride—including the white cloth that had covered her face—and donned the festival headdress of the married woman, which in this northern area was brown and decorated around the front with large silver and gilded spangles.[104] She and her matrons of honor now took their places by the oven. A meal was provided. After this, the dancing began, though at first the bride and her retinue remained sitting. When it was time for them to take part in the bridal dance (*Bruttdantz*), the elder of the two men who had arranged the wedding (*Schaffer*)[105] danced with the bride. Then it was the groom's turn, and then the other organizer's, and then his relatives' (*Frunde*). The older matron of honor was next brought into the dance, then the younger. The general wedding dance followed, and it was this event that especially exercised church authorities for its sexual license.

When it was time for the couple to go to bed, the bride's attendants took her to the bedchamber and got her ready. Then the groom was brought to her. The company drank to the couple. The older organizer raised a sword over the bed and repeated a set blessing three times over the pair, wishing them "as many sons as the church ladder has rungs" and daughters as well.[106] The bride and groom were left alone but surrounded by pranks and noise perpetrated especially by their unmarried friends; this uproar lasted until Friday morning. Adolfi indicates that this night was the couple's "Tobias night," which is to say that, like Tobias, they refrained from—had no choice but to refrain from—sex. Elsewhere it was acceptable for couples to become intimate after the drinking of the *lövelbier*, but after the Reformation authorities of church and state took great exception to this practice.[107]

Early Friday morning, the groom invited all the neighbors to breakfast and all the women to accompany his bride to church. When the bride emerged from the chamber, she presented her gifts, a reversed form of the ancient *Morgengabe*, to the groom and his relatives. Adolfi does not say, but usually this took the form of a handmade shirt for the groom and for the others a handkerchief or other small piece embroidered personally by her.[108] After breakfast, it was the custom in some places to put a red vestment (*Gewandt*) over the head and around the shoulders of the bride, and to lead her around the churchyard (cemetery) and then into the church.[109] There she said her prayers and listened to at least part of a sermon. She was then led back to her new home, where the midday meal, with many guests, took place. She again sat in the place of honor next to the stove, but this time her new husband sat by her in place of the matrons.

This meal was a great feast. Guests were seated throughout the house. The *Schaffer* and their helpers often came in with fresh goblets and compelled people to "dig in" (*tholangen*). When the roast meat was standing on the table, these words were spoken: "The Holy Ghost is hard by the door." Great and powerful (*gewaltige*) drinking vessels were brought in "so that the guests become merry." The *Schaffer* and their assistants now brought in the gigantic bridal bread and the huge bridal cheese, and the head *Schaffer* announced three times, "The honorable and virtuous bride has honored us with cheese and bread. What does she deserve for this?" The leading matron of honor answered three times, "Honor and virtue, happiness and health; and honor and virtue shall indeed be her reward!"[110] The bread and cheese were taken out to be cut into pieces and then brought back in. The first serving was given to the bride, the second to her two principal attendants, the next to the cook, the next to the musicians; and so on until everyone had had as much as he wished, in the name of the bride.

Periodically the two *Schaffer* and their helpers reminded the company to eat and drink freely, for "the Holy Ghost is hard by the door." Finally the *Schaffer* and the cook or the *Schaffer* and the groom brought in the "Holy Ghost," and admonished everyone to eat and drink more if they still desired to:

> Inasmuch as no one among you, honorable and virtuous women, honorable and worthy patrons and friends, desires any more of this food—for there is still meat, roast, butter [and] cheese, and these will not be removed as long as the mealtime continues . . .—we want in the name of God to bring in the Holy Ghost.

They raised three silver goblets, each man holding one in his hand, and had them filled up with beer from a fresh jug that had been filled from a fresh cask. They drank a toast to the bride, her matrons of honor, and the most prominent guests: "May you have a happy year with the Holy Ghost!" Everyone sang "O God, we thank you for your goodness." The goblets were then emptied, refilled, and surrendered to the next person, until all had drunk. At last, the food was removed, the tables and benches cleared away, and the floor swept so that the guests were able to dance. Beverages, at least, remained available.

This continued until the groom, who had been in another room some of the time with other guests who were not dancing, came in with his two *Schaffer*, each with a beer jug in his hand, and with a fresh goblet drank to the bride again and to her matrons. They then relinquished the jug to others and left the room. In the meantime, the bride put on her wife's shawl (*Kagele*) and together with her two attendants brought a fresh jug of beer and fresh bridal goblets into the room. They served each guest and made sure that their drinking vessels were clean and that everyone was drinking heartily. The groom and his men now returned and sat by the stove, and the entire company drank to his happiness. It was impolite for anyone to stand until he had been served beer by the bride. The musicians continued to play; the guests danced and sang. Adolfi surmises that this night, too, will be a "Tobias night" for the newly wedded pair. Saturday passed in the same celebratory fashion.[111]

On Sunday, the women escorted the bride to church as was their wont, and they were accompanied by musicians. In this region, the groom did not return to church with his new wife for a bridal Mass. Guests were invited once again. Adolfi remarks that it is fine to begin a marriage with such festivity, for the Saviour himself had celebrated at Cana and provided wine, even though some of the guests were already drunk.[112] He then admonishes people not to give in to excess and thereby to enrage God. The Holy Ghost goblet is intended to remind people that their gathering is for the purpose of honoring the Holy Ghost, and they should behave accordingly.[113]

Adolfi ends with the observation that changes in this nuptial practice do creep in and that there are certain variations, such as leading the bride through the street. But by and large, he says, what is described here is the custom in the leading places of Dithmarschen. Almost as an after-thought, he adds that on the Thursday following these observances, the new wife goes in a wagon to visit her parents and other kin. Her husband picks her up on the following Sunday.[114]

Spangenberg is far less tolerant than Adolfi. He thinks that wedding guests already enjoy themselves too much and do not require the ancient custom of the groom's urging the people through the suitors to eat and drink their fill. Already they "root around [*wülen*: like pigs], gobble down, and guzzle." He objects to the lavish expenditure on weddings. Even passing a dish around among the guests does not produce enough money to defray half the costs. Wedding banquets have become, he insists, entirely too elaborate. He specifically criticizes serving sweets and having images carved in butter or wax.[115]

On dancing, the *bête noire* of numerous pastors and parish visitors, Spangenberg decries the "vile running around, immodest turning, grabbing, and licking of lips," and he condemns these as "godless, sinful, and improper." He especially attacks the "animal" (*viehisch*) dancing that takes place at the seasonal *Lobetäntze*, once again contrasting the bestial and the human. Immodest dancing in whatever setting makes those who engage in it resemble God's subhuman creatures. In some places all the wedding dinner guests processed to another place for dancing, but in his area only the young people went to the dance hall, accompanied by the tune of pipes, drumming, and screaming. If their parents were there to watch, they would be more restrained, he is certain.[116] Spangenberg tells the story of a pastor near Stendhal who in 1203 himself played the fiddle for a wedding dance, was struck by lightning, and lost his right hand.[117] But this dance was so entrenched in the culture of every social class that the governors of church and state never dared to abolish it. All other dances they freely prohibited, with limited success.[118] Nevertheless, at these tolerated dances they posted officials to make sure that people did not dance lasciviously, fight, sing lewd songs, or stay beyond the legal hour.[119]

As in Dithmarschen, by the late sixteenth century nuptial vows seem to have been exchanged on Sunday. But in the County of Mansfeld, worldly celebration and the bedding of the pair were not postponed until the following weekend but went right on from Sunday into the new week; "yes, even on Thursday too." Spangenberg finds most offensive the vulgarity of putting the couple to bed. Young people escort the bride and groom to bed with piping and drumming, noise and obscene comment, and afterward they run wild and even commit acts of vandalism.[120] Husband and wife ought simply to kneel down and pray, and he gives an example of a fitting prayer. Spangenberg disapproves of contemporary wedding practices; Adolfi is content merely to describe them. Roper observes that, in late medieval and early modern Germany, Augsburgers "were often quite vague about the point at which a marriage commences." The taking of vows was not nearly as persuasive as sexual consummation, and this often occurred after engagement, even though the bedding ritual came later.[121] Legal considerations aside, I would like to suggest that in Adolfi's description of clothing and symbolic role changes we may detect, if not a single moment, at least a configuration of moments within which we see the transformation from a woman engaged to be married to the true matron. It is evident that vows exchanged in church had very little to do with this status. The initial symbolic defloration may have occurred with the notching of the silver wedding goblet: the groom notched it, after he and the betrothal guests had emblematically "quaffed" his future wife, and he then gave it to his bride, who was to safeguard it for ever with her trousseau goods. The denouement in the popular ritual occurred when the bride, her face and head veiled, arrived at hers and the groom's new home and he ceremonially led her onto the premises and into the bedchamber. Then the bride took off all the apparel of maidenhood and donned the headdress of the wife. The third step was the bedding of the couple, but the rite of putting to bed was the focus and not the accomplishment of the sexual act itself, which, Adolfi admits, may not take place on this night of raucous amusement. The ritual bedding of the pair had come to *stand for* the consummation. Little effort was made in northern Europe to examine the bedclothes on the morrow to determine whether the bride had been a virgin. This was in practice less important in the north of Europe than in the south, perhaps because in the north it was practically taken for granted that she was not.[122] Many people, as we have seen, expected the sexual relationship to have commenced with engagement. Fourth, dressed as a married woman, the bride (but not the groom) went to church—probably originally in an effort to be reconciled with the sacred after the loss of her virginity—and when she returned home, she took the housewife's seat of honor next to her husband. As evidence of her new status, the "bodies" of the giant bread and cheese were offered to the company in her name; they symbolize her newly "broken" body[123] and may even compensate the community for not being permitted to share in the "consumption" of her physical self; and finally, she as housewife must serve up beer to each and every guest. She would henceforward be in charge of food and drink in this domicile. The sexual function is prominent here, but it is intertwined with the socioeconomic position of the housewife, and this social role is important too. The fact that the bride attired herself as a matron *before* going to bed with her husband is evidence of this duality. Emblematically she had to be a woman before engaging in sex; the sex act itself did not render her an adult.

Particularly worthy of note is that in Dithmarschen this crucial set of rituals that changed a girl into a woman were at several days' remove from the exchange of vows in church. Those vows were for the people clearly not at the heart of the matter. Despite centuries of effort by the Catholic Church to make marriage a sacrament, with the coming of the Reformation it was still fundamentally a mundane transaction. Nonetheless, the people had made their ritual concessions—had no choice but to make them—to the church.

STATE EFFORTS AT REGULATION OF ENGAGEMENTS AND WEDDINGS

Church ordinances and visitation protocols alike show the growing determination of secular authorities to insert themselves into every facet of the lives of their subjects. In an expansive and determined mood, rulers wanted their vision of a thoroughgoing social order to prevail. They described this vision in disinterested terms, but today we see them as striving to consolidate in their hands as nearly complete power as they were able. The leaders of the church cooperated with them during the sixteenth and seventeenth centuries, even though (as we see it) their motives were somewhat different; both state and church strove to secure the same ordering of society. Theologians, superintendents, and other clerical visitors saw themselves as laboring to fulfill God's commandments on earth. Those in their congregations often lacking self-control, it was their bounden duty not merely through structural improvements to facilitate order but through incessant watchfulness and tireless participation in disciplinary bodies to impose it. As they saw it, nowhere was improvement so urgently needed as in engagement and marriage practices.

Traditional engagement and wedding customs were at the boundary dividing the wild, animal aspects of nature from the civilized existence of human beings. We think of boundary crossing in van Gennepian terms today, as the conveying of especially the "virginal" bride, but also in some sense the groom, from one state (and one estate) to another. This movement from one life condition to another was not lost on sixteenth-century people; popular marriage rites richly symbolized this transformation. Yet, although early modern leaders would not have articulated their fears in precisely these terms, I must argue that they did regard the unfettered, licentious celebration of the sexual union that underlay marriage as pressing men and women too close to the periphery, where the divinely ordained human mastery of the Creation began to blur and the as-yet-undomesticated animal world ever threatened to invade the pale. Just as towns and villages had to guard against the intrusion of wolves in deepest winter, just as they determined to exclude pigs and other foraging, wandering livestock in the sixteenth century, so the beast within mankind had to be watched, disciplined, and subdued.[124] In Germany, the Catholic fifteenth century had, to be sure, assigned the life of the flesh a lower status than that of the spirit, but it was not preoccupied with the punitive and public enforcement of its rules; for all but spectacular cases, the sacramental system and the eternal hereafter sufficed as remedies. Late medieval Catholics may have seen this permissive attitude as realistic, but Lutherans saw it as utterly corrupt. They had to exert themselves in drawing humankind back from the brink. The close links forged between church and state in the century of the Reformation enabled them to try.

All of the wedding and police ordinances (*Hochzeitordnungen* and *Polizeiordnungen*) of this period—and there are many—reveal authorities' more and more concerted efforts to bridle what was all too often unbridled. The metaphor of the bridle is an apt one, for it is used in this age and suggests once again the animal aspects of the association between men and women.[125] Prohibitions of various excesses, such as suggestive dancing, immoderate drinking, expenditure, dressing, and numbers of guests, become increasingly explicit and met with heavy penalties, and prelates and princes invent new bureaucratic means of keeping track of brides and grooms.[126] To prevent secret engagements, Dorothea Sophia, Protestant abbess of the convent of Quedlinburg in 1627, declared that every engagement must be witnessed by three men, and in order for it to be publicly announced—that is, to be valid—both bride and groom must demonstrate their knowledge of the catechism.[127]

In Emden in 1596, before they can marry the engaged couple must appear before the city scribe and have their names written down. No musicians may be present at the *lövelbier*, nor may anyone dance, on pain of a fine of ten gold gulden, a very large sum. Nor may the couple marry without a written license from the city secretary.[128] Marriage licenses would appear to have originated in the sixteenth century.

Whether couples wed during a regular church service, and thus before all members of the congregation who were there, or whether they arranged with the pastor to come with their family members and attendants, the behavior of members of wedding parties clearly left much to be desired. The regulations admonish, prescribe, and threaten. People arrive late, even in the middle of the sermon, and disrupt the service of God. Or they do not come at all and leave the pastor standing for hours at a time. Or they are drunken and rowdy, unbefitting a holy occasion. The musicians create a ruckus, over which the words of the ceremony cannot be heard.[129] The ordinances set onerous monetary penalties for these transgressions. The visitation records sometimes instruct pastors to lock up the church and refuse to marry on that day any bride and groom who are more than fifteen minutes late, or at the very least the tardy couple must pay a fine.[130]

Worst of all were couples who appeared before the pastor having already engaged in sexual intercourse.[131] The populace in the sixteenth century took it for granted that after engagement, bride and groom—for after betrothal they were so called—became intimate.[132] Rulers and clergy expected them to abstain till after they had been joined in church. No doubt, in order to make this demand mildly reasonable, Spangenberg thought that weddings should follow closely upon engagements; postponements were, according to him, chiefly to facilitate the amassing of splendor.[133] Beginning in the middle of the sixteenth century, along with other immoral behavior, premarital sex became subject to church discipline and in some places also civil penalties, including brief imprisonment.[134] Many common folk did not understand this harsh attitude. As late as the mid-seventeenth century in a village near Braunschweig, several mothers protested when authorities noted with intent to punish them that their babies had been born too early. The women insisted that one had to reckon from the engagement.[135] In his marriage ordinance of 1553, Duke Christoph of Württemberg declared that when people who could not marry had sex, the man was to be thrown in the tower for an unspecified period, to lie on the ground and to be fed on bread and water at his own expense; the woman was to spend a fortnight in a women's jail (*Frawengefencknuß*). If they were eligible to marry, the man must be imprisoned for eight days on bread and water, and the woman for four days in the women's jail. After that they may—indeed probably must—marry, but they may have neither music nor guests at their wedding, and the bride is forbidden to wear a wreath.[136] In the lands pertaining to the diocesan chapter in Magdeburg, such brides had to cover their heads.[137] In Rothenberg, the church ordinance of 1618 sets out a long pre-nuptial ceremony of public shaming and penitence that a woman and man must undergo before they can proceed to the proper wedding rite.[138] The pair must appear before the entire congregation on a Sunday morning and stand before it until the sermon and Holy Communion are over. The pastor then confronts them:

> Inasmuch as it is said and apparent [because of the woman's pregnancy?] that both of you have joined yourselves dishonorably under the influence of the Evil Enemy and your own sinful, evil lusts, contrary to God's ordinance and will; that you have lived unchastely and not waited for the Christian going-to-church, after which with God['s blessing], honor, and good conscience you would have been able to live together; you have thereby angered God the most highly praised Trinity, driven away the dear holy little angels and chaste spirits, injured your own consciences, annoyed the Christian Church and the dear youth, afflicted the office of preacher, offended the government, wounded the hearts of your parents, and fallen thus into the court and judgment of God.[139]

This development finds parallels through early modern Germany and beyond. It reflects once again the perceived need to confine and channel sexuality.[140] Robert Muchembled has argued that the harsh surveillance of sexual deportment in France during the sixteenth, seventeenth, and eighteenth centuries was an important feature of governments' efforts "to obtain the highest possible level of obedience."[141]

> By different channels, each individual learned that his body did not completely belong to him. In twentieth-century terms, he was persuaded that sexuality was a social function and not an erotic or individual function. But there was more: he was also taught to control his entire body in order to put it to the service of society.[142]

It may be that sixteenth- and seventeenth-century magistrates and princes, whether Catholic or Protestant, saw themselves as rendering their flocks for the first time truly Christian, as Muchembled states, following Jean Delumeau; but on this matter the anthropologically influenced historian, in my view, must agree with Natalie Zemon Davis.[143] A religion is far more than the sum total of its official definitions of orthodoxy.

INTERPRETATIONS

Ritual comparison provides an excellent example of the conflicting attitudes and ways of life between governors of church and state and many ordinary people. The disparity between the ecclesiastical formulae, whether Catholic or Protestant, and late medieval/early modern popular practice is striking. Official church sentiments as reflected in the rites have been engrafted onto folk customs whose values are close to the opposite of those of the clergy: they are material, social, and sexual, none of which—for nuptial purposes, at least—the people disapproved of. To them it was appropriate to strive to elevate family honor through lavish display, to negotiate a couple's (and thereby their family's) future provision, to admit that marriage was a sexually active estate on which the biological future of the kinship group, and to a lesser degree the community, depended. Popular observances dramatized all these features. They included relatives (*gute Freunde*) at every step of the way; they solicited their opinion, their presence, and their participation. They tacitly offered to relations and neighbors active reprocity. In the name of household honor, communal cohesion, and—not accidentally—personal gratification, they made free with food, drink, and ribald innuendo. In fact, the bride's father's—and the groom's—ability at specified stages to *provide* that gratification enhanced their honor. And so the people tolerated the transgressions that the resultant lack of inhibition produced; indeed actively took part in what might be regarded, along with Carnival, as a kind of anti-ritual, one deliberately overturning the stern ideals of the church. Indeed, prior to the Reformation, when the rural parish clergy were still of the class and mind of their charges, priests collected in person the "bridal soup" to which they were entitled, and entered into the spirit of the day.

Yet I do want to leave open the possibility that some of the people themselves welcomed a little more order. In 1570, in the village of Heber near Wolfenbüttel, members of the congregation told the parish visitors "with wonderment" that, at the last three weddings, no young woman had been raped, "which before was unheard of."[144] Now, of course, the former reality represents more than just gratuitous aggression under the influence of alcohol, and was probably a process of appropriating eligible young women. Even if this is the case, and even if the group as a whole passively condoned such behavior, unlimited beer consumption did facilitate this type of symbolic activity.

Examining the history of northern European weddings, I can only conclude that the church ritual and spiritual principles were the real interloper, the innovation, the force striving to reform the populace's outlook on and manner of relating to the cosmos. In the late sixteenth and early seventeenth centuries, leaders of church and state seemed oblivious to the anthropological roles that engagements and weddings, as practiced among the people, played. Ritual evidence shows that the Reformation, whether Lutheran or Calvinist, intensified the late medieval effort to spiritualize marriage. It attempted to an unprecedented degree not just to govern general marital and domestic comportment but also to interject the divine into the very psychic bond between husband and wife. Its doctrinal theories and Martin Luther's personal moderation aside, if judged by the actions of its representatives, the Reformation must be said to have tried to *sacralize* marriage. Its approach toward marital sexuality was not so very different from that taught by late medieval and early modern priestly confessors to that large segment of the laity that was unattracted to celibacy—except that Protestantism did not presume to "bracket" sex within that bond. Instead, it was determined to blunt sex's animal nature by subsuming it entirely within an unbracketed domestic and spiritual matrix. This was part of that concerted joint effort, especially pronounced from the second half of the sixteenth century, to inspect and gain control over every nook and cranny of subjects' lives. For three or four generations, the state employed the ideological language of the church in order to justify its cooperation. Nevertheless, during the course of these generations, the state's interests took on greater importance, and some today may find that their pious pronouncements sounded less dispassionate as time went on.[145] Yet both shared the attitude that all that was animal must be "harnessed," and human beings compelled to separate themselves more fully from the exterior, lower world of nature.[146]

At the same time, engagement and wedding practices afford perhaps the best example within early modern Germany of popular resistance to the imposition of ritual from above. One of the ways in which people protested was—where the ceremony was not held following the regular order of worship—not to go with the bride and groom to church. Parish visitors frequently brought this disobedience to their princes' attention. Their lament in Saxony-Weimar is typical:

> Up till now in many places almost no one...can be found who wants to help accompany the bride and groom to church, but the major part first come to church when the wedding sermon and rite are nearly over, [and] the rest probably present themselves after church, only for the dinner.[147]

If we reflect on what part these "laggards" heard, we shall gain insight into what was important to them. Certainly it was not the definitions of suitable Christian demeanor of husband and wife toward one another, whether these came from Scripture, sermon, or song. They missed, or nearly missed, these. What they came to hear was the pronouncement by the priest that the condition of the couple before him had changed; they came, in short, to witness the *supernatural* function of the clergyman, as circumscribed as this had now become. In their eyes—and, ironically, probably also in those of many pastors—the officiant was God's deputy and as such provided one link between the heavenly and the mundane. Clergymen may well have diminished in popular esteem as the

Reformation was seen to decrease their ability to tap the divine for their parishioners' earthly benefit. This sixteenth-century evolution notwithstanding, after several centuries many common people had accepted the church's impositions upon wedding observances to just this degree: that they accepted the validity of the priestly blessing.

Beyond this, they perennially refused to give up those secular wedding festivities that in their eyes were the crux of the matter. The ritual outlined by Adolfi is heavy with transparent significance. The substantial economic, social, and sexual interests of the couple, their families, and society stand before us in dramatic form; in these multiple acts with their symbolic accoutrements the creation of a new nuptial pairing is carried out, in a manner that prevents social disorientation. The luxury of cornucopian food, drink, and sensual license disposed the community to accept change. Most of the authorities' objections were alien to the people. To submit to bureaucratic pronouncements would have been, once again, to abandon the transactional patterns of their ancestors. This they were not prepared to do. In areas close to territorial borders, despite every pastoral prohibition, they took part in all the major events of their Catholic relatives' lives, including weddings. Their papist kin reciprocated by their participation in the secular observances, but they could not lead the bride into church.

As I shall, in the end, have to say in every chapter, no existing ritual theory can be laid down like a template upon early modern Germany. This is so not alone because those theories were derived as the result of studies of other societies; it is also because every setting is different. But several theoretical models hold out valuable insights that can enable us to explain the dynamics, the successes, and the failures of German engagement and wedding celebrations. Emile Durkheim's solidarity thesis could explain what it was that *Freyer/Werber* were attempting to achieve by consulting every relation and even friends of a young woman whom a prospective groom had in mind.[148] They sought to ensure before advancing a proposal that the family and the community harbored no grudges, no insuperable other visions of the said maiden's future; they sought the general consent to seek the specific consent. Throughout the ceremonies, the *Schaffer*, that man in charge of the execution of each step, took pains—if Adolfi is credible—to keep everyone satisfied. The unwritten script provided the formal words and gestures of inquiry and placation, but his personality undoubtedly entered the equation. If we used Victor Turner's concept of *communitas*, we could interpret the secular engagement and wedding processes as embodying modes of relationships among individuals that were potentially, and perhaps actually, fraught with tension but that in this setting were able to be bridged. The peasant collectivity within which a marriage occurs could be called the "normative" or "existential" *communitas* that mobilizes group resources and works toward social perdurance.[149] Here persons and groups with genuine differences manage to cohere via the ritual process. The bridal party's duty (in proportion to means) to send part of the wedding dinner to the homes of poor people, and the practice of letting guests bring (and thus feed) their servants and children, formed a small, extra-ritual element in bringing all neighbors together through the distribution of largesse. In the popular practice, as the visitation protocols often reveal, meal- and dance-crashers were widely tolerated. In these gestures, the hosts of the wedding meals seek that delicate balance between structure and *communitas*. Class differences are emphasized at the same time as, in another sense, they are overcome.

We would need to know more about the circumstances surrounding the rape of young women at German wedding festivities in order to understand it. This was clearly a rite of violence, and one for which in the countryside there seems to have been no recourse, if any was desired. The inebriation that was virtually required of every full participant in the engagement and wedding observances loosed stays that were not, in any case, very tightly bound; this and the openly sexual dancing led across boundaries that rural folk evidently did not intend to keep firm. By means of sexual familiarity, even if not rape, the young men demarcated their territory. This animal-like behavior was, of course, intolerable to the Protestant clergy. It seemed to them to have only destructive purposes, but we might hypothesize that it had a constructive side as well; one intended to delineate and enhance the community. What seemed to the authorities to have been chaotic may indeed not have been so.[150]

Mary Douglas in *Natural Symbols*, following Marcel Mauss, enunciates the principle that the human body is defined by the society within which it exists.[151] This pertains most certainly to sexual behavior. Inasmuch as the same clerical complaints about peasant sexuality existed among parish visitors all over Germany, we may be sure that, by convention, villagers fundamentally condoned their fellows' behavior at wedding parties. The villagers were produced by, and integrated into, their culture. The flirtatious interaction among eligible men and women was a waltz of come-ons and sexual aggression, before the eyes of married adults (including magistrates), that produced mainly acceptable results: new weddings and new households. Although young people could not violate the material and social aspirations of their families, before the Reformation the biological consequences of suggestive dancing did not unbearably stigmatize or commit their participants.

But urban life had begun to modify the body. Here, even before the Reformation, magistrates and princes had begun to press for greater corporeal restraint, whether this took the form of the more orderly disposal of human waste or the insistence on a more tranquil demeanor. Metropolises like Nuremberg looked to Italian cities like Venice for their fashions and manners, and their smaller urban satellites in turn imitated

these few great cities. Bodies became more constrained: more differ-
entiated by class, more regularly indoctrinated as by sermon and law,
more threatened with punishment.[152]

Two major influences shaped the post-Reformation body: the city and
late medieval monasticism.[153] Growing numbers of people living in ever
closer proximity to one another—as Nicolaus Hausmann put it for
Zwickau: on top of one another like the spawn of toads[154]—created a
reinforcing atmosphere for the magistrates who constructed the
institutions of order. New law codes, more precise definitions of class,
detailed lists of acceptable deportment, harsher and more certain
sentences, a greater reliance on imprisonment and even "bird-cages"
for disobedient children betokened a class of city fathers bent on control.
This bourgeois inclination coincided nicely with the second influence,
the Reformation itself, a prominent feature of which was the espousal
and dissemination of a monastic temperament. Jean Delumeau is correct,
in my view, in asserting that early modern Europe experienced a revival
of ascetic self-discipline, and this was true within Catholicism as within
Protestantism, differing only in the details.[155] The Protestant body was
expected to contract marriage on reaching adulthood, and to engage in
chaste and moderate sex, and the household within which this
relationship was lived out was in many respects a new monastery, a
metaphor aptly adopted by Johann Spangenberg.[156] The household was
the basic unit of an orderly society, instructing its members in Christian
piety, which included all the restrained virtues and abstinent lifestyle
essential within God's dominion. The Protestant body was modestly,
appropriately covered, but definitely covered; it did not eat or drink
more than necessary; it did not disrobe for sex; if masculine, it did not
wear codpieces or make suggestive faces or gestures; if feminine, it
stayed in the domestic sphere and was quiet, submissive, and assiduous.
Noblewomen's grave effigies epitomize the Christian woman's body:
their eyes are lowered, their praying hands are together, their clothing
comes at least to their chins, and, if they were widows, their mouths are
covered to show that they were *mundtod*, literally having "dead mouths,"
unable to represent themselves in the world but requiring a guardian
(*fürmund*). The men's gaze is placed higher: their hands may not meet
(for men must be expansive), they often wear the sword and perhaps the
armor of their office, evidence that they may be aggressive, but only in
causes compatible with their faith.[157] It will occur to some that this is
hardly different from the idealized Catholic body before the Reformation, and this, in part, is the point. Monastic ideals for women and
modified monastic ideals for men continued and were now inculcated
upon the entire laity with a new spirit of vigor and rigor. It did not matter
if the new theology was the same as that earlier teaching that had
elevated withdrawal from society. Lutheranism in the age of orthodoxy
sought to discipline all aspects of life in the world; small wonder that

Lutheran theologians during this period bitterly debated whether good works were necessary for salvation. In their practical lives, it was hard for them to imagine that godly behavior was optional for those who would attain eternal life.

It is, then, hardly conceivable that popular and pastoral betrothal and nuptial rituals should have blended together into a mutually satisfying amalgam. And they did not. The religious ceremony constituted but a fraction of the wedding observance, one in which, I have argued, the people often took part reluctantly. James Fernandez has concluded that various participants in the same ritual, observing the same symbols, can interpret what is occurring very differently.[158] Although Lutheran and Calvinist authorities had a good measure of success with the passing of generations in gaining public attendance at nuptial rites in the church, there is persistent evidence in the visitation protocols of lack of interest, or at least a lack of interest in anything except the pastor's pronouncement that a couple are now wed. In their eyes, I have asserted, this was persuasive because it was the supernatural moment. Many people's absence from or ill behavior in church betokened the yawning chasm that separated their worldview from that of the clergy. Future microstudies may reveal the extent to which this chasm narrowed during the late seventeenth and eighteenth centuries. Whether or not it did, the populace had little choice (à la Gramsci) but to consent to the dominating if not the dominant values—at least in church.[159]

But in their homes, they enjoyed somewhat greater scope for resistance. The prayers that opened and closed the wedding dinner did not really succeed in suffusing that event with sacrality, and pastors must have realized this. Increasingly they stayed away from this raucous merriment and preferred to have servings of the wedding repast sent to the parsonage or to accept a money substitute for it. Nevertheless, Adolfi does gloss over the festivities with biblical justifications, and so we might conclude that even in the secular arena (as the clergy and the laity witnessed the same ritual processes) they interpreted them differently. Spangenberg, on the other hand, had few illusions.

The questions of ideology and power within betrothal and nuptial rituals is possibly simpler to answer than in connection to other rituals I am examining.[160] With the few and tenuous bridges between them that I have outlined, the people's engagement and wedding observances were clearly separate from those demanded by the clergy and increasingly by other officers of the state. The Lutheran church elaborated its marriage rites more and more fully during the sixteenth century, but all the accounts based on actual practice suggest that religious ritual content alone would never have made significant inroads into the mentality of the people. Only the most unrelenting and severe effort by church and state together—including imprisonment, fines, and/or temporary banishment from the Lord's table with its threat of dishonorable burial or even eventual exile—may have won some compliance. At every socioeconomic level during the period under study, however, official and popular ceremonies failed to coincide.

Michel Foucault's observations about power relations in society seem to me to fit this setting particularly well, though I would not agree that in early modern Germany resistance to authoritarian advance arose out of its opposite: freedom. It would be historically naive to imagine that Germans of any class during the Reformation era exercised or even sought to exercise the kind of freedom that Foucault has in mind.[161] But, indeed, negotiations of power were played out in every community in which the state came to have its representatives—which is to say, before the end of the sixteenth century, in every community. Ritual was one of the means of negotiation, and of resistance. Nowhere did the cooperating church and state press more concertedly upon the physical *body* than in their efforts to establish their vision of sexual morality, betrothal, and marriage. They aggressively sought to contain, to moderate, to *civilize* the body. As suggested, they also had their eye on the familial "body" (Roper) and the body politic.[162] Catherine Bell has written,

> Ritualization as any form of social control, however indirectly defined, will be effective only when this control can afford to be rather loose. Ritualization will not work as social control if it is perceived as not amenable to some degree of individual appropriation. If practices negate all forms of individual choice, or *all* forms of resistance, they would take a form other than ritualization.[163]

Future studies of that appropriation will need to focus first on the upper bourgeois strata of German cities, moving only with time beyond this patrician culture to the less privileged urban classes and to the peasantry.

2 To beat the Devil
Baptism and the conquest of sin

As one of the only two Catholic sacraments retained by the
Reformation, baptism aroused deep discussion among the Reformers.
Already Christian humanists had stressed the need to purify texts, and
in their examination of Scripture had perceived what they regarded as
human accretions that over many centuries had embroidered upon the
rite of the early church. Within approximately two decades of the
beginning of the Reformation, Protestant churches radically altered the
ceremony that they had inherited. In their view, they succeeded in
recapturing pristine apostolic (and thus true Christian) practice. But I
shall maintain here, as elsewhere, that there was more to the story than
through imaginative theological smelting processes to refine the
precious metal of the divine will out of the dross of papal ore.
Whether they were aware of it, Lutheran and Calvinist liturgists reveal
in their innovations a profound concern for the shaping of earthly
society.

LATE MEDIEVAL BAPTISM

Late medieval Catholic baptism provides an excellent example of the
phenomenon I have called ritual archaism—that is, aspects of ongoing
rituals that have not kept up with, and thus do not reflect social reality. In
the early centuries, membership grew chiefly through the conversion of
adults, who, admittedly, brought their family members of every age, and
indeed their household staff, with them into the new faith. Even though
small children and infants were among those baptized at Eastertime, the
body of catechumens, preparing for membership in the church through
indoctrination and self-discipline, was made up of adults. For nearly a
millennium, the ritual as it evolved continued to address mature
individuals. Nevertheless, with the exception of certain interludes, such
as the Carolingian period, when once again whole populations were
brought into the Latin Church, from about the fourth century babies
predominated among the baptisands.[1] The inappropriateness of major
parts of the baptismal rite constituted ritual disjuncture. Because the

sacred proceedings were largely in Latin, perhaps people did not notice. But in part, too, the Church used the institution of godparenthood to mask unsuitability.[2]

As we recall from Saint Augustine's account of his own baptism, the sacrament was originally to occur at Easter.[3] With changes in time and circumstances, baptism was celebrated at every time of the year. So great were the protective virtues ascribed to baptism that parents were unwilling to risk postponing the ritual. In the fifteenth and early sixteenth centuries, throughout Germany the Catholic ceremony was still made up of two major segments, however. This was so even though the printed rubrics incorporated local customs.[4] Priests were first to exorcize and determine the preparedness of the catechumen to be received into membership in the mystical body of Christ, and, second, to perform the baptism itself. The traditional pattern was that the priest and the acolyte, clad in their vestments, went out to greet at the church door the infant on whose behalf baptism was sought. In keeping with the ancient instructions, the child was to be held precisely beyond the threshold, in larger churches presumably in the narthex or the galilee; baptism was quite literally a liminal transaction! The clergy positioned themselves just within the sanctuary, the sacred domain.[5]

The officiant first enquired of the baby what its name was.[6] Part of the disjuncture we perceive in this ritual is the ongoing practice of addressing a newborn child who could not possibly have answered. Some ritual handbooks had abandoned this fiction and frankly addressed the individuals bringing the infant to church. And increasingly they prescribed the vernacular—though there is no doubt that priests did put this and other questions in their parishioners' mother tongue, whatever the rubrics may have said. The midwife (serving as a godparent) and any other godparents, had to reply for their charge. The cleric then asked the midwife or others whether the baby had already been baptized, as in the birthing room, in case its life had been thought to be in danger.[7] If it had not, the priest then enquired what the baptisand desired of the church. The expected answer was either "faith" or "to be baptized."

Next the priest asked the sex of the candidate. The reply affected his or her physical placement during the ceremony as well as a number of prayers. From early times females occupied the lefthand side and males the right, and although in the late Middle Ages there was a tendency toward eliminating these instructions, in many rubrics they remained.[8] The outlook on which they were based, of course, persisted into the early modern period and beyond.[9] Then the officiant determined the qualifications of the godparent(s). They had to be baptized Christians who were neither excommunicated nor in a state of mortal sin; they had to know the Lord's Prayer, the Ave Maria, and the Apostles' Creed; and they could not be too closely related to the infant whose spiritual parenthood they were assuming.[10]

Presently the priest began the series of exorcisms that to our sensibilities dominated the first section of the ceremony.[11] Satan was indeed a powerful presence in the world. The cleric first blew upon the infant (this is called either insufflation or exsufflation), either once or three times for the Trinity, and commanded the Devil to "come out of this image of God" and to "give place to the living and true God." He made the sign of the cross on the child's forehead and on its chest, over its heart, saying, "I make the sign of the Savior, our Lord Jesus Christ, upon your forehead/breast." Placing his right hand upon the baby's head, he intoned one or more of five prayers set out in the late medieval rubrics.[12] The Breslau manual prescribes all three of the following, beautifully rendered in early modern English by the compilers of the Salisbury manual:[13]

Almighty and everlasting God, the Father of our Lord Jesus Christ, vouchsafe to look upon this thy servant (*or* this thine handmaid) N., whom thou hast vouchsafed to call to the first beginnings of faith: all blindness of heart drive from him (*or* her): break all the bonds of Satan with which he (*or* she) was bound. Open to him (*or* her), O Lord, the door of thy goodness, so that, wearing the sign of thy wisdom, he (*or* she) may be free from the defilements of all fleshly lusts: and rejoicing in the sweet odour of thy commandments may serve thee in thy Church, and may advance in goodness from day to day, so that he (*or* she) may be made worthy to attain to the grace of thy baptism having received thy medicine; through the same Christ our Lord. Amen.

We beseech thee, Lord, mercifully to hear our prayers: and this thine elect N. do thou guard with the power of the Lord's cross [here the priest again makes the sign of the cross on the child's forehead], with the imprint of which we sign him (*or* her): so that preserving the first beginnings of the worship of thy majesty, through the keeping of thy commandments he (*or* she) may be found meet to enter the glory of the new birth. Through Christ our Lord. Amen.

O God, who didst create the human race in such wise that thou mightest also restore it, look in mercy upon thine adopted people: and within the new covenant place the children of thy new race, so that that which they could not obtain by nature the sons of promise may rejoice that they have received through grace. Through our Lord.[14]

The dualism, the moral dialectic of the universe is evident here. Satan stands opposed to God, the flesh to the spirit, humankind's degeneracy to the perfection of the Deity. By means of these prayers and the rites yet to come, the officiant as intermediary prepares to open a channel between the creature and the Creator, but this can only be accomplished after provisionally vanquishing the Devil. So ubiquitous was this Evil One that the priest was obliged to exorcize not only the infantile "catechumen" but also in turn each of the physical media with which the sacrament was carried out: the salt, the font, and the water. The priest prepared the salt first:

> I exorcise thee, creature of salt, in the name of God the Father almighty, and in the love of our Lord Jesus Christ, and in the power of the Holy Spirit. I exorcise thee by the living God, by the true God, by the holy God, by the God who created thee for the protection of the human race, and ordered thee to be consecrated by his servants for the people that comes to faith, so that thou mayest be made a saving sacrament for putting to flight the adversary. There we ask thee, O Lord our God, that this creature of salt thou wouldst sanctify [sign of the cross] and bless [sign of the cross], so that for all who receive it it may become a perfect medicine remaining in their bowels [*in uisceribus eorum*], in the name of our Lord Jesus Christ, who is about to come.[15]

The salt was now more than purified; it had received supernatural power. The priest put salt into the baby's mouth saying, "Receive the salt of wisdom for a propitiation of God unto eternal life." He then prayed that the person seeking baptism and tasting this salt would "hunger only until he is filled with heavenly food."[16]

Throughout the history of medieval baptism, at this point in the preparatory observance, different prayers followed by renewed formulae of exorcism now had to be said over female and male candidates.[17] Why one content would originally have been appropriate for males but not females, or the reverse, is no longer clear. Indeed, it was not always clear to those who compiled ritual handbooks, for occasionally the formulae for one sex were prescribed for the other. Both the Breslau and Salisbury manuals begin with this prayer for little boys:

> God of Abraham, God of Isaac, God of Jacob, God who didst appear to thy servant Moses on mount [*sic*] Sinai, and didst lead thy children Israel out of the land of Egypt, appointing for them the angel of thy mercy, who should guard them by day and by night, we beseech thee, Lord, that thou wouldest vouchsafe to send thy holy angel from heaven, that he may likewise guard this thy servant N. and lead him to the grace of thy baptism.[18]

The corresponding prayer for girls in both these rubrics is as follows:

> God of heaven, God of earth, God of angels, God of archangels, God of patriarchs, God of prophets, God of apostles, God of martyrs, God of confessors, God of virgins, God of all that live good lives, God whom every tongue confesses and before whom every knee bows, of things in heaven and things on earth and things under the earth, I invoke thee, Lord, upon this thine handmaid N. that thou mightest vouchsafe to lead her to the grace of thy baptism.[19]

Perhaps the first, with its references to the founding patriarchs of the Chosen People, was seen as heroic and thus masculine; while the second focused on God and included categories, such as martyrs and virgins, that included women. The sex-specific exorcisms are equally unclear. The following was among those to be pronounced only over males:

> Therefore, accursed devil, hearken to thy sentence, and give honour to the living and true God: give honour to Jesus Christ his Son and to the Holy Spirit, and depart from this servant of God N. because our God and Lord Jesus Christ has vouchsafed to call him to himself by the gift of the Holy Spirit to his holy grace and blessing and to the fount of baptism.

The priest again made the sign of the cross on the child's forehead.[20] Both manuals prescribe the following exorcism for females:

> I exorcise thee, unclean spirit, by the Father and the Son and the Holy Ghost, that thou come out and depart from this handmaid of God N. for he himself commands thee, accursed one, damned and to be damned, who opened the eyes of the man that was born blind, and on the fourth day raised Lazarus from the tomb.[21]

More significant than the apparent lack of truly gender-pertinent language in the respective prayers and formulae of exorcism is the fact that throughout the ages of Latin Christendom girls and boys were put into separate categories from the moment of their baptism. By the end of the Middle Ages, that moment was often within hours of their birth. Thus began the great and lifelong inculcation of gender roles, prominently shaped by the conviction that males were superior and females inferior. Boys were treated first, if there were two or more infants, and were held on the priest's righthand side; girls came second and were held by a godparent on the priest's left. The pronouncement of separate invocations was itself a harbinger of lessons to come.

There is still more to the lengthy preliminaries of this first segment, all originally directed toward adult catechumens. The clergyman now read Matthew 19: 13–14: "Suffer the little children to come unto me, and forbid them not, for of such is the kingdom of Heaven." He continued with the recitation of the Lord's Prayer and the Apostles' Creed. In the early Middle Ages, adult catechumens had been expected to be able to recite these themselves. With infant baptism, their original function was lost. They served to instruct or remind the godparents of the essentials of the faith, which they were expected to transmit in due course to their charge, as she or he grew up. Then yet again the priest addressed the Devil at length:

> Be not deceived, Satan, punishment threatens thee: torments threaten thee: the day of judgement threatens thee, that day of eternal

punishment, that day which is about to come as a fiery furnace, in which eternal death will overtake thee and all thine angels. And therefore for thy wickedness, thou that art damned and to be damned, give honour to the living and true God: give honour to Jesus Christ his Son: give honour to the Holy Spirit the Paraclete, in whose name and power I command thee, whoever thou art, to come out and depart from this servant of God (*or* from this handmaid of God) N., whom today the same God and our Lord Jesus Christ has vouchsafed to call to his holy grace and blessing and to the fount of baptism, so that he (*or* she) may become his temple through the water of regeneration, unto the remission of all his (*or* her) sins. In the name of the same our Lord Jesus Christ, who is to come to judge the quick and the dead and the world by fire.[22]

This exorcism appeared in every German manual.[23] Closing the first phase of the ritual, the priest applied spittle to the ears and nose of the infant. The Salisbury manual provides greater detail as to just how the priest was to proceed, and these instructions are compatible with many of the German rubrics:

Then let the priest spit in his left hand, and let him touch the ears and nose of the infant with his right thumb with saliva saying in his right ear, "Effeta, which is Be opened." On his nose. "Unto the odour of sweetness." In his left ear. "Be thou put to flight, O devil, for the judgement of God is at hand."

Some German manuals provided for the touching of ears and nose, intoning the same words, without spittle.[24] The language contains another exorcism.

At length, the candidate had proved his or her worthiness for baptism. The party now proceeded to the sacrament proper, sometimes accompanied by a prayer or benediction. The most frequent was, "The Lord preserve your going in and your going out from now until the age to come. Enter into the temple of God so that you may deserve to see the son of the living God."[25] Many manuals state that "women" (*mulieres*) prepared the child for baptism.[26] This meant removing its clothing. By the late Middle Ages, font and water had normally already been blessed so that an intervening exorcism of these objects was not needed.[27] One godparent held the child while a second touched it with his or her hand. The presiding cleric now variously addressed the infant itself or the godparents, who spoke as though they were the child: "N., do you renounce Satan?" "I renounce him." "And all his works?" "I renounce them." "And all his pomps?" "I renounce them."[28] The Breslau manual specifies that the priest make the sign of the cross on the infant's chest and again on its back, between its shoulder blades, using holy oil or chrism: "I anoint you with the oil of health, in Christ Jesus our Lord, into eternal life." He then addressed "the baby," asking whether she or he believed the tenets of the Apostles' Creed. "The infant" responded to each question, "I believe."

Calling the child by name, the cleric asked, "N., do you desire to be baptized?" to which the answer was, "I desire it." He then took the infant—or if there were more than one and they were of both sexes, boys were baptized first—and, holding it with its face down toward the water, submerged it in the font three times, declaring, "N., I baptize you in the name of the Father, and of the Son, and of the Holy Spirit."[29] All the rubrics contain these essential words of baptism. This threefold immersion was sometimes to be carried out in such a way that in the end the priest made the sign of the cross with the baby's body: first directing its head to the east, then to the north, then to the south.[30] As the chief godparent held the infant over the font, the priest once more anointed its head—usually the crown rather than the forehead (the Breslau manual specifies *in medio capite*)—with oil, and applied a baptismal cap, or the baby was now dressed in the widely used white baptismal gown, the *Westerhemd*.[31] "Receive a white robe [*sic*, even if a cap was used], holy and unstained, which thou mayest bring before the tribunal of our Lord Jesus Christ, that thou mayest have eternal life..."[32] If a cap was applied, the infant was to keep it on until the second or third day; but if were a gown, it was to be worn for a week or eight days.[33] Thereupon a lighted candle was placed in the child's right hand, or if he was unable to hold it, as was now usually the case, a godparent received it on his behalf. The priest admonished, "Receive a lamp burning and without fault: guard thy baptism: keep the commandments, so that when the Lord comes to the wedding thou mayest meet him together with the saints in the heavenly hall, that thou mayest have eternal life and live for ever and ever. Amen."[34]

J. D. C. Fisher has described how, until the high Middle Ages, children were confirmed and received their first Communion immediately upon the conclusion of the baptismal service. The application of the chrism as the child was lifted from the font was originally performed by the bishop, the only person authorized to administer confirmation; this act was seen as bringing the Holy Spirit down upon the newly baptized and enabling it in its subsequent life to realize the fruits of the baptismal washing. Having been confirmed, the child was then eligible to receive Holy Communion and was carried by the priest to the altar, where the cleric dipped two fingers into the Chalice and inserted them into the suckling's mouth. As baptism came to be thought of as urgently needed after birth, and bishops were not able to fill this constantly required office, confirmation became separated from baptism and postponed until children were older—and, in many places, neglected altogether. At the same time, the Chalice was withdrawn from the laity during the twelfth century, but newborn babies were incapable of swallowing the Host. By the late fifteenth century, the "wine of ablution" was still applied in very few places, such as Speyer and Cologne, to the lips of the child after baptism, and this was not regarded as full-fledged Communion. Like confirmation, the first Communion was reserved for a later time.[35]

MARTIN LUTHER'S REVISIONS OF BAPTISM

By 1523 Luther had decided that Scripture warranted only two sacraments. Having eliminated all but two out of a field of seven, he and his fellow Reformers focused much attention on baptism and Communion.[36] In contrast to pure theology on the gamut of subjects, which could fairly well be confined to learned circles, these were regularly enacted before congregations and involved them at various stages in their lives. The way these two sacraments were carried out symbolized the differences in religious leaders' thought and came to be the most prominent features by which emerging denominations were recognized and described.

But 1523 was, nevertheless, early. At this stage, the Wittenberg nightingale was still treading lightly upon people's consciences and practices, confident that the Word of God would work changes in the human heart.[37] Two events would ultimately change his mind: the Peasants' War of 1525 and the Ernestine Saxon parish visitation of 1528–1529, in which he himself took part. These produced in him the first stirrings of militancy and a sense of the need to condone the efforts of the secular power, as Luther saw it, to assist the Word in taking root. This change of mood was in any case yet ahead when the epoch-making Augustinian friar translated the baptismal rubric used in Wittenberg into German.[38] He did not wish to hurry people, but above all, he was convinced, the Word could hardly penetrate hearts and minds if it was not articulated in a language that they understood. In preparing "The Little Book of Baptism in German" in 1523, his main purpose was to reveal to the masses not educated in Latin what in fact was occurring when their babies were christened, and to move them to greater devotion.[39] He stated in his postscript

> I haven't yet wanted to change anything in particular in the baptismal booklet ... To spare weak consciences I let it stay almost as it is, so that they don't complain that I want to bring in a new baptism and find fault with those who have been baptized up till now, as though they weren't properly baptized.[40]

Incorporating the vernacular into the ritual was a process already well underway in the late Middle Ages.[41] In the same epilogue, Luther gives a foretaste of the opinions that he would shortly assert more vehemently. He wrote that more than ritual exorcism and the use of salt, spittle, oil, chrism, gown, and candle were necessary to protect a child from the

Devil. For, he insisted, baptism could take place without any of these. To frighten demons, Christians needed to listen to God's Word with all seriousness and pray heartily with the priest for the baby's wellbeing.[42]

In the text of the rite, Luther did make three innovations nevertheless: he somewhat curtailed the number of exorcisms; he omitted the admonition to godparents and the recitation of the Creed; and he inserted a prayer of his own invention that stressed the (familiar) image of the Great Flood as the equivalent of baptism, by means of which Noah and his family were washed of their sins. Using this rubric, the priest was to pray to God,

> that you would graciously look upon N. and fill his spirit with the bliss of true faith, so that by means of this healing Flood all that was born in him from Adam and all that he has added to it may be drowned and may perish. And may he be set apart from the numbers of those without faith, and held dry and secure within the holy Arc of Christianity ...[43]

There is no question, however, of Luther's belief in the perpetual danger presented by the Devil. At this point, he was content to point out in his postscript that interior faith was more effective than either gesture or substance in combating Lucifer.

Three years later, the picture was quite different. By this time, owing to the disaster of the preceding year, Luther was beginning to see the need to be more aggressive—less attentive to fragile consciences—in articulating and promoting his vision. His practical competitors, among them Ulrich Zwingli, Thomas Müntzer, Andreas Bodenstein von Karlstadt, and early Anabaptists, had not been shy in asserting their leadership and in the process persuading numerous people of the correctness of their teachings. Karlstadt had publicly taken those to task who were slow about making changes out of purported fear that the people would be offended. To his mind, Christian truth mattered far more than human comfort.[44] Luther's close friend Nicolaus Hausmann, pastor in Zwickau, was pressing him, "so that there might be peace," to add a revised German baptismal liturgy to the "German Mass" that, also under Hausmann's urging, he had seen published at the beginning of the year.[45]

The "Little Book of Baptism Revised" of 1526 shows the boldness and strength of the Reformer's conviction.[46] He turned his previous epilogue into a prologue, excising the part about sparing weak consciences. Although a core of the old Catholic ceremony remained, Luther further shortened the service chiefly by eliminating several exorcisms and two traditional prayers that he had included in 1523. He retained, however, his "Great Flood" prayer. He also omitted the exsufflation, the application of spittle to the infant's ears and nose, anointing the child with oil before the baptism and chrism or oil afterward, and the burning candle, together with the words pertaining to the sacramentals. Although the baby was still to be dressed in its white gown—as it was in much of Germany throughout the early modern period—Luther now excluded the accompanying words, "Receive a white robe, holy and unstained..." A generous kernel of the old rite remained, then, but without the lengthy—in Luther's eyes gratuitous—non-scriptural additions of a millennium. He substantially reduced the proportion of attention to the diabolical presence and to magical measures taken to counter it.

Martin Luther believed that he was paring the ceremony back to its essential elements. All the same, it bears observing that both in his foreword and in his rubric Luther considered the Devil to be a threat. Twice the officiating clergyman must command the "impure spirit" to come out of the baptisand, and in the opening exorcism the wording is, "Come out...and give place to the Holy Ghost." Evil powers were still seen as so mighty that if they did not make way—if they were not ritually *forced* to make way—the divine Spirit could perhaps not have taken up residence in the child. In Luther's script, the sign of the cross is still applied to the infant's breast and back, as though it required fortification on both sides to frustrate Satan. These remaining acts reveal a persistent worldview, one that we know the Reformer continued to share with the masses of his contemporaries. Luther had closely examined and thought about the proper baptismal rite.[47] He was no longer in a compromising mood. He intended to include acts and words that were both scripturally acceptable and necessary to validity. At the same time, of course, the verbal makeup of the celebration reflects his more abstract theology—his conviction that baptism was a sign of interior washing, a "heavenly bath." Luther did not write of baptism as the entry of the infant into the Christian community, although in his prologue he stressed the benefits of the godparents' pious concentration and prayer for their charge. The ritual itself suggests to us that baptism was yet crucial to the child's lifelong spiritual wellbeing: it cleansed him of his inheritance from Adam, which is to say, original sin, and it permitted the Holy Spirit to enter him and begin its regenerative work. In his larger catechism of 1529, Luther wrote,

> Two things take place in baptism: water is poured upon our bodies, which can perceive nothing but the water; and the Word is spoken to the soul, that the soul may have its share also. Now, as water and Word constitute one baptism, so shall both body and soul be saved and live for ever: the soul through the Word, in which it believes; but the body because it is united with the soul and grasps baptism in such a manner as it may. Hence, no greater jewel can adorn our body or soul than baptism; for through it perfect holiness and salvation become accessible to us, which are otherwise beyond the reach of man's life and energy.[48]

Luther's closing benediction of 1526 sums up his view: "May the almighty God and Father of our Lord Jesus Christ, who through water and the Holy Spirit has given you a new birth and has forgiven all your sins, strengthen you with his grace to eternal life."[49] Theologically Luther ascribed all the good that occurred in baptism to the action of God. But if we leave doctrine aside for a moment and stand on the outside to examine the ritual, we see that to Lutheran baptism was ascribed tremendous power over the unseen world; it was indispensable. Whether or not it was God's chosen vehicle for bringing his grace to bear upon the individual, in the end it was necessary for salvation.

A feature missing from the Lutheran baptismal rite was the distinction between male and female baptisands. Neither "Baptismal Booklet" made reference to gender. Only Andreas Osiander, in his 1524 translation of the Latin rite for Nuremberg, kept the sex-specific prayers and exorcisms, but soon Luther's ritual was in use there.[50] In the subsequent ecclesiastical ordinances, prayers that had been for use with one sex or the other were apparently now said over infant boys and girls alike. Yet what we know about reformed practice in other rituals—especially marriage and Holy Communion, and the reinforcement of gender-specific order of sitting, of standing, of receiving the bread and the wine—makes me wonder whether at least the first generation of Lutheran clergy did not continue to place girls on their left and boys on their right and, by the direction of their faces during these and other prayers, continue the observances of the preceding ages. Still, it is significant that the handbooks no longer contain such instructions.

OTHER PROTESTANT VISIONS

Franz Lau once described the years from the beginning of the Reformation up until 1525 as a time of "wild growth" (*Wildwuchs*), when Luther was simply one, albeit an influential one, among a number of rebels against Catholic practice, each of whom thought himself divinely inspired. The teachings of these men, who preached openly within their cities and the country around and who were aided by the printing press, were not identical. On the contrary, they differed considerably.[51] Although ultimately Luther's second baptismal rite predominated in Germany from Nuremberg to the north, the situation was especially different in the southwest.[52] Here influences against which the north of Germany was temporarily insulated were at work, coming from France and Switzerland. Under the leadership of reform-minded clergy at Strasbourg, especially Martin Bucer, church ritual underwent more thoroughgoing alteration than it would in other areas.[53] Late in 1524 Bucer's work on liturgical revision appeared under the title, *The Reason and Cause... of the Innovations in the Lord's Supper..., Baptism, Images, and Song in the Congregation of Christ ... Undertaken in Strasbourg*.[54]

At this early date, Bucer and his colleagues were prepared to strip away tradition and, as they saw it, to restore baptism to its pristine condition in the early church. They proposed the summary abolition of all exorcisms, sacramentals, and "superstitious" gestures. They even toyed with the notion of ending infant baptism.[55] Bucer was blunt:

> We hold the external rite of baptism for a sign of the true baptism of Christ, that is, of the inner purification, rebirth and renewal, on account of which you should consider and think of yourselves and others as those who are committed to Christ and will obtain this inner new birth; and the washing away of sins and renewal of the mind will be attributed to Christ alone, who cleanses his elect by his Spirit, granting them faith and salvation...
>
> The other reform or innovation in regard to baptism is that we pay no heed to the teaching about chrism, oil, salt, clay and candles, nor do we use them. The reason for this is that they are human inventions without warrant in God's Word, which have been the cause of much superstition. Hence it has come to pass that this chrism and oil can be consecrated only by a bishop and only on Maundy Thursday. So also many people have not been allowed to bathe their children until the priest has been paid a penny or a groat to wipe off the chrism and oil. Such magic tricks ill become intelligent and rational Christians, who ought to pay heed to the word of their Lord and follow it alone. Therefore our practice is to baptize children without all this pomp after a short exposition of the nature and significance of baptism and common prayer that Christ will baptize the child with his spirit and cleanse him from all his sins, and to commend them to their godparents and the other brethren, that they may love them as their fellow members in Christ and lead them to Christ...[56]

The city fathers approved the adoption of rites that incorporated Bucer's advice; the simple, unadorned act of baptism remained.[57] The introduction to their rubric tells the clergy to discourage people from hurrying their sickly babies to baptism "as if the whole of salvation depended on an outward washing alone." It insists that salvation depends upon God's choices and not upon men's acts.[58] On the other hand, baptism should not be unduly postponed, for, like circumcision among the Jews, it represents the child's introduction into the body of Christians, with whom God had made a covenant.[59] In order better to represent to the people this joining of the Christian community, baptism was supposed to take place on Sunday before the congregation, "so that the baptism of the child, the presentation and entrusting of him to the church with the prayers for him may take place...in the presence of God's people."[60] Officiating clergy were to speak the words of the ritual in a loud, clear voice so that all in attendance could hear:

It is proper that all parts of the application of holy baptism be carried out in a loud and understandable voice and in that part of the church where everyone in particular can easily hear and understand everything. For the action and procedure of the holy sacrament affect the entire church and are not private...but are [the] collective and public action of the churches...

The explanations of the sacrament were no longer for the instruction of the "catechumens" seeking baptism, but were directed to the entire visible church.[61] These explanations, usually in the form of long, sermon-like prefaces to the actual ritual, indoctrinated all the faithful. During the sixteenth century, baptismal services exceeded their early Reformation models in length until they were every bit as long as the late medieval ones. But the material that took the place of the repeated exorcisms was now explanatory and exhortatory, pressing proper understanding and virtuous behavior upon the people gathered in the church.

Practical circumstances moved administrators of the church to permit baptisms on weekdays too, but only after a regularly scheduled sermon. However few they were, then, members of the congregation were there as observers and represented their absent neighbors. For this sacrament introduced the individual into Christendom, not an abstract list of members but a community whose behavior, an outer manifestation of true sentiment, was to include proper, compassionate, helpful interaction. God gave children through their parents as a gift to the entire congregation and church.[62] Private baptisms were improper in that they failed to embody the communal principle inherent in the sacrament. It would not be far-fetched to think that even in the organization and exposition of the baptismal ceremony we can see reflections of the greater southwest German focus upon those communal ideals to which Peter Blickle has drawn our attention.[63]

The words of the service embodied this intended emphasis upon membership in the Christian collectivity. No longer did the officiant ask the baby if it wished to be baptized, but he straightforwardly addressed the godparents: "Are you willing that this child be baptized?" On learning the infant's name, he then instructed his listeners that faith was a gift, and it could not grow except "only by the operation of the invisible power of God." He prayed that the little one might enjoy this regeneration by the Spirit, signified by the outer washing of the sacrament. He called upon the entire congregation to ask God to confer faith upon this child and make him "a fellow heir, fellow member and fellow partaker of the promises in Christ." He charged the godparents and also everyone who was present to "teach this child Christian order, discipline and fear of God." Baptism joined the individual to the group of his neighbors; if the Holy Spirit successfully worked upon the child, he would mature and live in a way that manifested order, discipline, and fear. These were, as I have suggested, qualities that were now given greater priority across Europe than ever before; even the words of the common baptismal rite testified to this. The rubric closed with an admonition to the clergy not to let any usage become a fixed custom: "For the minds of the simple immediately descend to that level and they will put their trust in them, which is contrary to a pure faith in Christ."[64]

The Strasbourg ritual, then, constituted a much more complete break with late medieval patterns than Luther's second "Baptismal Booklet" did. It dismissed nearly every past practice, including the leading into the sanctuary, exorcisms, the sign of the cross, and the baptismal gown. Its spirit was more optimistic concerning the relative might of God and the Devil, for the Devil was not even mentioned. God alone, through the work of the Holy Ghost, had the capacity to make the developing individual, enmeshed in the community, triumphant. Sacramentals were not only superfluous but they challenged God's omnipotence! Later in the century, Calvinists held similar views, which translated into ritual practice. They insisted on an end to exorcism, the sign of the cross, directing baptismal questions to babies, emergency baptism by women, and much more.[65]

The Strasbourg prescription was, as Hughes Oliphant Old has recently shown, more influential than had previously been thought. Even the Zurich baptismal rite incorporated some of its language as religious leaders there, confronted with the specter of Anabaptist voluntarism, sought formulae that stressed the divine rather than the human will.[66] They also produced long, detailed rationales for infant as opposed to adult baptism. Revisions made in the Strasbourg order of baptism reflected the emphasis upon children. The preliminary prayers taught the listeners that indeed infant baptism was the sign of the new covenant, the old covenant with Abraham having been sealed by the circumcision of baby boys.[67] The words reflect the conviction that Christians must *care* for their children, not only those of their flesh but those of all the congregation:

> In this faith, O heavenly Father, grant that we may baptize this infant (*these infants*), that we may accordingly all be moved and ever led to regard him (*them*) henceforth as our fellow member(s) in Christ in all things, that we may faithfully pray for him (*them*), carefully bring him (*them*) up and assist him (*them*) in every way, so that by him (*them*) thy name may be hallowed and thy kingdom extended, and that both here and everywhere he (*they*) may delight to live in accordance with thy will . . . We also pray thee to keep him (*them*) in health of body, to provide for him (*them*) in every necessity, and of thy fatherly love to deliver him (*them*) from all evil . . .[68]

The implication may well have been intentional that Anabaptists did not cherish or properly provide for their offspring. Baptismal prayers may be an underutilized source for studies of ideal attitudes toward childhood. In addition to these prayers, baptismal services in Switzerland and southwest Germany gradually made references to children's parents in their services, bringing into prominence a bond that the medieval rubrics noticeably neglected.[69] Nevertheless, every baby had godparents (usually at least one woman and one man), and these, as under Catholicism, held their spiritual progeny and assisted during the service. Their duties of instruction in the Christian faith as their godchildren grew were regarded very seriously, more so than in the late Middle Ages. The Hessian church ordinance of 1566 called godparents "guarantors"—that is, in the legal sense, people who were legally liable for the fulfillment of promises made "by" their charge: "Now, in worldly matters no one would take on as guarantors any other than trustworthy people whom one could count on to be able and to want to keep faith."[70] They were sternly informed that "with and next to his parents as coparents" they were to undertake the child's Christian education.[71] In one of two ritual forms provided, the godparents were asked to swear that they desire from their hearts to baptize the infant. They had to reply, "I desire it from my heart, to the honor of God [and] the improvement and increase of the Christian church; I am also willing to swear for this child and to pledge my faith."[72] In each of the godparents' replies to several queries, they had to affirm "from the heart." A merely positive answer was not enough. The official church regarded theirs as a solemn oath and, in case of the parents' death or dereliction, an onerous responsibility. During the late sixteenth and early seventeenth centuries, the state played an expanding role in enforcing its vision of the proper godparent. A father had to tell the pastor in advance whom he had selected to hold and represent his child, and the clergyman was to make sure that these were adults and morally upstanding individuals.[73] In 1610, Count Ludwig of Nassau ordered his visitors to inquire, among many other things, if the godparents of children who could not pass their catechism examinations were allowed themselves to take Communion, implying that they were barred from doing so.[74] If carried out, this could even have ended in the exile of godparents who did not fulfill their obligations.

One of the procedural details that engrossed the Reformers was whether infants ought to be immersed naked in the font or basin, or if it was sufficient to sprinkle or pour water over their heads (with no regard to whether their bodies were clothed or not).[75] Practices already differed prior to the Reformation. The Catholic ritual handbooks showed a preference for either sprinkling or pouring holy water on the head of the infant (*aspersio* or *superfusio*), although the Cologne rubric of 1485 maintained that babies should be dipped in the font unless they were too weak to endure this, or unless the priest were not strong enough to perform the immersion.[76] When immersion was used, there was a tendency from the later medieval period on not to submerge the baby's head.[77] Both of Luther's "Baptismal Booklets" prescribe immersion, which may well have followed the Magdeburg precedent.[78] Luther's ruler, Elector Johann Friedrich, ordered in his general ecclesiastical ordinance that either babies could be dipped in the font or water could be poured over them (*begiessen*), but by no means was it permissible simply to apply a drop or two to their bodies or foreheads.[79] Bucer's early Strasbourg rubric provides for the pouring of water, and its successor of 1537 agrees with this, adding the detail that the application of water is threefold (*trine*) and that the baby is undressed. But, when Johann Bugenhagen arrived in Hamburg in 1529, he was surprised to find that aspersion was in use there and that the babies remained clad in diapers or other clothing. He personally thought the clergyman should cup water in his hand and pour it over the bare child's head and back.[80] Lucas Cranach showed Melanchthon doing precisely this in the Wittenberg altar of 1547.[81] The Hamburgers did not alter their custom, and this form gained in currency first in southern Germany and then also in other parts of the north.[82] Elector Ottheinrich of the Rhenish Palatinate noted the diversity of practice in his ecclesiastical ordinance of 1556, but he concluded,

> Because in the church everything should happen in an orderly and improving manner, we have thought it useful that the infants be unswaddled, except that, in order to avoid danger, they should not be dipped in the water but rather, water should be poured on their bare bodies.[83]

In the administrative district (*Amt*) of Neuffen in the duchy of Württemberg at the beginning of the seventeenth century, the visitors found that every village pastor poured water three times upon the forehead of the baptisand. A couple of them also poured water on the child's bare chest, but this was uncommon.[84]

From the start of the Reformation, territories in the German southwest tended to carry out a more drastic revision of inherited usages than those in the north. Eventually inclining toward the Calvinist view that baptismal fonts themselves were superstitious objects, some even had the fonts replaced by simple brass basins.[85] We may speculate that such alterations reflected in part the more radical change radiating out of Switzerland—including, from mid-century, Geneva—and in part because of the concentration in that region of humanistically oriented church leaders, intent upon recovering New Testament "purity." Too, in the cities of the southwest, preaching services, with the emphasis on the sermon but with a brief Mass at the end, were familiar and offered the precedent of simplicity. No doubt the reasons were woven of these strands and others (such as dynastic politics) besides.

Another matter that exercised leaders of church and state during the sixteenth century was baptismal exorcism.[86] The Reformers in Strasbourg and Württemberg (and Zurich) eliminated it very early on, along with every other "superstitious" act and object.[87] As Bucer had said, "Such magic tricks ill become intelligent and rational Christians." But in the more thoroughly Lutheran territories, exorcism, however abbreviated, was retained; in these areas criticism of it tended to link the critic, to his peril, with one or another of the forbidden southwestern varieties of Protestantism—with Zwinglianism or, later, Calvinism, or even with Anabaptism. Partly for political reasons, Elector Joachim II of Brandenburg retained the elaborate, multifold exorcism of the Catholic rubrics in his ecclesiastical ordinance of 1540.[88] And, in fact, any move to omit exorcism was associated with the "second Reformation" of the second half of the century, usually Calvinist in nature. In Saxony, for example, Elector Christian I succeeded his father, August, in 1586 and immediately set about introducing Calvinist changes in the liturgy even though technically never publicly repudiating the recent intra-Lutheran Formula of Concord. Among many other Calvinist impositions, he insisted that exorcism cease. Pastors had to submit on this, as on every other point, or go into exile. Remarkably clear, and highly relevant to the theme of this book, is that many common people, above all those who had not undergone a humanist education, vehemently opposed the omission of exorcism. In Zwickau the elite, including city councilors and the clerical staff of St. Mary's Church, the leading church of the city, supported their prince; arrayed against them were the clergy of St. Catherine's Church, traditionally a gathering place for discontented members of the working class, and most guildsmen and tradespeople. In the Holy Cross Church in Dresden, a butcher forced the pastor, threatening him with a cleaver, to include the words of exorcism in the baptism of his daughter. Other people all over the land chose to take their newborns to a neighboring principality where exorcism was still in force.[89] Christian's death in September 1591 brought this Reformed episode to a precipitous close, and ecclesiastical rituals reverted to their Lutheran forms—with the notable exception that exorcism remained abolished. Under the leadership of the nobility, but including people of every class, anti-Calvinist "storms" temporarily shook the land.[90] But one aspect of the storms was an effort to restore exorcism! The visitors in Liebenwerda learned from the city council in 1592 that the people would have been willing to let their babies "lie there" without baptism for over six weeks rather than forgo exorcism. In fact, one woman had undergone churching several days before her infant was christened.[91] One burgher in Delitzsch was reported to have said on a social occasion that he wished the Devil had taken all of those who were doing away with exorcism. The mayor reported him for this. Another man stated that the nobles in his area had resisted abrogating exorcism.[92] There were differences of opinion. Yet popular pressure might help to explain, along with a tendency in the sixteenth century to return to "high" liturgical forms, why the Württemberg church ordinance of 1553 reintroduced exorcism. This also came at a time when Calvinist theology, even without the help of state governments, was spreading beyond Geneva and posing questions to theologians that had to be answered. Political factors were at work as well.[93]

Saxony was not alone in experiencing an upheaval over the issue of exorcism—which had become a symbol of loyalty to Luther. In 1589, Dukes Joachim Ernst and Johann Georg of Anhalt, father and son, decreed an end to exorcism. It began seven years later, following the latter's marriage to a daughter of the Calvinist Count of the Rhenish Palatinate, Johann Casimir, a thoroughgoing revision of all ecclesiastical ritual, in accord with Calvinist teaching. From there the controversy infected much of Brandenburg, where it simmered into the second half of the seventeenth century.[94]

Underlying this conflict were, at least on the surface, diametrically opposed doctrines of baptism; and for propaganda purposes each side asserted that this was so. When Reformed clergymen accused their Lutheran colleagues of carrying on a Catholic theology of works—and "superstitious" works to boot—they were not altogether off the mark. The insistence upon exorcism did suggest to learned and less educated citizens alike that this act was somehow necessary to a child's salvation. The urgency with which babies, even those born out of wedlock, were to be brought to baptism, as well as the Lutheran retention of emergency baptism by women in the birthing room, undergirded this impression.[95] Ironically, before the argument between the parties grew heated, and also later, when despite inter-credal strife some principalities did away with exorcism, Lutheran leaders could concede, following Martin Luther himself, that exorcism was an *adiaphoron*, an act that was not part of the essential scriptural core of the rite. But when the level of anger rose, the possibility of compromising on the basis of a common theological base became remote. Lutherans accused Calvin's followers of making baptism ineffective for most of Christian humankind and thus of abandoning the Word of God. In the turmoil in Saxony after the death of Christian I in 1591, when recently arrived Calvinist pastors were forced out or compelled to sign Lutheran articles of the faith, several key points focused on baptism. They had to agree that "baptism does wash us of sin"; that baptism effects such a cleansing that "we persist [*beharren*] in such covenant and trust unto the end" and are not lost but obtain eternal life; that all who are baptized have drawn to Christ; that "unless a person is born of water and the Spirit, he cannot enter the kingdom of God," except in cases of death before baptism.[96] In the early seventeenth-century anti-Calvinist broadsheet, "The Calvinist Disguise, That is, a True Depiction of Calvinist Precepts That Are Now Gaining Ground"

("Caluinisch Deckmantel, Daß ist: Warhaftig Abdildnus [*sic*] des itz einreissenden Caluini"), Lutherans accused Calvin's successor Theodore Beza of teaching "that in baptism the power of new birth is not ascribable nor applicable to all children."[97] Exorcism aside, then, their theological conceptions of baptism did differ. To Lutherans, baptism did effect change, a newness of life, that overcame original sin (but not non-original sin) and without which no one could be saved.[98] To Calvinists, it was an outward sign of an election that had already occurred, a faith that already existed within the individual and that required no ecclesiastical observance to set it in motion. Nevertheless, God had commanded Christians to undergo baptism. Calvinists perceived and adopted as their own the substantial social significance of baptism that their Zwinglian and southwest German predecessors had expressed in their own ceremonies.[99] Social historians have learned not to expect complete consistency between theological precept and practice. These discrepancies will appear again when we come to the subject of confession/absolution. For both Lutherans and Calvinists, baptism was an outer washing accompanied by the interior working of the Holy Spirit. Had they concentrated upon the shared elements in their theology, they might have achieved conciliation. But each sought conciliation strictly on its own terms; the sixteenth century did not look kindly on compromise. Nonetheless, late medieval and early modern European Christianity ever sought means of "washing" souls regarded as sullied by their humanity.

POPULAR PRACTICE

Among people of all ranks, including the nobility, baptism held out the promise of two advantages, the one supernatural and the other earthly. First, as with other rituals, this initiatory observance, through its occurrence in sacred space, its administration by a man empowered to manipulate the unseen, and by its inclusion of exorcism and sacramentals, afforded every infant a degree of lifelong divine protection against evil forces. Such forces were, of course, implicated in every misfortune. Above all, baptism was prerequisite to salvation, although only a person's subsequent behavior mediated and mitigated by the rest of the sacramental system could virtually guarantee one's final entry into paradise.

Just what the non-privileged members of society may have thought about baptism is easier to base on impressions gleaned from myriad kinds of sources than it is firmly to document. However, parish visitors in Saxony-Weimar at the end of the sixteenth century were dismayed to discover that in the village of Altenberga the people continued to recite a request for baptism that, the pastor reported, had already been in use when he had arrived forty-two years before; and everyone knew it by heart even though they could not remember what the catechism said about baptism. The godparents arrived at the church bearing the child. They recited,

> Worthy [and] dear sir, I come here together with this company and bring a small, poor baby that was conceived and born in sin in accordance with the flesh of Adam, where it wantonly would remain and would die in sin, so that it would have to be eternally damned and lost. But because the Lord Christ has commanded that children be brought to him and promises them the kingdom of Heaven, so we beg you, a servant of God, to bring him [the child] into the communion and merit of Christ, so that it is thereby freed from God's wrath and may become a child of eternal blessedness and remain with us forever.[100]

This was a rite of popular participation in the pre-Reformation baptismal ceremony, when the priest greeted the infant "seeking" consecration at the threshold of the church and subjected it and its sponsors to the long preliminaries for the catechumen. Here the people spoke a part resembling half of a dialogue in a mystery drama. Theirs was an active role. It corresponds to the elaborate grave prayers that parishioners said in parts of Germany, kneeling at the burial site in the cemetery.[101] Visitors ruled these impermissible. The visitors doubtless found here, too, that this lay petition was incompatible with the uniformity that rulers now sought to impose on every ritual. Above all, though, it suggests that the people still accepted the Catholic teaching that baptism was a precondition of safety here and of salvation after death.

Further, the belief was very widespread that the water in (or with which) a baby had been christened was a powerful remedy for any ailment of man or beast. Other kinds of blessed water also had curative virtues, from the basic holy water that the priest consecrated on Sundays to water associated with particular saints' days, such as St. Blasius (February 3) and St. Stephen (December 26).[102] But baptismal water possessed even greater potency. In theory, prior to the Reformation it had had to be blessed by the suffragan bishop (*Weihbischof*), who was supposed to travel around the diocese rendering this and other objects sacred. But, by the end of the Middle Ages, the baptismal rubrics themselves often included the necessary exorcisms of font, water, salt, oil, and chrism. In any case, the people were especially eager to obtain this substance for their own purposes, and the Catholic clergy were content that they should have it. The Lutheran visitation protocols, however, reveal authorities' determination that they should *not* obtain what now was considered a superstitious element that the people would only employ in their ungodly magical rites. They repeatedly required pastors and sextons discreetly to pour out the used water of baptism in the churchyard or into a creek, where no one could retrieve it. Typical is the command for the lands of the archchapter of Magdeburg in 1585 that any sexton who made baptismal water available to people to use in trying to cure their livestock, or for other magical purposes, would lose his job. The water was to be poured out immediately after each baptism.[103] Official and popular worldviews clearly diverged.

Second, situated within a network of family and friends by means of the reality of blood ties and the selection of godparents, baptism also afforded the newborn the hope—or rather, their parents' hope—of future benefit. Godparents named children in the christening ceremony, often after themselves. Godparents were supposed to give their spiritual offspring a present on the first anniversary of their birth or of their baptism (these dates usually being very close together) and on other occasions such as Christmas or New Year, Easter, or on the child's first Communion. Red-dyed Easter eggs were typical gifts.[104] Occasionally a knight served as godparent to many of the infants born in his villages and made a monetary gift to the parents that was so desirable that, if the nobleman were away or ill, fathers sought to postpone Christian initiation despite the risks of death and damnation. This was the case in a village in Württemberg, and in 1585 the members of the pertinent synod told the pastor that he must not let his parishioners put off baptism, "for if an unforeseen death without baptism should occur, this would place not a small burden upon the parents' consciences."[105] Parents may well have tried to obtain godparents who were of sufficiently high socioeconomic station that they could afford to grant favors.[106] An era that was as poor in catechetical instruction as the late Middle Ages presumably did not hold godparents to their technical duty to see that their charges were taught the basic tenets of the faith.

Before as after the Reformation, the midwife was characteristically prominent among those adults who carried the newborn to church. She was a woman of humble standing who nevertheless enjoyed the mystique of someone privy to the great mysteries and trials of the birthing room—and who herself, each time she bore a child to baptism, relinquished her unique privilege of administering the sacrament in cases of emergency. Among the poor, the midwife was sometimes the only godparent. Higher up the social echelons, however, the numbers of such sponsors increased, sometimes exceeding any reasonable moderation as families sought to seal a bond with as many potential patrons as possible. Catholic and Protestant churches objected to this excess. In general, they limited the number of sponsors to no more than three. The social reality was, nonetheless, that godparents were carefully selected, and obtaining the best ones might mean postponing baptism long enough for someone to travel to distant residences, obtain their consent, and accompany them back.

Childbirth being fraught with the risk that it was, successful reproduction was a cause for rejoicing. If godparents, friends, and relatives came from neighboring towns, a father was bound to entertain them whether he could afford to or not. And he did. Officially the mother was still confined to childbed, and other women would have prepared as lavish refreshments as the Host could afford. Most of the party would have escorted the midwife and the baby to the church and observed as the priest (and later the pastor) performed his office. Yet, the parish visitors decried the fact that fathers did not attend their children's christening. As late as 1622 in Weimar, they were still having to fine men for this infraction.[107] Women bound protective herbs in the baby's clothing to give it additional protection against danger.[108] Before the Reformation, baptism was likely to occur at many times of day and hardly before the assembled community. Afterward, as we have seen, this changed. Under Catholicism, after half an hour or so, family and friends returned to the infant's dwelling or other abode to drink and to frolic. Under Lutheranism, this recreation would have had to be postponed by the length of a sermon. The hour of fun arrived, in any case. In the countryside, celebrations, including excessive food and drink, are said to have gone on for "three and four days."[109] If the mother were ill, she may not have appreciated the cacophony; but the sources never give us a sense of the mother's desires.

It was the custom, before and after the Reformation, for friends and neighbors to give presents to the newborn. Women also made gifts for the mother. Sometimes these were given on separate occasions, three weeks after parturition, the mother's friends and neighbors calling specifically on her and putting their offerings on her bed. These often took the form of nourishing food such as eggs, or a source of food (a hen—as egg-layer, also a reproductive symbol) that would help the mother regain her strength. Some presents were given during the post-christening festivities. Civil authorities began to express their disapproval in "police" ordinances during the later fifteenth century. They objected to the postponement of baptism so that relatives would have time to arrive; they criticized the scale and lavishness of the parties, which often undermined the economic stability of the newborn's household; they sought to limit the size of gifts that women or anyone could give either the mother or the child.

Enforcement first became effective after the Reformation, as one aspect of the process that we call confessionalization. Or perhaps the volume of complaints in the visitation registers indicates that it did *not* become effective. What is certain is that state and church exerted themselves. Princes and magistrates set limits according to social class on post-baptismal entertainments and the size of gifts. In the early seventeenth century in Thuringia, the poor and day laborers could offer the godparents of their children (and no one else) at most "cake and a drink." Violators were to suffer imprisonment.[110] In Geneva, the authorities outlawed the conferring of names that were associated with Catholic "superstition," angering the populace through what seemed to be an arbitrary curtailment of family naming patterns and the crucial relationships to living friends and relations that underlay them.[111]

All in all, the populace at large continued to regard baptism as possessing two levels of utility. It was the indispensable fortress against the Devil and facilitator of eternal bliss, and it cemented beneficial alliances in worldly society. In order to secure the second advantage, families *had* to look beyond the village or town confines to a territorial radius of as much as several days' travel time. Lutherans even reached into Catholic and Calvinist lands, for their circles of friends knew no political boundaries, but those in authority perpetually combated this.[112] Parents expressed not only their satisfaction at obtaining an(other) heir but also their need to consolidate a kinship network that might improve their and their children's material outlook. This kinship could be spiritual as well as biological. For their part, infants' fathers were bound by standards of etiquette to entertain those who agreed to the forging of this bond. Fathers had to demonstrate their generosity toward the baptismal party by means of plentiful food and drink. This demonstration was clearly a ritual of its own, one that the authorities failed to appreciate. But because it was essential, and indeed at every level of society, the wielders of power probably failed to eliminate it. Their prohibitions increase in severity into the seventeenth century, with threatened penalties growing ever harsher. These bespeak a popular determination to retain practices that they found to be in their own and their children's best interest.

Before the Reformation the outlook of average parish clergy, to judge from ritual contents, coincided quite neatly with that of a majority of their parishioners. Very few of either category had any familiarity with theology and little education. Both groups generally believed in the efficacy of baptism as a channel of divine grace. Exorcism and sacramentals were hardly objectionable, but properly forfended trouble. The similarity in the socioeconomic provenance of the priest to that of his neighbors meant, too, that both understood the societal dimensions of the larger celebration of baptism, including its worldly and its churchly portions. Priests probably attended many a christening breakfast.

The Reformation strove to alter the picture. In the name of New Testament purity, theologians and other urban and lettered people now undertook to eliminate the ritual accretions of the ages. Even where they were able to enforce their versions of proper baptism, the visitation literature shows that through much of Germany people adhered to their own interpretation of even the transformed baptismal liturgy. And in their collective interaction they resisted what they saw as policies that jeopardized their social and economic wellbeing.

REFORMED CONFIRMATION

A lengthy treatment of pre-Reformation confirmation is not needed, for with the separation of this rite from that of baptism it fell into neglect.[113] Its status as one of the seven sacraments is surprising, for it elevated that anointing and invocation of the Holy Spirit that had concluded baptism to the highest status, at a time when in practice it hardly seemed to matter any longer. The catechumenate faded away, and in most places all that remained of a serious effort to indoctrinate the next generation was the briefest questioning, as a preliminary to confession, concerning one's familiarity with the Lord's Prayer, the Ave Maria, and perhaps the Ten Commandments. Technically, the Apostles' Creed too should have been a prerequisite for receiving the first Communion, but without a formal instruction process the people could hardly have learned it. Priestly confessors used their office almost wholly to detect and liberate the penitent seeker from the burden of sin.[114] Thus, confirmation had all but been subsumed under the sacrament of penance. What remained was a cursory rite—made up of the application of holy oil to a child's forehead and the laying on of hands, performed by the bishop on those infrequent occasions when he toured his diocese—of admission to adult Christianity. It was a vestigial remain of the personal episcopal cure of souls, which in its other aspects had been firmly delegated to the parish priests. It served to remind people of the technical source from which the priestly authority sprang.

Prominent by its absence from this observance was the requirement that children be familiar with the basic doctrines of their faith. Some city men noticed this lack. The urban demand for preaching grew out of the burghers' desire to be taught. A number of related developments converged in the late medieval city: outrage over the moral abuse of the confessional; government satiation with ecclesiastical tax and jurisdictional exemptions; the desire of a more literate citizenry for direct access to the scriptural message; an economic and cultural milieu that fostered humanist ideals. The Reformation emphasis upon preaching the unadulterated Word of God bore the imprint of a complex cultural matrix. Perfectly suitably, then, in educated burghers' and in the Reformers' terms, young Christians had to be indoctrinated. Baptism having been foreshortened in the century of Constantine, the church needed to fulfill its obligation and resurrect the amputated ritual. Protestantism did more than bring confirmation back to life: it amplified and extended it in such a way that, in the age of confessionalization, the subsidiary parts of which it was constructed came to serve both church and state. Many streams fed the impetus to instruct parishioners in some formal way.

Luther—and this he shared with many humanists[115]—early on saw the didactic element in preaching. It was not only the crucial method of making the spiritually transforming Word available to those who were receptive through faith; it was also food for the intellect. He would quickly perceive the valuable role that a restored and revised confirmation ritual qua ritual could play. His first critique of this Catholic sacrament appeared in 1520 in "The Babylonian Captivity of the Church." At that date, he was concerned to show that it was non-scriptural and did not fulfill the principal criterion of a true sacrament, that it be accompanied by a divine promise.

> Here it is to be noticed that the apostle [Paul] knows nothing of the sacrament of confirmation. For he teaches that the Holy Spirit is given in baptism, as Christ also teaches, indeed, in baptism we are reborn by the Holy Spirit. We read in the Acts of the Apostles that the apostles laid their hands on the heads of the baptized, so that they might receive the Holy Spirit, which is analogous to confirmation; but there it happens that the Holy Spirit is given with outward signs and causes men to speak in many tongues in order to preach the gospel. But this was a temporary measure and does not continue any more.[116]

As the 1520s went on, and Johann of Saxony launched parish inspection, Luther's abstract convictions took on a practical urgency as he realized at last how thoroughly dismal conditions throughout the territory were, among clergy and laity alike. He prepared his "Short Catechism" in haste in 1529, for it was badly needed. He exclaimed in the introduction,

> Dear God, help us! What misery I have seen! The common man, especially in the villages, knows absolutely nothing about Christian doctrine, and unfortunately, many pastors are practically unfit and incompetent to teach. Nevertheless, they are all called Christians, have been baptized, and enjoy the holy sacraments even though they can recite neither the Lord's Prayer, the Apostles' Creed, nor the Ten Commandments. They live just like animals and unreasoning sows . . .[117]

Luther himself did not draw up a rite of confirmation, but he left the possibility open that each pastor would teach and examine each child before admitting them to Communion, and that this was a kind of confirmation: "I allow," he wrote, "people to be confirmed as long as we know that God did not say anything about it."[118] But first of all the pastorate had to be taught. The early Lutheran church made a good beginning by means of the catechisms, eventually disseminated to every cleric. These helped, together with the 1528 "Visitors' Instructions to the Pastors in Electoral Saxony," the intermittent execution of parish visitation itself, and the creation of superintendencies to continue the oversight begun by itinerant inspectors. But bringing the entire pastorate up to an acceptable level of knowledge took the rest of the century; and improving the laity, especially in the villages, went on through the entire early modern period.[119]

By the 1530s, pastors were to see that their charges knew the fundamentals of the faith. Clergymen were to preach from the catechism, or at least expound on portions of it, to parishioners of all ages at least once a week. It quickly became evident that adults refused to attend, and haranguing seems not to have achieved the desired results. Church administrators concentrated on the children. They prescribed catechism classes for Sunday afternoons, after "the sermon," which had come to denote the service of worship with or without Communion. Householders were unfailingly to send both their offspring and their young servants. Laments concerning people's failure to do so fill the visitation registers, although conformity grew more widespread as penalties became more severe.

One of those penalties was public shame. The juvenile catechumens, generally between the ages of ten and thirteen or fourteen,[120] quickly had to demonstrate their prowess before the entire congregation, and those who failed the test could not begin to receive Communion. Martin Bucer, perhaps inspired by Erasmus,[121] wrote the first surviving ecclesiastical ordinance that provided a formal examination as an appendage to the Sunday service. On the day set for this quizzing on the catechism, people needed to come to church an hour earlier than usual. Children, their parents, and their godparents took places on the chancel dais. One child was asked in detail concerning the articles of the faith and about Holy Communion. He or she swore to believe all this, and in particular made the connection between baptism and the present ceremony; he or she vowed to remain in the Communion of the church and to attend divine services regularly. Each child in succession took a similar oath. A pastoral admonition and a prayer followed. Then the cleric laid his hands on the head of each child and said, "Receive the Holy Ghost, your protection against all that is wicked, strength and help toward all that is good, from the gracious hand of God the Father, Son, and Holy Ghost. Amen."[122] The entire congregation, including the newly confirmed, took Communion.

Later ordinances demanded far more of each young person, not just of one select child. In the plan drawn up by Martin Chemnitz in 1569, once again candidates, parents, and godparents arrayed themselves before their neighbors. The superintendent was to charge the children to do now what they were not able to do at baptism, namely to confess their faith publicly. Only then could they be admitted to Communion. Each child recited Luther's catechism from memory—the shorter one, I would guess!—and the clergyman pressed for further information, as proof of understanding, on specific parts. He praised the industry of those who had succeeded in their study. He asked them collectively if they renounced the Devil, as had been done at their baptism on their behalf, and if they would abide by their faith until the end of their lives. His homily requested the adults of the congregation to provide good models of behavior to the youth. It was left to each superintendent to decide if he would perform the laying on of hands. Then all sang "Come, Holy Ghost" and received Communion. This ordinance urges parents and godparents to enjoy this sacrament together with their children.[123]

The ecclesiastical ordinances are replete with provisions for the holding of confirmation. It is ironic that a ceremony that had fallen into desuetude prior to the Reformation was revived, reshaped, and given some prominence even though, the Reformers insisted, confirmation was not a sacrament. By the second half of the sixteenth century, it occurred before the altar, that most sacred space, with as much regularity as population growth warranted; but those who administered the territorial churches affirmed that, theologically, it was not as sacred an act as either baptism or Communion. Bjarne Hareide has given us a most useful study of the inner-Lutheran struggle over confirmation during and after the period of the Interim, when those who followed Flacius and those who agreed with Melanchthon argued passionately on either side of the issue of adiaphora. Flacius accused Melanchthon of going too far to accommodate the emperor and the pope. Melanchthon replied that although confirmation was an indifferent matter (adiaphoron) it had been founded by the early church.[124] I would argue that debates among the elite aside, confirmation filled two essential needs. The first was to rationalize the centuries-old preponderance of small children being baptized, who, as we have seen, were completely unable to testify to their own faith. At last the children had to speak for themselves. The ritual completed their initiation into the local Christian community, and it theologically concluded, by their consent, their baptismal engraftment onto the body of Christ. The second was to force each coming generation to learn the fundamental precepts of the faith. Until young people knew what it meant to be a Christian, discipline lacked any defining standard. The moment they sinned, confirmation made individuals violators of their *own*—not their godparents'—promises and declaration of faith. Even the southwest German divines who eliminated exorcism from their baptismal rites believed in the ubiquitous minions of Satan. Only by means of confirmation, in the course of which each person publicly demonstrated a personal understanding of those precepts being accepted, could they hold each person responsible for renouncing the Devil in the daily vicissitudes of life. In early modern Germany, oaths were solemn transactions, and confirmation possessed the character of an oath, for in it the individual confirmands committed themselves to the Christian faith. Henceforward, misdeeds were more than the breaking of civil and/or ecclesiastical law; they were a reneging on one's pledge to God. Civil crime was apostasy, and apostasy was civil crime. Confirmation as it evolved in Germany formed an essential part of the foundation upon which confessionalization and social discipline reposed.

CONCLUSIONS

James Fernandez has written that the analysis of metaphor seems to be the very nature of anthropological inquiry.[125] I have described above the fairly radical changes in structure and content of the baptismal rite in the transition from Catholicism to Protestantism in those lands that adopted either Lutheranism or Calvinism: the end of the priest's greeting the baptisand(s) at the door of the church, effectively barring him/her/them until subordinate rituals of purification and qualification were performed; the greater stress upon the community, to some degree everywhere but most especially in the German southwest; the elimination of the sacramentals of salt, oil, chrism, and candles. All of these changes contain within themselves their own metaphoric shifts. Yet the most dramatic alteration in metaphor stands revealed in the abolition of exorcism—in much of the southwest almost immediately and later in the century in parts of the north as well. Even where it was retained or reintroduced, its form and extent had undergone moderation.

In the late Middle Ages, Satan was the metaphoric category into which all but a few theologians deposited misfortune and human ills of every kind. We cannot presently know whether the masses were cognizant of the theoretical possibility that the Evil One was the instrument of God. It is more likely that they thought of the satanic as opposed to and by the divine, God's ultimate triumph over Lucifer occurring only at the end of the world. Even then, diabolic forces would simply be assigned to preside for all eternity over hell. Certain human beings, however, by virtue of their special knowledge and their office, could assist human society in fending off the otherwise ubiquitous battalions of darkness. These were the bona fide clergy, but they were also fortune tellers, soothsayers, potion makers, and the speakers of ritual blessings. The clergy grudgingly shared a modest but "real" influence over the supernatural sphere with all of these, and the rural clergy also often agreed with the cosmic view of these "colleagues." When the Reformation began, parish visitors found, indeed, that some pastors were dispensing medications along with their more conventional ministrations.

In general, the Reformers and their late-century successors disposed of the old satanic metaphor and replaced it with a different one. This displacement met with some popular opposition, but the state lent its very persuasive muscle to the administrators of the churches. The Devil was no longer the objectified, exterior force, striving to frustrate all constructive human endeavor from without. Sinners could no longer point outside themselves and exclaim, "The Devil made me do it!" Rather, the impetus toward evil lay within human beings and among people in their interactions with one another. Religious revision in the sixteenth century included the internalization of sin and the imputation of personal responsibility for it. The attitude of ecclesiastical leaders was now, more thoroughly than before, that the source of human ills lay within the guilty individual. Even collective injury, as the result of natural disaster or war, was attributable to a heaping-up of individual transgression until it became a collective burden, when in his wrath God brought calamity down upon his people, including the innocent. This alteration in the landscape of religious metaphor coincided very nicely with the scrutinizing, accusatory, subduing behavior of the early modern state.

If we "frame" the Catholic and the various Protestant baptismal services in our mind's eye, we can detect this tendency. The onus of self-discipline falls upon each infant, later to be underscored and personalized at its public confirmation. In the "high" Lutheran ritual, with its retention of an abbreviated exorcism, the child must assume at least equal answerability with the forces of evil; in the more "cleansed" rite the small Christian stands before God, with, however, the additional fortification of intensified community assistance. The baby's fellow citizens, including parents, godparents, clergy, neighbors, and appointed magistrates, will watch, aid, detect, and, if need be, punish.

We know that the Reformers themselves believed in the slings of Satan. In chapter 5, on dying and death rituals, I shall suggest that the observances of the dying chamber indicate that people felt vulnerable to his ungodly might until they had breathed their last. But there, as well as at the baptismal font or basin, the Devil no longer occupied the bedposts or hovered above the waters; rather, he was within the departing Christian just as he was within the infant being joined to the body of Christ for the first time. For the educated men who ran the churches, Satan was becoming steadily more figurative and thus, in one sense, more abstractly metaphorical. Many of the less educated still perceived the Devil as a concretely encroaching presence against whom they were prepared to take action. He was outside themselves. Their familiar and much favored remedy of exorcism having been withdrawn, they were now asked to thwart evil themselves, by reforming their lives. Judging from the hordes alleged to have visited every available cunning-man, wise woman, prophet, and passing gypsy, many ordinary people rejected the elite solution. In short, they refused to internalize their superiors' judgment that they and their lifestyle were bad. Not a few of them had to endure government-imposed penalties for their cultural self-esteem.

3 Churching, a women's rite[1]

In contrast to England, churching in Germany has received little attention.[2] Robert Scribner has noted the early Lutheran clerical and magisterial ambivalence toward the postnatal rite of purification, but it is apparent to him, as it is to me, that Protestant authorities quickly came to insist that women undergo some sort of ritual, the particulars varying from place to place.[3] Churching (*kirchgang* in New High German) is a particularly promising rite for the anthropological historian. Its forms both before and after the Lutheran Reformation, and, more to the point, the failure of Reformers to abolish it, provide additional evidence of the deteriorating position of women in late fifteenth- and sixteenth-century society.[4] That is one way to interpret the evidence. But as we know, every ritual is viewed differently by each individual observing it.[5] We cannot recover the perceptions of discrete participants—whether priests, new mothers, their relatives and friends, or other members of the congregation—but it is plain that elite men's aims were likely to diverge from the purposes of the women themselves who were churched. Underlying this divergence are distinctions both between masculine and feminine moieties and between magisterial and popular ones.

BACKGROUND

The New Testament account of the Virgin Mary's adherence to the levitical prescription for postnatal ritual purification assured that in some way Christianity would take note of this Marian event.[6] However, even in the Bible, Mary's conformity to religious law is hardly the focal point. Central to the story is the presentation of the infant in the temple, where the aged man Simeon recognized the Messiah. Secondarily, the ancient widow Anna, a "prophetess," also knew who Jesus was and began to tell others who were there. Thus, Mary's purification per se is the tertiary occurrence, little emphasized. It is not mystifying why Mary's act should have been subsumed under the more important presentation (*Hypapante*, or *Occursus Domini*) of Christ with the highly significant insights that ensued.[7] The iconographic account, dating from the eighth century, bears this out.[8] In the great majority of the representations that I have examined, the baby Jesus' and Simeon's epiphany are the central elements. Mary is usually the other principal figure, significant as the mother of Christ and not as the protagonist in a purifying rite. If her offering of two turtle doves is present at all, it is only a symbolic detail, lending greater authenticity to the scene. The doves are carried either by Joseph, who in some versions has accompanied his wife, or by an unidentified woman.[9] At Simeon's side but toward the periphery, Anna may appear. The artists who created such images did not take as one of their purposes to relate the biblical episode either to the medieval manner of observing Candlemas or to depict the ceremony that by the fifteenth century parturient women throughout Europe underwent.

Several artists, however, did set the Presentation against a background that would have been more familiar to late medieval onlookers. A fourteenth-century statuary group attributed to the school of A. Beauneveu includes a woman holding what appears to be a candle.[10] A Presentation by Jacques Daret, a densely symbolic painting, shows, besides the usual personae, two women carrying tapers.[11] Stephan Lochner's Presentation (1447), compared to its predecessors and contemporaries, is exceedingly ornate, filled with people, and above them God and numerous angels. Yet, for all that, it bears a close resemblance to actual Candlemas and churching practices in north European late Middle Ages.[12]

The feast of *Hypapante, Purificatio virginis*, or Candlemas was observed at least by the late fourth century in the Greek church, on February 14, which was the fortieth day after Epiphany, the day on which Christ was thought to have been born. Justinian promoted this festival and changed the date to February 2, to correspond to the transfer of the Nativity to December 25.[13] Dorothy Shorr speculates that the observance was established in Rome under Pope Gelasius I (492–496) to serve as a counter-attraction to the pagan Lupercalia (February 14), which was originally an occasion of ritual purification, in the course of which the participants carried torches in procession.[14] The Venerable Bede (d. 735) recounted how in his day, in honor of Mary's purification, the people and priests processed with candles in the churches.[15] During the eighth century, the candles were blessed and were alleged to symbolize Christ as the light of the world. Such candles, like many other objects used in sacred rites, became sacramentals in the eyes of common folk; they were thought effective in averting storm damage and curing illness. Ordinary priests, too, thought the candles to have such powers, for, in contrast to prelates, priests were and remained until the Reformation "of the people." Through the rest of the Middle Ages, although with regional and local variations, Latin Christians honored the Virgin on February 2 with candlelight processions. Lochner used this fifteenth-century practice as the setting of his Presentation painting. A veritable throng of children and townspeople, especially women, hold their tapers at the altar as Mary makes her offering of the doves. Simeon, depicted here as a priest attended by an acolyte, holds the Christ child. In this scene, the Virgin is not just pictorially equal in importance to Jesus and Simeon, but also psychologically so.

This evolution of Candlemas is closely related to that replication of Mary's penitential act that we call churching. In German-speaking lands, the first manuscript evidence of a particular liturgical blessing for new mothers dates from the eleventh or twelfth century.[16] The introduction of churching may correspond in complex ways to a deterioration in women's position in society, to the triumph of Catholicism within a heavily folk milieu, and to the expansion of the cult of the Virgin.[17] As Adolph Franz presents the liturgical record, the earliest formal benediction was administered on the eighth day after the birth, in the home of the parturient (*Wöchnerin*, *Kindbetterin*). In the five variations found, the cleric first read Psalms (40, 66, 81, 112, or 127), John 1, or other versicles; he then proceeded to administer a blessing closely resembling that used for any sick person, asking God to restore health to his faithful servant.[18]

There is little sense of women being specifically unclean or impure here as a result of pregnancy and giving birth. Nearly all primitive societies attribute some special status to women in their reproductive roles—during menstruation, pregnancy, and after giving birth—which is often a combination of dangerous and sacred.[19] Is it possible that Europeans had cast off such attitudes? Franz states that this was indeed so—at least as far as the church itself was officially concerned. Only in the Lambach formula, dating from the twelfth century, does a residual concept of impurity in childbed appear:

> Holy Trinity and true unity, omnipotent God, who made heaven and earth, who established the unmovable mountains, Yours is all the heavenly kingdom: into Your holy and excellent care I commend the soul(s) and body(s) of Your servant(s) and all her (their) thoughts and deeds, so that You may defend her (them) from evil spirits and never deliver her (them) into their power, either now or in the future ...[20]

The word *unclean* may not occur in the text, but we do encounter the idea that new mothers are especially vulnerable to the Devil. In Psalm 81, which is prescribed in the Lambach formula, God reprimands Israel:

> Do but listen to me, O Israel:
> you shall have no strange god
> nor bow down to any foreign god;
> I am the Lord your God
>   who brought you up from Egypt.

But my people did not listen to my words
and Israel would have none of me;
    so I sent them off, stubborn as they were,
to follow their own devices.[21]

Particularly in the twelfth century, when Christianity's hold on the populace was not uniformly firm, this passage could be interpreted as a criticism of women who had not entirely stopped invoking non-Christian powers. Women who did so were spiritually sullied. According to Franz, the Greek prelacy, as reflected in prescribed prayers, adhered much more strongly to notions of childbearing as polluting. Amusingly, he recounts how at a synod held just before 1200 the Syrian church announced that henceforward, menstruating and parturient women did not have to keep away from religious services, including Communion, inasmuch as "after baptism among Christians there is no more impurity"; the fathers added the qualification that, strictly out of reverence, such women should avoid Communion.[22]

Another aspect of the Lambach formula deserves comment. The plural forms of the nouns, pronouns, and adjectives are placed in parentheses. If priests were by the twelfth century only blessing mothers in childbed, (privately) in their homes, these plural alternatives would not have been needed. Women already were coming collectively to a public place, probably the church, to receive their benediction. This development marks a transition toward the late medieval rite of churching.

Pope Gregory the Great (590–604) had proclaimed unambiguously against the uncleanness of women who were either menstruating or had just given birth. They must be admitted to the sacrament. If she wished, a mother might come to church on the very day of the birth and give thanks for her delivery. Jewish law, he said, did not bind Christians.[23] Subsequent ecclesiastical decrees did not necessarily follow this pattern. The 227 Synod of Trier instructed priests to receive women who wished to be blessed immediately after giving birth, but this did not mean that they could resume sexual relations until the traditional period of confinement had expired.[24] We must remember that the period of confinement entailed a prohibition on sexual relations. A synod held at Cambrai in 1310 forbade clergymen to pronounce the blessing over women until one full month after childbirth—unless, that is, a mother's life were in danger.[25] The Manual of Sarum (1506), however, did state the women could return to church without committing a sin. If they chose, out of reverence, to stay away for a period of time, their devotion should not meet with disapproval.[26]

THE LATE MEDIEVAL CATHOLIC RITUAL

By the fifteenth century, a festive ceremony marking the mother's return to church was found everywhere in Germany. Its spread stands in contrast to the official view of prelates and theologians that women were not impure and not subject to Jewish law. Franz comments, "Laws that impose this ecclesiastical blessing as a duty upon women in childbed are not to be found. One always speaks only of a *consuetudo*."[27] We are confronted, then, with an instance of considerable distance between formal doctrine and the beliefs of adherents (including, probably, most ordinary clerical adherents) of Catholicism. Here is where, in my view, the analysis of ritual can perform a service. The canon law may be silent, but the symbols and symbolic actions in the ceremony itself can be made to yield something of the cosmic and societal perspectives of those who took part.

The liturgical formulae provide valuable information. The rites reproduced by Franz date from the twelfth century, and they were the basis for subsequent ceremonies. The medieval ritual that I shall reconstruct here is a montage of pieces gleaned from a variety of sources. Every parish will have had its own variations on the patterns described here and, indeed, each enactment of churching within the same community will have been slightly different from every other.

At the end of a forty-day period (give or take a day or two: often the German word for the parturient woman is *Sechswöchnerin*, which literally denotes forty-two days), the mother was met at her home by the midwife and others who had attended her during delivery, usually relatives and close friends, and accompanied her to the main entrance of the church. The infant having already been baptized a day or two after birth, in the mother's absence, its presence now was not required. If it was brought to church—as it routinely was in Germany in the fifteenth century—it was acknowledged in a prayer for its wellbeing.[28] In contrast to the Marian episode, the medieval repetition was principally a women's ceremony. Some Netherlandish churches had a special door on the north side (the direction associated with the Devil) of the west end, the *kraamvrouwdeur*, through which these women entered the sanctuary.[29] They carried burning tapers in their hands, as they did on Candlemas. Their heads were covered (as married women's always were), as a sign, the sixteenth-century preachers Johannes Mathesius and Cyriakus Spangenberg asserted, of their subservience to men because of the Fall.[30]

They did not enter, however, until greeted and led in (*Einleitung*) by the priest together with his attendant. The priest, wearing alb and stole, first sprinkled the new mother with holy water. He recited prescribed Bible passages, customarily Psalms. The extant liturgies mention Psalms 50, 112, 120, 122, or 127. After these, he said the *Kyrie eleison*, the Lord's

Prayer, and a brief responsory in which he referred to Mary's inviolate virginity and asked for her intercession.[31] He then intoned a prayer, such as

Almighty and everlasting God, who has freed this woman from the danger of bearing [a child], make her devoted to Your service so that, having passed through the course of temporal life, resting under the wings of Your continual mercy, she may attain perpetual rest.[32]

In another rubric, this variant was used:

Lord God, who through Your servant Moses commanded the people of Israel that when a woman had borne a son, she should refrain from entering the temple for forty days, consider this your servant worthy to be strengthened from every pollution [*inquinamento*] of the flesh so that with a clean heart and pure mind she may deserve to enter into the bosom of [our] mother, the church.[33]

It is clear that an element of impurity remained, and this is identified with receptivity to Satan.[34] The celebrant took her right hand in his left and led her, followed by her retinue, into the church and to the altar. Or he extended to her the lefthand end of his stole, which she grasped with her right hand. Before the altar, the priest recited further prayers, begging God's mercy for the woman. Sometimes Mass was said, but more often it was not. In some areas, the mother being churched walked around the altar once or even three times, followed by her companions. She then made an offering of money or goods, sometimes yarn that she had spun during her confinement, often placing it upon the altar. Spinning was the proverbial female occupation, and however necessary it was to the domestic economy, in providing it the housewife simultaneously testified to acceptance of the "distaff" role. Whatever the woman gave during her churching was for the use of the priest, as apparently was at least that candle that she herself bore. In a few cases, the mother kissed a Gospel or reliquary, or the priest touched her on the head with a reliquary.[35] He pronounced a final blessing, and either he or his acolyte again aspersed her with holy water. Occasionally, the priest or his helper swung a fragrantly smoking censer around her.[36]

There are few records of the treatment of a woman who had had a miscarriage or a stillbirth. In Schleswig in 1512, it was stipulated that such a one should go through the customary ritual—but that her candle would be unlighted.[37]

Churching was a privilege that could be denied either to an unmarried or a disobedient woman. Not to undergo this ritual meant to remain tainted by the several stains of reproduction, including to be vulnerable to evil influences. For married and submissive women, churching was a festive event, one for which they dressed up as much as they were able and after which they entertained the women in their train with cake or a meal. So convinced were they of the efficacy of the observances that families pressed to have churched the corpses of women who had died in childbed. The church tolerated a practice that it regarded as superstitious. In these ceremonies, women bore the body of the deceased into the church. A synod of Ermland in 1610 found it necessary to forbid the popular practice of carrying the corpse three times around the altar before committing it to burial.[38] Relatives feared that their lost loved ones could not enter paradise unchurched. Men and women alike thought it dangerous for pregnant or impregnable females to look upon or pass by the grave of a woman who had died while giving birth. Partly because of the sympathetic effects that any trauma was believed to exert upon a fetus, and partly because the souls of dead women were thought likely to try to claim a surviving infant, such graves were deliberately placed in a remote corner of the burial ground, and sometimes outside consecrated earth.[39] This suggests, additionally, that the opinion lurked in the background that unchurched women's bodies remained impure and potentially contaminating to others.

REFORMATION CHURCHING

Martin Luther explained the origin of churching in the sermon he gave on Candlemas 1521. He took the obvious biblical text, Luke 2: 22–39, and after recounting the Bible story, he commented,

> Because the human society in which we live demands that no one anger or injure another, but instead help him when there is need, we must follow the same principle. For God put us on earth and gave us our bodies and temporal life so that we could live like one another in a common manner. And if that is not the case, then our temporal existence cannot go on. On that account, we have to do here what the others do, as though we were in a foreign land. This is just what the Virgin Mary did. She was not obligated to purify herself and bring an offering, for she had never become impure, By right she could have abstained. But because she was in another place [*gepiet*], she had to observe what the others did.[40]

Two years later he spoke in the same vein:

> Mary does this work [purification] for the honor of God and love of her neighbor. She does not want to use her liberty, but instead, through her act she strengthens the obedience of the others, who had to be subject to the law because of their impurity.[41]

The Reformer did not advocate an end to churching. He regarded it, just as Catholic theologians had, as a custom that could well be retained. It was, after all, validated by its inclusion in the New

Testament. Whether he regarded women in his own time as impure is not clear. He certainly adhered to a number of popular beliefs.[42]

Church ordinances and visitation records of the sixteenth century reveal that, whatever Luther may have thought, other reforming voices and some women and their husbands had ideas of their own. In Ernestine Saxony, Elector Johann (and Luther and some of his Wittenberg colleagues) insisted in "Unterricht der Visitatoren an die Pfarrherrn im Kurfürstentum zu Sachsen," the instructions for the first great parish visitations beginning in 1528, that women were to continue in the traditional six-week confinement, during which they did not work, take part in public life, or engage in sex. The preliminary visitations had revealed that some pastors were preaching an end to churching, and as a consequence some husbands were compelling their wives to return to their secular labors prematurely and—we take it from the oblique reference—to resume sex:

> For the period of six weeks is ordained in the law of Moses, the third book and twelfth chapter. Even though that law has now been suspended, this particular piece, which is taught us not just by the law but by nature too, is not suspended ... For that reason, women shall be spared until they return to their full strength, which cannot well happen in less time than six weeks ... So in this case, one should consider the needs of the body and do what is proper and not use Christian liberty to injure the body or for lewdness.[43]

In this case, men were calling into question their wives' prolonged confinement ended by churching. In the vicinity of Halberstadt, some pastors had done away with churching, and the visitors in 1589 insisted on its reestablishment where it was lacking. One rural clergyman told them that his predecessor had eliminated it, but that he himself, who had been in place for twelve years, had brought it back, for "this authority is good."[44] In other instances, women themselves rebelled against post-partum isolation and churching as it had been practiced before.[45] It was necessary to insist in Mansfeld in 1580 that,

> Because it happens that in some places one or more women do not observe their Christian churching after their six weeks, as other pious women do, but for no reason except contrariness disdain the blessing and the prayers said over them and their little children, the pastor in such a place in accordance with his office can discuss the matter with them, dissuade them from such mischief, and warn and admonish them to maintain similarity and uniformity with other Christian matrons and not so flippantly to refuse and despise these prayers. And if after such warnings they do not behave properly, he should inform the superintendent and the consistory.[46]

Evidence of this is sparse, however, and may suggest that most women preferred not only tradition but the retention of sacramental offices that they regarded as efficacious in promoting their wellbeing.

Whatever women may have wished, throughout the ecclesiastical ordinances of the sixteenth century runs the prohibition of the pastor leading the new mother into the church. This was now widely but not universally condemned as superstitious, on a par with sprinkling holy water, blessing salt and water (and the candles used in churching), and ringing the church bell to avert storm damage.[47] The political dividedness of the Holy Roman Empire translated after the arrival of the Reformation into wide religious variation even at the official level. The several exceptions that can be found may be taken as proving the rule.[48]

The Lutheran ritual, generally obligatory for all married women, typically ran as follows: as under Catholicism, the midwife and birthing-room attendants, attentively dressed for the occasion, greeted the mother at her home and went with her to church. They entered and sat together, possibly in a pew designated for them by tradition. After Communion or the sermon, the pastor called them to the altar, where the mother knelt. The clergyman instructed her and the congregation that women were not unclean after bearing children nor *more than normally susceptible to the Devil* (my emphasis); marriage and reproduction were instituted by God, and honorable. He recited parts of several Psalms—many different ones are cited now, such as 22: 10, 127: 3–5, 128 (all), 139: 14–18—which emphasize the wonder of birth. In Wolfenbüttel in 1569, this prayer was given as a pattern for ministers to follow in churching women:

> On account of sin this curse went out to all the daughters of Eve: "I will increase your labor and your groaning, and in labor you shall bear children"—which still remains as a reminder that children are conceived and borne in sin. All the same it is a special work of grace of God's creation, that a woman is blessed with the fruit of her body, that a little child is formed in the mother's body and is nourished and maintained, that the mother is delivered with great anxiety and labor pains, and is made happy with the joyous sight of a living, healthy fruit....[49]

He was to invite the congregation to express the same sentiments with him in prayer. Finally, the mother, together with her child, if present, received a benediction: "The Lord bless you, etc." The women apparently left the sanctuary with the other members of the congregation.[50]

In 1543 in the Duchy of Pfalz-Neuburg, the preacher was to inform the people that new mothers were not in the power of the Devil, as many thought. Marriage and the bearing of children were sacred, *even if* (my emphasis) Satan dared "to tempt the woman in childbed more than he does other folk."[51]

In these instances, nothing is said about the mother's offering. In others she was to go to the altar and lay her gift there, or she gave it to the pastor; it was still for his and/or his deacon's or sexton's use. One of the developments of the late sixteenth and early seventeenth centuries was that authorities placed ever greater emphasis on payment for clerical action. In Saxony, particularly in the seventeenth century, women collectively were urged to pay for a prayer (*Fürbitte*) for their safe delivery as the birth approached, again for the baptism of their new baby, once again for the pastor's giving thanks (*Danksagung*) from the pulpit for their survival that far, and, finally, again after six weeks at their churching. By the late seventeenth century, the fees had risen steeply, as high as six *groschen* for churching alone.[52] In some poor parishes, the pastor offered a package whereby a woman could obtain all pertinent services for a flat payment of six *groschen* or other amount.[53] Sometimes the parishioners were so impoverished that even this exceeded their means, and lower fees were set. Even so, people avoided paying, and their clergymen complained to the visitors.[54] Some husbands were mocked by other men for allowing their pregnant wives to be prayed for by name from the chancel, but this was not the usual attitude.[55]

The visitors of the village of Schöna near Schlieben were amazed to discover in 1672 that when a woman was ready to return to church six weeks after giving birth, she circled the altar, followed by her female retinue.[56] This phenomenon of circling is well known, but what is exceptional here is that Protestant leaders had permitted the Catholic practice to continue.[57]

Afterward, just as throughout Germany during the late Middle Ages, the mother entertained her attendants and close women relatives with a meal. The writers of the ecclesiastical ordinances, as well as parish visitors, complained loudly about what they considered to be exorbitant expenditure on such fetes. The Saxon visitors in Weimar had explicitly to bar men in 1614, for these meals were strictly "a women's conventicle" (*ein weiber Convent*).[58]

AN ANTHROPOLOGICAL APPROACH

In his famous essay, "Thick Description: Toward an Interpretive Theory of Culture," Clifford Geertz (drawing on Gilbert Ryle's concept of "thick description") admits not only the diversity of act and meaning within any scene witnessed by the ethnographer, but also the inevitability of the ethnographer's imposing his (or, in this case, her) interpretation.[59] Analysis, he says, and this can apply to a ritual as well as to the larger configuration called culture,

is sorting out the structures of signification—what Ryle called established codes, a somewhat misleading expression, for it makes the enterprise sound too much like that of the cipher clerk when it is much more like that of the literary critic—and determining their social ground and import.

I do not claim any objective (much less eternal) validity for the evaluation I here offer; it is similar though not identical to Adrian Wilson's analysis of English churching.[60] Wilson sets out three alternative conclusions concerning churching in England: one based on the Dutch anthropologist Arnold van Gennep's analysis of rituals as rites of passage;[61] one derived from Keith Thomas's assertion that folk beliefs persisted even in the face of elite efforts at suppression—churching, then incorporating such persistence;[62] and Natalie Zemon Davis's perception that lying-in customs put the woman temporarily "on top" and thereby inverted the usual male-dominated social order.[63] Wilson ultimately sides with Davis. Germany, however, is not England, in addition to which it would be impossible to approach this or any ritual interpretation without grounding in the many-sidedness of late medieval and early modern German life.

In both the medieval and the reformed ritual, an official ecclesiastical—that is, a dogmatic—conviction is perceptible, and yet it is less so in the earlier era than the later. Gregory the Great's rejection of feminine impurity never succeeded in permeating the church even to the level of the writers of liturgy. Such prelates and their staffs continued to regard women in their reproductive capacities as impure no matter what the pope said. The clergy of all grades were, when compared to the post-Reformation period, more closely attuned to the worldview of the populace, and more willing to accommodate it. I am convinced that Robert Scribner has got it right when he depicts the relationship and nature of clerical and popular views of ritual, both under Catholicism and after the Reformation.[64] Denunciations of superstition were only halfhearted. As has often been said, one of the great strengths of the medieval church was its readiness to tolerate elements of folk religion that it did not perceive as absolutely incompatible with the essentials of Christian belief.

I cannot avoid seeing late medieval German churching as a classic instance of van Gennep's transitional rite. What is it a transition from, and what is it a transition to? At the moment when she perceived her pregnant condition, a woman began a less ritualized and as much psychological as physiological transition, from the bond with her husband and household functions to one focused upon other women. Apart from the pregnant woman, the other central figure in the group was the midwife, who also served as the source of various gynecological and obstetrical ministrations throughout her clients' fertile years—most women did not live till menopause, and so we might say throughout her clients' lives. Second, close women relatives and friends, several in number, filled out the cohort of those who would render advice and consolation during pregnancy, and who would attend the mother during her labor and delivery. With the becoming-mother as its nucleus and its raison d'être, and with the midwife possessing a power that contained sacred and supernatural (as well as merely secular) aspects, this small society enjoyed a veritable exemption from the rule of male preeminence in society.[65] No-one could or would properly gainsay the legitimacy of their "cell," and yet it could arouse unease among men.

This privilege of sorority extended to some degree to all other mothers of the community, who informally rendered their advice on nausea, swollen limbs, fatigue, untimely bleeding, and the wellbeing of the fetus. Men doubtless overheard these conversations, but they were excluded.

Men were excluded sexually as well, though no doubt practice contrasted greatly with theory. As delivery became imminent, men were peripheral. Their wives dreamed unaccustomed dreams, were moody, and yearned for special foods. Such behavior was sufficient evidence to both sexes that women were more than normally susceptible to the Devil's influence. Perhaps this was why the enceinte sought the Eucharist more urgently than any other group in society, except the dying. Perhaps as much because of this belief, common to men and women, women turned with the church's blessing to female saints for succor and sustenance. The Virgin, Margaret, and Jesus' grandmother Anna were the particular and passionate objects of their devotion. These were the heavenly female patrons of the reproductive sodality on earth, who could help to overcome diabolical inveiglement as well as physical dangers. Both ephemeral and fleshly helpers met in the birthing room, the scene of a drama (including numerous small rituals) that was the culmination of this society's efforts. Only in this extraordinarily charged setting did a female person have the dispensation, *in extremis*, to administer a sacrament of the faith. This itself is a measure of the excludedness of men and the sanctity/pollution of the birthing process.[66] After the Reformation, Lutheran authorities took pains to circumscribe the midwives' exercise of this privilege, and the Calvinists eliminated it altogether.

After the birth, this circle remained intact just as the parturient's health, given the unhygienic practices of that day, remained precarious. A member of this group was probably frequently among the godparents and attendants who accompanied the baby away to church to its own purification through baptism. Until the mother's survival was assured—the relative certainty of which was seen to coincide with the cessation of her flux of blood or paler fluid—the society of participant women could not be dissolved. Nor could the mother endanger others by precipitously invading the larger sacred sphere. The inner sanctum was, of course, the church itself, inasmuch as both laity *and* clergy attributed sanctity to this edifice and the space it enclosed. In the popular mind, the bleeding, postpartum woman should also avoid wells, livestock, and newly planted fields—which in rural Germany took in most of the village space. The new mother was thus decisively confined.

On the occasion of her churching, the midwife and other members of her birthing circle, who themselves had never given up their ties to the world outside and were only felt to be threatening in their relationship to the mother, escorted her from her door to the door of the church. Candles in hand, they humbly awaited admission, accorded them by priest and deacon or acolyte. The mother's impurity was rendered harmless to the congregation through the immediate application of holy water. With this act, carried out by a man, she was rejoined to the society of men. It is possible that the water is in this instance a symbol not only of cleansing but of fertility.[67] From her churching, a woman was again obliged to accept her husband's sexual advances. The woman's dangerous position and the priest's power to purify and to protect others is shown in the cleric's extending the lefthand (sinister) end of his stole for her to grasp in her right hand (dexter). By this device, he was able to lead her into the midst of the people without incurring diabolical forces; and before the altar, where she knelt, the mother was least able to do harm. Sanctity was ubiquitous but not evenly distributed, even within the sanctuary.

On her knees before a human man, the priest, and God the Son, the woman had her special character further reduced through the recitation of formulae. Some of these reminded her of her humble position and the gratitude that she owed the divinity; others reflected the thankful attitude of the community for her surviving the clear and present dangers of childbirth. If she now received the Host, the body of Christ, she was reunited in at least three senses to the body of man (to her husband, to the Son of God, and to the male-dominated community)— for unless her life threatened to ebb away, she did not receive the sacrament, just as she did not have sex or perform her normal part in the communal body during her confinement.

At approximately this point, she (and sometimes her attendants) laid her offering on the altar, as a seal of her gratitude and submission. To do this she had to touch the altar, something lay people did not do in the normal course of events. She may already have done so in placing her candle there, or the other women may have held it for her. The people regarded the altar as the holy of holies, a most efficacious sacramental that was bound to facilitate the mother's physical, spiritual, and social healing. Similarly intended was the offering to her of the Gospel or a reliquary, themselves mighty sacramentals. The final sprinkling with holy water complemented the initial one, completing the purification. The priest's final benediction dismissed the women. Their circle therewith lost its supernatural enhancement; its bond was broken. The women ended their months-long interlude with a repast, a familiar act of solidarity. In this instance, it was the mother's gesture of thanks and farewell.

Medieval churching transferred a woman from one state to another. Pregnancy cast women into a status fraught with uncertainty, and society expressed its ambivalence in religious as in secular terms. The enceinte withdrew into a circle of their own, which reinforced the mystery of birth. Within the small space of the birthing room, women interacted directly with the divine. Having had such a dispensation and having been so segregated, they now required reintegration into the community. Churching ended women's social and sacred privilege; it made them normal again. Normalcy included being subject to men. Men as priests mediated between them and God; men as husbands and magistrates ruled the tangible world.

I have already indicated that during the Middle Ages most clergy would have shared their parishioners' beliefs, including those that theologians then and afterward labeled as superstitious. Thus, it is not necessary to distinguish between clerical and lay attitudes toward what was done during the churching ritual. Both clergy and laity saw in this liturgy the subduing and casting out of threatening powers that through the pregnant woman had invaded their midst.[68] Nonetheless, it may be useful to distinguish between men's and women's estimations of churching. I am convinced that, in general, women absorb the valuation that society places upon them; in the period under discussion, they were not "feminists," women seething with frustration at a culture that so hedged them about with negative judgments and limitations on their prerogatives. Pregnant women found it credible that they were vulnerable to Satan as they underwent the strange transformation of pregnancy; they consented to avoid church, animals, fields, and water sources after giving birth. It is easy to imagine that they found strength in the society of familiar, related, and experienced women as they faced the dangers of motherhood, and that they entered into the feminine sodality with enthusiasm. Their gratitude for survival encouraged them to accept the transition represented by churching back into "normal" ("disexual") society, and any reluctance they may have felt toward the dissolution of this close association with women was minimized by the knowledge that in their capacity as relative or neighbor they would shortly be members of another such circle, one whose life this time was not at imminent risk.

In addition to ending one phase and reintroducing another, churching provided one of the two occasions when a woman was prominent in the public eye. The other was when she married for the first time. Whether she enjoyed this attention depended on her temperament.

In the first decade or two of the Reformation, Germany was in a state of religious confusion. Needless to say, churching was not exempt from that condition. Some Protestant women rejected churching; most apparently did not. Some princes, prelates, pastors, and magistrates abolished churching; most only altered it. Here we must deal with averages and with the outcome after most religiously motivated unrest had calmed itself or been quelled.

As seen, the Reformers insisted that childbirth rendered women neither impure nor more than usually susceptible to evil. Lutheran pastors continued to regard women as more successful targets of Satan's darts than men, but this had, they thought, been consistently so even before the Fall.[69] This weak state had nothing to do with their reproductive capacities. They looked on women as being perpetually the Achilles heel of Christian society, one through which the threat of disorder might be realized. There are three reasons why reformed communities retained churching. First, it was a firmly embedded tradition that the common people in their care refused to give up inasmuch as they continued to regard it as a means of defeating those swirling, invisible forces that could undermine health and wellbeing. In addition, many ordinary folk *did* regard new mothers as tainted, and the official church failed to root out this conviction. The leading in and aspersion may have been eliminated, but the people were still able to look upon the ritual that remained, carried out in the sacred theater, as an acceptably effective individual purification and collective defense. Second, as we can see in the reformed ritual, even while officially, parturient women were no longer impure (having been so intimately and unavoidably in the company of women), they had to be reintegrated into the life of the community. The Protestant rite, by means of its continuities with its Catholic predecessor, marked this reunification. Third, having been in the company of women, they had to be reimpressed with their humble station, with their subordination to men. Liturgical references to Eve's punishments—conceiving in sin, bearing children in pain, and being subjected to her husband—conveyed the message that woman was not fully trustworthy and had to dwell under the watchful authority of her mate. The Devil was best combated not through magical acts but by socially controlling that sex, the "weaker vessel," that most readily became Satan's instrument.

Church authorities were conscious of the first point; Luther referred to it himself. But when asked to justify why they now insisted that women observe a confinement of six weeks and then be churched, they answered in practical rather than religious terms: new mothers needed six weeks' rest to recover and attend to their infants. God had ordained that people should multiply and replenish the earth, and they ought to do so in a responsible way, not endangering their health. For this reason, men must spare their wives sexual intercourse until after churching. But the authorities' motives were surely more complex, as our growing awareness of women's deteriorating position in early modern Germany would suggest.[70] The new genre of wedding sermons, and other sermons that explicated pertinent parts of the Bible, often articulated an ecclesiastical ambivalence toward women.[71] The message reiterated from the chancel, whether or not precisely on the occasion of churching, was feminine subordination; Protestant churching must be seen in this context of concerted indoctrination and social disciplining.

The typical Lutheran churching rite can be interpreted as supporting these conclusions. Its enactment is still a ritual of transition, from a society of select women initiates back to integrated, male-dominated life. But, officially, the reformed community had been desacralized—or, rather, its sacred aspects, its supernatural potency and authority had now been concentrated in one center, that of God. By the early seventeenth century, this official view had been inculcated on the parish clergy as well. In general, they were willing to represent this view of the universe even to the rural laity, which constitutes more of a reformation of the clergy than it does of their ordinary parishioners. No matter what the pastors (from whom they now felt increasingly alienated) told them to do, the people at large adhered to their earlier semi-animistic, magical, "superstitious" outlook. In Matthias Zender's *Atlas der deutschen Volkskunde*, we see that such views were still present in the 1930s.[72] As a result of the Reformation, outside of major towns, clerical and popular religion diverged. Catholicism had been content to accommodate folk practices, but Protestantism was not and strove with energy and determination to edify and discipline the parish flocks. Evangelical leaders must have perceived that they could impose rules governing practice, but that they could not as easily transform the cosmic view of those under their direction. Many people went on affirming the special vulnerability of the pregnant woman to evil, and regarding ritual acts and sacramentals as effective measures with which to counter this influence and to transform mothers into normal people again.

The Reformation consigned all manner of nonconformity to the realm of disorder, which is to say to the purview of the Devil. Every departure from the new orthodoxy and from freshly reinforced concepts of hierarchy had to be harshly dealt with. Churching was now, in the unarticulated elite view, more simply a measure in support of hierarchy and order. Not women, men, or children should regard parturient women as exceptional. Despite being essential to the propagation of the species, despite having undergone severe risks to their continued existence, they had to be impressed with their lowliness. Both the maintenance of confinement and the reformed churching ritual contributed toward that end. In studying English churching, Wilson probably need not have chosen from among the three interpretive possibilities that he delineates. The place of churching in both pre-Reformation and Lutheran society is best understood if we regard the ritual as multiply symbolic; it could not be eradicated because to each segment of the population—women and men, magistrates and ordinary citizens, clergy and laity—it bespoke and preserved a desired cosmic order. Each group had its own perceptions of churching, its own structures of signification, but even though these perspectives did not fully coincide, the ritual was indispensable to a majority.

OTHER INTERPRETIVE CONTEXTS

The debate on whether men throughout the world have attributed to women a special affinity for and closeness to nature has gone on among anthropologists for some time. Sherry Ortner concludes that every society places women in a special relationship to nature.[73] I recall hearing a paper by a historian of medicine in which she or he included a slide of the late medieval hierarchy of earthly being. At the apex was a man; on the next level down was a young woman looking in a mirror and combing her hair; and on the step below her was a horse.[74] Indeed, in primitive societies women mediate between nature and culture by converting nature to culture—by, for example, raising and civilizing children.[75] Edwin Ardener writes of the same attitude, noting that many societies "bring women in from the wild" by means of a puberty or nubility rite.[76] Against this theoretical backdrop, churching might be interpreted as a means of returning women to their proper human condition after their interlude with nature. Their transition is, then, not only from the company of women to that which includes men, but from the semi-animal sphere to the human one.

We can place the shift in churching that we have witnessed into another, related, context that goes beyond the confessional and theological. Carolyn Merchant has provided such an interpretive framework in *The Death of Nature: Women, Ecology and the Scientific Revolution*.[77] Her thesis is that during the sixteenth and seventeenth centuries Europeans ceased to look upon nature as a benevolent and maternal order, of which they were a harmonious part. They came to objectify the world outside themselves as something to be mastered and exploited for profit and pleasure. Nature objectified (requiring masculine dominion) included women. Merchant is too ready, in my opinion, to romanticize the Middle Ages, to exempt that era from exploitive intent, and to assign blame for trends that were deleterious for women to capitalism rather than to elements intrinsic to human nature.[78] Indeed, feminist scholarship does not take kindly to the idea that there is "human nature" per se. Nevertheless, Merchant does convince me that there was a shift toward the more intensive and rationalized exploitation and control of nature. The vagaries of the wild could not be left untrammeled but needed to be taken in hand, to be domesticated for the use of the "husbandman." Before the end of the period Merchant treats, even the intimate sorority of the birthing room will have been intruded upon by the male physician wielding forceps and casting aspersions at the midwife. Even women's unique role had to be dominated by men.[79] Forceps themselves become a symbol for nature not being thought capable of taking its course.

It is no coincidence that, parallel to this evolution, city fathers began to deliberate over midwives' alleged incompetence and to suspect them more regularly and irritably than before of trying to defeat rather than facilitate the reproductive process. They ranted about what they considered excessive expenditures on post-churching entertainments, and they set specific limitations on numbers of guests and courses that could be served.

What happened to churching is thus emblematic of larger trends on both the theological and the worldly plane. Men struggled to master the diabolical, the aberrant in their midst and move it outside domesticated zones. With double predestination, in which even the wild and the diabolical are under divine Providence, Calvin achieved this mastery more successfully than Luther. With an omnipotent God, churching was no longer needed, and he abolished it. The churches in Germany that came under his influence followed suit; eliminating churching was one of the essential marks of becoming Reformed.[80] The sacral sphere of women was proportionately diminished. Nevertheless, new mothers were to remain in seclusion for six weeks. In Lutheran circles, women, perceived with marked ambivalence yet indispensable to human perpetuation, could not be excluded, but they had to be subdued. Evangelical churching represents an increase in masculine hegemony, both over evil and over society. No one who has followed the scholarly discussion of confessionalization can doubt that concrete efforts to effect dominion over every facet of society and polity might well extend even to the level of so modest a transaction as churching. No exchange between God, the Devil, and mortals was, after all, truly modest. Under the humble surface of the liturgy, Protestant churching continued to be about the interplay of cosmic forces.

The English poet Robert Herrick (1591–1674) wrote the following poem, "Julia's Churching, or Purification." Even though it pertains to English practice, it is pertinent to Germany. It is, in any case, too revealing to omit:

PUt [*sic*] on thy Holy Fillitings, and so
To th'Temple with the sober Midwife go.
Attended thus (in a most solemn wise)
By those who served the Child-bed misteries
Burn first thine incense; next, when as thou see'st
The candid [white] Stole thrown ore the Pious Priest;
With reverend Curtsies come, and to him bring
Thy free (and not decurted) offering.
All rites well ended, with faire Auspice come

(As to the breaking of a Bride-Cake) home;
Where ceremonious Hymen shall for thee
Provide a second Epithalamie.
She who keeps chastly [*sic*] to her husbands side
Is not for one, but every night his Bride:
And stealing still with love, and feare to Bed,
Brings him not one, but many a Maiden-head.[81]

POSTSCRIPT

On March 26, 1788, the gentlemen of the Oberconsistorium in Leipzig wrote to Elector Friedrich August III, giving their opinion on the question of whether churching should continue to be obligatory for all married mothers. As recently as 1745, they observed, a woman, Susanne Schmidtlin, who had failed to bring her child along with her to be blessed, had been punished with one day's imprisonment. There was always some regional variation as to the form of the ritual and whether the baby's presence was required.[82] An accompanying letter from the superintendent in Helldrungen, who avidly supported churching, noted that the ancient practice still obtained throughout the county of Mansfeld, including those portions that lay in the Saxon electorate and in royal Prussia, and the entire district (*Amt*) of Arnstein.[83] Both documents reviewed the benefits of churching, with special emphasis on maintaining high moral standards in the community by admitting married women and their legitimate babies to churching while barring the unmarried, and on the deacons' need to retain the income that the women's offerings provided.

The learned men of the consistory nonetheless recommended to the prince that churching be made optional, provided that those mothers who chose not to undergo it made their monetary gift to the church anyway. The elector accepted their advice and made this official in his instructions to them of August 27, 1788.[84]

4 Repentance, confession, and the Lord's Table

Separating the divine from the human

In his art history film series, *Civilisation*, in the 1970s, the late Kenneth Clark (*seliger gedechtnis*) spoke of the great creative exuberance of Western Europe beginning in the eleventh century and culminating in the thirteenth. He referred, of course, to art and architecture; but in many other spheres of cultural and economic life, Europeans were indeed astir. Theology was no exception. Precisely in these times the precepts and practices that would typify late medieval Catholic Christianity matured and took their characteristic pre-Reformation forms. There emerged a system of penitential doctrines, from requisite auricular confession through purgatory, indulgences, and the Treasury of Merit to vicarious satisfaction for sin—in short, many of those allegedly non-biblical teachings to which Martin Luther and the other Reformers so vehemently objected.[1]

At the same time, the celebration of the Eucharist, with all its intertwined history, dogma, and liturgical refinement, drew toward itself, in those who performed as in those who merely partook, an utter concentration of thought and emotion. The phrase "God with us" now became quite literally, palpably, edibly true as before the eyes of the faithful, the priest replicated Christ's very sacrifice and placed his very body into their hands under the form of bread. In the high and late Middle Ages, heaven and earth interpenetrated.[2]

Instead of reviewing the evolution of the medieval sacraments of penance and the Eucharist, in order to capture the transformations wrought by the Reformation in Holy Communion, including preparation for it, I want to take a holistic view of the drama of the Mass both before and after the advent of Luther. In both pre- and post-Reformation sacral settings, what transpired in the multilayered process of repeating the Last Supper of the Lord? I want to consider in their turn not only the official processes, which were determined by ecclesiastical leaders, but also, as far as possible, the perceptions of the laity as the winds of change in the sixteenth century blew upon them. As I shall show, the transactions of the Eucharist, writ large enough to encompass the shape and intent of the whole service of worship within which this sacrament existed, altered its shape as the Reformers intended that it should. The fundamental configuration (*Gestalt*) of the most holy worship was entirely different in the post-Reformation churches than within Catholicism, though in varying ways and degrees. We today may detect layers of meaning other than those articulated by theologians in their articles of belief and their tracts. We may also perceive alterations in the nature of lay participation in official ritual.

LATE MEDIEVAL PENANCE, A QUEST FOR PURITY

Merely to look upon the Host after its substantial conversion into the body of Christ conferred spiritual benefit. For a receptive, even if unshriven, soul to witness (and in a lifetime to witness repeatedly) one of the greatest miracles of the faith was a privilege, to be sure, but in the eyes of the people it could even help one's standing in the unseen world. But to go still further and enjoy the grace available through the communicant's ingestion of the Redeemer's body and blood required the most fulsome admission of one's unworthiness. I am thinking here of private as well as public sinfulness; of that serious variety that the Church came to define as "mortal," or worthy of hellfire. Mortal sins included lustful thoughts, and thus it was impossible for most people to live inwardly as well as outwardly in a way that was reasonably sure to meet with heavenly reward.[3] To receive the Eucharistic elements, the Christian needed preliminary purification, and the sacrament of penance was a means to this end. The two sacraments were inextricably bound.[4]

The early Church was content to deal with gross visible violations of Christian principle, and it did so in a public manner, excommunicating the guilty. Most private sins remained private and did not bar one from Communion unless they became known. There was no fixed penitential procedure, and a person could make confession to a Christian layperson.[5] Under the influence of Celtic Christianity, a more rigorous enumeration and punishment of sins arrived on the continent during the Merovingian era and left the mark of its minute self-scrutiny upon Catholicism.[6] From the Carolingian era, a clericalism and a move toward liturgical uniformity asserted themselves, in the context of which Alcuin insisted that the laity confess only to priests; the theology of penance developed apace.[7] Such issues as the doctrine of the power of the keys, and its delegation via the bishop to parish priests entrusted with the cure of souls; of contrition, attrition, and condign justice; of the priest as physician of the soul; of the boundary between one sin and its repetition in the enumeration of sins; of the confidentiality of the confessional—these and many more claimed attention from nearly every major theologian during the remainder of the Middle Ages and beyond.[8] The thirteenth century, the age of Bonaventure and Aquinas, was decisive as to both theory and practice. Canon 21 of the Fourth Lateran Council in 1215 ordained,

> Every person of the faith, whether male or female, having arriving at the age of discretion, must themselves truthfully confess all their sins at least once a year to their pastor, and attentively carry out, within the measure of their means, the penance imposed upon them; [and] receive with respect, at least at Easter, the sacrament of the Eucharist, unless, on the advice of their pastor, for a valid reason, it is advisable for them to abstain temporarily. If [they do] not [do this], they are to be forbidden entry into the church during life, and deprived of Christian burial after death. This salutary decree is to be announced frequently in the churches, in such a way that no one is able to disguise their rashness as ignorance.[9]

The arrival of the mendicant friars meant that in each parish more clergymen than just the curé were able to preside over the sacrament of penance. This and the growing scrutiny of each Christian's state of mind on coming to confess inclined many scrupulous individuals (including, as we know, Martin Luther) to confess often, even though they were not required to do so every time they wished to partake of the increasingly readily available Eucharist. Keeping one mortal sin secret, or even entertaining reservations in the contrition that a person felt for a single sin duly confessed, could invalidate the sacrament of penance and propel one headlong into Satan's sulphurous pit.[10] For such as these, no number of Eucharistic Hosts, seemingly piously consumed, could provide relief. The one sacrament, if ingenuinely partaken of, guaranteed that its successor was equally illegitimate, so closely were penance and the Eucharist tied to one another during the late Middle Ages. And the hypocrisy, the betrayal inherent in such invalidating attitudes, compounded the transgression.

If, however, someone in a genuine state of contrition—or, as the Church conceded, out of fear of God's wrath—managed to describe the who, what, where, with what helpers, why, in what manner, and when of every mortal sin committed since the last confession, and to convince the confessor or his or her interior remorse, the confessor must then exercise the power of the keys and pronounce absolution—the remission of sin.[11] The words "I absolve you" sufficed, although confessors' manuals did suggest additional remarks that the average priest could use.[12] In a liturgical sense this absolution concluded the sacrament of penance. But in a spiritual sense it did not, for the confessor imposed an appropriate punishment or penance upon the sorrowing sinner, and this penalty had to be carried out in order to render effective the absolution granted. Absolution was, then, provisional. The modern person thinks chiefly of prayers and fasts as the constituent elements of the punishment, designed not only to take up time but to focus the penitent's attention upon his or her flawed spiritual existence. At the end of the Middle Ages, confessors often employed such measures. They also had at their disposal the imposition of other penalties, such as fines, philanthropic deeds, and the undertaking of pilgrimage. In reality, the powerful and well-to-do were in the best position to carry out such acts of penance as these.[13]

In medieval and much of early modern Europe, only the greatest churches had an architecture of penance.[14] After the Fourth Lateran Council at the latest, to whom a person made confession was far more important than where it was made. The miniature edifices called confessionals, with curtains or grills between the cubbyhole for the priest and that for the penitent, are of more modern invention.[15] The German word *Beichtstuhl* ("confessional chair") originally referred to the arm-chair in which the listening priest sat. Confession could also be made in the open or, obviously, in the privacy of one's bedroom in case of serious illness or imminent death. In an emergency, any place sufficed. Ordinarily the conscience-laden Christian sought out a confessor at the parish church. Particularly during Lent, when, as we have seen, the Church enjoined all the adult faithful to perform their paschal duty, parishioners lined up as the high holiday approached. The pictorial evidence suggests that confessors stationed themselves in the choir in larger urban churches, but waiting penitents seem to have been close enough to overhear even whispered confidences. In Rogier van der Weyden's luminous *triptych of the Seven Sacraments*, a priest sits before a simple rood screen hearing the sins of a bare-headed old man kneeling before him; the two look into each other's faces, and the priest's gesture suggests that he is consoling and instructing his charge, perhaps shriving him at that very instant. A waiting woman, her hands together in prayerful anticipation, kneels so close to the pair that she could easily crush the elderly gentleman's hat on the tessellated floor.[16] In the countryside, where few parish churches had or needed great choirs, confessors may nevertheless have sat near the altar, subtly pointing out the relationship between a good confession and the efficacy of the Eucharist. After the Reformation, pastors waited in the choir, the sacristy, or elsewhere at the front of the sanctuary.

LUTHER AND PENANCE

The Wittenberg Reformer at one and the same time preserved tradition and broke with it.[17] For several years he retained penance within a group of three scripturally warranted sacraments, and then he abandoned it, leaving baptism and the Eucharist as those rites that were made up of the sacramental requisites, a sign instituted by God and accompanied by His promise.[18] By the time he wrote "The Babylonian Captivity of the

Church" in 1520, Luther had already stated his opinion concerning penance as defined by Holy Mother Church. The "Ninety-Five Theses Against Indulgences" had attacked one side of the issue: the fanciful avoidance of temporal (including posthumous) punishment for sin— even, in its most extreme form, without contrition.[19] In 1517, Luther had challenged not the power of the keys, not the existence of purgatory, not the validity of the concept of the indulgence. At that early date, he had questioned chiefly the Pope's ability to affect the status of the dead, the sale of indulgences as a corrupt business transaction, and the implication that Christians could only gain access to the merit of their Savior through letters of indulgence. In 1520 Luther had moved on and was exploring the ramifications of his fundamental insight, that those with faith are justified before God. In "The Babylonian Captivity" he insisted that ritual penance (though at that time still a sacrament in his estimation) could only be effective for those whose faith had moved them to contrition, and he asserted that Christ had conferred the power of the keys, including the right to hear confession and grant absolution, "to Christians individually and collectively." Hence, a person could confess to any other brother (or sister?) in the creed.[20] From a sacramental angle other than that of the Eucharist, Luther was undermining the exclusivity of the priesthood. The following year he unrestrainedly attacked the Pope's claim that he alone possessed the power of the keys.[21] Luther's idea of the lay confessor did not meet the needs of those in authority at the time, and it did not take hold.[22]

Luther's view of the nature of humankind and of salvation was that, owing to their corrupt nature even after baptism, people could never be free from sin.[23] Each Christian was *simul justus et peccator*, simultaneously justified and a sinner. Taking justification by faith to its logical conclusion, he insisted that what was important about confession was heartfelt regret and the resolve to improve one's life. Only those with faith in Christ's atonement would be saved no matter how often they confessed, but the truly faithful would benefit from confession nonetheless, for it would both foster reflective penitence and console them for their human frailty with the message of divine forgiveness. To confess was to come face to face with the enormousness of God's gratuitous mercy.

It may be that in the face of Andreas Bodenstein von Karlstadt's attempt, among much else, to abolish auricular confession in Wittenberg, Luther came firmly to retain that which he had contemplated making optional. In the "Formula missae et communionis" of 1523, Luther already specified that only those would be admitted to the Lord's table who had come to the pastor in advance and indicated their desire to commune; who had expressed awareness of their sinfulness; and who had been able to explain exactly what the sacrament meant and to recite from memory the words of institution. Nevertheless, he continued, private confession was not absolutely requisite.[24] At that same time, Johannes Bugenhagen, the Wittenberg city pastor and Luther's close associate and friend, rejected compulsory auricular confession.[25] In the end, Luther came to regard individual confession as necessary. He himself found confession to be a source of reassurance and consolation. "I know what comfort and strength it has given me," he wrote in 1522.[26] Bugenhagen either changed his mind or was compelled to give in.[27] Eight years later, the *Augsburg Confession* stated,

> Confession has not been abolished in our congregations. On the contrary, it is the custom to offer the body of the Lord only to those who have been heard and absolved beforehand. And we most carefully instruct the people concerning faith in connection with absolution, about which a great silence has dominated until now. The people are taught to value absolution most highly, for it is the voice of God and is proclaimed by His command. We praise the power of the keys and point out what great consolation it brings to the frightened conscience; and [also] that God desires faith so that, believing, we may take up that absolution as His own voice sounding from heaven; and that faith in Christ actually attains and receives the forgiveness of sins. Earlier, works of satisfaction were boundlessly emphasized, but faith, the merit of Christ, and justification by faith were never mentioned.

The text continues that the signatories of the *Augsburg Confession* tell their congregations that it is not necessary to recite all sins. First of all, it would be impossible. Though they did not say so in this document, others would admit that they wished to eliminate the titillation of either reciting or hearing sexual details, and they did not want the confessional to be studiously avoided as a place of torment.[28] Above all, in addition to faith, the *Augsburg Confession* insists, one requires a penitent heart. It concludes, "We retain confession, for one thing because of the extraordinary benefit that lies in the absolution, and then also on account of the usefulness that it has for the conscience."[29]

Luther came to stand by this. Only those who possessed faith could come to true contrition and so benefit from absolution. Lutherans did, as the *Augsburg Confession* said, concentrate upon the faith of the penitent rather than on confession and penal assignments as works. This was indeed a break with past practice. Protestant confessors did not require their charges to perform particular acts in order to effectuate a sacrament. Instead the clergy were to listen, advise, teach, comfort, and reprove. This was the ideal.

So great was his horror in the Ernestine Saxon visitation of 1528–1529 at discovering the profound ignorance of both laity and clergy, that Luther may have come to regard confession as the only means available for individually instructing the masses of adults, who, as quickly became clear, refused to attend catechism classes.[30] By the 1530s, confession to a priest-turned-pastor was required. Philip Melanchthon's notations are many in a thick book of the visitors' findings and ordinances in the Saxon visitation of 1529–1531, and throughout this volume decrees similar to the following are found:

> In all ways we forbid anyone to be given the holy sacrament of the body and blood of Christ unless he can recite from memory the Ten Commandments, the Creed, and the Lord's Prayer; and [unless he] reports what he seeks in the holy sacrament, including what causes or presses him to receive the same; and unless he laments his misdeeds beforehand to the pastor or the deacon.[31]

The pastors themselves had to confess periodically to a neighboring cleric if they had no deacons in their own parishes.[32] To the relief of troubled consciences had clearly been added the purpose of indoctrination, an intention present in medieval penance though usually neglected owing to the ignorance concerning their faith of the parish clergy themselves.[33] Adults might fall asleep during the sermon, but they could not do so in a private, personal consultation with their spiritual guide, of whom a higher level of information was now expected. Further, among those who attributed significant benefit to the Eucharist, being barred from it on grounds of lack of knowledge was hardly healthful. Some late-century divines were even inclined to restrict the disabled. When the visitors in a Württemberg village in 1584 learned from the local pastor about a retarded or senile man of eighty who, his confessor knew, could not memorize the Ten Commandments, they debated long and hard about whether he should be allowed to receive Communion, and they decided that he should not, unless he deeply desired it. He should be held up as a cautionary example to all.[34]

Under Lutheranism, a person had to confess before each instance of receiving Communion. The "Artickel gemeiner verschaffung" that governed the Thuringian visitation in 1533 commanded,

> One is to make sure that the pastors adhere to a uniform use and order in confession, and that each person who laments his sins is given a separate absolution; and if in some places it should happen that people receive the holy sacrament without having confessed, or if somewhere a pastor lets people who have decided to commune come forward in a group [*in einen haufen*] and speaks a general absolution, this shall in no way be [allowed to continue].
>
> Rather, the holy sacrament of the altar shall be administered to no one who has not indicated [his desire to commune] to his pastor in advance, and who, as a penitent lamenting the pressure of conscience and his lack of spiritual virtues and qualities [*güter oder habe*], in general or in particular has them heard and receives consolation about this;[35] and if the curer of souls [the pastor, *seelsorger*] should doubt

whether people can recite the articles of the faith, they should examine them otherwise on the catechism, so that no one at all, no matter who he is, who is ignorant of who he is or what he believes about faith or the sacrament is admitted to it [the sacrament], to its disgrace.[36]

A name frequently given the ritual of confession is "private exploration" (*privat exploration*), suggesting a widely ranging examination that could be very personal.[37]

So important were Lutheran confession and absolution that the governors of the churches often found it desirable, as with other key rituals, to provide pastors and their clerical helpers with a script for them to follow in relieving parishioners of their burdens of conscience. The widely influential agenda of Heinrich of Saxony in 1539 told confessors exactly what to say when a hypothetical penitent sought them out. The pastor should inquire, "Dear friend, do you know the Ten Command-ments and what God demands in them of all human beings, that they should do and have done?" The penitent is made to answer, "No, sir, unfortunately I cannot, for under the papacy few clerics [*pfaffen*], not to mention the poor laity, knew the Ten Commandments."[38] The pastor ought to continue, "Dear friend, inasmuch as you don't know the Ten Commandments, it is all the more certain that you have not kept them." He should go on with his admonition:

Such is the greatest sin of all that a person could commit, never at all to inquire after God, even though you go on for twenty, thirty, forty, or more years, using every day so many of God's gifts and goods, and letting yourself be given body, soul, sense, reason, food, drink, and everything necessary; yes, you let yourself be served by His dear Son, with His suffering and death, for your salvation and blessedness; you let yourself be preached to about this every day, and you go around nevertheless not ever thinking or asking what you could do for God by way of praise, thanks, and service for such great and many-sided goodness...Just think: if you were to die now, you could never answer before His strict judgment seat for such gruesome contempt for God and His holy Word. You would have to despair and be eternally lost.

The verbatim harangue recommended here to pastors goes on for several times the length of the passage cited. The confessor finally prepares to give absolution:

My dear friend, this word of absolution that I transmit to you [based] on God's promise, you should regard as if God, by means of a voice from heaven, granted you grace and forgiveness of your sins; and you should heartily thank God that He has given such power to the church and to Christians on earth.

Then follows the formal pardon:

> The almighty God and Father of our Lord Jesus Christ wishes to be gracious and merciful to you, and wants to forgive all your sins for the sake of his dear Son Jesus Christ, who suffered and died for this [purpose]. In the name of the same Lord Jesus Christ, at His command and by the power of His Word, where He says, "Whatever sins you remit, these are remitted," I pronounce that you are free and quit of all your sins, so that they are as fully and completely forgiven as Jesus Christ has earned through His suffering and death...[39]

The reprimand of the admonition comes very close to the Catholic view that if a person were to die unshriven, his position before God the Judge would be precarious indeed.

The Eucharist, to be sure, was available less often than it had been in Catholic churches where canons, multiple altars, and altarists fulfilled the testamentary instructions of their patrons, and where, in cities, the many churches of the mendicant and other orders offered full Masses.[40] Nonetheless, control of the link between confession and Eucharist increased. From the ecclesiastical ordinances of the 1530s, we see that rulers of the church were already providing scripts that confessors must use in granting absolution. Already the tendency toward a revived ritualism, with its inherent mistrust of the slightest deviation from approved procedure, is visible.[41] In granting absolution, the pastor stated explicitly that he was acting in God's stead, with His authorization, an idea that theologically had long been present in the doctrine of the keys, but whose new emphasis during the post-Reformation era underlay the renewed, the Protestant, clericalism of the mid- and late century.

Neither confession nor the sacrament of the Lord's Table was reserved to the Lenten and Easter seasons, though for some time former Catholics inclined toward the tradition of confessing and receiving the sacrament then (if at no other time).[42] Other favored times were Pentecost and Christmas, just as they had been in the late Middle Ages. The church ordinances and visitation records reveal that pastors sometimes waited in vain on Saturday for penitents to come to them in the sanctuary (*never* in the pastors' homes!),[43] and that at numerous Sunday services, where the Eucharist might have been celebrated, there were no communicants. But around Easter, people jostled one another to gain access to the confessional.[44] In the county of Nassau-Dillenburg (senior line) in 1538, a village pastor was reprimanded for allowing a boy to help him hear confessions before Easter![45] Judging from contemporary comment, pregnant women sought the Eucharist, and thus also the confessional, more regularly than any other category of the population.[46] Next were the seriously ill.

PENANCE BEYOND THE CONSOLATION OF TROUBLED CONSCIENCES

In the German southwest, under the influence of Zwingli and then of Calvin, auricular confession was available, virtually as a type of pastoral counseling, but it was often not required. In this region, with its pronounced tendencies toward a communal concept of society, cities and territories in the Swiss Reformers' sway favored a collective confession of guilt as part of the Eucharistic ceremony.[47] Amy Nelson Burnett has described superbly well Martin Bucer's ideas, and his efforts to impose a rigorous discipline, including auricular confession, in the churches of Strasbourg, which the city fathers thwarted out of residual anticlerical and more complex political motives.[48] In Regensburg, the 1544 formula for the Saturday afternoon vesper is fundamentally a service of collective repentance, scheduled for the day when auricular confessions had traditionally been made. The pastor's admonition is long and severe, stressing that anyone who took the sacrament on the morrow without due penitence was betraying the clergy and earning himself God's wrath.[49] Toward the end of his life, Calvin regretted not having maintained a general absolution after this, to be spoken by the minister.[50] The Heidelberg Catechism, adopted by the Calvinist elector Friedrich III of the Rhenish Palatinate in 1563, does not refer to confession.[51] As Basel experimented with Lutheranism after mid-century under the leadership of Antistes Simon Sulzer, one of the specifically Lutheran features that were readmitted was private confession.[52] During the 1570s, when the county of Nassau-Dillenburg underwent its second Reformation, from Lutheranism to Calvinism, one of the numerous ritual alterations imposed on the churches was an end to private confession and absolution.[53]

Auricular confession, then, constituted one of the lines of structural as well as theological demarcation between Lutheranism and Calvinism. Southwest German Lutheranism represents something of a hybrid, reflecting its proximity to Switzerland as well as the intricacies of politics.[54] Bodo Nischan has described the debate over this form of confession in Brandenburg in the early seventeenth century, as Elector Johann Sigismund tried to convert his dominions to the Reformed faith.[55] Bernard Vogler has examined Lutheran prayer books for the period 1550 to 1700 and found that 10–30 percent of their contents dealt with repentance, confession, and Communion—a considerable portion. He notes that every prayer book contains "numerous prayers before confession, after absolution, and before and after the Lord's Supper." These, however, often formed part of the ritual of collective abasement and pardon that was more common in the southwest.[56] Within the increasingly orthodox Lutheran world, confession became something more than an avenue of priestly instruction and consolation. It became, too, a means of gaining information on the private lives of citizens and at the same time of effecting their submission, if not remorse. Luther's successors returned to the confessional as a means of purification, but not in the abstract terms of guilt and punishment in the afterlife, but on earth, in present society, and in terms of concrete modes of behavior. Scholars have made the same assertion about the late medieval Catholic Church's exploitation of the confessional.[57] Hervé Martin has hinted that Thomas Tentler was too mild in his critique of the Church's uses of the sacrament, perhaps too confident in the genuineness of its desire to comfort.[58] Tentler rejects the pejorative characterizations of sacramental penance by the sixteenth-century Reformers, insisting that many Europeans felt that they benefited from it.[59]

A salient point of contrast (and, indeed, a crucial one) between late medieval Catholic and early modern Protestant efforts to shape the moral behavior of parishioners is that in the earlier period the clergy had to work toward these ends without the cooperation of the state. The two great competing corporations of the high and late Middle Ages, church and state, eyed one another suspiciously and cooperated wholeheartedly only in cases of the most exceptional and public concern to both. But before the 1530s were out, in lands that had accepted the Lutheran Reform, civic and religious leaders had begun that close cooperation, albeit wary, that characterized the remainder of the sixteenth century and much of the one that followed. Their collaboration underlay the process now called confessionalization, including, after Gerhard Oestreich, social disciplining.[60] The churches found in princes and magistrates more than an emergency bishop (*Notbischof*). They gained an indispensable enforcing arm in helping to produce a godly society; while the Janus-faced civil authorities, looking heaven- and earthward at the same time, found in religious discipline that very encouragement of the docility and orderliness that they sought in the people they governed. Needless to add, the temporal sword was also able to cleanse the rust of public, and sometimes private, debt from itself with sequestrated ecclesiastical wealth.

Scholars have looked upon Calvinist church discipline—with its carefully placed elders, its consistory, its threat of excommunication—as the more effective counterpart of the Lutheran rite of confession.[61] It is true that Calvinist cities and city states were able to adopt a more highly structured, efficient ecclesiastical polity, but I would argue that a similarly reliable oversight could and often did evolve in the monolithically Lutheran city as well. The key to supervisory success was the geographic setting, in addition to which politics played a sizable role. Calvinist divines, prior to the conversion of the elector of Brandenburg in the seventeenth century, generally existed in that part of the Germanophone lands that was shaped by a sense of communalism; and public, congregational confession in unison, with or without general absolution following, corresponded well to that tradition of the residents' federation. Similarly, any serious violation of group mores was seen as an offense against the local Christian society, one that was suitably dealt with publicly and, if persistent, by exclusion from the commonalty. We have seen this heritage and this cast of mind reflected in baptism as well. Guilt was equally the inheritance of all. None were more holy than others. Those who distinguished themselves on the negative side of the scale, and did not repent in prescribed ways, found themselves excised like a wart from the metaphorical body of Christ.

Even without quite the same communal identity, Lutheran territories behaved differently only by shades and hues. Their directorates of church and state interlocked, and consistories quickly arose at the superintendent or territorial level to deal with knotty problems of faith and morals—an expansive category. Elders, with their assignments to pry and to visit, may not have existed, but pastors informed the visitation committees (that arrived as often as annually, to every few years) as to who was intractable in sin and thus not responding to confessorial pressure. The visitors in turn sternly interviewed malefactors and, where they could not or ought not provide rectification, they brought instances forward to the prince and/or the synod or consistory. In addition, local officials, including city councils, had to lend their support to the detection and punishment of sin; they and the pastors were supposed to cooperate.[62] In Lutheran as in Calvinist lands, the former competitors now worked together unprecedentedly closely, even if not lovingly. In a Württemberg village in 1585, a servant who had contracted plague confessed on his deathbed that he had had an adulterous affair with the mistress of the household. The pastor told the visitors, and she was punished.[63] In the age of intense confessionalization, the confidentiality of the confessional was not dependably secure.

One could argue that in a village anyone could detect neighbors' sins without resort to the confessional. Nevertheless, even in the countryside secrecy is possible, and neighbors, in any case, may well not have counted as sinful such things as ignorance of the Ten Commandments or the Creed, immoderate drinking and bald flirtation at weddings, or bumptious self-indulgence. The Lutheran confessional was designed to root out these evils along with the worse ones. As in the Calvinist "theocracy," Lutheran administrators intended to create a godly society by assiduously molding the individual Christian.

Occasionally, nonetheless, the visitors thought a pastor was too harsh with his parishioners in the confessional. In Oberbatzingen in Württemberg in 1586, they told the cleric to "behave more moderately."[64] Pastors ought not, for instance, prevent their charges from entering the church, for they needed to hear the sermon whatever the state of their soul.[65] In Jena in 1560, the consistory ordered a pastor never to use absolution as a weapon against his flocks. He had refused to absolve a woman who would not let water from her land flow over onto his.[66] In Quedlinburg in 1627, the (Lutheran) abbess told her clergy that when someone made a genuinely contrite confession they were not to be denied absolution. But if these same parishioners afterward persisted in their sin, pastors were to admonish them with increasing degrees of severity, and finally refer them to her consistory. Abbess Dorothea Sophia was moderate in not hinting that she would ultimately ban intractable people from her lands. She stated simply that they could not serve as godparents and after their death could not be buried with the usual observances or within consecrated ground. In these measures, she simply continued Catholic practice.[67]

Usually, however, pastors were encouraged to be strict. Lutheran clergy, like their Calvinist counterparts, could and did avail themselves of excommunication. They could (and they did) bar recalcitrants from Communion. In the Württemberg village of Thonningen in 1584, a widow named Adele was not allowed to receive Communion because she harbored envy toward her stepson, an attitude that could have been confirmed in confession.[68] In Nassau-Dillenburg at the end of the sixteenth century, someone complained to an unnamed governor in the secular sphere that the clergy were hindering people from taking Communion who had undergone punishment for such infractions as prostitution (*hurerey*) and who had felt regret and reformed their lives. Some had been barred from the Eucharist for two years even though they deeply desired to take part, it was alleged: "If one [the clergy] were to deal in this way with every transgressor, there would be no Sunday when he did not have to present twenty or thirty [miscreants]."[69] Excommunication was not an entirely satisfactory measure, however, for, as the visitation protocols reveal, many parishes across Germany had at least a few residents who neglected their Eucharistic duty. This meant, of course, that they did not present themselves at confession so that their misdeeds and misapprehensions could be discovered. But in no place was this kind of nonconformity tolerated for long. The visitation committees invariably asked for the names of everyone who stayed away from the Lord's Supper and thus also from the confessional. In 1557, Duke Johann Wilhelm of Ernestine Saxony told officials of both church and state in Altenburg to provide him with a list of every single person who had not been receiving Communion.[70] In 1572, Duke Julius of Braunschweig-Wolfenbüttel demanded the name of every man and woman in his lands and how many times and exactly when since his entry into office each had received Communion. He wanted this list written in a fine and orderly manner with the data for each person clear and separate.[71] As in Geneva, sacrament scoffers could quickly undergo an excommunication that excluded them not only from the Communion table or altar (which they might not have minded), but under some strict regimes also from membership in the body politic. Yet, it appears that in most Lutheran territories those who refused to take Communion (on whatever grounds), or who were prevented from doing so, were not exiled but suffered lesser forms of pressure such as pastoral and visitorial harassment and being buried apart from their godly fellow citizens.

If the Lutheran institution for detecting and punishing sin was not as efficient and uniformly effective as that in Calvinist city states, this was owing to structural weakness rather than worldview. In any far-flung territory that was in large part rural, geography was an impediment to persistent, consistent oversight of the individual. The determination of each prince to rule in person also tended to hinder operations, for not only did princes differ in temperament from generation to generation, but they were ill or absent, or they were distracted by myriad other concerns. Ecclesiastical government most nearly attained its ends in those places where visitation committees, superintendents, and consistories were appointed and allowed to function with little regular princely intervention. These places were most likely to be free imperial cities including their surrounding dependencies, which had the added advantage of compactness.

Some will think that I am being too harsh, even cynical, in my approach to Lutheran use of the confessional. They will argue that the chief purpose of confession was to permit each pastor to console (*trösten*) his parishioners who were deeply worried that their inability to suppress their sinful nature would lead them to alienation from God and finally to damnation. There is indeed an element of truth in this. Pastors in their role as confessor were able to minister to the burdened consciences of those who were able to perceive and to worry about their spiritual as well as behavioral ills. To such as these, the sensitive cleric was able to respond with assurances of God's love and the certain applicability of Christ's atonement. But I remain convinced, on a close reading of numerous visitation protocols from all regions of Germany, that the Siamese twin of comfort was discipline—namely, to wield auricular confession, with its explicit threat of denying the sacrament, in order to produce an entire society that was uniformly as worried about personal corruption as those few who (through individual temperament) were already spiritually attuned and compliant. We must, in the end, see the institution of confession within its historical context, and that context is distinctly characterized by the multifaceted efforts of authorities to gain docility in those subject to them.

POPULAR OPINION

It is difficult to know just what the laity thought about the penitential system. Modern scholars have not been able to agree whether the late medieval confessional burdened or unburdened the sinner. Steven Ozment is either famous or infamous, depending on one's point of view, for having taken the position—characteristic of nineteenth-century pre-ecumenical Protestant partisans—that there was "a swelling popular desire to be rid of the psychological and social burdens of late medieval religion," characterized by the confessional.[72] He rightly reviews the salient clerical diatribes—of Luther, Oecolampadius, Jakob Strauss—against the abuses of the Catholic confessional.[73] But he insists that the problem lay not in misuse but rather in the condoned Catholic teachings and practices.[74]

The evidence is at once more varied and more ambiguous. Luther's acknowledgment that many people from Wittenberg and its environments were rushing across the Saxon border into Brandenburg to purchase indulgences suggests a widespread popular desire to find a means of avoiding the painful consequences of sin, particularly in the next life.[75] But others felt ambivalent toward the clergy, who in one habit or another always seemed to have their hands outstretched to receive money, and could easily be persuaded of the grafting intent of all men of the cloth. The silver miners of Freiberg rioted against the indulgence king, Johannes Tetzel, in 1517.[76] The widespread anti-clericalism at the end of the Middle Ages has multiple other layers of explanation. I suspect that with the firm implementation of Lutheranism ordinary Christians allowed themselves to be homiletically weaned away from a reliance on expensive and clerically tainted sorts of works like the acquisition of indulgences. At the same time, in confronting the crises of their present lives, they persisted in consulting cunning people, fortune tellers, and a wide variety of self-appointed healers; people like themselves but who claimed to have access to nature and/or the supernatural. Present wellbeing took precedence over the posthumous future.

As for the act of confession itself, in the early Reformation laymen wrote pamphlets attacking auricular confession. Pamphleteers among the lower nobility singled it out as an abuse and asserted that one should confess to God alone. Adam von Schaumburg, a knight, saw in Communion the proper mechanism by which Christ forgave sins. Other writers advocated confessing to a pious friend or acquaintance or in a general congregational rite.[77] Artisan authors, too—such as the weaver Utz Rysschner of Augsburg—perceived a discrepancy between Scripture and confession to priests. They considered that the Bible advised the collective admission of guilt.[78] During the upheavals that accompanied the introduction of Calvinism in the Rhenish Palatinate (1563), Saxony (1586–1591) and Brandenburg (1613), although people did lament various ritual aspects of the change—such as the elimination of bell ringing and of exorcism in baptism—I have not detected any popular complaint about the abolition of auricular confession.[79] In the early

Reformation, Catholic abuse shaped much dissident opinion, especially the non-theological; after the middle of the sixteenth century, the setting was different.

Recently Hans-Christoph Rublack has examined the place of auricular confession especially in late seventeenth- and early eighteenth-century Germany.[80] He concludes that leaders of the church failed to attain their disciplinary goals. The people accepted confession as a ritual act that entitled them to absolution and admission to the sacrament, but it did not move them to introspect, much less to regret. Confession, Rublack notes, became integrated into local social processes and structures, so that status differences are visible in the treatment meted out to sinners. In many instances, as during the week before Easter, the clergy simply gave in and applied a foreshortened admonition to people in couples or groups that appeared before them. I think these conclusions entirely likely. However, during the late period that Rublack treats, confessionalizing fervor was abating, and princes' enforcement of church ordinances was growing somewhat lax. My own concerns here are the aspirations and methods of the generations before the Thirty Years' War, and the kinds of reponses that they may have elicited then.

Until much more research is carried out on the Catholic laity of the early sixteenth century, I shall provisionally conclude that, even within a Lutheran polity that had excluded earlier misuse of the confessional, the laypeople found the procedure painful but not so painful that they would not tolerate it. In many parts of Germany, in any case, they had no choice. At least they no longer had to tell all their sins and every detail of them, and that was a relief. Luther opined at his dinner table that people were afraid of private confession, and he recommended that pastors inform their parishioners that, via their clergyman, they were really speaking into Christ's ear.[81] This should alleviate their fears. The parish visitors in Württemberg said that some people avoiding Communion stayed away because of the prerequisite confession, and they must have known. Parishioners did not invoke their financial difficulties. In most places where individual confession remained, parishioners had to pay their *beichtpfennige* or eggs (originally Easter eggs) for it. We may be certain that, in other places as well, some monetary substitution made up for the loss of this form of pastoral income.[82]

What voluntary Communion shirkers often did say was that they harbored ill-feeling toward a family member or a neighbor and that without purging themselves of this hostility they dared not approach the altar or Communion table.[83] Their prior confession would have been invalid inasmuch as it was not made in a genuinely repentant spirit. They retained this opinion from Catholicism and were in part encouraged to do so by the Lutheran stress (audible in Luther's own early commentary) on the essential penitent, conciliatory attitude of the communicant and on the reform of his earthly demeanor.[84] In

Württemberg in 1582, the parish visitors encountered several people who attempted to excuse their absence from Communion (and from confession) by saying that they harbored envy and hate toward others "which they had not conquered spiritually." They were reported to the superintendent and were ultimately dealt with by the prince's chancery.[85] David Warren Sabean has written a most perceptive essay based on several Württemberg cases.[86] In 1583 in Braunschweig-Wolfenbüttel, a family involved in a blood feud stayed away from the sacrament.[87] Such excuses may well have been a veneer, crafted of ideas and language that the laity expected ecclesiastical authorities to accept, attempting to conceal a genuine distaste for individual penance. They also said that they did not have the proper clothing to go to church, revealing what was probably a genuine social concern.[88]

Finally, people's experience of auricular confession depended on the manner of their pastors' application. This wide personal variation is beyond the historian's scrutiny. Clearly many parishioners would not have enjoyed their private exchanges with a hostile, domineering man of the cloth, perhaps a resentful, city-born-and-educated, persistently urban-oriented man unhappily residing in the countryside. Relations between sheep and shepherds were doubtless of every cast. Some of the laity may well have shared Luther's sense of comfort at receiving assurance of God's enduring love and pardon from the mouth of a compassionate clergyman. They could then proceed to the even greater consolation of the Eucharist itself. For others, confession and receiving Communion were social observances; for others still, conforming was a means of avoiding confrontation. After all, no one could see into another person's heart.

THE CATHOLIC SACRAMENT OF THE ALTAR

Going to church before the Reformation was a sensuous experience.[89] Indeed, the Mass (together with the sacred space within which it was celebrated) made use of every human sense. Even in rural churches and chapels, the devout heard the sound of the bell, the intoning of the ritual prayers—mesmerizing in their unintelligible, monotonous Latin—and the special words of consecration, *"Hoc est corpus meum"* and *"Hic est sanguis meus,"* by which the mundane elements of the bread and wine underwent transubstantiation.[90] They often saw the altar with its cloths and retable, the corpse-laden crucifix, the sheen of paten and Chalice, the glint of candlelight, the ceremonial vestments sometimes even in simple parishes worked by nuns in flowers or scenes of the Savior's life, the transfixing motion of the priest's hands as he raised up the Host and by God's permission effected a miracle.[91] They smelled the sweat of their neighbors and at the same time the heavenly fragrances of beeswax and incense. They felt holy water on their fingertips and the very flesh of Christ sacrificed as the priest placed the wafer into their mouths at the rood screen or the altar steps. And they tasted, besides the plume inhaled as the acolyte swung the censer, the body of God's Son as they closed their lips.

This degree of actuation of the senses was the bare minimum. In the great urban and monastic churches, where no restraint in expenditure had impeded the decoration of sanctuaries and altars, church interiors did convey, as they were meant to, devoted and skilled Christians' best idea of heaven to come. They assaulted the senses in their attempt to arouse religious fervor. Yet religious fervor had elaborated these interiors in the first place.[92] Each generation sought to assist in the pious inspiration of the next. As tourists we tend to forget today that nearly every surface was painted in vivid hues, as were the moving statues whose bare wooden simplicity so charms the modern eye.[93] Churches were marvels of dramatic contrast with the mundane environment. The rich stimulus they intended to present to the faithful cannot have gone totally unnoticed.

Just as important, church interiors conveyed the lives of Christ and the saints. They did this explicitly by means of paintings, frescoes, pictures in stained glass, sculptures, and seasonal artifacts such as the baby Jesus for use in the nativity scene and the woodcarved and painted Jesus on donkey back (*Palmesel*) that was rolled or carried into the churches on Palm Sunday.[94] They achieved this implicitly by means of layer upon layer of symbolism that informed the churches themselves and every object in them. The late medieval mind was irrepressibly allegorical. It is, however, impossible for us to know how much of this symbolism remained the product and possession of erudite minds, and how much may have sunk down over the centuries to the sensibilities of the ordinary laity.[95]

The focal point of every church was the so-called high altar, a term used to distinguish it from the numerous side or low altars that coexisted in the nooks and niches of every affluent church. From the early Middle Ages the altar had been thought of as the tomb of Christ, that sturdy plane upon which the parish priest offered up the repeated sacrifice of the Lord, called the Mass.[96] In the early Middle Ages, saints had been buried under it, and in later centuries every parish of means acquired relics, which were preserved within it (or at least near it).[97] Every eye focused upon this altar because of its prominent, visually inescapable location at the east end of the sanctuary. The exception, one from the Protestant viewpoint all too readily encountered, was when a rood screen had been erected that was actually intended to protect the holy of holies from lay profanation. Usually in such cases choir monks or canons occupied the elongate choir immediately before the altar, psychologically reserving to themselves this most sacred site in the larger church. In such cases, the consecrated Host was distributed to the people in front of the rood. In the humble churches of the countryside the congregation was more likely to have optical access to the altar.

The church in its entirety contrasted with the simple materials, the humble aspect of the workaday world. Prominently placed, often the only stone structure within the agrarian community, it demanded attention. Knightly manor houses and castles were commonly outside and, if possible, above the village. The church with its churchyard, the burial place of ancestors, represented the presence, the accessibility, of the divine to even the lowliest members of society. Rain running from its eaves guarded the pious yet still vulnerable dead. Its after-humming, penetrating bell extended the supernatural umbrella into distant fields, orienting consciousness toward itself, calling to regular remembrance and to prayer. It informed about the dying and dead, the weather when severe, the sacral time.[98] In and around this plain or fancy edifice, heavenly power was more concentrated than it was afield, where the forces of evil contended on an even footing with those of good.

When the pious citizens entered its premises, they found themselves surrounded by a solidity that bespoke the unshakeable arm of God. They crossed themselves with fingers dampened in holy water and went to stand in shifting, disorderly ranks within the holy space. In the late fifteenth century, only princes, city counsellors, and other august personages had pews. In this stratified society, however, it is likely that standing places became customary and, like the proliferating seats of the sixteenth century, reflected one's position in society: the better off and the prominent had the best available view of the *pièce de résistance*, the transubstantiated bread, the Body of Our Lord.[99] In great city churches, where there were endowed preacherships and consequently regular sermons, women and elderly or ill men brought collapsible three-legged stools and set themselves up in relative comfort close to the pulpit.[100] The poor stood at the back. Because pre-Reformation Christians were not compelled to attend church, even if they were devout they did not strain the capacities of the parish churches except at high holidays. In larger and especially wealthier parishes, Masses were readily available, and people could attend one that met their needs.[101] But the majority of altarists who fulfilled endowers' instructions to read or say or sing Masses for the repose of their souls did not actually consecrate and distribute the Eucharistic elements. Instead, they read shortened or "dry" Masses (*missa sicca*) that left this essential core out.[102] Even in the villages, the peasants were likely to have access to a weekly "wet" Mass. But, as after the Reformation, it would seem that the majority of the devout preferred to receive the sacrament only on a few major holidays.

The faithful who gathered for Mass entered a sacrally charged atmosphere. While we know that some ordinary Europeans doubted the veracity of the Mass as taught—a number of inhabitants of Montaillou, for example, under the influence of itinerant *perfecti*[103]— many others appear, through their piety and their avid participation in confraternities and processions, to have accepted the Church's teachings. They expected to witness the miracle of the Eucharist, and they felt confident of gaining personally from it even on those numerous occasions when they themselves did not ingest the Host.[104] Every ritual object and transaction contrasted this setting with that of their ordinary lives. They found themselves surrounded by representations of the divine that, rather like the eyes of the Neoplatonist's beloved, were intended to draw the worshipper from the contemplation of individual and earthly beauty—as in a painting or a lighted candle—upward to recollection of the spiritual reality symbolized by it.[105] The problem that so exercised the Swiss Reformers, who opposed the retention of images, was that people did attribute divine potency to the objects themselves. Zwingli and Calvin were correct in their perception. In late medieval Catholicism, not only the common laity but the ordinary parish priests shared a view of the universe within which rituals and objects, properly wielded, did tap the divine and facilitate its healing flow into human lives. What transpired in the performance of the Mass could bring blessing upon all.[106]

As is well known, then, the accurate recitation and enactment of the sacrament of the altar was the priests' signal act. Standing between the altar and the congregation in the theater of the Most High, they were structurally as well as functionally the link between God and the community. By priestly privilege, they were able to bring God the Son into a more immediate presence than otherwise existed within the nonetheless electric milieu of the sanctuary. There was, thus, an aura of expectancy as the people waited for the processional, for the appearance of the high priest. It is unfortunate that information concerning the processions into the churches in Germany has not been preserved, if indeed it was recorded. These would have resembled in type and variety those of the great English church of Sarum (Salisbury).[107] Rural parishes would have had far less elaborate equipment, and possibly no more clerical personnel than the priest and an acolyte or two. The great churches, in cities with boys' Latin schools, already had organ music and choirsong, adding to the sensual and ethereal dimensions of the event.

However deeply modern Protestants are convinced that the use of Latin was one of those forces alienating Christians from Holy Mother Church, the social historian can imagine that the language of Scripture, of the erudite, and of the clergy did itself help sustain a mystique of the Mass's special might. To be sure, where understanding was essential, the Church had long since made concessions to laypeople in the form of vernacular songs and, of course, the sermon. We have seen that key questions of the baptismal and wedding rites were asked in the language of the people. It is likewise unthinkable that medieval preachers preached in Latin to any but clerical audiences; for if they had, they would have wasted their breath. Should one even take the position that ecclesiastical transactions all were designed to exert social control upon the laity, then use of the popular tongue would have been indispensable in attaining this goal. But in ritual matters that were not to be laid bare to the vulgar gaze—and the priesthood did regard itself as a caste above—Latin was the language of choice.[108] The people were accustomed to it and, in the church as well as out, often believed in the magical potency of "hocus pocus." They accepted the "fruits of the Mass," harvested alike by the unlettered as by those who understood Latin. These were summarized by Johannes Nider (who was also the author of the anti-witch treatise, *Formicarius de malifici*[109]) in the first half of the fifteenth century as: the person does not age while hearing Mass; he or she is freed of physical bonds; the Mass restores good health; it protects against death; it effects indulgence—the reduction of temporal punishment for sin; it frees the soul from purgatory; it earns forgiveness of sins; it sometimes turns the lives of great sinners around; it increases faith; it strengthens hope; it sets one's neighbor a good example; it reminds us of the suffering of the Lord.[110] The vision here of clergy and many of the laity coincided. The attribution of such virtues to Masses said or heard explains the endowment of private Masses by those who could afford them.[111]

Despite periodic crusades to make the ritual of the Mass uniform throughout Latin Christendom, wide regional and local variation persisted until the Council of Trent. Certain standard parts of the rite were in different order from place to place, or the prayers used in the dioceses were not the same. Nonstandard, unofficial prayers called tropes, on subjects of local interest or reflecting local traditions, also embroidered and expanded the ceremony.[112] Like the processionals, Masses changed with the religious calendar, reflecting the singular characteristics of one major saint or another, one event or another in the life of Mary or of Christ. In times of emergency, special Masses were said that were directed toward that heavenly figure—such as St. Sebastian or St. Rochus—deemed most likely to help his afflicted devotees.[113]

The fundamental quality of the Mass, that which set it apart from every Protestant rendition, was its orientation toward the miracle of transubstantiation. What the priest and his assistants did before the elevation prepared the congregation for its privilege of bearing witness to the arrival of the supernatural; and afterward, in the brief concluding observances, all were drawn together before dismissal in the aura of the physically as well as spiritually present Christ. If to be baptized was in a metaphorical sense to be engrafted onto the body of Christ, to commune was to be joined more physically, palpably, to the divine. The ideal was to *feel* this concession in a semi-mystical state of deep humility, reverence, and awe. Not everyone could be transported, for that extreme experience was usually reserved for saints.

The priest, as the instrument of this wonder, bore a heavy responsibility. He had to be whole and in good health; no castrate could be ordained, and no sick or condemned cleric could say Mass.[114] The celebrant was supposed to be cleanly, carefully attired, aware of the significance of the alb, the long, plain linen underdress to be worn at Mass; the chasuble, the sometimes ornately decorated overgarment worn over the alb; and the stole, some of whose attributes I have noted elsewhere. In a small church, he entered without fanfare, but in a prominent church with some pomp and choirsong. Two candles burned on the altar. All was ready for the oblation, near the altar—the wine and the water with which it would be mixed, and the wafer of bread, round like a giant coin and usually impressed with a crucifix.[115] The acolyte would bring them to the priest. The first part of the Mass included the priest's greeting the people, a penitential rite based upon the clergyman's confession of sin (*Confiteor Deo*, "I confess to almighty God") and the *Kyrie eleison* ("Lord, have mercy, Christ, have mercy," uniquely retaining the Greek phrase, not its Latin translation); usually a recitation of *Gloria in excelsis* ("Glory be to God on high"); a prayer or prayers (*collecta*) before a reading from an Epistle and thus varying with the occasion; a reading from the Gospels; and a brief homily if the priest was capable of delivering or reading one. At this point, in the early church, the catechumens were dismissed, for they were not yet qualified to proceed to the Eucharist.[116]

During the second part of the Mass, the creed was now sometimes pronounced, followed by the offering of the bread and the wine, the officiant's washing his hands before touching the elements that would become Christ's body and blood, and the priest's "secret" and silent recitation of preparatory obsecrations.[117] After a prefatory thanksgiving and recitation of the *Sanctus* ("Holy, Holy, Holy"), the long Eucharistic canon began with prayers for the living. A small bell was to be rung before transubstantiation occurred so that the onlookers could prepare for the miracle. The people knelt and the men removed their hats. Facing the altar, the priest then softly intoned the words of consecration of the bread and wine. He kept the formula to himself.

> Who the day before He suffered took bread into His holy and venerable hands, and with His eyes lifted up towards heaven, giving thanks to Thee, almighty God, His Father, He blessed it, brake it, and gave it to His disciples, saying: Take ye all and eat of this, for THIS IS MY BODY.

In like manner, after He had supped, taking this excellent Chalice into His holy and venerable hands, giving Thee also thanks, He blessed, and gave it to His disciples, saying: Take ye all and drink of this, for THIS IS MY BLOOD.

His back to the onlookers, he held each element aloft so that all could observe the Son's arrival and his simultaneous sacrifice, with the eyes of faith even if the visible accidents remained unchanged, and could adore Him. As Lee Palmer Wandel has described in the context of Zurich, the priest's every gesture, indeed his extended posture during the elevation, contributed to his reenactment of the Crucifixion. These were charged moments.[118]

Next usually came prayers for the dead and the Lord's Prayer. After the *Agnus Dei* ("Behold the Lamb of God that taketh away the sins of the world"), members of the congregation, particularly (but not exclusively) those who had confessed the day before, came forward to receive the Host. The Chalice, as we know, was reserved to the clergy. The priest and his helpers seem in the early sixteenth century to have placed a smaller wafer in each person's mouth, though this may have varied from place to place. The pictorial evidence suggests that this practice continued within the Lutheran Church. A special cloth was held under each person's chin in turn, to catch any precious crumbs that might inadvertently be allowed to fall.[119] One could not degrade the Body of the Lord. Calvinists, however, insisted that communicants feed themselves.[120]

In Christianity's early centuries, women and men occupied separate parts of the church: the women the north side (with its negative associations), and the men the south.[121] This meant that they received Communion at their respective corners of the main floor before the altar steps. Depictions from the late Middle Ages are less conclusive, and it is likely that an earlier segregationist discipline had relaxed.[122] Society's more important personages probably went forward first. There was, however, room for spontaneity and pushiness. The Lutheran visitation protocols mention the earlier disorder in receiving the sacrament; a wrong, they state, that must be corrected.[123]

After the incomparable denouement, the priest ritually cleansed the sacred vessels, storing unused but consecrated Hosts in a pyx (to be used in administering the sacrament to the seriously ill), draining and wiping out the Chalice. The Lord's Prayer and the *Sanctus* were recited, followed by a prayer for peace. Then came the kiss of peace, mediated by the pax board so that people did not actually kiss one another. After post-Communion prayers, the dismissal (*Ite missa est*, from which the Mass took its name), and the benediction, he and his attendants quickly recessed, and the people departed. The performance was at an end, the medley congregation dispersed. Not only an ambience of sanctity remained behind. The nave's ceremonial function, reinforced by the presence of Christ's flesh in the pyx and the relics and images of saints, sustained a sacral ether until the next celebration.

THE LUTHERAN REFORMATION OF THE MASS

The Wittenberg divine's rejection of salvation by works carried with it the categorical denunciation of the Mass as Catholic theologians understood it. As Luther examined the complex implications of his reading of Romans 1: 17—as he thought further about his insight concerning first his own and then others' salvation—he found it necessary to carry the teaching of justification by faith alone over into all the subdivisions of his doctrinal worldview. If works could avail a person nothing toward salvation, then the Mass as *opus operatum*—that is, as an act with salvific validity in and of itself—was dead.[124] Following conviction where it led him, he condemned votive Masses, still Masses, and private Masses. All of these were presumed to possess beneficial power, for those who read or sang them, those who heard them, and for any souls for whose repose they were intended.[125] As a clergyman familiar with run-of-the-mill citizens in his part of Saxony, Luther knew that the popular mind attributed miraculous power to the Mass; he knew all about the alleged virtues of the Mass.[126] Luther and other Reformers in German-speaking lands so often applied the phrase, *abomination of the Mass* (*greuel der messe*), to the papist ritual that it became a kind of antipapal stock in trade.[127] In the first phase of his writing on the Mass, Luther opposed the Catholic concept of the sacrament as a sacrifice and all that went with it.[128] As the above description argues, however, this was the very marrow of the pre-Reformation Mass, and to eliminate this was to do away with its essence. Gone for him was the sacrifice, gone the priestly presidence over the miraculous, gone the sacramental efficacy of all the equipage of the altar, gone the virtues of the Mass with their far-reaching implications for the cure of sin and for the afterlife. The Mass stood at the cultic center of the faith, and to besiege it was to attack this indispensable core.

Nonetheless, in his "Formula missae et communionis" of 1523, Luther wrote, "We are not able to deny that Masses and the rite of the communion of bread and wine were divinely instituted by Christ."[129] Not only this, but in the Lutheran understanding the physical presence of the Lord remained. That Luther taught consubstantiation as the type and manner of Christ's being in the Eucharistic elements is so well known as to require little commentary here. He began to expound his theology long before the confrontation with the Swiss sacramentarians that produced that failed effort at conciliation, the Marburg Colloquy. He had already differed with Andreas Bodenstein von Karlstadt. At about the same time, the Bohemian Brethren were circulating unclear opinions, including that the bread and wine should not be adored as Christ but the evident suggestion that the Lord was in fact only spiritually present in the sacrament. Luther wrote to them in 1523, in "On Adoring the Sacrament of the Holy Body of Christ," that the heart of the sacrament lay in the Word of God—and here he means the words of Jesus as he distributed bread and wine to his disciples in the upper room. "It is highly necessary," he wrote, "that in the sacrament one leads the people to the Word and accustoms them to give much more regard to the Word than to the sacrament." This attention to the Word would result in true honor of the Eucharist, in contrast to the outward sham of "bowing, bending, kneeling, and adoration." Those who hear the biblical words of institution with faith may believe the assurance given—that in partaking of the elements their sins are truly forgiven them.[130] This faith is able to believe not only that God forgives the sinner but also, in a way that defies mere human understanding (*vernunfft und witze*), the body and blood of Christ do exist in the bread and wine. Without the assurance of the Word, Christians would be left with bread and wine as simple signs. But the Word is clear. "This *is* my body" does not mean "this *signifies* my body."[131] Luther argues that faith can test the Word to see whether literal acceptance is possible or whether a figurative sense is intended. In Matthew 16, Peter, a man, could not be a physical rock upon which Jesus could build his church. But in the accounts of the Last Supper, in Luther's view, Christ was speaking in "dry and clear" terms of his physical body and blood.[132] He rejects in turn the idea that those who partake of the sacrament are joined in Communion with Christ—though he admits that such interpretations might "have an attractive appearance to reason." The only sense in which communicants are joined, he insists, is in the literal, transitory simultaneous reception of the sacrament, and this has no profound meaning. In all these matters, he places the burden of proof upon those who would promote a figurative understanding; they must prove that the scriptural passages they adduce *must* be taken as they take them and in no other way. If they cannot offer proof, then one must stand by the literal text.[133]

The Reformer then turns to the question of adoration of the sacrament. Citing John 4: 21–24, he explains Jesus's admonition to the Samaritan woman that "God is spirit, and those who worship him must worship in spirit and in truth" (*geystlich und rechtschaffen*). He draws a distinction between the Catholic outward worship and the true Christian inner devotion. Christians can engage in the latter in any circumstances. They do not need to be in attendance at Mass. They require no outward symbols to validate their interior disposition. Their hearts bend, not their bodies. Genuine worship is the faithful person's trust and reliance upon God. Such a one believes that Christ's body and blood are present in the sacrament, for His Word does not lie. Just as the three kings adored Christ in the manger, so may Christians adore Him in the Eucharist. They are, however, not required to. Adoration is a spiritual state and need not be reflected in gestures. Those who perceive the sacrament in terms of the Word of God forget about postures: they sit still, listen, and reflect.[134] Theirs is not to investigate or to know how God the Father, Son, Holy Ghost, or the soul of Christ is in the sacrament. It should be enough to be convinced that the Word that is heard and the body that is received are in truth those of one's Lord and God. Let the faithless sophists look into such things![135]

At this early date, well before his main encounter with the Zwinglians, Luther had outlined his fundamental precepts concerning the Eucharist. When he set out later that same year (in Latin) and again at the end of 1525 (in German) to draw up a new liturgy of the Mass, he intended it to embody these ideas.[136] Nicolaus Hausmann, pastor in Zwickau and Luther's abiding friend, had repeatedly asked for an outline of the new practice, and the Reformer finally sat down and described to him what was being done in Wittenberg. He said that for the sake of those who were weak in faith (*propter imbecilles in fide animos*) he did not want to undertake radical change.[137] He would examine all the parts of the ceremony and retain that which was good.[138] Even though he perceived that changes had been made in the service of worship throughout the ages and that many of them were deleterious, he thought that such segments might be maintained as the *Kyrie eleison*, the Creed, and of course the readings from the Epistles and the Gospels. But the canon of the Mass, the Eucharistic ritual itself together with its equipage, he regarded as execrable, wholly the invention of self-promoting bishops and priests.[139] He would eliminate many feasts of the saints but would keep, in addition to those that celebrated events in Christ's life, others such as those of St. Stephen and John the Evangelist; he considered Purification and the Annunciation to pertain to Christ, and they should remain. He advised, then, keeping (in this order) appropriate Sunday introits, the *Kyrie*, the *Gloria*, untainted collects, and readings from the Epistles that could not be understood superstitiously but that promoted faith in Christ. Next should come the gradual, a pair of verses sung after the Epistle, perhaps the *Alleluia*, but the officiant might choose others that pertained to the church calendar.[140] Then was to follow the reading from the Gospels. Here Luther added, "We do not prohibit either candles or incense nor do we decide on them. This matter is free." Pastors might exercise their judgment in including or excluding these parts of the divine service.[141]

At this point, Luther became much more directive and, indeed, emphatic. Above all, everything suggestive of oblation must be removed, and only that which is "pure and holy" should remain. Proceeding to the bare kernel of the rite, Luther maintained a brief remnant of the prefatory dialogue between the officiating clergyman and the congregation:

P: The Lord be with you.

R: And with thy spirit.

P: Let us lift up our hearts.

R: We lift them up unto the Lord.

P: Let us give thanks to the Lord our God.

R: It is meet and right so to do. It is meet and right, just and availing unto salvation that we should at all times and in all places give thanks to Thee, holy Lord, Father almighty, eternal God; through Christ our Lord.

Luther then moved to the familiar biblical words of institution: "Who the day before He suffered took bread..."; "In like manner, after He had supped, took the Chalice, saying..." The cleric should pronounce these words in a voice such that all those standing around (*a circumstantibus*) can hear. Or, if the minister desired, he could bless the bread and distribute it and then bless the wine and proceed likewise. This alternative proved to be impractical when many communicants were at hand. However this was done, the celebrant must stand before the people and speak loudly enough that all could hear.[142] The blessing being finished, the choirboys should sing "Holy, Holy, Holy," while the officiant elevated the bread and the wine, which was done in order to spare the weak, who might be offended by too rapid a change in observance.[143]

Then the Sunday prayer was to be read, followed by the Lord's Prayer. Specifically to be omitted was the succeeding prayer of the Catholic Mass, "Deliver us, we beseech Thee, O Lord, from all evils," and all the gestures that had been made over the Host and the Chalice. Nor was the Host to be broken or a piece of it submerged in the Chalice. Instead, the words of absolution were to be pronounced in full voice, the clergyman facing the people. While "Behold the Lamb of God" (*Agnus Dei*) was sung, the pastor should take Communion and then administer it to members of the congregation. The old prayer, "Lord Jesus Christ, Son of the Living God," could be said, but the singular pronouns, "Deliver *me* by this Thy most sacred Body and Blood from all *my* iniquities," must be changed to "*us*" and "*our*." Likewise, the ministrant ought to change "May the Body of our Lord Jesus Christ preserve *my* soul to life everlasting" to "*thy* soul." Similarly, the concluding benediction was altered to remove the singular: "The Lord bless *us* and keep *us*..." The pax board was not mentioned. The words *Ite missus est* were to be eliminated.

Finally, Luther admitted that local variations were many, and he did not rule them out. One of the salient features of his "Formula missae" is its flexibility. Pastors should, above all, be guided by the Gospel and dispense with every hint of the Mass as sacrifice. In addition, pomp and luxury must be pared away. He did not insist on priestly vestments.[144]

By the time Luther prepared his "Deutsche Messe und Ordnung Gottesdiensts" in 1525, others had paved the way.[145] Luther was a latecomer, even though in 1523 he had stressed each pastor's freedom in ordering much of the Mass and suggested the propriety of using the vernacular. His contretemps with Karlstadt, who seemed to insist that all Latin should be removed from the order of worship, may have given Luther pause.[146] In any case, as Luther told his parishioners on October 29, 1525, people, including those in authority, desiring a German Mass from his hands had put so much pressure on him that a vernacular service must have been the will of God.[147]

One of Luther's chief concerns in bringing the Mass into German was to render the often traditional words well sung. For to Luther the Mass was a musical event, and it would be so all over Lutheran Germany by mid-century.[148] Masses in the late Middle Ages could be said or sung, and priests often did sing them, or rather considerable parts of them. Luther sought the advice of the elector's experts on music in deciding which notes to use, and he departed from Catholic practice, which made his version literally less monotonous.[149] To the modern sensibility, it is strange that pastors were encouraged to *sing* every Epistle and Gospel text, but this evidently did not trouble early modern Germans.[150] In his introduction, Luther described two somewhat contradictory principles: pastors should enjoy their Christian freedom to modify the Mass; but out of love for our neighbors we should strive to be the same in sense, manner, and gesture, "just as all Christians are of one baptism and have one sacrament [Eucharist]." He thought it would be a good idea if there were uniformity within each territory, or if the villages and hamlets around a city adhered to the urban observances.[151] It would be useful to have a firm order of worship so that one could more easily teach simple people and children. In 1525, Luther declared that a catechism was badly needed. In the meantime, the sermon was a principal means of training Christians in their faith. And indeed it was. Luther was more explicitly than before moving the preached Word to the center of the churchly performance.

Every day's Epistle, every day's Gospel lesson could be sung. Luther provides notes for I Corinthians 4: 1–5. Wherever possible, the presiding clergyman should turn his face toward the people rather than to the altar. The people should participate regularly in the ritual through their own singing. Luther had begun to compose and to gather hymns for the congregation's use. First came the liturgical hymns that embodied essential portions of the service, such as the Creed: "We believe in one God." But many others remained to be translated, as Luther himself admitted.[152] He interjected pastoral explanations to the people of the Lord's Prayer. It was not enough to memorize it; one had to understand it.[153]

The officiant was to sing the words of institution. Luther again urged the retention of elevation, and it was not eliminated in Wittenberg until 1542.[154]

In preparing a vernacular Mass, Luther did not intend that the use of Latin should die away. Indeed, wherever there was a boys' school, which by definition ought to have a classical curriculum, the boys should regularly constitute the church choir, and they should perform their liturgical roles in Latin. Only when they were called on to lead the people in singing a German hymn should they revert to their mother tongue. As the sixteenth century wore on, the importance of Latin in the Lutheran order of worship grew.

Although Luther made his chief revisions in the celebration of the Mass early on in his career as a Reformer, he faced an ongoing theoretical challenge from those who disagreed with him, especially on the question of whether and how Christ was bodily present in the bread and wine. In his definitive treatment, "Vom Abendmahl Christi, Bekenntnis. 1528," he presented the concept of *unio sacramentalis*, the sacramental union of flesh and bread, blood and wine, that did not literally involve the communicant in "eating" their Savior.[155] Be this as it may, in the popular and public (including the average priestly) mind, those who partook of the Eucharist did consume their Lord. Erudite distinctions were beyond their ken. With the restoration of Lutheranism in Saxony in 1591 and after, the people were told, concerning the bread and wine, that

> by means of the words, "This is my body, this is my blood"—which one otherwise calls the sacramental union—it is right and well said that the body and the blood of Christ are received and enjoyed with the physical mouth by all who take the sacrament, the worthy and the unworthy alike.[156]

This besetting, divisive issue, despite its interest, is beyond the scope of this study.[157]

LUTHER'S CONTEMPORARIES AND THOSE WHO CAME AFTER

In the course of his labors in Braunschweig, Hamburg, Lübeck, Herford, Bremen, Pomerania, and Denmark, Johannes Bugenhagen disseminated (though he did not slavishly imitate) the basic vision of Luther.[158] A feature of Bugenhagen's program is the explicitly incorporated admonitions, as, for instance, in the form of a collective confession and before the Communion itself. These could be seen as the counterpart—the elaborative opportunity—of the medieval tropes, though the purpose of the Protestant innovations was indoctrinational and moral. Doubtless Bugenhagen and Luther had informally made such statements in the Wittenberg city church, but Luther had not found it necessary to make these formal parts of the liturgy. Bugenhagen, however, knew that his time was limited in those places where he sojourned, and he wanted to leave behind as explicit a guide as he could. His Masses, then, represent a transition into the detailed ritual prescriptions, including a number of admonitions, required of all presiding clergymen before (or at the latest shortly after) the middle of the century.[159] Already in 1533, the Ernestine Saxon ecclesiastical ordinance, issued under the authority of Elector Johann Friedrich, declared,

> In addition, they [pastors] shall see that the high feasts...and all Sundays and other holy and evangelical days are held in an orderly and honorable way, with great seriousness and reverence, with divine office and the service of God, with sermon and song, as history [books] depict it, so that they adhere to the churches in Wittenberg and Torgau or Zwickau, and so that they establish no new holiday or ceremony, according to their own pleasure on their own initiative, other than those that are presently in use in our churches.[160]

Every trace of Luther's preferred flexibility had disappeared. Nonetheless, at this early date many differences remained, which authorities would make a concerted effort to erase within their domains.[161]

Another practice encountered in Bugenhagen, and widely found in urban and other large churches throughout northern and central Germany, was that of the communicants going into the choir to receive the sacrament. Because during much of the year so few people wished to receive the Eucharist on any one Sunday, it was possible for them all to fit into the choir and to sit or kneel in prayer between the distribution of the Host and that of the Chalice. They came forward at the pastor's signal (the women on the left, the men on the right)[162] and then returned to the choir, where they remained until the final benediction. These were without exception in proximity to the high altar and—noteworthily— separated from and elevated above their non-communing neighbors.[163] In case a ritual community was either forged or reinforced during the sacrament, those who did not partake were deliberately excluded from it.

What the people came forward *to* deserves comment. As increasingly pastors were ordered to face their congregations while they pronounced the words of institution, they required a new kind of altar that permitted them to do this. Ordinarily the old "high" altar remained in place, and a new tablelike altar was erected in front of it. Officiants could stand behind it as they consecrated the Eucharistic elements, and the people could, according to gender, be fed at their respective corners of it. The visitors in Thuringia in 1555 shed light on this process in their report to the sons of Johann Friedrich:

> Because everywhere in the land, as a result of Your Princely Graces' father's blessed command, and otherwise for good reasons and causes [he] ordered the altars in the churches to be built and set up so that the priest could carry out his entire office facing the people; and

as everyone regards Weimar as the master and model, so we humbly request that Your Princely Graces have this ordered for this area [*alhir*] too.[164]

As influential as the pattern adopted in Wittenberg was, all over Germany the leaders of church and state negotiated in the production of orders of worship that reflected their own traditions, theological convictions, and political realities. Although this book is a treatment of ritual, we must remember that the theoretical interpretation of the manner of Christ's presence in the Eucharist was the single most knotty problem, more than any other factor preventing the unification of the major Reformers and thus of the Reformation movement. Martin Bucer did his utmost to mediate among the parties but in our own century has continued to draw criticism for failing to incorporate the indispensable essence of Luther's Eucharistic thought.[165] Bucer himself favored a spiritual understanding of the partaking of Christ.[166] But in the current ecumenical environment, his quest, which temporarily succeeded in uniting Germans (though, of course, not the Swiss) by means of the weasel-worded Wittenberg Concord of 1536, seems praiseworthy. Nonetheless, political motives loomed prominent in the background and lent their encouragement.[167] Likewise, Philip Melanchthon in our own time has continued to suffer the slings and arrows of confessional partisans, for the concessions that he was willing to make to a Calvinist view of Christ's Eucharistic presence. Certainly, in the sixteenth and early seventeenth centuries, compromise was not honored; it was equated with betrayal, or at best pragmatically seen as unavoidable.[168]

The leaders of every major metropolitan and territorial church attempted to symbolize their theoretical position in the milieu, words, and gestures of the service of worship. Whatever modifications they decided upon, they kept a tight rein on every parish in order to ensure that rituals were performed just as prescribed, and completely uniform. To judge from the visitation protocols, rulers became preoccupied with ceremonial uniformity. In Nassau-Saarbrücken, for example, the prince wanted to know, among many others, if a hymn was sung after the collect and the Epistle; if there was a song after the sermon and if it was long or short; if in the collective confession and absolution every single word of the proper text was used; if the Lord's Prayer was said after this in silence or aloud, and with the people kneeling or not; if the proper vesper lection was used; if the pastor always preached the catechism at midday on Sundays; if, when the pastor said the words of sacramental institution, he grasped the bread and the wine and elevated them; whether the Hosts were large or small, whole or broken; whether the Eucharistic napkin was still being used;[169] whether after dispensing the sacrament the pastor turned toward or away from the people; if the hymn continued during Communion; whether communicants stood or knelt; if they still laid their offerings on the altar; if public penance was in use and for which misdeeds; how the clergy dressed, including how they wore their beards and hair; whether people knelt in prayer in the church and if they [the men] bared their heads; how the church bell was rung and when; and if people sat in church in the order of their station in the world.[170] In Württemberg, too, visitors asked the clergy to tell them precisely how they performed every ceremony, and they paid special attention to the administration of baptism and the Eucharist. Did the celebrants face the people? Did they stand in front of or behind the altar?[171] Did they elevate the bread and wine? Did they repeat the words of institution? Did they use the collective confession and absolution?[172] Ernst Walter Zeeden has correctly observed that many of them, even if unwittingly, preserved substantial remnants of the Catholic liturgy.[173]

The most drastic contrast with the pattern laid down by Luther was, of course, that introduced as part of the Calvinization of a few territories during the sixteenth century, most notably in the Rhenish Palatinate in 1563.[174] Even here the prince, Friedrich III, an imperial elector, got himself in trouble inasmuch as the Peace of Augsburg of 1555 accorded legitimacy only to Catholicism and Lutheranism. Nevertheless, Friedrich pursued his religious program, attempting to extend it to the city of Amberg north of Regensburg and east of Nuremberg as inheritance and dynastic politics allowed. On January 10, 1567, he forbade the wearing even of simple cassocks (*chorrock*, literally a choir robe) by presiding clergy; the use of Communion napkins that in some places were still being held under communicants' chins; turning in the direction of the Eucharistic elements during the words of institution; any exorcism; Latin songs; altars; all images including crucifixes. In Calvinist services, only psalms were sung, and organs were silenced and removed (though restored in some places at the end of the century).[175] In the Sunday service, instead of the Epistle, any suitable part of the Bible could be read. Latin was eliminated.[176] Reformed liturgists, then, broke more completely with Catholic precedent, as they were aware. When Johann Sigismund was attempting to introduce Calvinism into Brandenburg beginning in 1613, he wrote,

> Touching on Herr Luther, we recognize him as a chosen instrument of God, through whom the churches have experienced very much that is good. It would grieve us to censure or think otherwise of him. But nevertheless you will agree with us that he was stuck very deep in the darkness of popery, and for that reason it is not to be wondered at that he was unable sufficiently to extricate and unwind himself from all human teaching.[177]

In Reformed churches, the sensuality of the Catholic Mass was now entirely gone. Church interiors were whitewashed and every seductive image removed.[178] The experience of the worship service, finding no outward distraction, had to concentrate on the Word preached—hardly a tangible object—and on individual interiority. What is more, during the course of the century, in many Reformed churches the focal point—the Eucharistic table—shifted to one side of the nave, as though to underscore the papist superstition inherent in altars. The people could no longer contemplate even a bare remnant of the site of earlier devotion.[179] This kind of service was much more intellectually demanding than that in which visible symbols were rife; and whether average people, including the masses of the uneducated and not particularly motivated, were able to rise to the challenge of the theologians is unavailable to our scrutiny. In order to avoid punishment, the people had at least to pretend. In their orderly echelons—now sitting in the comparative comfort of pews, their bodies held in place as they had not been before—they listened, they received, they submitted.[180]

Much ritual territory lay between the lands that adopted Luther's rubrics and preferred ceremonial environment and those that ultimately accepted (and kept) the Calvinist pattern. And, as in other instances, the majority of those lay in the south and southwest of Germany, the region where Lutheran, Zwinglian, and Calvinist strains intersected. They varied greatly from one another in the specific liturgies they developed, though all revealed their greater or lesser historic debt to the Catholic Mass. Inevitably, too, they did look to see what Luther was doing or had done in Wittenberg; they read his treatises, including those on the Mass, and often included at least some of the liturgical hymns that he had made available. Those churches that adhered to the Augsburg Confession employed rituals that were reminiscent of Catholicism and at the same time recognizably Lutheran. The city of Augsburg was a maverick, needing perhaps to establish its independence of that summation of the faith to which it had lent its name.[181] The ingenuity and individuality of their choices can be symbolized by Regensburg's decision around 1567 to remove a painting of the coronation of Mary from the altar—even though it had been kept covered so as not to lead simple folk astray—and to replace it with a painting of words considered to be the summation of the teachings of the Old and New Testaments. The people were to regard the literal Word.[182] During Saxony's brief Calvinist interlude before Christian I's death in 1591, a sympathetic knight had a similar word-painting installed in a country sanctuary.[183]

All churches under the Lutheran umbrella removed many paintings, statues, reliefs, frescoes, and other depictions of saints that did not have (in the authorities' opinion) firm biblical or historical substantiation.[184] Indeed, very few holy figures who had lived after the age of the Church Fathers continued to enjoy respect—and certainly not veneration. Incidences of iconoclasm were very rare and confined to the beginning of the Reformation.[185] Whatever their views on images, few governors of church or state would brook popular aggression. But they themselves progressively, inexorably, had most images removed during the course of the century, leaving in place (or adding) only those that illustrated either the life of Christ or major points of Lutheran theology.[186] These were intended to edify the people, not to arouse even pious emotion. Economic motives were as important as religious conviction in determining what came away and what was done with it, for many ecclesiastical treasures possessed objective value.[187] It is perhaps ironic that, even as the images were being removed in the northern and central parts of Germany, fancy clerical vestments were often not disposed of and were sometimes used and then replaced as they wore out.[188] Brandenburg was "highest church" of all.[189]

How successful were Reformation leaders and their successors in persuading the populace that the Eucharistic elements and attendant acts did not have supernatural powers? Once again, we are thrown back upon clues that initially seem rather small until one perceives that they recur. In a rural parish in the Rhineland, the congregation was distressed when the pastor dropped some Hosts at the altar.[190] In a village pertaining to Halberstadt in 1589, the people were upset by the sexton's having seen that he was running out of wafers (Hosts) during Communion and having broken some of the remaining ones in half. They reported it to the visitors, who interrogated the culprit—for they, too, thought it wrong, but probably for different reasons.[191] To the members of the congregation, it may well have seemed that the cleric was desecrating Christ's body, while the visitors probably regarded this act as too reminiscent of Catholic practice. Nonetheless, officiants were to know in advance how many communicants there would be, so that they did not prepare too many Hosts. This suggests a traditional concern with the treatment of extra consecrated wafers (which is to say, with the Body of Christ). One could not easily affirm the bodily presence and at the same time ascribe no special status to the embodying bread. The Lutheran retention of the specially formed wafer also doubtless reinforced the tendency to ascribe the same miraculous properties to the Protestant Host as one had to the Catholic. The Zwinglian and Calvinist use of common table bread marked a radical visual break with the past that helped to bolster their leaders' respective theologies of the Eucharist.[192] But no attitude was characteristic of all. In a village in the dominion of Magdeburg in 1562, a man mocked the sacrament, taking a jug of beer and pretending to perform Mass with it. He had to do public penance.[193]

BEYOND RITUAL FORMS

One of the curiosities of the liturgical history of the sixteenth century is that the word *Mass*, where it was retained and not thought tainted by papal associations, became detached from the celebration of the Eucharist. The great majority of Protestant services all over Germany were not the scene of the sacrament of the altar. Nearly all ecclesiastical ordinances that lay down a pattern for divine worship describe procedures for Communion "if communicants are present." In fact, Communion was often unavailable, whether or not some people might have liked to partake of it. The increasing use of the phrase *service of God* (*Gottesdienst*) reflected these circumstances, and the word *Mass* was gradually reserved for occasions when the Eucharist was available. The frequency of Holy Communion varied with both time and geography. Also, if no one had approached the pastor for confession and expressed the wish to receive Communion, then the sacrament was not held. But as a generalization we can say that it occurred at least several times a year, for the authorities considered this to be a minimum and urged the pastors to press their flocks to partake. Near Stuttgart just after mid-century, it was held on average six to seven times a year.[194] The 1552 Mecklenburg church ordinance tells pastors, when no communicants have appeared, to take the opportunity "to admonish the people to come to Communion more often."[195] The Catholic Mass, then, had been denatured, not simply in the manner in which the Lord's Supper was now celebrated but also in the sense that this sacrament was very seldom available. Non-Eucharistic Protestant services, with the sermon as their centerpiece, could trace their lineage back to the late medieval preaching service (*Predigtgottesdienst*), at which nevertheless the Eucharist had often been celebrated. On the other hand, many Lutheran church services are described in the Lutheran ecclesiastical ordinances and visitation protocols at which exclusively prayer, song, and readings from the Bible took place.[196]

The sermon, then, that near-eponym for the reformed order of worship, frequently did not occur.[197] At other times it was nothing more than a clerical explication of the text for the day or of a particle of Luther's catechism. To be sure, the parish visitors ensured that on Sundays pastors preached, and in the larger towns there was a sermon in at least one church virtually every day. We may be confident that the early morning sermon (*frühpredigt*) in the cities was essentially a postil or homily, by the standard of the day quite abbreviated, for the laypeople's mundane duties called. What mattered to the theologians was that the Word of God was inculcated on the populace, and every service embodied this principle. On major feast days, some of the ancient litany was indeed brought out, even though on regular occasions such long prayers were omitted. One of these is the full litany of the *Kyrie eleison*, in which the people call upon God to save them and their rulers from all manner of specific troubles.[198]

We need to expand our concept of the sermon in order to gain an accurate picture of the predicatory function of the Lutheran clergyman.

As more and longer admonitions and exhortatory prayers were added to the official liturgy, often to be read verbatim to the people, these took on the aspect of new homilies. The catechism, too, found its niche in the revised service. Many people would not come to catechism lessons set at a special time, and one remedy for this was to have the pastor teach the catechism during the Sunday service, inserted between the sermon and the sacrament (if held), or between Gospel reading and sermon.[199] While a principal and proper "sermon" had its prominent place in the service— a place that it shared in time and psychological importance only with the Eucharist on days when this was celebrated—the new disciplinary principle, borne on the homiletic vehicle, spread into parts of the service where it had not been before. Other territorial ordinances required pastors to preach on the catechism at specified weekly services, usually on Wednesday, or on Sunday afternoon. In some areas, ministers confined their treatment of the doctrinal summary to the Lenten season, perhaps unconsciously following the ancient pattern of preparing catechumens for examination and baptism at Eastertime.

Furthermore, as Luther's preferred flexibility was abandoned, pastors found themselves increasingly bound by prescribed biblical texts in accordance with the post-Reformation church calendar. We erroneously think of the preaching duty as an opportunity for any pastor or deacon with the capacity to be creative. Although certain stars like Luther himself could ascend the pulpit and expatiate at will on Scripture, visitation committees and superintendents cultivated in their clerical charges a studious imitation of their betters, some of whose sermons were printed. Very few of the sermons of run-of-the-mill rural ministers have come down to us, but where they have, we find tediously similar expositions of the biblical passages associated with particular days of the church year. In Braunschweig, I came across the sermons of a number of rural pastors from 1573, which strongly bear out these generalizations.[200] Needless to say, the words of Luther's own postils resonate strongly within them. This was thought proper, a sign of well-directed assiduousness. Individualism was condemnable. In the Hohenlohe of 1578, we find a rather extreme example of prescription that goes beyond the reading of brief admonitions before the sacrament. In that county, the prince's religious advisors set out entire sermons about the Eucharist that pastors were to read verbatim.[201] In 1625, the visitors in Calenberg-Göttingen complained, "Some pastors and servants of the church want to be different from everyone else [*singular*] and not follow the super-intendents' directions in official matters."[202] They were doubtless not smiling as their scribe wrote that down. These "official matters" definitely included sermons and all aspects of the liturgy.

Taken altogether, Luther's Mass was shorter and more edificatory than its Catholic predecessors. It was designed to be comprehensible to the masses and not to enchant them. Yet its provenance was clearly visible. The sequence of its parts remained almost entirely as under Catholicism, though Luther emphasized pastors' right to elect one prayer, one hymn, one biblical passage over another as well as the adiaphoristic nature of such matters as whether to retain candles, altar cloths, images, and vestments—even the ringing of the altar bell before elevation.[203] Nevertheless, as is well known, Luther made two radical changes: the elimination of the Mass as sacrifice and the expansion of the homiletic moment into a prominent, time-consuming aspect of worship.

Luther's followers noticeably lengthened the religious service through their addition of various admonitions and catechism lessons. It may be for this reason that some rulers thought it desirable before the end of the century to rule on the permissible length of the sermon per se. Wolfgang of Hohenlohe wrote to his court preacher in 1585 that the sermon could not last more than one hour.[204] In 1594, he shortened this to three-quarters of an hour.[205] The parish visitors radiating outward from Magdeburg did likewise.[206] The visitation protocols leave the distinct impression that the main Sunday sermon was supposed to be no more than one hour in length—but even this greatly surpassed the Catholic homily.

On the one hand, it is true that the priest was demoted to the level of parson, whose role was now strictly to be played out on earth and among men, without mediatory access to the divine. On the other, however, as we who have followed the discussion concerning confessionalization are aware, Protestant pastors compensated for their loss in two ways: through their responsibility to carry out—not just to pay lip service to— the religious education of each person in their charge; and through their alliance with the authorities of both church and state. What they sacrificed in the supernatural sphere they made up for in the earthly. Everywhere in Germany, pastors were integrated into a disciplinary network that combined church and state, and this showed itself in ritual. As the Count of Hohenlohe declared in 1553,

> Constantine, Theodosius, and others have also taken on [governance of] the churches and the service of worship. By this means, God helped them [presumably their subjects] toward their souls' blessedness and to temporal happiness and wellbeing.[207]

Everywhere admission to the Eucharist came to depend on individuals' fulfillment of moral and ritual prerequisites. Gradually (but definitely) citizens had not only to attend services an absolute minimum of every Sunday morning, but often at least once more. They also—at any rate, in Lutheran territories, as shown above—had to submit themselves to the pastor for scrutiny of their doctrinal mastery and their genuine regret for even interior sinfulness, for their lack of thankfulness toward God and their small charity toward neighbors. Not just in theory, but in real and detectable ways, every person was unworthy. There were, after all, no more earthly saints to be canonized. The eye of the governors fixed each one. This, at least, was the ideal that princes, magistrates, superintendents, and consistories strove to attain. The Count of Nassau-Dillenburg went so far as to have the annual civil court convene on the same day each year as the parish visitors undertook their investigation, so that the two powers could coordinate their efforts.[208] The ordinances are filled with language like that approved by August of Saxony in 1557:

> The parishioners of every place must behave blamelessly and in a Christian manner in every aspect of their lives, and especially in the hearing of God's Word and the reception of the most worthy sacrament. If in opposition to this one or more should be found who live an unchristian life and despise God's Word, and who, in particular—now that the Gospel has been preached loud and pure— have never or not in many years received the most worthy sacrament in both kinds, or who in other ways are openly scornful of God's Word and have been admonished on that account by their pastors and diligently taught and instructed but who have stubbornly and without repentance stayed in their prior annoying and bad life, these shall be pointed out to the authorities in each place, and should these not undertake a suitable punishment, then the despisers of God's Word shall not be admitted to any baptism or Communion without having properly regretted and repented. Or should they depart or die, they are to be buried with none of the usual solemnity [accorded] other Christians.[209]

Others were more pointed about guilty parties' prospects for exile. Johann Friedrich's successors in eastern Thuringia, still Saxon dukes and the cousins of August, told their subjects in Altenburg and the surrounding countryside that same year that if miscreants' behavior did not improve such that they could and would receive the sacrament, the local official (*Schosser*) was to see that they sold whatever they owned and moved out of the land within a set period.[210]

In the prevailing atmosphere of close supervision, sin was a more besetting problem than under Catholicism; not because it was more frequent, but because the standards for admission to Holy Communion were now higher, the tolerated discrepancy between theology and worldly life smaller than before. As we have already seen, barring from the Communion table became a weapon often wielded by the pastorate. Where the clergy were reluctant to perform their harsh duty, parish visitors insisted.[211]

Procedures for punishing people within the church became harsher as the sixteenth century wore on. In parts of Germany, as Heinz Schilling has written, sin became criminalized.[212] Before as after the Reformation, the transgressor met with certain civil penalties for acts of violence or sexual misconduct. With the establishment of the Reformation, malefactors also faced public humiliation in the form of pastoral accusation from the chancel and relegation from Communion, and, should they repent, in the form of self-display in church as a penitent and a scripted upbraiding and questioning before the entire congregation. Religious thinkers considered themselves to be reviving the legitimate practice of the early church. In Merseburg, a lengthy ceremony held up the serious sinner for observation. After the sermon, the penitent knelt before the altar. The pastor was to tell the people,

> Dear friends in Christ, you know that this N. N., by means of the sin he [or she] committed, his [or her] manslaughter[213] or public adultery, has greatly enraged God our Lord, and has troubled and vexed our Christian congregation. On this account, he [or she] has made himself [or herself] unworthy of the Communion of saints and the congregation of God and unable to receive the most worthy sacrament, and has earned God's rage and eternal damnation; by such sin he has cut himself off from Christ and His holy body and become a member of the Devil, which is horrible to hear...

The clergyman then announces the sinner's change of heart. He interrogates him or her:

> So I ask you now whether you committed such manslaughter or adultery, and if you did this, that you confess this same sin publicly before God and this congregation...

On receiving the confession, the pastor inquires,

> Are you heartily sorry for this sin, by which you enraged God and troubled and vexed this holy congregation?...Do you also intend with God's help to improve your life and to sin no longer in this way?

After much more comment, at last the pastor pronounces forgiveness:

> Dear N. N., now that you have confessed your sin openly before this congregation, and more than this, asked for absolution, so we wish most heartily to dispense this to you, and this your repentance makes the angels in heaven high rejoice.

The pastor withholds absolution, however; the sinner must stand at the front of the church after the sermon on eight days. At the end of that time, absolution will be granted, and the sinner may again receive Communion. In the meantime, he or she must demonstrate a commitment to the upright life.[214] The final ritual of absolution prescribed in Merseburg is over one and a half pages of fine print, and would have taken perhaps half an hour to perform.[215] Finally the pastor proclaimed,

By the command of our dear Lord Jesus Christ, and through the merit of His holy suffering and dying, and in accordance with the admonition of the dear St. Paul, we want, in God's stead, to absolve and acquit this poor sinner [masculine singular] N. of their [*iren*, or *her*] sin, which was publicly committed, and to free and loose him from the bands of the devil and of eternal death into which he has fallen.[216]

Such scenes as these could be found throughout Germany in the second half of the sixteenth century and beyond.[217] A short list of the named offenses would include—in addition to manslaughter and adultery— blasphemy, usury, children's striking or cursing their parents, incest, and excessive drunkenness. In 1576 Philip Ludwig of Pfalz-Neuburg decreed that at the end of the ceremonial denunciation in church, members of the congregations were to lead guilty parties to the church door and turn them out. Such evildoers were not only to be banned from the Communion table, baptism, and Christian burial, but also from the social life of the villages, including taverns and weddings.[218] The Leipzig consistory concerned itself with the problem of pastors' skipping public church discipline as a favor to prominent citizens.[219]

Because these measures were part of the divine service, they represent a Lutheran alteration in its complexion, one that set it apart yet further from the usual late medieval Catholic Mass. Of course, it would be going too far to assume that just because these scripts were on the books, and just because visitation committees enjoined pastors to employ this means of enforcing church discipline, such episodes were commonplace. Yet the visitation protocols suggest that they did occur and were thus familiar.

DIVINING THE MASS

It is one thing to describe the ritual changes that occurred in the transition from the Catholic Mass to the Protestant Masses and services of worship. It is another to arrive at an interpretation of the shift in meaning that the entire transactions meant, from confession and absolution, where pertinent, to the benediction and dismissal of the devout. As promised at the outset, I shall return to the concept of configuration, the overall shape, sight, and mood of the ceremonies. Analyzed from this point of view, the technicalities of whether the *Gloria* or *Alleluia* remained are no longer as important as the overall effect that the churches intended to have on worshippers.

The late medieval Catholic Church believed that it brought the human and the divine together. The priest—at his (sacramental) ordination given an indelible mark upon his soul—claimed to negotiate that layer of the cosmos that was a little lower than the angels and, in administering the other six sacraments, to introduce the presence of the deity to humans. Between his sacramental functions, and however flawed his life was, he was intended to represent God even in the remote hamlet. As men of generally little learning, of a similar provenance to their charges, priests shared a worldview in which not only they, but various processes and objects, could serve as channels of heavenly power. The words that they spoke, the cultic objects that they wielded, the very clothing they wore in the performance of their official duties: all had an impact on the mundane such that it could be transformed. The power of the keys was no mere phrase but conveyed their ability to influence who could and who could not reach paradise.

Late medieval priests were not stingy with their sacral power. They lent it not only in ritual settings—as in, for example, extending their stole to a woman being churched or applying holy oil to the baptisand. They believed that the water, the salt, the candles, the animals, the fruits of the field and every other object that they blessed did gain in sanctity as a result. They often gave the baptismal water to parishioners to take home, undisturbed that these simple folk intended to apply it to their cows and their corns. They encouraged people to bring their candles to church on the feast of Mary's purification, Candlemas, so that in making sacred gestures over them they imparted to these tallow and waxen household objects the strength to ward off demons at the deathbed of family members. The clergy were happy, for the price of a loaf of bread or a small coin, to sprinkle holy water on the humble abodes of their neighbors, certain that this ministration lent protection during the following year to all who dwelled therein. It did not disturb them that popular rituals were often an informal extension of Eucharistic efficacy into the profane world. After all, they, the priests, were the delegators to the laity of this kind of magical craft.

The signal privilege of their station was to bring forth the Most High in the canon of the Mass. The scrupulous among them, like Martin Luther, worried that if they erred in the performance of this crucial ritual they would invalidate that Mass or even bring God's displeasure down on the community. This is why the principal qualification for priesthood was the ability to execute the liturgy of the Church with utter correctness. To say this is not to assert that priests (whose training had often amounted to little more than an apprenticeship with an already ordained clergyman) actually did fulfill every jot and tittle of the rites impeccably. Nor is it to say that, however humble their background, they thought of themselves after ordination as the equal of those they served. Early modern Europe was acutely hierarchical.

Officially, the Reformation completely undid the fundamental assumption that human beings could in any way wield or influence divine favor. Even where such traditional phrases as *the power of the keys* remained, when we look at the *configuration* of penance and the Mass, when we study it in the context of theology, liturgy, and political environment, we see that the confessor and officiant could in no way sway God. Even speaking "in God's stead," the pastor pronounced his conviction, grounded in doctrine, that the deity would regard kindly the truly repentant sinner. Christ's atonement would cover those who sorrowed and struggled against sin. The clergyman did not *cause* God to look kindly or to mitigate punishments due the living and the dead, for in contrast with Catholic views, God had never relinquished any of his authority to human beings—not to Peter, not to St. Francis. This, at least, was the Lutheran position. Calvinist teaching, as we know, compromised even less with human frailty.

The Reformation doctrinally eliminated the tangible, perceptible points of prior contact between the human and the divine, including priestly privilege and the sparks that had charged church interiors and all manner of sacramentals. All good fortune, all virtue (including that of the saints), all health, all benefit derived—along with that ultimate favor, salvation—from God alone. No human activity could affect or effect outcomes.[220]

This theologically based conclusion, however, is hardly useful in the mundane sphere. In everyday earthly society, rewards and punishments must exist as incentives. In the early modern there-and-then, people could not avoid attributing illness and deformity to personal sin, and collective tragedy (such as war and epidemic) to God's wrathful response to human disobedience. Thus, sensitive educated mortals could have been torn between the teaching that works availed them nothing, and the socially influenced value that works were essential to the individual as well as the collective wellbeing.[221]

This ambiguity played itself out in the Lutheran sanctuary. To enter the church was different from entering one's home or workshop, by virtue of the church's dedication to the contemplation of higher things. If some places were more or less sacred than others, it was not the result of God's action, but of human consecration versus desecration. *People* rendered (say) houses of prostitution impure, and *people* made churches sacred. This Protestant process of removing concentrations of divinity can be evaluated in opposite ways. One could regard this as a Protestant secularization of society, which is the preferred approach at the moment, or one could see it as an attempt to extend sanctity to every niche and corner of human activity. I am strongly inclined toward the latter, even though we know by virtue of hindsight that this neo-monastic endeavor failed. But having said this, I must note that the images, the colors and textures, the candlelight, the Latin, the vestments, the organ music, and above all the real presence of Christ's body and blood in the Eucharist, particularly in the traditional wafer-shaped Host, conveyed semiotically to worshippers that the divine was still among them and likely to be concentrated more in the church and its grounds than outside. Psychologically it made little difference if all of these liturgical elements had undergone some alteration in their official forms and meanings. A painting of Christ on the cross above the high altar was still an image of the Savior, to which simple people could impute a certain potency of its own. The Virgin still appeared, though strictly in her role as Christ's mother. How much did it matter in its effects that St. Sebastian and St. Rochus were gone? The candlelight carried the late medieval symbolism of light and spirit forward to later generations. Vestments and liturgical function still created an aura of pomp and the elevation of the clergy above the laity.

Lutheranism, as Martin Luther in his way intended, continued to make concessions to "weak consciences." I must interpret this to mean that especially in Brandenburg and parts of Saxony, where many "high" (near-Catholic) ritual forms were still in use, the official cult compromised with the popular need to offer a rich symbolism, despite the risk that much of the populace would decipher these emblems in ways that the leaders of the church did not approve (which is to say, in traditional ways). Lutheranism accepted this tension the moment it put forward the tenet that communicants ate Christ's body and drank His blood. This profoundly sacral assumption could hardly exist—and this is probably an esthetic judgment—stripped bare of ancillary symbols of the divine presence: the high altar, altar cloths, Communion napkins, bright-hued clerical garments, the joyful noise of voice and organ, the generous employment of Latin. The Lutheran service writ large held out to the individual access to God far more than the Reformed one did.

Inherent in this still recognizably Catholic-derived Mass, then, was the message not only that God was still approachable (if in a more limited way than before), but also that human beings, including but not exclusively the clergy, could still act in ways that obtained His benefit. In abolishing the sacrifice of the Mass and the priesthood as a separate caste, Luther on one level concentrated all *action*, all *effect*, in the godhead, thought of most of all as the Son. But on another level, by leaving a generous residue of sensuous cultic objects and processes behind, he allowed his followers to go on affirming a more diffuse and available sacrality. Calvinism, by contrast, presented congregations, in their sternly ordered ranks, with the unadorned Word, free of distraction. The message implicit in the bare Word and the denuded sanctuary was that God, the Creator and the repository of all sanctity, had withdrawn from the concrete world. God was a spirit who could not be conceptualized in any human terms. He could only be approached by means of interior concentration of an abstract nature. The Holy Spirit, the least easily defined aspect of the Trinity, prevailed. Holy Communion was presented in the form of ordinary table wine and bread, and Christ's flesh and blood were there strictly spiritually. Calvin did not accommodate the weak; he challenged them to abandon their material crutches. Encoded in the Reformed Mass and its setting was the lesson that mortals were helpless to propitiate God. They ought not even to pray for the living or for the dead—and these segments of the Catholic ritual were rejected early—for to do this suggested that they might persuade God to act other than as He in His eternal Providence had ordained. Nor must they presume to act in ways that suggested that they might elicit any favor. In effect, God was separate and remote.[222] Calvinism, in trying to unite theology and earthly life, avoided Lutheran tensions; but with its implacably disciplinary ideology it trod upon flawed humanity. If Calvinists in the end promoted the secularization of Europe, they did so unwittingly by rendering God entirely spiritual.[223] Without perceptible representation, God vanished from the lives of the masses who could not conceive Him exclusively in the abstract.

John Bossy and Virginia Reinburg have written of the late medieval Catholic Mass as an institution that incorporated a number of social functions. To Bossy it represented the unity (though sometimes a vengeful one) between the living and the dead with its prayers for both categories of relations and neighbors; it symbolized the wholeness of society by means of the wholeness of Christ. He devotes much attention to the Mass as sacrifice, contrasted to the Protestant sacrament, and what this means.[224] The medieval Mass possessed a carnivalesque aspect and was essentially an "annual reception, occurring at Easter after the asceticisms of Lent...a more plausible embodiment of the unity of Christians than the more frequent and more devout communions of the Counter-Reformation."[225] In between these infrequent Communions, the *Pax* (the kiss of peace) served the laity as a substitute ritual expression of their oneness, which otherwise had the function of receiving the Eucharist in the symbolic environment of social peace. In Protestant services, the *Pax* mainly disappeared.[226] Bossy concludes that the Protestant Masses, and ultimately those of the Counter-Reformation Catholic Church, were individualistic and asocial, and with this I am inclined to agree. Reinburg draws on a more diverse body of evidence, including depictions. Turning around the view that in many extra-ecclesiastical rituals the people tapped the power (and in part the form) of the Mass, Reinburg sees socially familiar social gestures brought into the church and incorporated in the rites surrounding elevation and communing—standing, hat doffing, saluting at the Gospel reading; societal almsgiving and feudal donation in the offertory procession; the taking of communal oaths in the greeting and the *Pax*.[227] In an effort to derive a *configuration* of Catholic and Lutheran Masses from the study of a broad range of materials, I have to reiterate that, while at the formal level late medieval clergy and laity constituted two separate castes, in the domains of background and outlook the parish priests had a great deal in common with their parishioners. Despite the drawing apart of elite and urban clergymen, in other settings the people and those who cured their souls understood one another well. In coming together for Mass, and in the celebration of it, they formed, as ministrants and recipient/observers, a complementary whole. They had quite a successful symbiotic relationship, until in the later Middle Ages that relationship began to deteriorate under the pressures of excessive clerical populations and jurisdictions, and of economic competition.

As for the laity, the sociological assumptions of late medieval society could serve as fault lines along which eruption occurred, or they could facilitate cooperation. Laypeople constituted no unified whole, nor in towns did they wish to. Princes and magistrates were the first groups demanding and receiving acknowledgment of their special status in the form of views and pews (and burial places) inside the sanctuary, and they came forward first to receive the sacrament.[228] But the hoi polloi stood, knelt, and sat around the late medieval church interior, shifting their weight, physically unconstrained (and likely also socially so). They could easily come and go, and no one threatened to punish them for doing so. In this comparatively unstructured setting, they could press forward to see as much of the transubstantiatory moment as internal church structures permitted. They tolerated one another, at least occasionally—and formally, in their testaments—submitting to the imprecations of the beggars standing outside the doors. The social dimensions of the Mass can only be rightly interpreted in the context of the community in which it took place.

The Masses of the Reformation occurred somewhat further along in the processes of social differentiation (hierarchization), discipline, and condoned clericalism. Increasingly in the sixteenth century, with the full consent of Protestant authorities, church interiors were divided up into rows of pews, which the burghers often personally owned but sometimes leased, and the flowing social body now became the ordered, ranked, gender-separated *bodies* containing individual souls.[229] Custom and tolerance gave way to legal disputes over pews, and the consequences of restlessness could include official disapproval. People were forbidden to leave the church before the final benediction without good reason. At the same time, as popular confraternities were banned and many types of craft gatherings were forbidden or closely overseen, social subdivisions (a basis of medieval identity) broke down. This is a secular concomitant of changes in the Mass that cannot be overlooked. At least men increasingly faced God as individuals just as they were individually answerable to the magistrates. For most purposes, women were subsumed under them. All were now to come forward to the Eucharist according to sex, standing, and marital status. This tendency may have existed in the late Middle Ages, but after the Reformation regimentation grew apace. Although in one sense falling into line and barely distinguishable, their places in that line coincided with inner and outer circumstances that the pastor, through his confessorial role in the Lutheran Church, knew well. No one could slip through to the Lord's

Supper without his approval. Many factors beyond the historians' reach bore on these approvals, but in the second half of the sixteenth century, and the first half of the seventeenth—the period of the most concerted social disciplining—visitors, superintendents, and princes pressed the clergy to be firm. They preferred strictness to compassion, and prescribed admonitions and sermons bear this out.

Order and personal responsibility gained new emphasis not just in the messages conveyed by the service of worship itself, but by interior decoration and arrangement. The increasing admonitions spoken by the pastor, in addition to his formal sermons, were delivered from the pulpit that now protruded into the midst of the rows of people. In the late Middle Ages, chiefly the great urban churches already had these pulpits, designed for their specific purposes, but many other churches did not. With the Reformation, they became part of the standard design of every sanctuary. Just as important as to see the altar was to see the preacher, and in the Calvinist sanctuary the altar was gone.

One of Martin Luther's most heartfelt teachings was that Christians must love and serve their neighbors. In his own sermons—and in those of his followers who were likewise disposed—Christian charity received prominent billing. The atmosphere created by such a pastor itself would enhance a communal spirit, sealed by the Eucharist when it was served. Lacking such pastoral inclinations, however, the new services of worship would not have conveyed an ideal of social unity. Even though the reformed liturgy included a collective confession and, sometimes, absolution, its purpose in the context of the whole was to abase oneself before God, not to foster cohesion on earth. Bossy has noted that the unison singing of vernacular hymns "did surely achieve something of the immediate and unproblematic unity at which they [the Reformers] aimed."[230] However, we need to think about this seeming unity in the light of intense confessionalization, which used congregational singing, and specifically the carefully crafted lyrics, to indoctrinate the people and to gain their conformity to the elite-defined norm.[231] Conformity and community are not the same thing. They are based in very different feelings. We might see the changes introduced into pre-Eucharistic discipline and in the worship service itself as part of what Hans-Peter Dreitzel has characterized as the second phase of the European civilization process, that of the internalization and generalization of compulsory standards of behavior throughout burgher society.[232] In the form of parish inspection and synodal oversight, the urban elites carried out their *Drang nach außen* in the countryside. Through the forcible improvement of the clergy—which was much more successful than their efforts among the laity—authorities of church and state separated the pastors and deacons from their congregations at least as much, and in rural parishes far more, than Catholicism ever had. The ministry became an implement of official control (though it doubtless comforted as well) and the laity a mass of potentially eruptive, daily disorderly under-miners of the Christian polity. Ordinary Christians became objects to be acted upon by the publicly admonishing, disciplining deliverers of the Word. These shifts of intention are evident in the reformed Mass and service of worship.

5 Banning the dead and ordering the living
The selective retention of Catholic practice

CATHOLIC DYING

In the eyes of many Protestants and some reform-minded Catholics, the late medieval rituals of dying (*ars moriendi*) were little short of infamous. As a private exercise, Erasmus satirized the deathbed rituals of the affluent burgher of his day in the colloquy "The Funeral." Although not intended to be either a serious or fulsome description of contemporary deathbedside manner, the dialogue does encompass major features of Catholic practice, not to mention the ways in which it anticipates Reformation critique.[1] The about-to-be decedent George Balearicus has first of all sought medical remedy for his bodily ailment. By the sixteenth century, this was thought obligatory if one had the means, for not exerting oneself to postpone death blurred the boundary between suicide and the hour of demise ordained by God. Second, Balearicus makes confession to a member of the clergy—that Erasmus has that cleric be a Franciscan and that other clergymen dispute his right to hear confession need not detain us here. Third, the parish priest arrives to administer extreme unction and holy Communion. Fourth, the dying man makes testamentary provision for his wife and children as well as philanthropic bequests to various religious orders and to the poor. Fifth, he gives instructions for his (elaborate) funeral. Sixth, the Church, through its representatives, assures George of salvation; he has done what is required of him. Seventh, George is covered in a Franciscan tunic and laid upon a pallet strewn with ashes—symbols of his renunciation of the world and the flesh. A crucifix and a taper are extended to him. Some of the people in the room chant Psalms. Until he finally expires, clergy speak loudly into his ear, demanding some sign of confirmation of the commitments he has just made. It is necessary that he not fall away in the brief time remaining to him. Finally, a priest speaks the absolution. This is obviously not the sort of departure that Erasmus advocates, for he immediately proceeds to describe a properly pious death; nonetheless, the "bad" death contains elements both of structure and conviction that were quite typical in the larger towns of pre-Reformation Europe.

Dying was an art form at the end of the Middle Ages.[2] The deathbed drama was not something that just *happened* after people realized that their end was near. Learning one's role took an adult lifetime of preparation. This, at least, was the ideal. Medieval people were extremely vulnerable to disease and infection, and even in times when plague was not rampant—as it frequently was—they could not be certain of living from one week to the next. Childbirth alone was a life-threatening event. Understandably, then, in this environment keeping mortality in mind was not seen as a morbid preoccupation. It made sense. The sacramental system of the Church led people through every crisis, with the ultimate goal of delivering souls who persevered in seeking salvation to the righthand side of the Judgment Seat. But how in an inveigling world could one foster that essential perseverance? In addition to pastoral counseling, in the confessional and from the pulpit, in the fifteenth century a genre of book spread that instructed the unlettered laity in the art of dying. Vovelle states that of the religious books published by the ten leading printers between 1400 and 1600 (presumably not just in France but in Europe), between 0.5 and 2 percent were on the art of dying.[3] Arthur Imhof describes one such twenty-four-page booklet stemming from the upper Rhine in the second half of the fifteenth century but which was widely printed and sold in Europe. This example is in Latin, but its eleven woodcut illustrations convey the essential message even to the illiterate. The first ten appear as five dichotomous pairs, the first picture in each pair showing a dying man being tempted toward a bad, ultimately damning, end; the second depicting a dying man manifesting saving virtues. (It is a fact that each of the subjects is male, although some of the saints clustered around the bed and the occasional kinswoman and servant are female.) In the first pair, the temptation to abandon one's faith is juxtaposed with the strengthening of faith. In the latter, Christ and the multitude of saints press upon the bed, an angel ministers to the dying, and the ubiquitous demons slink away in defeat. In the second pair, the urge to despair stands adjacent to trust in the grace of Christ's death as conveyed by Church and saints. Christ's arms are contorted around the horizontal member of the cross, and his legs flail; his head is thrown back.[4] In the third, impatience with one's condition is contrasted with bearing one's illness submissively, aided by reflection on the agonies of the martyrs, several of whom hold their symbols out for him to contemplate. In the fourth, haughty ambition (as devils offer crowns to the dying man) is opposed to the consolation of humility; souls who were not humble are tormented in hellfire.[5] And in the fifth, the desire to retain one's earthly wealth is next to the relinquishment of this world and concentration upon the next: even the gathered relatives beam approvingly down upon the invalid.[6]

The eleventh and final woodcut stands alone. In it, death comes to a man smiling and at peace. The burning taper that was often placed in the hand of the nearly dead is caught by an attendant monk. Angels receive the infant-like soul as it rises up, and the beastly demons at the foot of the bed writhe in frustration. The ranks of saints pour out their grateful adoration at the foot of the crucifix.[7] Christ has died, and his body hangs slack.

The ritual of dying, then, included not alone a variety of prescribed acts as depicted by Erasmus and reflected in the images set out in the woodcuts. Just as important was the cultivation of a spiritual state that by the hour of death was utterly unshakeable. This state consisted of persistence in faith, confidence in the power of Christ's death upon the cross to make satisfaction for the sorrowing sinner, acceptance of the pains of illness and death, humble submission to God's wishes, and a willing relinquishment of this world.

None of this was supposed to be possible without the aid and participation of the Church. Two of the seven sacraments, channels of divine grace, were brought to the dying in their homes. The Catholic rite of extreme unction at the end of the fifteenth century closely resembled that prescribed in the early fourteenth century by Bishop Heinrich I of Breslau, though Heinrich does not mention that it was customary to toll the church bell of the parish in which the person to be attended resided. The priest comes to the dying person dressed in surplice and stole, preceded by holy water and lighted candles, and followed by the cross and another cleric, who carries the holy oil and tow or wool cloth for wiping off the oil, which a priest must afterward burn. When they arrive, the officiating priest says, "Peace be to this house," and the accompanying clergymen reply, "Amen." The priest asperges the ill one with holy water and says,

> The Lord be with you. Let us pray. Lord God who through your apostel James spoke saying, "Is one of you ill? He should send for the elders of the congregation to pray over him and anoint him with oil in the name of the Lord. The prayer offered in faith will save the sick man, the Lord will raise him from his bed, and any sins he may have committed will be forgiven" [James 5: 14–15].

> We ask, Lord our redeemer, that you heal the feebleness of this infirm [person] by the grace of the Holy Spirit and with salubrious remorse, and forgive his sins; expel from him the combined pains of heart and body and mercifully return to him full internal and external health, so that by this work of your mercy he may return restored and healthful to his former duties. Through Christ.

The sick person now humbly asks the priest and the others who are present, out of fraternal charity to forgive any offenses he may have committed against them. If he does not know the words of the prayer of contrition (*Confiteor*) or does not wish to say it, he is to strike his breast, declaring, "I am to blame for all my sins; I beg you to pray for me," and all say the prayer for mercy (*Misereatur*) together. The priest now pronounces absolution and remission of sins. He then extends the crucifix to be kissed. After an additional prayer, the seven penitential Psalms (6th, 32nd, 38th, 51st, 102nd, 130th, and 143rd) are recited. The priest then applies the holy oil with his thumb, making a cross on the eyes, ears, nostrils, mouth, hands, and feet of the dying. He speaks to each of these members in turn, "I anoint your eyes [etc.] with sanctified oil in the name of the Father, Son, and Holy Spirit, so that if you have sinned through illicit looking [etc.], it is expiated by means of this unction." This prayer is then repeated: "Through this unction and his holy and most kind mercy, may God forgive you whatever you have sinned by looking, hearing, smelling, tasting, touching, or going."

Although there is no sign of it here, the priest might also touch any body part that was especially painful. The bishop continues his script:

In the name of the Father, Son, and Holy Spirit, may this anointment with holy oil serve to purify your mind and body and as a fortification and defense against the darts of unclean spirits. Through Christ. God, who gave to your servant Hezekiah three times five years' [more] life [II Kings 20: 1–11], by your power raise this your servant from his death bed to health. Through Christ. Behold, Lord, your servant laboring in the infirmity of his body, and revive his soul, which you have created, so that corrected by your punishments it may feel itself saved by your medicine. Through Christ. God, who always governs with pious affection, incline your ear to our supplications, and grant your suffering servant refuge from his adverse health of body, visit him with health and show him the medicine of your heavenly grace. Through Christ. God, matchless defense against human infirmity, spread the strength of your assistance upon our infirm one, so that, aided by your act of mercy, he may deserve to be rewarded uninjured in your holy church. Through Christ the Lord. God, who bestowed upon humankind a medicine for health and the reward of eternal life, preserve the gift of virtue in your servant N. and concede that he may feel your remedy not alone in his body but also in his soul. Through Christ our Lord. God the celestial virtue who dispels all languor and infirmity from human bodies by the power of your precept. Be propitiously present to this your servant so that, having fled his infirmities and rejoined human society, he may bless your holy name from the moment his health is restored. Holy Lord, Father omnipotent, eternal God, who strengthens the fragility of the human condition with an infusion of the virtue of your merit, so that by healthful remedies our bodies and members are invigorated, kindly wait upon this your servant, so that every corporeal infirmity having been removed, the perfect grace of pristine health is restored to him.

Through Christ. Lord Jesus Christ, who said to his disciples, "Every one whom you shall bind upon earth will be bound in heaven, and whomever you shall loose upon earth will be loosed also in heaven," in which number He wished to have as many unworthy persons included as they desired, He himself absolves you by means of our ministry of all your sins, even those that you have carelessly committed in thought, word, and deed; and He deigns to lead you, absolved, from the violence of your sins, to the realms of heaven...

At this point, the priest may administer the Eucharist. He concludes with a blessing upon all the members of the house (*in hoc habitaculo*). The dying person is once again sprinkled with holy water. The Psalms and prayers being finished, the priest may depart, joined by the deacon, and with two candlebearers (*duobus ceroferariis*) he carries away the Communion.[8]

In these Catholic rituals of death, the use of particular objects and substances had its roots in venerable tradition. Persuaded that death was the just reward of sin—that sin established for all human generations in the Garden of Eden—the ministers of the Church found it necessary to wield their most potent weapons. The items they carried to the dying were sacramentals, and by their nature possessed of varying degrees of power against sin. All reveal the inherently dialectical outlook of the age: The sacramentals break the prevailing dark, sin, and death of the bedchamber, pouring into it the figurative light of redemption—sin and redemption, the ubiquitous dialogic elements of late medieval religiosity.

Wearing surplice and stole sets the cleric who is performing extreme unction apart, not just from the laity but from his own everyday self. Being garbed in sacred vestments confers sanctity and special powers on him. The stole in particular has supernatural abilities to thwart the forces of darkness, as we saw in the churching of women, when the priest led the woman into the sanctuary by giving her the lefthand end of his stole.[9] The holy water signifies cleansing. Priests sprinkled it on myriad occasions when spiritual purification was called for. They aspersed dwellings at Christmastime to protect them from evil, and fields in the spring, during the Rogation Days, to make them fertile. Holy water dispersed the powers of evil, and this is precisely what was expected of it in the presence of death.[10] The Host, a special wheaten wafer usually baked by members of religious orders but blessed implicitly even before its elevation and conversion into the True Body of Christ, was, of course, the mightiest sacramental of all. Partaking of the sacred feast of the Eucharist consoled the sincere and frightened with the promise of life everlasting, and by the late fifteenth century pious people whose lives seemed precarious, such as pregnant women, received this sacrament as often as possible.[11] The crucifix derived its strength from an affinity with the scene it represented. Sacred images drew the minds of onlookers to the contemplation of their subject. The sick and dying were thus reminded that Christ's agony had been at least as great as their own, and that his sacrificial death atoned for their sins. And, iconographic canon law notwithstanding, the observer regarded holy artifacts as channels of divinity. The oil of extreme unction harked back to biblical chrism. Durandus, bishop of Mende, a contemporary of Thomas Aquinas, finds plenty of New Testament precedent for applying holy oil to the sick. He cites James 5: 14–15:

> Is one of you ill? He should send for the elders of the congregation to pray over him and anoint him with oil in the name of the Lord. The prayer offered in faith will save the sick man, the Lord will raise him from his bed, and any sins he may have committed will be forgiven.[12]

Durandus elucidates:

> The oil of the sick [i.e., applied to the sick] serves as a medication. Because pains accompany illness, the blessing of [i.e., that is in] the oil administered to the sick says, "Grant, o Lord, that it [the oil] drive out all pains and bodily illness."

Durandus explains the annual consecration of the oil.[13]

Except at the end and almost incidentally, the ritual handbook of Bishop Heinrich I of Breslau does not refer to candles. Yet, not only does the *ars moriendi* of the upper Rhine depict a taper in the hand of the decedent in the final frame of the proper Christian death, but virtually every one of the numerous portrayals of the death of the Virgin Mary contains these as well. Candles were typically consecrated on the feast of Mary's purification, in English fittingly called Candlemas (February 2), and were considered to be powerful sacramentals. They brought light into all manner of worldly darkness, even into the stalls of sick livestock.[14] I have encountered no adequate scholarly treatment of the evident practice of placing a lighted candle in the hand of persons who were just about to breathe their last. Potentially pertinent light metaphors are legion. Suffice it here to mention four very likely ones. First, fire has lustral qualities. Sin and death are inextricably linked in the dying chamber, and the lighted candle both cleanses the protagonist and helps protect against the diabolical forces acknowledged to be present. Second, it lights the way into another (unknown) world. For both these reasons, a burning candle stood through the night by the corpse of the deceased. Third, it represents the radiance of Christ's presence at the end of this journey. And, fourth, it symbolizes the human spirit: the moment when the dying person releases the taper is thought to be the instant when he or she gives up the ghost. The telluric dangers of fire being manifest, someone must be there to catch that candle. Numerous pictures of the death of the Virgin show one of the disciples, perhaps John, to whom Christ had entrusted his mother, with his hand too on the candle.

Bystanders often stare intently into Mary's face, presumably to be witness to her departure. The artistic evidence is not compelling; it is improbable because impracticable that the dying always grasped candles. The ideal that they should have is significant.

It is perhaps unfortunate that the most renowned surveyors of Western attitudes toward (and practices of) death have come from a Catholic country. One thinks here especially of Philippe Ariès and Michel Vovelle.[15] Their commentary on late medieval convention is valuable, and confirms the tradition outlined above, but these authors neglect the alterations made in ritual practice and outlook on death that the Reformation is alleged to have ushered in.[16] Ariès draws attention to the shift beginning in the fourteenth century in the time and place of the Last Judgment. Although Christ is still depicted as rendering his final verdict on the destination of each soul only at the end of the world, in a prominent counter-scheme each soul's fate is determined at the moment of death.[17] The eschatological denouement takes place every day and all around us even if we do not hear Gabriel's horn with our mortal ears. The drama depicted in the *ars moriendi* manuals is thus no minor one. Nor did even the post-Tridentine Church reconcile the millenarian and the bedchamber patterns of judgment. The message conveyed to individual Christians is that they hold their destiny in their hands. All that they may have done during their lifetime, whether preponderantly for good or for evil, they may now nullify by their manner of dying. This is a consummate theology of works—to which Erasmus juxtaposes the "good death" in "The Funeral"—and leads me, for this purpose only, to sympathize with Steven Ozment when he writes of the terrible burden of late medieval theology.[18] Nevertheless, mere laity wielded some influence over their fate, and they did not face the future without help. The Church with its sacraments stood as a powerful help in time of trouble, a heartening companion on life's final journey. And their departure was a social event, an occasion for the gathering and talking, singing, and praying of relatives, friends, servants, and neighbors.[19] Yet, on the left or swarming all around were Satan's minions, and late medieval people thought them mighty indeed.[20] Just how much power they had was a matter of one's theology and discussion, but it was understandable, if nonetheless fatal, if a mere human being succumbed to their relentless wiles. The most important place *not* to succumb was, clearly, at one's "appointed hour."[21]

The observation that death, personified as a skeletal Grim Reaper, becomes eroticized in the fifteenth and sixteenth centuries deserves comment.[22] The sexual element is indisputably present in such paintings as *Death and the Maiden* and *Death and the Matron* (Kunstmuseum Basel) by Hans Baldung Grien. The grisly, decaying figure of death prepares in the first instance to haul the naked and pleading young woman away by her hair; and in the second he bites the weeping matron's cheek as his fingers touch the side of her breast. It is implied that the imminent sex act will be the occasion of the women's death. In both paintings, the women's pale bodies, with genitals plainly visible, are the focus of attention. Bob Scribner understands this genre and aptly labels it a "pornography of death." Such paintings ostensibly warned onlookers of the sinfulness and vulnerability of the sensuous person, but I agree with Scribner that in fact the torment of death is strictly subordinated to the display of the "eroticized female body."[23] Patrons could rationalize ordering such works by reference to their edifying layer of meaning—and then, perhaps unconsciously, indulge their senses in the visually erotic. This is not the image of death projected in the *ars moriendi* manuals, nor, likely, did most people, Catholic or Protestant, look upon death as a sensuous experience. For dying persons who were conscious, and for those of their household who were present, it was an acute experience of the senses, nevertheless.

MARTIN LUTHER

Martin Luther's opinion was the strongest formative influence upon fledgling German Protestantism. In turning to Lutheran belief and practice, we must begin with what he said and wrote. He did not devote a great deal of attention to dying, and addressed the subject chiefly in his 1519 "A Sermon on Preparing to Die," a time when he himself was beginning to think about martyrdom.[24] Although it is true, as Rudolf Lenz maintains, that in this sermon (subsequently printed over and over again and disseminated widely), the Reformer connected seamlessly with the *ars moriendi* literature of the late Middle Ages, Luther had at this early date not yet formulated his mature views. His was a mind still in transition.[25] As Craig Koslofsky has shown, Luther retained a belief in purgatory up to 1530.[26] It is, then, not surprising that he places much stress on the offices of the priest in administering extreme unction and Holy Communion, or that he frequently refers to "all the saints," including specifically Mary.

Luther compares death to a leave-taking and a rebirth. It is "just as a child is born, with danger and anxiety, out of the small dwelling of its mother's body," for this earth, as big as it seems, is much smaller than that heaven, a "great space," into which one goes.[27] Death is also like giving birth in that "a woman, when she is in labor, suffers anxiety; but when she is delivered, she never thinks about the anxiety, for a human being has been born into the world through her."[28] As preparation for this journey, a person makes confession, especially of major sins, and arranges for the sacrament of Christ's body and the (extreme) unction. "For the sacraments [*sic*] are nothing other than signs that serve to stimulate faith." We should imitate Mary, who said to Gabriel, "Here am I...as you have spoken, so be it." God speaks and gives signs through the priest, and a person could pay him no greater dishonor than to doubt whether his message is true, and, conversely, no greater honor than to believe him.[29] Those individuals who are lucky enough to die in their beds and to enjoy the benefits (*tugenden*) of confession, absolution, unction, and the Eucharist "have great cause to love, praise, and thank God and to die happy."[30] For these—and Luther here still includes them under the rubric of sacraments—are a great comfort and sign, and they constitute a staff (*als an eynem guten stab*) *on which one can lean in faith for support*.[31]

A prominent theme in this sermon is the human temptation to doubt whether one is chosen by God for salvation. In this phase of his career as a theologian, Luther was more concerned with election than he would be later on; his interest in predestination eventually faded nearly away—or else he took it so much for granted that he did not expound on it further at length. But in 1519 he repeatedly reminds his hearers and readers that anyone who is intent on knowing what God's providence is desires to know as much as God, and this is a great sin.

The salient message is, not surprisingly, that one is saved by unswerving faith in the efficacy of Christ's sacrifice. This cannot be obtained at the last moment but should be cultivated and reflected on all one's life:

> All one's life one ought to ask God and his saints for right faith in the final hour, just as is beautifully sung at Whitsun: "Now we pray the Holy Ghost, for that faith we need the most, when we leave this wretched life."[32]

The dying Christian must cling to the image of Christ the Redeemer. This faith gives the sacraments validity. This faith banishes death, sin, and hell. Armed with this faith, the soul shall be borne by angels, "of which there are countless," into eternity. He should pray to the angels, the mother of God, all apostles, and the dear saints.[33]

Luther's next works that deal with death are his funeral sermons for, respectively, Saxon elector Frederick the Wise (May 1525) and Frederick's brother and successor Johann (August 1532). While the content of these is not parallel to that of 1519 in that they treat of the consequences rather than the process of death, they do suggest major changes—the changes that we know had occurred from Luther's many other writings—in his stance. Priests are now referred to as pastors or clergy (*Geistlichen*), and they are now chiefly preachers of the Word instead of intermediaries between God and humankind. In keeping with this demotion, and with Luther's revision of the sacraments, they no longer perform extreme unction. When Frederick the Wise was dying, however, he not only received Holy Communion, but, as is well known, he received it in both kinds for the first time.[34] According to his advisors, he was is a state of devotion (*Andacht*, a word to which we shall return), and he first made his confession. Thus, in 1525 we may be quite sure that the holy water and the consecrated oil were gone, but auricular confession and Communion were part of the prince's preparation for death.[35] Princes are few in number and their life- and deathstyles hardly typical. Change in practice elsewhere in 1525, before the first Saxon visitation of 1528–1529, depended entirely on local personalities and conditions. Luther, at least, in 1525 and 1532 was more intent upon the Christian's unshakeable faith in Christ, the key to salvation, than upon what he now rejected as hollow works or crude superstitions. In keeping with his expectation of the millennium, Luther insisted that preparation for death encompassed all of life. Death was the penalty for Adam's sin, transmitted to all his (and Eve's) progeny, and one should always be ready for the Lord's call. People ought to confess and commune regularly, be reconciled to their neighbors, and make a will early.[36]

In Luther's funeral sermons for the Saxon princes, the medieval sense of devils and deities warring for the individual soul can be detected but in a much lower key. Both demons and angels were everywhere, including the scene of dying, but the tension between these parties was no greater than it was in all the transactions of life. Without reference to divine providence, Luther implicitly teaches that, for most Christians, the outcome of their encounter with death was known before they fell sick. During their lives, they had either striven to conform to God's wishes and cultivated faith by every spiritual means, or they had given in to the pressure of the Prince of Darkness and sought worldly gratification. Luther did not anticipate that radical conversions were likely to occur at the last moment. Death was not a jolt, an occasion at odds with life, but merely a concluding event. And it was concluding only in a limited respect. It marked the end of the earthly stage and form of existence. A person went to sleep in Christ.

What has happened to the medieval strain of thought that placed the Final Judgment effectively in the deathbed chamber? There the emphasis was not on the sleep of souls until some perhaps remote (if cataclysmic) millenarian episode. Notwithstanding the ongoing Catholic millenarian tradition, manifested among other places in the Sistine Chapel in Michelangelo's *Last Judgment*, the practical decision was reached precisely in the moment of death. The *ars moriendi* manuals place the souls of the successful directly in angelic arms in paradise; others proceed to hell—purgatory does not receive prominent billing. But Luther clearly believes that the dead slumber in their "little beds of rest" (*Ruhebettlein*) until the last trumpet sounds. He tells his listeners in 1525,

You should...be certain that your dead friends (if they otherwise have believed in Christ) are not dead but that they are sleeping in sweet, lovely peace, and that on the Last Day they will surely be resurrected and have a body that is lighter and brighter than the sun.[37]

According to their faith, they shall be saved, but not before the end of the world. By 1530, this seems to have been the Reformer's *theology*.[38] In his personal and emotional life, he clung to less rational and more satisfying modes of explanation. When Katharine's and his beloved daughter Magdalena died, he spoke of her as being with God and as becoming a star in the firmament, a traditional metaphor and a popular source of consolation. We need see no conflict between these two versions of life after death.[39]

In 1532 Luther distinguishes between the bitter death of castigation and derision that Elector Johann had suffered at the Diet of Augsburg in 1530, and the "mere" death of the body:

> Our dear Lord God was thinking: The good prince has already gone through his real death at Augsburg; therefore I have included him in my death and henceforth he shall nevermore die, except physically. So that he passed away as in a sleep, as children and irrational animals die, except that animals have no hope of another life. Therefore it is a comforting death when a person dies so gently, his five senses simply dying away, if only the person looks upon it rightly; when he passes on so wrapped in our Lord Christ's suffering [rather than the Franciscan cowl of Erasmus's colloquy] that our Lord God says: I will allow the Devil to destroy you only physically; therefore do not look so steadily at your death, but look at the fact that my Son died for you and the fact that you have already been spiritually killed. So now I will send death to you only in the sense that you will die as far as your five senses are concerned, as in a sleep.[40]

Luther insists that those who die in Christ are simply sleeping sweetly, dreamlessly; Johann, he is confident, is "one of the holy sleepers."[41]

When the Reformer speaks of the saints, he means all human beings

> whom God has sanctified, without any of their works or cooperation whatsoever, by reason of the fact that they are baptized in Christ's name, sprinkled and washed clean with his blood, and endowed and adorned with his dear Word and gifts of the Holy Spirit.[42]

He specifically refutes the Catholic and popular notion of the "bad" death for such as these:

> Now those who are such baptized Christians, who love his Word, hold fast to it, and die in the same, no matter whether they are hanged, broken on the wheel, burned, drowned, or perish of pestilence, fever, or the like, simply include them in Christ's death and resurrection . . . [43]

In official Lutheranism, then, the violent and/or unexpected death conferred no disadvantages on the soul. In popular opinion, however, such a dying continued to be most unfavorable, for such people had not had a final opportunity to be sacramentally reconciled with God. In addition, sin and the Devil were thought to have played a central part in bringing about these "bad" deaths, an indication of the flawed spiritual condition of their victims. Such attitudes were very hard to root out during the sixteenth century and beyond. Pastors preached against these beliefs.[44]

What of those Christians who succumbed to unbearable pain and committed blasphemy in their final hour? Could this divert their souls away from God? Luther insisted that if in great pain and distress a Christian uttered something that was "untrue," God would forgive him or her, provided that that person had confessed his or her fundamental faith and desired to hold fast to it. The Devil had created this temptation anyway, and God would not let him triumph.[45]

As Luther grew older and felt his own demise draw nigh, he referred more often than before to a Christian's desire for death. At table with students and friends, he remarked, "The hour of our death is a heavenly gift for which we should constantly ask God and daily prepare ourselves so that with Simeon and Paul we look forward to our departure and our gain with pious longing."[46]

> Christians look at it [death] as a journey and departure out of this misery and vale of tears (where the Devil is prince and god) into yonder life, where there will be inexpressible joy and eternal blessedness. Diligently they study the art of looking at death in this way. Daily they practice it, and earnestly they ask our dear Lord Christ to grant them a blessed hour of departure and to comfort them in it with His Spirit, that they may commit their souls[47] to Him with true faith, understanding, and confession. To such people death is not terrible but sincerely welcome, especially in this last, dangerous time. For, as Scripture says, death takes them away before the calamity comes. They enter into peace and rest in their chambers.

Luther himself had no fear of death. For him the true *ars moriendi* was the *ars vivendi*—preparing throughout life to meet one's Maker. Technically, this was the Catholic Church's position, too, but it weighted human preparation more heavily than Luther did; it accorded to human beings a greater role in deciding their fate, and they had to act this role at no time more flawlessly than in death's throes. If sin crept in again, as well it might, between the deathbed sacraments and the moment of expiration... well, who could be sure of the soul's destination? Luther chose instead to rely upon the corollary of predestination, which is justification by faith, without, however, repeatedly drawing the link between them that on occasion he admitted was there. The rest of the time, he made it seem as though Christians could have faith on their own, and in this spirit he appeared to enjoin them to do so. So far as death was concerned, his was a doctrine not of whether sin occurred after the final ritual act, but of *averages*. Despite perpetually falling into sin, did the individual *usually* struggle, *usually* profess the true faith, *usually* maintain control of personal behavior? Such people merited the comfort and support that Protestant clergymen could muster. Ultimately, only God knew whether they were saved. Owing to the dual nature of the visible church, it was their neighbors' duty to give them the benefit of the doubt.

Martin Luther was more interested in promoting faith and preaching the Word than in shaping ritual practice. In general, he mocked Catholic rites of all types for the theology of works inherent in them, for their lack of biblical foundation, and for the superstitious elements they incorporated. But once he had witnessed, during two complete Ernestine visitations, the elimination of intolerably papist liturgy, he professed to be content to let each pastor render decisions about matters not essential to the faith—whether to wear a choir robe, which hymns to sing, within certain boundaries how to decorate the sanctuary. Consequently, and because ordering the Mass and baptism (the two remaining sacraments) seemed more urgent, during his lifetime no uniform deathbed practice arose. Luther saw the function of the pastor as relieving tormented consciences by hearing final confessions, assuring the dying of God's pardon, helping the seriously ill to cling to the comforting image of Christ's atonement for the sins of all believers—in short, as facilitating Christians' transition out of this life. The pastor, albeit in that hierarchical society on a higher social plane than many of his flock, was not a mediator, not a channel of grace, but an informed professional and a compassionate neighbor within the parish. Luther, then, his 1519 sermon on preparing to die notwithstanding, abandoned many defining features of the *ars moriendi*. He did not return to them.

AFTER LUTHER

Luther's perspectives were influential but, as we know, not all defining. The ecclesiastical ordinances of the sixteenth century reveal at once the uniqueness of the Reformer's authority and the determination of each territorial ruler to be master in his own house.[48] The princes regarded ritual uniformity as essential, and their leading theologians and advisors were not far behind.

Shortly after elector Heinrich of Saxony succeeded his elder brother George "the Bearded" in 1539, he launched a general parish visitation. Looking to his cousins' prior example, but being his own man, he had a detailed order of worship drawn up. It included two segments titled respectively "How One Should Inform and Console the Sick" and "How One Should Administer Communion to the Sick."[49] The main points of information for the sick are: that sin, including original sin inherited from Adam, is the sole cause of illness; that Christ frees us of sin provided that we believe in him, and he does this first through Scripture and the sacraments, and second by cleansing our lives (*wesen*) of sin; that God does not send us sickness as a sign of his anger but rather in an effort to turn us to true repentance and faith; and that having heard Christ preached, you (switch to second person singular) may be sure that your sins are paid for and that God shall have only salvation in store for you. Before giving the sacrament, the clergyman shall instruct the sick person through God's Word and speak the words of absolution. Confession is implied but not explicitly required. He then prepares the communion table with a cloth and puts the bread and wine upon it. He begins with "a fine, consoling prayer-Psalm, such as the twenty-fifth."

> Unto thee, O Lord my God, I lift up my heart.
> In thee I trust: do not put me to shame,
>> let not my enemies exult over me.
>> No man who hopes in thee is put to shame...

Then follows an appropriate text from the Gospel, as, for example, John 3: 16: "For God so loved the world, that he gave his only begotten Son, that whosoever believeth in him should not perish, but have everlasting life."[50] At length the pastor turns to the communion liturgy, reaching the invalid the bread and the wine. He concludes with the 111th Psalm, "With all my heart will I praise the Lord, in the company of good men, in the whole congregation." In other copies, the 103rd Psalm, the 117th Psalm, or the 91st Psalm are suggested.[51] Or the Lord's Prayer may be recited. And finally, the blessing:

> The Lord bless you and keep you,
> The Lord make his face to shine upon you and be gracious unto you.
> The Lord lift up his countenance upon you and give you peace. Amen.

A particular departure from the Catholic ritual is the almost complete omission of the seven so-called penitential Psalms (listed above).[52] These are all desperate pleas for God's mercy by people mired in wretchedness, to wit, Psalm 38: 1–7:

> O Lord, do not rebuke me in thy anger,
>> nor punish me in thy wrath.
> For thou hast aimed thy arrows at me,
>> and thy hand weighs heavy upon me.
>> Thy indignation has left no part of my body unscarred;
>> there is no health in my whole frame because of my sin.
>> For my iniquities have poured over my head;
> they are a load heavier than I can bear.
> My wounds fester and stink because of my folly.
>> I am bowed down and utterly prostrate.
>> All day long I go about as if in mourning,
>> for my loins burn with fever,

and there is no wholesome flesh in me.

For such as this, the Saxon ordinance substitutes, among others similar, Psalm 103: 1–5:

Bless the Lord, my soul;
   my innermost heart, bless his holy name.
Bless the Lord, my soul,
   and forget none of his benefits.
   He pardons all my guilt
   and heals all my suffering.
He rescues me from the pit of death
and surrounds me with constant love,
   with tender affection;
he contents me with all good in the prime of life,
and my youth is ever new like an eagle's.

The Saxon formulae remained influential during the sixteenth century. Many territorial churches simply modified them to suit their convictions, the times, and local tradition.[53] And with time, as auricular confession and private absolution gained in importance, this, in its full-blown form, was inserted between a somewhat diffuse, broadly applicable pastoral admonition and the distribution of the bread and wine.[54]

The changes in prescribed Psalms, even taken alone, are strong evidence of a fundamental alteration in the intention of the ritual in 1539. The medieval Catholic Church urged seeking redemption through extreme self-deprecation. The early Lutheran authorities sought to reassure the dying that those people whose faith was unflagging would find themselves surrounded by God's love and mercy. At the same time, the traditional attitude that an unexpected and sudden death was dangerous remained. Among the texts of prayers for all occasions that simple pastors could draw upon is one "Against a Fast Death in Times of Dying": "Almighty and merciful Lord God [and] Father, we heartily ask you graciously to incline yourself to your people, who submit themselves to your majesty, so that we are not precipitated [*übereilet*] into a hasty death . . ."[55]

What about the many who in their prime had not behaved in a pious manner, nor attended church any more often than they had been forced to? How were the clergy to deal with these when they became desperately ill? The ordinance of Kassel in 1539 provided that pastors could not administer the sacrament to the unrepentant. These must first be brought "to recognition and regret" concerning their godless existence. They must convince the ministers of their "true and heartfelt sorrow" and beg for mercy and pardon. They must wish that they were able to receive communion in church.[56] In their extremity, the people continued to believe in the power of the sacrament to effect their salvation; they feared to die unshriven and uncommuned. For their part, the clergy gained the submission of the recalcitrant in the end.

Most people did not fall into this extreme category. They were mediocre, and lax in their spiritual life. As in the case of confession, it now became the duty of the clergy to *instruct* Christians. This is usually referred to as the "admonition" (*Vermahnung*). The Lutheran pastor enters the sickroom and admonishes and instructs the invalid in theology—usually in elementary form, based on Luther's catechism. The section of Veit Dietrich's Nuremberg *Agenda* of 1545 that has to do with providing holy Communion for the sick begins thus: "One should instruct [*unterrichten*] and comfort sick people who desire the Lord's Supper." Upon analysis, we see that what the sick and dying actually wanted was communion itself. The authorities were aware of this in Augsburg in 1537, and in the Rhenish Palatinate in 1563, when they ordained that when people were ill, the pastor and his helpers were to instruct them that they were not to receive the sacrament for superstitious purposes, in order to heal their outer selves, but in order to strengthen their true faith in Jesus Christ.[57] The elimination of extreme unction had concentrated all sacramental power in the remaining Eucharist. What the Lutheran clergy had to do first was inform them of the teachings of the faith and *then* comfort them. The instruction, of course, had largely to do with sin as the cause of illness and death, the source of sin, the sacrifice of Christ, and the requisite faith in his atonement. The sick person then must confess in a spirit of true repentance and submission to God's will, receive absolution, and only then could the clergyman distribute the sacrament.[58]

As the sixteenth century wore on, the ecclesiastical ordinances put ever greater emphasis on death as recompense for sin. Even if six of the penitential Psalms, tainted by their Catholic associations, were not reintroduced, the Protestant scripts included ever longer, more emphatic homilies on sin, to be delivered at the deathbed and *before* the sacrament. This lesson was explicitly to benefit family and household members who were standing around. Indeed, one example, from Augsburg in 1555, seems more directed to them than to the dying.

It is a special work of God's love, dear Christians, toward us poor, sinful humans that God presents to us, in addition to his dear and holy Word, daily examples of sick and dying people, in order thereby to keep us in a state of repentance and not to let us quickly and in large numbers to be ripped away in his fury, as every day we so richly deserve. Therefore, we Christians should gladly be around the sick and the dying, in order to take their example to heart and to learn all manner of things [from their experience], as Sirach teaches [Ecclesiastes 7: 35]: "Do not hesitate to visit the sick, for by such visits you will win their affection." And the preacher Solomon says [Ecclesiastes 7: 2–

4], "Better to visit the house of mourning than the house of feasting; for to be mourned is the lot of every man, and the living should take this to heart. Grief is better than laughter: a sad face may go with a cheerful heart. Wise men's thoughts are at home in the house of mourning, but a fool's thoughts in the house of mirth."

The ensuing themes are the familiar ones: sin as the cause of death, Christ the Redeemer, and God's mercy to those to believe. But their articulation is far longer than earlier; they now constitute a veritable sermon for that small segment of society gathered in the chamber. In this instance, the invalid is not the focus of attention, but merely a reason.[59] In a local visitation near Weimar in 1594, the parish inspectors insisted, indeed, that others *must* be present when communion is brought to those in failing health.[60] The ordinance for Lindau of 1573 baldly states that before administering communion to the sick, the pastor must first *preach* (my emphasis) to him about repentance, so that he comes to a recognition of sin and the applicable punishment of God's anger and is brought to heartfelt regret and sorrow.[61] Nor should a person wait until the very last hour to request the sacrament, for there must be time beforehand for the clergyman to examine, instruct, and comfort the dying.[62] Nevertheless, some families *did* fail to call a clergyman even to the dying, and this was no longer permissible. Parish visitors in the countryside of the county of Nassau-Dillenburg in 1590 commented that the people did not call the pastor when they became sick, which had to stop.[63] In evangelical parishes in the second half of the sixteenth century and beyond, one did not have the option of dying unvisited.[64] Every conscience had to be examined and taught. Because, obligatory or not, families had to pay for these services, poor people may have had economic motives for letting relatives die unnoticed.[65]

What if an invalid self-righteously refused to forgive those whom he bore grudges? The pastor could then deny him the sacrament. In 1586 in Grauwinckel near Weimar, one Caspar Gretz (who obviously had not succumbed as had been expected) complained to the visitors that the pastor had refused him communion on his sickbed. The cleric retorted that he had gone to Gretz at 1:00 a.m. and found him unwilling to abandon his quarrels: "He slandered many people even in such an hour."[66]

As in every church ritual, during the second half of the sixteenth century those who governed the churches felt less and less secure entrusting ritual decisions—including the content of sermons and of admonitions to the dying—to individual clergy. If every religious service throughout a given territory were to be absolutely identical with others of its category, then more and more of what the clergy were to say and do had to be set out virtually verbatim in the ecclesiastical ordinances. In the villages of Württemberg in 1601, the visitors found several pastors who, when visiting the dying, made up their own admonitions instead of reading that which was prescribed. The visitors, at least, who were making the most detailed survey of ritual practice, appear not to have been pleased by this, although they could see that differing circumstances could make small alterations in the lesson advisable.[67] They left the ultimate decision to the prince and his closest advisors, but all feared that the comparatively unlettered rural cleric would not expound essential doctrine fully and accurately. Completeness and correctness were imperative. Every subject must experience the *same* religious regimen insofar as that was administratively possible. We have already witnessed this development in other contexts. The great theological controversies that divided Lutheran divines in the "age of orthodoxy" moved princes to attempt to ensure that any pastors who even inadvertently taught doctrines other than those that they (the princes) espoused were either corrected or fired. Especially rural pastors did not understand the various shades of meaning and required close scrutiny. Fixing scripts to be read by all solved this problem.[68]

One detail of visitorial concern was the ongoing ringing of the church bell whenever the pastor or another delegated clergyman took Holy Communion to a sick person. Some rural pastors had taken it on themselves to eliminate this, as they thought, remnant of papist "superstition," which in their eyes evidently enhanced and drew attention to the alleged supernatural powers of the Eucharistic elements. In the Württemberg countryside of the late sixteenth century, residents complained bitterly to the visitors about the cessation of bell ringing. The visitors decided, here and elsewhere, that a modest tolling was acceptable. They justified it on the grounds that neighbors should know that one of their community lay in danger of death so that they could pray for recovery, and so that they could contemplate their own mortality and reform their lives.[69] Here, then, is another ritual act that the Lutheran Church tended to retain even as it taught against aspects of the Catholic rationale and the widespread popular belief. We may be sure that most ordinary people clung to its familiar associations.

DEATHBED ETIQUETTE IN FUNERAL SERMONS

Church ordinances and visitation protocols are valuable sources, as we have seen, for both evangelical theory and behavior in the parishes. The funeral sermons that rose in importance during the second half of the sixteenth century and that were seen as ritually and socially indispensable throughout the seventeenth form the third and major genre.[70] They went gradually out of vogue during the eighteenth century because, one scholar has explained, the Christian community ceased to be synonymous with the secular community; religion increasingly became a private rather than a public affair.[71] Funeral sermons were initially given in the tradition of the classical encomium whenever a person—especially but not always a man—of exceptionally high standing died.[72] Martin Luther's sermons for Electors Frederick the Wise and Johann the Constant fit squarely in this category. On similar occasions prior to the Reformation, honorific speeches were given at the burials of princes and luminaries. With the Reformation and the dramatic rise in the importance of the sermon, the Reformers used every public opportunity to preach the Word of God. At first, Luther was certain that the Word alone, preached in church, would effect the changes in people's hearts and understanding that he desired. After participating in the Saxon visitation of 1528–1529, Luther, grievously disheartened, accepted the application of electoral authority to the multiple problems of rural and urban parishes, and he sought with even greater energy than before to use every occasion to instruct the abysmally, often unmotivated laity. The visitation committees imposed a rigorous, frequent burden of preaching on the pastorate, specified which parts of the Bible each sermon was to focus on, and closely examined each village cleric in order to be sure that his interpretation of the Bible coincided with their own.

But it was only after Luther's death that two new genres, wedding and funeral sermons, came to be expected of pastors. The pious and affluent burghers regarded such sermons as an amenity, something that, along with special music, enhanced their image in society, and they were glad to pay extra for them, just as they paid for family pews and prestigious, scarce inner-city burial places. Inside the church, society became more formally, lavishly, hierarchical during the late sixteenth and early seventeenth centuries. These new sermons, originating within and for the upper echelons of society, came to be recognized as yet another valuable means of inculcating Lutheran piety upon the masses. By century's end, most parish visitors in Germany compelled *every* pastor to preach at *every* funeral (other than at the punitive "still" burials of heretics and criminals),[73] whether or not the objects of their elocution could afford to pay.[74] Sometimes for the impecunious and humble, set texts were available for reading aloud. The sermons that were subsequently printed, and roughly 250,000 have survived for us to examine, were almost exclusively those produced for the higher social ranks. Rudolf Lenz is specific: 61.5 percent were given for men, 34 percent for women, and 4 percent for children; 87 percent of these were from the elite level of society, 8.5 percent from the middle section, and none from the lower classes.[75] Their usefulness to the modern scholar has been shown to be considerable. Numerous studies have now been made of funeral sermons, and indeed, Lenz has built his whole career upon the analysis of this literature.[76] But one ought to exercise caution in drawing conclusions about all of society based on what is manifestly an elite genre. Yet, we do want to know about elites as well as non-elites.

The funeral sermons were based on myriad biblical themes and gave Germany's leading preachers a chance to display their rhetorical and scriptural mastery. A few of them are splendid, imaginative, and moving. But of special relevance to the subject of the Lutheran manner of dying are the biographies that quickly came to be tacked onto the funeral sermons. In and of themselves, these descriptions are hackneyed. Part of each life summary is also a description of the manner in which the decedent died. I suspect that these are not wholly accurate. They were given for effect. One is reminded of the saints' lives composed during the central Middle Ages. Both the medieval saints and the early modern dead share a number of stock (though different within their category) characteristics. The Lutheran deceased seem to share a number of perfect and therefore artificial patterns of behavior in taking their leave. These dying are shown to have fulfilled a religious ideal and to inspire the audience (whether hearers or readers) to conform to that ideal themselves. Secondarily, they are to comfort survivors by showing that the manner of dying indicated that the dead were destined for heaven.

Like Jesus's and Mary's deaths in the late Middle Ages, throughout the sixteenth and early seventeenth centuries princes' deaths provided the fundamental model, even though these, as thoroughly public figures, were well known as having sinned boldly.[77] Two excellent examples come from members of the geographically dispersed Hohenzollern family. Jacob Herbrandt's summary of the death of Albrecht, the 35-year-old son of Margrave Casimir and his wife Susanna of Bavaria, in 1557, is deliberately detailed.[78] Herbrandt was the clergyman presiding over the ritual of death. The nobleman, otherwise a "pugnacious hero and mighty warrior prince" as was expected of him, had endured a drawn-out illness. When the attending physicians saw that his end was near, they called Herbrandt, who came to his chairside—Albrecht could not lie down—and delivered a sermon on repentance and faith in the Gospel (message), on Christ as Redeemer and other unnamed texts. The cleric informed Albrecht that God sent illness and other trouble especially to move Christians to acknowledge and heartily to regret their sins. He asked for the sacrament, and before he received it he asked the physicians and nobles who were gathered around to witness his death. He made a speech of forgiveness:

> Although I have been highly and heavily offended by many people and have been driven away from my land and people, nevertheless I forgive and pardon them from the heart... For today I want to die like a German prince who has been driven out, and like a pious Christian...

Herbrandt talked to him about the sacrament. Albrecht confessed his sins still further even though he was in such pain that he could hardly talk. He affirmed his faith. The clergyman then pronounced the absolution and proceeded with the rite of Holy Communion, which he prefaced with still further admonition and prayer, read aloud "from the ecclesiastical ordinance." Before receiving the bread and wine, the prince thanked God that he had lived long enough to do so. The nobleman then asked Herbrandt to stay with him. He commended his wife to her brother, Margrave Carlin of Baden and Hochburg. He spoke individually with the other nobility who were there. At 5:00 the following morning, Herbrandt began to read him comforting Bible verses. Seeing that the end approached, he asked Albrecht, "Do you believe?" and the reply was yes. He read more verses. Again he inquired if Albrecht remained in the faith, and the prince answered, "Why not?" Herbrandt urged him to commend his soul to God. Albrecht stated that he had already done so:

> He raised up both his hands, struck them together twice, entwined them and said, "Lord Jesus." He went out quietly like a little light, as though he were asleep, his hands still together as if he prayed...He gave up his spirit entirely gently and quietly, without any ugly or hideous expression of the sort one sometimes sees on the dying...[79]

Andreas Musculus's account of the death of Joachim, Margrave of Brandenburg, imperial elector, and treasurer of the Holy Roman Empire, in 1571, is in certain respects a departure from the norm, for there was no pastor at his bedside.[80] The 66-year-old elector had, Musculus tells us, celebrated Christmas with the greatest reverence and devotion (*Andacht*), had at that time confessed his sins, was absolved, and had received "the true body and blood of Christ." During this season, he had had Scripture, along with Luther's commentaries, read aloud to him at meals and was in the process of consulting his theologians as to how a summary of doctrine or excerpts from Luther's writings could be prepared for distribution to all the pastors in his lands. Here Musculus makes oblique reference to the doctrinal controversies that raged in his day—and the goal of making sure that pastors represented the official, that is, his own, position on such matters as good works and salvation. After the Christmas holiday, Joachim went hunting and attended church in the village where he happened to be, and at dinner afterward he again discussed theological matters and showed especial devotion. That evening at dinner, he had a young nobleman read the three [*sic*] Gospels along with Luther's commentary on each. They got into such a discussion "about the prophecy of Simeon...about Christ's circumcision...and about Christ's baptism" that they stayed there for three hours:

> And everyone was amazed that his electoral grace in this long dinnertime did not mix in one discussion about worldly concerns but stuck to the treatment and discussion of Christian matters, which does not otherwise happen at the tables of princes.[81]

Musculus explains this unusual behavior as "God's marvelous ordinance." After dinner, Joachim went on for nearly three more hours, in an attitude of devotion continually talking about God's Word and reading further from Luther's books. He finally went to bed after 2:00 a.m. He had slept for hardly an hour when he was awakened by an attack of coughing. He became somewhat afraid, and "because the Lord Christ cried out to his grace, his electoral grace, even though sickly, affirmed this twice; and without any grimace, just like a light going out, he fell asleep blessedly in the Lord Christ..."[82]

A typical and a model scheme underlies both these accounts. Herbrandt had had an opportunity to preach to his charge, to instruct him on the proper state of his soul, to examine his conscience, and to pronounce the absolution. Musculus had not. Joachim had, however, made his confession and received communion just prior to his demise, and the effects of recent partaking of the sacrament are always seen to bear on such cases. He had lived in such a way, including his interests and behavior, that was compatible with a pious death. Second, a crucial aspect of the proper dying is summed up in the key words, *repentance* (*Buß*) and *devotion* (*Andacht*). I would venture to guess that nearly every Lutheran funeral sermon refers to the sorrow and to the devotion of the decedent. This is a fundamental attitude and not something that is taken on when one is at church. But even if these had been somewhat lacking in life, they *must* be in evidence on the deathbed. It appears that Albrecht had more immediate cause for regret than Joachim, but these life summaries are not conclusive proof of that. Third, the dying person must reflect on, indeed *meditate* upon, passages from the Bible. Herbrandt was able to preach on and later to read aloud various passages from Scripture. Joachim himself fulfilled this requirement without realizing that he was going to die. As Musculus remarked, this was a wonderful decree from God. Joachim had had read to him, discussed, read himself, and thought about several Gospel stories, and immediately before dying. Fourth, both princes verbally affirmed their belief in the Lord Christ twice when they were at the point of death. Joachim was afraid, and a state of fear is just that condition out of which the dying must keep themselves from falling into doubt or despair. Declaring one's unshakeable belief is the approved antidote of devilish temptation. We wonder, of course, how Musculus knew what had happened to his prince in the middle of the night, and the logical answer is probably that servants were present and awakened by Joachim's coughing. The less logical answer is that it simply *had* to have been so. Fifth, neither prince made the slightest grimace, the smallest gesture of pain or resistance to death. Just what this means in the funeral sermons is never explicit, but implicitly it signifies several things. The dying person completely accepts and submits to God's will; he does not resist pain but receives it humbly and in peace. The invalid is not tormented in spirit by doubts of Christ's atonement for sin or of His intention for this individual; the omnipresent Devil has gained no inroad, not even at the last frightening moment. To grimace or to contort one's body in any way casts doubt on one's salvation in this truly liminal moment, when what lies on the other side of the threshold may actually be visible to the transitting soul. Albrecht's lifting up his hands to Christ is a gesture often described. It is a sign both of extremity and of trust. Sixth, one is expected to die as a candle going out, like a child falling asleep, without sound, motion, or fury. Again, the smooth, practically undetectable departure is a sign of salvation. Although the Catholic taper is no longer present, a candle remains in the ubiquitous verbal simile of the Christian death. A seventh element that is often included is a heartfelt exchange with family and friends, as we see both in Erasmus's "good" death and in Albrecht's. To the extent that this entails forgiving offenses, this aspect may be subsumed under confession of sin and profound feeling of regret, for to bear grudges, as well as to cause them, was sinful in that day.

Herbrandt felt it necessary, as many other pastors did, to keep questioning Albrecht about his faith, which seems almost torturous under the painful circumstances. Theology aside, the psychological reality behind this, as well as behind the intense scrutiny of the gestures and facial expressions, even the postures of the dying, is the irresistible conviction that the completely good death indicates that the decedent is saved. To my knowledge, there is no learned treatise—nor even a simple explanation—of this minute, close examination of the faces, hands, and general bearing of the dying. Yet the prayerful, silent repose of all one's features and body parts is praiseworthy and comforting to those who remain behind. Even those in agonizing pain were expected to be fully composed. For if they were not, the Devil was taking his toll. The attending clergyman must keep asking, "Do you believe in Jesus Christ?" sometimes shouting it into the ear of the departing soul (as satirized by Erasmus apropos of this Catholic practice), and search for bodily affirmation where speech is no longer possible. Those who die the good death are bound for paradise.

Princes' deaths may have set the standard beginning in the mid-sixteenth century, but pastors held out this ideal of dying to all souls in their care. Increasingly, they described the success of eminent neighbors (for whom the funeral sermons were printed) in attaining this ideal. Werner Friedrich Kümmel has shown in convincing detail how the characteristics of the proper death permeated the funeral sermons given for upper-bourgeois citizens.[83] His examples are predominantly from the seventeenth century, but there are many similar cases from an earlier date. In 1590, Nicolaus Selnecker the former Leipzig superintendent and professor of theology, who had been dismissed by the Calvinist elector Christian I, brought out 170 of his Leipzig funeral sermons from the years 1576 to 1589 in two volumes.[84] Sermon 35, given October 29, 1579, for

Barbara, wife of one Christophor [*sic*] Seeman, is not only detailed but adds to our picture some of the special traits that women were to exhibit. The account of Frau Seeman's death was provided by her husband, for his wife had been ill of a flux for seven years and had been abed for the last two, so that clergy could not attend her continually. Her limbs became weak and feeble (*schwach und matt*, words often used to describe the sick), and she realized that she was about to die. She asked for Holy Communion and received it. The next day she was unable to eat further, and she thanked God that she had received the sacrament before reaching this condition. She sent a note to church to be read from the chancel, requesting her neighbors to pray that God treat her in accordance with His will. She called her husband and her children to her and told them of her imminent death and urged them to adhere closely to God's word. She told the children to practice the good breeding, virtue, and decency that she had raised them to, and not to quarrel among themselves. If they did this, her blessing would remain among them, "as among the blessed children of Jacob," and among their children. She admonished the servants to do their duty and profession.

> Following this "business," she exhorted her husband and children not to cry. She said, "Oh, dear children, if only I could reveal to you that great joy and splendor that I already feel in my heart. How gladly shall I die! How I yearn for eternal bliss! How I wish to be freed and to be with my Lord Jesus Christ...He is my bridegroom, and when he comes, I shall go with him to the wedding in eternal joy...Death is coming ever closer to me...I have been through the desert [and] now I am going through the Red Sea, through the earthly death into the land of the living. I lean on the staff of Aaron and shortly will step out into the Promised Land and [shall see] how God drowns all my enemies, the Pharoah [*sic*]—that is, death, Devil, and hell—in the Red Sea."[85]

After a drink of small beer, she tells her family,

> I see in faith the ladder of Jacob, by which I shall climb to heaven: it is Jesus Christ...Dear children, whenever you hear sung in church the words of the Creed, "the resurrection of the body," think about your dear mother...[I]n this flesh I will see you again. Think only how I have gone to see Grandfather and won't come back to you. But you will come to me...

She reminded her husband and children not to forget to give the food to the poor boys at the St. Thomas School as long as they live, as she has done for thirty-eight years. She exclaimed, "Oh, in what a blessed time I have lived, in which I have heard many splendid and lovely sermons, which my parents under the pope did not hear!" She begged them to pray with her, that her bridegroom come and get her, and as they consoled her and assured her that he would take her to the heavenly wedding in paradise, she responded, "Amen, amen," and in a Christian manner gently fell asleep.

In Frau Seeman we have a woman who has taken charge of her own departure. In addition to having fulfilled the Lutheran requirements that she avail herself of confession, absolution, and the sacrament, she has so concentrated upon the Bible during her years as an invalid that she knows passages well enough to use them metaphorically, and certainly to apply them continuously to her own spiritual benefit. She concentrates on scriptural images without clerical help, and she turns these images to the comfort of her family. If we analyze this death story, we see that the essential parts are there. Frau Seeman had regularly received instruction from "lovely" sermons and from the Bible—and no doubt also from clerical visits during the long months she had lain in bed. She had received the sacrament the day before her death, and a precondition of taking communion was confessing with genuine sorrow and hearing the words of absolution. She meditated on numerous Bible verses that held special meaning for her, and she applied them to herself; she continually affirmed her faith in Christ the "bridegroom." She lovingly took leave of her family and her servants. She yearned for death and thus submitted totally. She died without grimace or noise, just like a candle going out.

In this woman's death, additional qualities are present that could well be associated with (and the alleged result of) her femininity.[86] Particularly the loving care with which she consoled her children and helped them to prepare for a future without her could be labeled as maternal. She urged them to continue to live up to the standards of behavior that as their mother she had set for them. She also specified that her family continue, in what may strike us as a very medieval Catholic style, to give food to poor students. Medieval wills nearly always included provision for the giving of alms. Finally, some may wish to detect womanliness in her adoption of the metaphor of Christ the bridegroom—and clearly, in worldly society, bridegrooms were male and brides female. In theology, nevertheless, Christ was also the bridegroom of men, for as members of his Church they were included within the metaphor of his "bride." I have not read any funeral sermon per se in which a dying man refers to himself even figuratively as the bride of Christ. From our post-Freudian perspective it is curious that Frau Seeman chooses to repeat this theme to her husband, and that he consoles her with it at the very end, assuring her that the bridegroom is about to come for her.[87]

THE LUTHERAN ART OF DYING

The Lutheran etiquette of dying reached a milestone in the compendium of Martin Moller, head pastor in Görlitz. Moller actually wrote two works on preparing to die. The first one, initially printed in 1587, is actually about the passion of Christ, but as the title reveals, contemplation of Christ's ordeal helps others to prepare to live and die properly themselves. The title in translation is *Soliloquy on the Passion of Jesus Christ. How Each Christian Person Should Observe in His Own Heart the Most Holy Suffering and Death of Our Lord Jesus Christ, and Should Derive from it Many Lovely Lessons and Healing Comfort and Usefully Use These in Daily Prayer and Yearning Toward a Christian Life and a Blessed Death.*[88] This went through two subsequent editions during the remaining years of the century.[89] But his true handbook on the theme of dying was his *Manual on Preparing for Death. Healing and Very Useful Observation, How from God's Word the Christian Should Learn to Live a Christian Life and to Die Blessedly,* first published in 1593 and still enjoying popularity eighty years later.[90] The use of this book thus coincides with the maturation and enforcement of dying rituals in Lutheran Germany.[91]

As the author states at the outset, in 1593 he had been a "preacher" for twenty-one years. His pastoral experience convinced him that the simple layperson (*der einfältige Laie*) needed an equally simple guide. He organizes this little book into straightforward questions and answers, each pair followed by a prayer. He asks, "What does it means to die blessedly?" and replies,

> To die blessedly means to end one's life in the correct and true faith, to commend one's soul to the Lord Jesus Christ, and with a heartfelt desire for eternal blessedness, to go to sleep gently and happily and pass on over.[92]

Some answers are more elaborate than this brief one, and on some occasions the author assumes the voice of the reader who is preparing for death and addresses his soul:

> You don't know, my soul, in what condition the Lord your God may find you, whether sleeping or waking, happy or sad, in worldly or spiritual occupation, drunk or sober, angry or peaceable...O dear soul...do not let yourself be found for a single moment in a condition in which you would not gladly die!

People cannot be sure that they will become sick before they die and have a chance to prepare themselves.[93] The prayer that ends this section is especially direct:

> Lord Jesus, my Savior, protect me from painful illnesses and a horrible death. Do not overtake me in my sin, and do not let me die without repentance. Grant me a quiet, gentle end, without great anxiety and pains, so that in possession of reason, with the ability to reflect, I can make a good end, confess your name up until my

departure, and commend my soul into your hands in a reverent and heartfelt manner.[94]

The centrality of repentance inspires the question, "What is, then, proper, true Christian repentance?" The answer is, "Repentance is nothing other than that a person abstain from sin and turn in heart to God." The steps are three: first, to recognize one's sins and heartily regret them; second, that one not become despondent over sin but believe in Jesus Christ, who has paid for our sins; and third, that one give daily evidence of faith through new obedience, both to God and to human beings (*Menschen*, in authority).[95] Moller draws on mystical strands of contemplation when he urges the soul to contemplate its helplessness before sin. The guilty soul berates itself at great length: "O anxiety, o horror, o you filthy, sinful, stinking soul! I am angry with myself that I have become such an abomination before my God!"[96]

The next step is, in this pitiful state, to call upon Jesus. "See, my Lord, I am coming to you. Yes, I come and bring you a greatly troubled, contrite, battered, frightened heart. O refresh my wretched soul, o heal my sinful conscience!" Then follows the reconciliation with Christ. The soul asks then if it can do as it pleases until the moment of death, but Moller assures it that it will not be minded to do so:

If true faith is in your heart and you have been reborn through the Holy Spirit, you will have other intentions, for newborn people desire a new life. And faith always protects against mischievous sins and is the enemy of all godless behavior. And if a faithful person is overtaken by Satan and because of inborn weakness takes a false step, that one picks himself up quickly, regrets this fall every day, and comforts himself in his Lord Jesus. And as a result, there is nothing damnable in him because he clings through faith to his Lord Jesus Christ.[97]

How does a person avoid losing this faith? Hold tight to God's Word every day; remember your baptism every day; receive communion often; have the proper understanding of suffering and pain; stay in your proper place (*Beruff*, the condition in which God has placed one);[98] and pray without ceasing.[99] Contemplate the hour of your death day and night. When you become ill, remember that the cause of it is your own sins.[100] The sickness of the flesh reflects the sickness of the soul. Moller compares bodily affliction to the rod parents use to spank naughty children. Indeed, sometimes God visits sickness upon young and innocent children in order through anguish to bring their elders to contrition.[101] Moller has the soul pray,

With broken and contrite heart, I confess to you, my Lord Jesus, that because of my sins I have well deserved this illness, and I am heartily sorry that I have angered Your Majesty and have brought such misfortune upon myself.[102]

"My God, I send a messenger back to you, namely my poor prayer and my sighing. O Lord, receive my supplication and let my sighing come before you."[103]

Moller urges people to consult doctors—but never people who use forbidden (that is, "superstitious") substances as medications or who pronounce blessings over people.[104] Nor should one improperly yearn for death, for to take one's own life results in eternal suffering.[105] Nevertheless, all Christians shall give themselves over to death in a spirit of joy and happiness. The soul is God's temple and dwelling and is assured of salvation in faith, and it is so tightly bound to God that it is bone of his bone and flesh of his flesh; nothing can separate the soul from the love of God. What, then, can death do except to bring one closer to the Lord Jesus. Death is thus like nothing.[106] "Hear, my soul, how graciously and sweetly the Lord calls to you, how he draws you to him like a brood hen her straying chicks, and like a true shepherd his straying lambs."[107] The faithful heart does not need to worry about the disgusting dead corpse or the unfriendliness of the cold grave, for our bodies are "God's grains of wheat, which he sows in his field [in the cemetery, *Gottes-Acker*], and when God's spring arrives and the warm temperature comes, when the son rises up, then we will grow forth and arise and bear eternal fruit."[108]

> Lord God, Holy Spirit, take my heart and fill it with the comforting grace of my Lord Jesus Christ, teach me here again to distinguish between the law and the Gospel, subdue in me the fear and shock in the presence of death, and teach me your healing and consoling evangelical language [*sprache*]; grant that I do not only hear with my ears and imitate with my mouth, but that I believe and feel with my heart, and that, when the hour of my death is here, I do not die but rather gently go to sleep; and that I am not laid in the grave but in my little chamber [*Kämmerlein*]; and that I do not decay but have peace and rest, until you shall awaken me again.[109]

Moller goes on to provide a number of verses and prayers, not only for the dying but for the people who are in the dying room. They may be spoken or sung by the invalid if possible, but otherwise by the clergy, family, and household staff. The author calls brief inspirational utterance "sighs" (*Seuffzer*), a word often encountered in funeral sermons. In its context, it refers to two fundamental, strongly recommended attitudes: sorrow for sin and the yearning to be with God. The true Christian should sigh regularly in life, and at no time so fervently as when dying. Dying people should speak simple verses as long as they are able, up to their very last breath if possible. He recommends brief biblical passages of resignation.[110]

One longish verse sums up Moller's main points:

Here lie I poor little worm,
Can lift not hand or limb,
My heart in chest beats hard from fear
My life with death contends,
Reason and all sense are weak,
I am tired and sick of life
I cannot hear or see,
To die well is now my gain,
So haste, Lord Christ, to me
Drive out the devil's fiery arrow,
He growls all around me now,
Just like a lion and gruesome bear;
Let no temptation, fear, or pain
Separate me from your love.
But let me in your kingdom serve
As your very humblest slave.
Grant to me unyielding faith
So that I'm justified and bless'd,
Purchased by your precious blood
From sin, death, and glowing hell.
When now my final hour arrives,
Let your angels stand around
And lead out of this vale of tears,
My blissful self to heaven's hall,
That I along with all your saints
In the dear angels' choir may praise
Your name forever. Amen.[111]

In the early seventeenth century, Zachaeus Faber, pastor and superintendent in Chemnitz, looked back mockingly upon the deathbed practices of Catholicism.

> The papist blockheads thought up and invented amazing physics against death, such as, at the very end, smearing and anointing the forehead, hands, feet, nose, ears, mouth, and other members that they might have sinned with; and they thought that all would go well with the person who was well smeared. They also regard monks' cowls and scapulars [?*Schepler*] as powerful cuirasses and helmets that death and the Devil have to be afraid of, [and] especially, when a dying person takes a consecrated light or candle in his hand, no devil can let itself be seen, and death has to take it easy.[112]

Whatever Lutheran clergy may have thought, the Lutheran rituals of dying in the second half of the sixteenth century bear comparison with those of the Catholic Church during the late medieval and Reformation era. There are some significant differences, obviously, but there are also a great many similarities, more than either Erasmus or Luther would have desired. A salient mark of contrast is, as Faber said, the elimination of extreme unction and penance as sacraments, and all of the sacramentals associated especially with the former. The clerical procession with its vestments, incense, candles, crucifix, holy water, and chrism are no longer present. From the Lutheran point of view, this meant that the deathbed scene had been purified of papist inventions and the superstitious attribution of magical powers to objects. The priest and his acolyte are no longer magicians. The sacral world has now been split in a new way, one that attempts cleanly to exclude the elements of "folklorized ritual."[113] Additionally, the saints are no longer present at the bedside. *Saints* now denotes *all* God's faithful: those few heroic persons attested biblically or historically merely lived out the gifts that God himself had given them; they had no supernatural or intercessory powers. Another distinction, as noted, is the near-abandonment of the penitential Psalms with their underlying mood of despair. The only one retained, and that usually in hymn form, was "Aus tieffer not schrey ich zu dir" (*De profundis*).[114] This shift represents on the face of things a move from an allegedly Catholic reliance on a theology of works, on the duty of all Christians to behave, both non-ritually and ritually, in ways that earn them salvation, to the official Lutheran position, that Christ's atonement is all-sufficient for those who believe, even if, as the warring divines of the age of orthodoxy finally agreed, "good trees always bear good fruit." And finally, in late medieval Catholic practice, the officiating priest did not feel himself to have the signal duty of instructing the dying in the precepts of the faith before hearing their confessions. We have seen that Lutheran authorities, by means of ecclesiastical ordinances and parish inspections, compelled reformed pastors to use every opportunity to teach parishioners, in particular including those of their flocks who were on the brink of death. As we saw, this was partly for the sake of the dying and partly for the betterment of the sometimes many others who stood around the room.

If we now look beneath the surface, we may find that the changes made in Lutheran rituals of dying, by late century, in any case, were fewer and less substantial than we have thought. First, it was highly preferable in both Catholic and Lutheran conviction that an ordained clergyman attend the dying. Although Luther "demoted" the clergy— removed the indelible mark of ordination from their souls—in the years after his death, and continuing on into the seventeenth century, the earthly governors of church and state actively sought to raise the pastorate above the laity. Symbolic of this is frequent use of the word *admonish* among the ministers' duties. This term strongly implies the act of a superior in relationship to an inferior, and indeed the growing distance between pastors and their flocks has been documented.[115] Although neither church maintained that clerical ministrations were a prerequisite of salvation, both entertained prejudice against a precipitate, unprepared death. Lutheran sources consistently reflect the desirability of pastors' attending those who might die, and the very best death, so important in both faiths, includes clergy. While Frau Seeman departed in the absence of her pastor, he had visited her regularly during the last two years of her illness and had recently heard her confession and administered the sacrament to her. The chronically ill, in any case, had ample warning of their demise and were able to ready themselves.

Second, although Lutherans removed extreme unction, in both manners of dying an essential sacrament remains: that of Holy Communion. In either case, this has to be preceded by confession to a cleric. It is incumbent on the layperson to convince the confessor that he or she is deeply contrite, and only then does the confessor speak the absolution. In Catholic belief, the priest, who has received the power of the keys from the successor of St. Peter via his bishop, actually has the power to forgive sin, or at least to remit temporal punishment. The view of the common layperson did not, of course, confine this ability to the temporal sphere, and this greatly exercised Erasmus, Luther, Zwingli, and other pious men. The Lutheran lay position may be somewhat more elusive, but the evidence of the dying chamber is that average citizens and average pastors believed that they, the pastors, could indeed forgive sin. The pastors saw themselves as God's delegates and mouthpieces in this; they spoke the authorized Word of God in the church sanctuary, so why not also in the presence of the dying. The life and death summaries attached to the funeral sermons bear witness to this throughout the late sixteenth and the seventeenth centuries. The cleric was to arrive at the bedside, *admonish* the invalid by means of a sermon or extemporaneous lecture, point out their sinful nature, and bring them to desire to confess. In fifteenth- and sixteenth-century eyes, every physical malady and deformity is itself proof of the presence of sin. The order of the Lutheran pastors' obligations are, then, first to admonish and inform concerning the cause of infirmity and only then to comfort. The dying, confronted with their guilt, then make their confession, after which the minister questions them concerning their contrition, and when convinced of this he may pronounce the absolution. Sometimes the dying confessed to unlawful acts that got their partners in sin in trouble with church and state. One man in a Württemberg village admitted to adultery, and the information was used against the woman involved.[116]

Without this combined confession and absolution, no Eucharistic meal could occur. We have seen how important it was to the laity to receive communion and that they attributed great healing and conciliatory powers to it. Throughout the sixteenth century and beyond, average people sought the supernatural palliative of the Host and the Chalice. If someone died without repentance, and hence without absolution and the sacrament, he must likewise undergo burial completely without ceremonial—without knell, procession, song, or clergy—stuck quietly into the ground in the presence of any relatives who wished to be present.[117] And often he was laid in unconsecrated ground, tapping thus the remaining conviction among the people that sanctified earth contained protective power.[118] It symbolized the unrepentant person's being morally, spiritually, beyond the pale. This treatment bespoke the certain damnation of the recalcitrant; after the final judgment, he or she would be placed beyond the pale of paradise. The visitors in Württemberg parishes in 1584, church leaders all, had to seek advice when they encountered an 80-year-old man, a former shepherd, in the village of Grubingen who had either been retarded all his life or who was afflicted with Alzheimer's disease or other dementia. This man, Jacob Kurtz, could not learn the Ten Commandments even though he went to the pastor for instruction every Sunday. The question put to the higher authorities was whether Kurtz should be permitted to receive the sacrament and, if not, what if he died without it. Should a funeral sermon be given, or should he receive a still burial? The answer written in the margin later is that if he is childlike, he should be treated like a child. He should not receive Holy Communion (on his deathbed) but should be comforted with words, unless he particularly wanted the sacrament. In that case, perhaps God would grant him sufficient understanding. By all means, the pastor should hold a sermon afterward in which he uses this man as an example to young people who are not diligent in learning their prayers.[119]

The structure of Lutheran bedside ritual tells us that the pastor guarded the entry to heaven. His role was virtually indispensable and his position by late century nearly as high in the earthly echelons as that of the Catholic priest. While it might be tempting to maintain that the Catholic cleric did not adhere as fiercely as the Lutheran did to the redeeming power of Christ's crucifixion, the *ars moriendi* illustrations discussed earlier certainly concede a central position to the cross. *Fiercely* is perhaps not the best word; *exclusively* would be better. For, while the Catholic Church taught the efficacy of Christ's atonement, it lent the people other aids besides. The Lutheran Church took several of those aids, the unction and the intercessory prayers of Mary and the saints, away. Yet the ritual reveals what works of theology did not, namely that even *it* failed to rely entirely on the saving power of faith in Christ's payment for sin. It demanded proper action, including not just upright behavior but participation in the new church's foreshortened but nonetheless existent sacramental system. The pastorate presided over this system.

Around both Catholic and Lutheran invalids, quantities of demons and angels gathered. Nicolaus Selnecker is speaking more than emblematically when, at the funeral of a little girl in 1577, he preached, "Death is swallowed up in victory, and the abominable, hideous enemy [death] has been turned into the sleep of a child and must with his leashed black dog the Devil leave us poor children unbitten."[120] It would be erroneous to think that Catholic authorities conceived these literally and the Lutheran authorities only figuratively. We know that Luther believed in the ubiquity of devils and angels, even if at the Wartburg he did not really throw his inkwell at the Evil One. The spiritual struggles of the dying as described by Lutheran preachers, and particularly these clerics' perceived need to keep loudly inquiring of the dying about the steadfastness of their faith until the very moment they expired, clearly suggests that, theology aside, in popular belief the Devil had an opportunity to draw the soul away from God.[121] This was one of the practices that Erasmus mocked. Until losing consciousness, the dying were expected to affirm their faith, by sign language if not by mouth. If they made faces, if they struggled against overpowering pain, if they groaned or cried out, they cast doubt on the triumph of the angels.[122] If people wanted to tarnish the reputation of someone who had just died, they had only to suggest that he had roared like a beast before expiring. This indicated that they were not among the saved. In evangelical circles, the rumor went round in 1568 that Duke Heinrich the Younger of Braunschweig, "Hans Wurst," whose lands the Saxon elector Johann Friedrich had conquered in 1542, had bellowed like a bull as he died. Peter Ulner, his court preacher, pointedly refuted this slander in his funeral sermon. Ulner insisted that the prince had expired just like the flame of a candle going out.[123]

Catholicism and Lutheranism alike urged upon their adherents an art of living (*ars vivendi*) as the initial preparation for death (*ars moriendi*). Early modern Lutherans prided themselves on the complete break that, as they saw it, they had made with corrupt medieval Christianity. In resisting a new spirit of rigidity, Luther himself inclined toward a greater degree of departure from tradition than did his successors. The authoritarian spirit of the later sixteenth century, however, was attracted by some of the very features had that rendered Catholicism objectionable in the first place. By scrutinizing the bearing of the dying, they sought to know the soul's destination.[124] By reimposing a rigorous art of dying, they sought to oversee the behavior of the "soul" on earth. By insisting on the submissive and obedient life as the only adequate preparation for salvation, they hoped to gain docility in human society. Whether the participants were conscious of it or not, in Lutheran Germany deathbed transactions constituted another small arena where the forces of worldly domination and surrender contended.

THE EARTHLY REMAINS

Funeral rites under Catholicism constitute a classic van Gennepian *rite de passage*. They contain segments of separation, transition, and incorporation, or so it seems to me. Ironically, Arnold van Gennep himself, who was looking at mainly non-Christian cultures, saw them only as acts of separation.[125] But as we shall see, in the Christian scheme—and even more pronouncedly in the Catholic version of that scheme—the living and the dead are, in the opinion of the living, reincorporated into a new, vital, enduring relationship.

Our beginning point is at the moment when life had passed out of the ultimately not very solid flesh. It is probably best for us to disregard the accounts of body preparation and funeral observances for kings and other dignitaries.[126] Everything from embalming, to lying in state, postponing the funeral sometimes for weeks, and burying innards and the rest of the corpse separately was not performed for ordinary people. Common folk on the eve of the Reformation were buried simply and quickly, within one or two days of death.[127] In the towns and villages of Europe, women—whether family members or others whose special function this was (*Seelweiber, Leichenfrauen*)—usually washed the body, an initial post-mortem act of lustration, and either dressed it in the clothing it would wear in the grave or sewed it up in a sack of ticking.[128] Sackcloth worn as an act of penance was in fact a reminder of death. Sometimes those who prepared the bodies were Beguines; this was one of the ways these women supported themselves, for the families of the dead paid them for their work. Sometimes this task was carried out under the auspices of a religious confraternity, to which by the end of the Middle Ages many urban dwellers belonged. In either case, women cared for bodies, an extension of their nurturing, curative, and reproductive roles in the household. They oversaw life coming into the world, and they helped it to leave; they stood at thresholds.[129] Preparing bodies was a "dishonorable" task, just like others connected to liminal states.[130] Despite official prohibition, even after the Reformation some women (*Klageweiber*) continued to serve as official mourners and to wail.[131]

If there was an overnight delay before the corpse could be put in the ground—as before the Reformation there usually was—women sat at watch, and candles burned. Both clergy and laity could see in the candles things that appealed to them—flame as symbol of a spiritual presence (as it had been used during the last moments of the life of the deceased), the cleansing qualities of fire, the supernatural strength against evil spirits of candles that had been blessed by the priest.

The fourteenth-century funeral ritual prescribed for the diocese of Breslau suggests the presence of a large number of ordained and lower clergy, and it was clearly intended to guide the cathedral canons when one of their number died. But a scaled-down version of the same rite was used in parishes churches, too. According to this manual, the bells in the belfry sound as the procession enters the church; first come the holy water, incense, candles or torches, and a crucifix. Then the clergy enter; and if there are several of them, they proceed in the order in which they stand in the choir. A deacon wearing a stole follows these. The dead person (*defunctus*) is carried in by four men, and then the populace may enter. The corpse lies upon the litter by means of which it was transported, or on a simple catafalque. It must be placed in the middle of the sanctuary and thus before the altar. Those who bear in the holy water and other sacramentals stand by the head, in their proper order. The deacon begins to intone, "From the gate of hell," followed by the prayer, "Incline thine ear to me, O Lord." The cross and the candles are placed by the deceased "with incense," probably meaning that the censer is swung over or around the body. If the departed needs to be absolved, this is performed by Psalms and prayers: "Out of the depths," "Lord, have mercy," "Christ, have mercy," "Lord, have mercy," "Our Father," "And lead us not," "From the gates of hell," "The Lord be with you," "Absolve, o Lord, the soul of your servant." The Church regarded posthumous absolutions as effective. If the burial Mass is not to be celebrated until the following day, canons change off in keeping watch through the night, first those who stand on the right in the choir, then those who stand on the left. They recite in particular the Psalms, by which is meant the so-called penitential Psalms, but the entire ceremony is rich in other Psalms, too.

When the time comes to bear the dead to the grave, the bells are rung and stoles distributed to the priests. The officiant and those who bear cross, light, censer, and holy water arrange themselves at the head of the deceased. They recite a brief liturgy here made of up four parts and interspersed with recitation of *Kyrie eleison, Christe eleison, Kyrie eleison*. First, "Do not enter into judgment upon your servant, Lord, since no man is justified in your eyes unless remission of all sins is bestowed on him by you." Second,

> God, in whose house all the dead live and in whom our bodies in dying do not pass away but are changed into something better, forgive the sins of your servant; may you absolve him by your mercy and may you order his soul to be borne up by the hands of your saints and angels and led into the bosom [*in sinum*] of your patriarchs, Abraham, Isaac, and Jacob.

Third, "Have mercy, we ask, Lord, upon your dead servant, disregard the sins of this one who adhered in his vows to your will, and let him be joined to the throngs of the faithful." And fourth, "Incline your ear to our prayers, Lord, in which we beg for your mercy so that he may be with your saints in the realm of peace and light."[132]

In leaving the sanctuary for the place of interment, the cross-, incense-, light-, and holy-water-bearers go first, followed by the clergy in their proper choir order, then the deacon at the end of the convent. These prepare the way like the proverbial canary in a mine shaft, rending safe the passage of the others. "But four men should be provided, who carry the body." It seems that the body is last, although in this case the populace is not mentioned, and it would undoubtedly have come at the end of the procession. As they walk, the cantor begins the antiphon, "Open your gates," and the brothers follow with the Psalm, "Let us confess." Just at this point the bells resume their dirge. When they come to the open grave, the officiant and other participating clergy stand at the head (of the *fossae*, meaning where the head of the dead will repose). The antiphon resumes, "Open your gates." Meanwhile the priest goes through the office. This is a repetition in varied wording, asking for God's mercy and forgiveness for the dead "brother:"

> We beg for your mercy, omnipotent eternal God, who deigned to create man in your own image, receive kindly and mercifully the spirit and soul of your servant, which you have today ordered to be released from human affairs and summoned to you. Let not the shadows of death overpower him nor the chaos and darkness of hell cover him, but, cleansed of all sin and gathered into the bosom of Abraham the patriarch, may he rejoice that he has attained the place of light and refreshment, so that when the Day of Judgment comes, you may order him to be resuscitated with your saints and the elect.[133]

On reaching the place of burial, the officiating priest asks once again for quiet sleep (*quieta dormicio*) for the dead until the resurrection. He then asperges the body and the grave with holy water. Two of the bearers of the body then descend into the grave to receive the corpse, with the other two remaining above. The officiant prays that the soul of the dead person may not be afflicted with the torment of death nor affected by the grief of a terrible vision nor tortured by fear of punishment. He then throws earth upon the body and afterward recites, "Lord, you have tested," to which the others respond, "You have formed me from the earth, you have covered me with flesh, my Redeemer, revive me at the Last Day." Afterward, the priest stands back from the grave while other men cover the body with earth; other priests who hold the manual, standing in pairs, pray quietly. One of these prayers is:

> Let us pray, dearest brothers, for the spirit of our dear one, whom the Lord has deigned to release from the snare of this world, [and] whose little body today is borne to the grave, so that the love of the Lord may consent to gather him in the bosoms of Abraham, Isaac and Jacob, so that when the Day of Judgment shall come, he may be revived among the saints and [God's] own elect [and] placed at the right side...It is with a certain temerity, Lord, that a man dares to commend another man to you, our God—a mortal being [commending] a dead person, a being of ashes another being of ashes. But because the earth raises up earth and dust is converted into dust, so all flesh is returned to its

origin. Tearfully we seek your affection, most loving father, so that you may lead the soul of this your servant, from the foul whirlpool of this world to the land of Abraham, your friend; may you admit him to his bosom and sprinkle him with the dew of refreshment [*refrigerii*].[134]

They beg that, if the dead man should deserve punishment, God will remit these sins by his grace. At the end of the final antiphon, those in attendance kneel and recite the prayer "Lord, have mercy" and others:

We ask, Lord our God, that the prayer of Mary, the holy Mother of God, of the blessed John the Baptist and of all your saints, for the soul of your servant, our brother, and the supplication of his humble family here present may obtain the pardon...of all his sins...for you have redeemed him by the precious blood of your Son, our Lord Jesus Christ.

The cantor then begins the Psalm, "Have mercy upon me, God," and the clergy return to the church in the order in which they came, and if necessary (because of distance, I take it, from the cemetery to the church), the Psalm, "Out of the depths have I cried," or else "May God be merciful." In pronouncing the benediction before leaving the place of burial, the officiant makes the sign of the cross three times: "The blessing of God the Father and of the Son and of the Holy Spirit descend upon this place and upon this body. Amen." The brothers sing numerous other songs, including "Naked I have departed [from the world]." Bishop Heinrich specifies at various places that alternative prayers and songs may be used, without always stating what the alternatives are.[135]

Even if this model, with its explicitly familial language, pertains to a monastic community, we can mentally substitute worldly friends and relatives for those canons or monks who did not carry the sacramentals—the incense, holy water, and candles. Laypeople naturally formed an earthly community, too—whether one most strongly imprinted by kinship, neighborhood or village, trade, or, in the case of women who died in childbirth, gender. Death seemed to invade and weaken that community. Catholic theology and Catholic practice, before the Council of Trent still prominently the product of close priestly relatedness to (and prelates' accommodation of) commonly held beliefs, reaffirmed the existence of a new, higher community, one that joined those living to their dead and that fostered continual interaction between them. The sacred dead were, we well know, easily reachable by prayer, and they had the extraordinary privilege of interceding for those still alive. The living, unable to desist totally from sin, actively required that saintly obsecration, quite in addition to the sacramental ministrations of the Church. But what of the non-saintly, the normal, dead? In the widely held popular view, the dead could communicate with the living and even haunt them. Winter was the favored time of the "walkers," and during the period between Christmas and Epiphany, the dead appeared especially to women.[136] *Resciescat in pace* was in fact a formula designed to keep the deceased in their place, underground, as well as a wish for their spiritual wellbeing. This far along in our analysis of late medieval rituals, the specific gestures, and many of the words prescribed in the manual of Bishop Heinrich, will be transparent. "Open the gates" has not appeared before, but in the setting in which the brothers intone it it is a command to the earth to open in order to receive the body. The sense of the brothers' continuing relationship to the deceased is plain, and their recognition that the dead must enjoy the benefits of the prayers of the living. In the context of Catholic belief, this ceremony is in one sense an act of separation, but it entails, too, the rededication of the living both to living properly and to doing their part to ensure the safety of the dead. At the same time, they acknowledge their own dependence upon the saints—that is, the very best of the dead—and upon the grace of God for their eventual salvation. The institutional Church taught that the dead and the living were bound together in a common endeavor: that of gaining the salvation of humankind.[137]

Jean Delumeau's *Sin and Fear: The Emergence of a Western Guilt Culture* is not—as others of his works had prepared us to expect[138]—very friendly toward late medieval Catholicism. Concepts of overpowering sin and the need to control it dominated both this world and the next. In his view, the late medieval Church was as tightly under the domination of monastic ascetic ideals as it had been during the eleventh to thirteenth centuries, and the Counter-Reformation Church continued passionately in this tradition.[139] The connection between the living and the dead was thus a troubled (if intimate) one.

In popular belief, it is true, the dead could hardly rest in peace, burdened by their sin, for which they had not succeeded in making satisfaction in life. They required the incessant prayers and Masses of the living in order to repose at last. At the end of the Middle Ages, it was customary to hold Masses on the anniversaries of someone's death, especially one week, thirty days, and one year afterward. So that those left on earth would not forget their duty to the departed, they appeared. Mothers who had died in childbed might try to take their babies with them to the afterworld. Criminals and other marginal people had to be buried at crossroads so that the very form of the cross might contain their malevolent purposes, or under the gallows, which civilized people avoided.[140] The attitudes and practices of the common people in relation to death and the dead were numerous and take up much space in the Bächtold-Stäubli *Handwörterbuch des deutschen Aberglaubens*.[141]

Unquestionably, late medieval people were ambivalent about death, but they were equally so about many aspects of life and the living. Human existence, on this side and the other, was a mass of gradations from threatening to non-threatening; there were times and places of danger and times and places of comparative safety. There were places, as in the church before the altar, where sanctity was concentrated, and places, as in the tavern, where it was exceedingly diffuse. Life-and-death was a seamless network of transactions and negotiations, with relatives, with those in authority in the here and now, with the priest, with God. A measure of the integration of death in life is symbolized by the locations of the dead within the medieval town and village: at the heart. The cultic center of the city/the neighborhood/the peasant community was the church or chapel, and its geographic placement was more or less in the area of intense lifetime activity. Within its crypt, walls, and floor, and under its eaves (the rainwater absorbed sacred power in its contact with the roof and drained beneficially onto the graves along the walls), initially prelates and then other clerics and elite citizens were laid to rest. Certainly large urban churches by the late Middle Ages were one of those places where the living and the dead regularly encountered one another. By the south side, whether in town or country—the north, with its diabolical associations was not an auspicious burial place[142]—lay the cemetery (*Friedhof*). The word *graveyard* might give the wrong impression, for until the early modern period the dead were deposited there without permanent markers. A wall or fence was supposed to demarcate it from the workaday world, for at their founding burial grounds underwent a ceremony of dedication, and only after that were they suitable for use; only in such ground could the holy dead rest in peace with fair certainty. The reality was, however, that walls and fences were expensive to build and maintain, and in times of population growth and scarcity of land, the people used what was near at hand. Sometimes houses were built onto the cemetery wall, and the inhabitants regarded its spaces as their own yard and even built sheds there. Some cemeteries contained fruit trees, probably around the periphery. Pastors thought that *they* had the right to cut the grass as hay, while sextons often thought *they* ought to have it. In the meantime, the people let their livestock graze there, which during muddy times turned the area into a stinking mire. It is likely that the people themselves ducked into the cemetery when they needed to relieve themselves, so frequent in the Protestant visitation registers are the pastors' and civic leaders' complaints about the noisome smells emerging from the cemeteries, and their enjoinders to the sextons to remove filth. Decaying corpses laid too close to the surface were not the only source of the stench, and they did not produce new filth.[143]

The point to be made here is that the living intermingled daily with the dead, and they thought very little about it during daylight hours. Even though individual graves usually did not exist, the physical remains of the dead were continually in evidence. Every time the gravediggers broke the earth, they came up with the remains of previous burials. For one thing, they were characteristically too lazy—the more so when the ground was frozen—to dig as deep as they were instructed to.

For another, after hundreds of years' use, the earth was literally saturated with skeletal remains. Every larger church and, surprisingly, every village church possessed a charnel house or ossuary. It was usually attached to the church wall, or at least the cemetery wall, and constituted a separate small building. Here the gravediggers deposited the skulls, femurs, tibias, scapulas and ulnas of the dead when they were denuded of flesh, and when they got in the way of a new excavation. Although there are some spectacular examples of non-German ossuaries being painstakingly *decorated* with flower mosaics of even the small bones of feet and hands, in general German *Beinhäuser* contained only the skulls and femurs of the dead.[144] This seems to reflect the persuasion that these were the potentially dangerous parts of the physical remains of the dead—the parts they required to move around—and to preserve these in the ossuaries was a mild precaution. Be this as it may, these bones were daily in evidence. We have tended to interpret them as macabre, as evidence of the late medieval preoccupation with death. I prefer to see them as testimony of the integration of human existence on either side of the grave. Late medieval people were nonchalant about the bodily relics of their ancestors, nor did it visibly disturb them that these bones were not kept separate and whole according to person.[145] The dead were part of the human collectivity, their community, and community still overrode individuality. Ariès and Vovelle are perhaps not wrong to maintain that the charnel houses existed as places to deposit bones that were in the way in overfilled cemeteries.[146] But they were more than that. They—and all those prominent, public places where the dead were in evidence— were the meeting places of those who had gone before and those who were temporarily still drawing breath. They were the symbols and substance of the eternal Christian community.

Nevertheless, Ariès is correct in drawing attention to one of the official Church's motives in consenting to this display of skeletons. In its eyes, this exhibition promoted the reflection on death as an incentive to lead a more upright and preparatory life. Graves and ossuaries, like death knells and funeral processions, served to edify.[147] They also reminded the faithful to pray for the souls of the departed and, if they could, to finance Masses—for prayers and Masses, the Church taught, reduced the time that salvageable souls spent in purgatory. The enthusiasm with which many Germans purchased indulgences in the early sixteenth century indicates their concern for the eternal rest of the dead. The people *did* absorb the doctrinal instruction of the day. At the same time, they retained traditional motives. A sense of community obligation, reinforced by the daily visibility of the very dead for whom one prayed, lent greater persuasive power to clerical admonition. We find here, then, another example of the integration of differing configurations of motives.

Despite the usual neglect of the individual in the deposition of corpses, the station of the dead remained important. It has been amply demonstrated that the structure of society showed through in the structure of burial.[148] Clergy and wealthy people assumed the few spaces within the church, with those near the altar enjoying more of the umbrella of sanctity than those farther away. Needless to say, men far more often than women and children are buried within church edifices. These men, by virtue of their fame, were not disinterred, for they in their cubbies were spared the indignity of displacement; elite men's bones are far less likely than those of ordinary citizens to show up in charnel houses. Outside, too, status conferred certain initial honors—deposition near the south wall of the church or under the eaves. All bodies outside were likely to make their way to the ossuaries in due course. Inspection of medieval cemeteries makes it appear probable that the gravediggers did lay people to rest on the north sides of churches, too. Unfortunately, we have no way of showing that these derived from lower socio-economic levels. It may well be that certain unfavorable categories rested there—women who had died in childbed without undergoing churching; practitioners of dishonorable trades such as animal skinners and linen weavers, prostitutes, executioners, and the very gravediggers them-selves.[149] During the late Middle Ages, babies who died unbaptized were often consigned to the earth completely outside consecrated ground, as were criminals, who (especially if executed) lay under the gallows on a distant hill. Grave allocation roughly recapitulated social position, and social position reflected not just the vagaries of the marketplace and inheritance but prevalent attitudes as well.

LUTHERAN RELEGATION OF THE DEVIL

The Lutheran Reformation, and indeed the Reformation in all its prominent early forms, ended the community of the dead and the living: it separated them. The dead departed and could not return. Nor did the living any longer have access to them. Nevertheless, to a considerable degree average Lutherans in the sixteenth century very likely continued to feel a sense of relatedness to the dead. They complained bitterly when their city fathers relegated their burial places to new, extramural cemeteries.[150] This shift of the depositories of the dead from inside to outside the cities occurred all over early modern Germany. The oligarchs justified this move with reference to the expanding populations that the ground now had to accommodate. There was no more room in the medieval churchyards. This was, of course, true. They also talked about the unhealthy vapors rising up from the graves (*dünst*), which, if more than their imagination, indicated that the graves were not being dug deep enough. But the transfer of urban burial places away from the scene of daily activity coincided neatly—too neatly—with the newly prevalent theology that the dead were no longer present. Initially, it is worth noting, the patricians ensured that they themselves (as members of the august few) would be buried in or near the central urban church; initially the common folk and plague victims were exiled to the periphery.[151] Naturally, the wealthy had to pay for their privilege: 50 *Reichsthaler* in Quedlinburg by 1627, a considerable sum.[152] In the placement of corpses, we can see the growing separation of the elites from the rest of their fellow citizens. Previously they had at least shared common ground, though their places within it differed. Now the high and the mighty had their own, close-in little beds of rest (*Ruhebettlein*), and hoi polloi reposed, to be sure, but at some little distance.

During the sixteenth century with its economic pressures, ecclesiastical authorities were more and more precise in their instructions about what each sort of person had to pay for which clerical services. In the vicinity of Magdeburg, the visitors ordained in 1583–1584 that for accompanying a corpse to the grave, the nobles would have to pay 0.5 Taler to the pastor, the same amount to the deacon, 6 groschen to the schoolmaster, 3.5 groschen to the cantor, and 2 groschen to the sexton; and for a funeral sermon 0.5 Taler to the preacher. A burgher funeral cost 3.5 groschen to the pastor, 3 groschen to the deacon, 2 groschen to the schoolmaster, 2 groschen to the cantor, and 2 groschen to the sexton, plus 6 groschen for a sermon.[153] The poor were buried for free. Similar fees were imposed and periodically raised virtually throughout Germany.

In addition, the Reformers strove to eliminate all ossuaries. In Göttingen, for example, a large *Beinhaus* was almost precisely in the center of the city.[154] The dead were thus not only present, but at the heart of daily transactions. Most Protestant leaders regarded ossuaries as associated with papist superstition. They had the bones taken out and buried, and in some cases the edifices themselves torn down. In reality, it often took longer to attain this goal than they had hoped, and in some places (even the towns) the charnel houses remained, but with the dead discreetly concealed.[155] Calvinist visitors were unpleasantly surprised in 1590, when inspecting lands of the earls of Dietz, that every village still had its ossuary. They ordered their removal.[156] In another important way, then, the living no longer encountered the dead every day. Increasingly there were "two kingdoms," that of this world and that of the next, and the twain were not to meet.

When after the Reformation Lutherans died, women still washed and dressed their bodies, but there was to be no delay, except that occasioned by the wait for daylight to arrive. Ordinarily, funerals followed death within a day's time, which guaranteed that more distant relatives could not even be notified, much less attend. Women continued the tradition of inviting neighbors to the funeral (*Bittfrauen*).[157] But burial was to ensue without the burning of candles or the application of other "superstitious" substances or rites. The Protestant position—and this was even more rigorously true of the Reformed faith—was that, all power residing in God's hands alone, no human action could affect what was now finished business. The dead were dead. Their future was shaped alone by God's providence and Christ's atonement, and what was done was done. Sometimes, pastors held no service within the church but accompanied the body directly to its burial. The visitation ordinances in Saxony and Thuringia followed the pattern adopted in Wittenberg. The clergy accorded different treatment to the dead, in continuity with Catholic custom, according to socio-economic status:

> First, when a common man dies, the bell is not to be rung, but the closest neighbors go with the body to the grave.
>
> Second, when a middling burgher dies, the relatives arrange for the schoolmaster with his schoolboys to be at the funeral, who sing all the way to the grave, among other [songs], "Out of the Depths Have I Cried unto Thee," etc. When one has come to the grave . . . the schoolmaster or one of his assistants sings with the people who are present, "We Believe in God the Father Almighty" because of the article [in the Creed] about the resurrection of the body . . . but bells are not to be rung, and for that reason the deacon is not requested or called.
>
> Third, when an honorable person [*von redlichen leuten*] dies, the body is buried with a procession, [and] all the clergy take part, not out of obligation but at the request of the relatives; the schoolmaster together with his pupils is there, and in addition, the great bell is to be rung. Nevertheless, it seldom happens.[158]

Class differences are visible practically throughout Germany. The visitors of the parish of Seehausen (Brandenburg) specified in 1541 that family members could decide whether they wanted the small bell, the large bell, or both together sounded for their relative, but they would have to pay the sexton accordingly; if they had both rung, they would have, in addition, to contribute 0.5 florin to the community chest.[159] This was essentially a luxury tax.

Initially, as we have seen, funeral sermons were given only for heads of state and their families. The Agenda of Heinrich of Saxony (1539), which had ongoing influence in Germany, prescribed simply that, when there were bodies to be buried, the people who were present should sing the song of Simeon, "Lord, Now Lettest Thy Servant Depart in Peace" ("Nunc dimittis," "Mit Fried und Freud ich fahr dahin"),[160] or "In the Midst of Life We Are in Death" ("Media vita in morte," "Mitten wir im Leben sind"). "It is not necessary that a sermon be held at the cemetery by the grave." Otherwise, the Agenda simply states,

> In cities corpses should be honorably led by the schoolmaster and the schoolboys, in accordance with circumstances, with the songs

specified above; similarly, in the villages by the pastor and the sexton, in the presence of some of the neighbors, and such burial shall be honorably observed, to honor [the dead] and to acknowledge the resurrection of the dead, which is Christians' highest, final, and certain consolation.[161]

The processions for local nobles, civic leaders, and the wealthy could give an impression of pomp and circumstance; not very different, indeed, from Catholic funerals for people of similar quality, though without papist sacramentals. Even without cross and candles, the bells rang (beforehand, at least, and in many places during the train to the burial ground), and the schoolmaster and his retinue of child singers filled the lane with their march and their hymns. They and the clergy met at the dwelling of the deceased; the body was borne aloft by designated men, the litter or coffin covered with a black cloth. Increasingly relatives and friends took to wearing black emblems of mourning on their clothes, such as armbands or ribbons on their hats or veils for the women, and thus they had a somber effect.[162] The schoolmaster and the boys went first, then the clergy, followed by the body and family and friends. Of the last, the men as a group preceded the women. High-ranking women had no part in elite funerals, but humbler women, while not at the center of such ceremonies, were not quite at the periphery either. Hiking out to a newer, more distant cemetery in rain or winter could be a numbing, chilling experience, and there were reasons why the requisite admonition or sermon was sometimes held in the church, *after* laying the dead to rest. The danger evidently was that people might go directly home or back to their work without stopping off in the church for the continuation of the service, and presumably on that account in some lands these homilies had to be presented at graveside. The collection box for the poor stood in the church, and everyone was supposed to drop a coin in; the tradition of giving alms to the poor after a death had changed its form somewhat, but still continued.

One of the hymns added after mid-century and recommended for regular use is "Nun laßt uns den Leib begraben" ("Now Let Us Bury the Body"). Elisabeth Blum has noted the cold mood, the emotionless detachment of this song, and she speculates that it is the product of the "emotional asceticism" of the circles of the Bohemian Brethren out of which it came.[163] When considered against the other ritual evidence of Protestant separation of the realms of the living and the dead, this assertion rings true. The hymn bespeaks the separation between the living and the dead. The *real* person is no longer present, and there should be little sentiment attached to taking the earthly residue to its grave. Verse 7 enjoins,

Now let us leave it [the body] sleeping here and all go home or go our way,

With industry let us do what we ought; death will come for us in the very same way.[164]

As princes, in consultation with ecclesiastical leaders, made their instructions for pastors more and more detailed, they increasingly specified exactly what was to be said. In 1580, Saxon elector August not only required that funeral sermons be given, but his advisors provided the texts of three entire homilies from which pastors might choose.[165] Each of these could be read in ten to fifteen minutes, and each presents the origin of death in human sin and the hope of salvation to those who have believed in Christ; each one is a concentrated lesson in Lutheran doctrine on death and resurrection. In addition, the visitors were to inquire in each parish whether each had a proper and clean cemetery, whether the graves were being dug deep enough (as deep as the height of the dead person), whether the people attend funerals and behave respectfully to the pastor, whether the families of those who have died pay the pastor and other official participants promptly and honestly.[166] The many variations in the territorial ordinances are noticeable. Indeed, the ordinance of Anhalt of 1575 prohibited funeral sermons, a sign that the controversy about them never wholly ceased.

> For a variety of reasons, funeral sermons are to be completely discontinued, and instead, at the funeral of a head of household or adult, the pastor shall read the old admonition; and at the funeral of children or young people the collect that one used to read before the houses [of the dead]; and immediately afterward the benediction should be pronounced so that the people aren't held up too long and the young people don't neglect their schoolwork.[167]

In most lands, however, funeral sermons were required beginning shortly after the middle of the century. Either at the graveside or immediately after the burial back in the church, the pastor delivered a brief sermon, never more than half an hour long,

> either about dying, where death originated, the many kinds of death, what Christian and unchristian deaths are, how a person can die well and blessedly and how one can prepare for this, and whatever similar teachings there are. Or he may do a sermon of consolation, which would not only comfort the relatives of the person who has just died but in general everyone in their time of death.[168]

The edifying purpose of these sermons is well summarized in a prayer to be given after such preaching in the Bavarian Lindau in 1573:

> Give us grace and understanding so that having heard this description of our dead brother, whom we have accompanied [to the grave], we may be reminded why we were born into this world, how fragile and transitory [*zergenglich*] our life is, and what the end of all of us will be;

so that we are truly humbled and all haughtiness, arrogance, self love, and false self-reliance dies out of our hearts, and that we commit ourselves to sincere repentance and the improvement of our lives ... to the end that, when you call us out of this mortal life, dear Father, we will be found to be your true servants, and along with this departed brother, at the resurrection of the justified [*der gerechten*] will be received into eternal life with you ...[169]

The sixteenth century was a time of transition in the use of coffins. At the beginning of the century, only the wealthy were regularly interred in purpose-built containers, and the masses contented themselves with sacks for their family members. Frequently, indeed, people were laid to rest in simple clothing. The visitors in the lands pertaining to the Halberstadt cathedral chapter noted with interest in 1589 that in the town of Ostewick, when a woman died in childbirth, the other women in attendance dressed her in all her clothes, including her best dress, and carried her to the grave themselves; the women dug the grave and lowered her into it, holding a shroud (*Grabtuch*) in front until the body was covered with dirt. Well, this was not exactly *simple* clothing, and this the visitors objected to. The women could continue their custom, but the dead had to be attired with less luxury.[170] But the point is that treatment of the cadaver was not yet uniform. The poor might have to borrow a shroud from the church, which every parish was supposed to have available and which was returned after use. It is evident from this that bare or clothed bodies, with no other covering, were put in the earth. The rich increasingly bought coffins, of various qualities of wood depending on their means, until, in the early seventeenth century, the city council of Braunschweig outlawed excessive decoration of the coffins with wreaths and garlands. How much one could decorate a coffin varied according to class and sex, the coffins of females warranting less attention than those of males.[171] It was harder to dig a grave for a coffin than just for a body, and the diggers had to be paid more to do it—and more still in winter when the ground was frozen.[172] In some areas, the church bell sounded when someone died, but not again before or during the funeral; in others, as under Catholicism, the bell was rung before the procession to the grave, to summon the people; in still others, also as before the Reformation, the knell occurred as relatives and friends accompanied the body. In general, the bell remained, but in more restrained usage. The people would not tolerate its elimination. Where there was more than one bell—two or the full panoply of three—both or all were sounded simultaneously.[173] This tintinnabulation was surely enough to ban the Devil, some may still have thought.

After the funeral, the people were accustomed to meet for a meal, either at the local public house or at the home of the deceased. Lutheran authorities disapproved mightily of this indulgence and consistently strove to do away with it—with only partial success. The people's practices tried to mend the torn social fabric, but those in authority wished Christians to focus yet a little longer, unsmilingly, upon their sinfulness and their mortality. They protested that families ruined themselves financially through these entertainments. Delumeau is right: there is a monastic tenor to the clergy's and the state's goals.

Both ecclesiastical ordinances and visitation protocols reveal that after the Reformation people began to be reluctant to attend burials. This troubled the clergy for two reasons: First, they wanted to exploit the confrontation with death for purposes of instilling the fear of God, and of the state, in all citizens. In both Catholicism and Lutheranism, the symbols and procedures of the rite reminded Christians of the imminence of death and strove to inspire reform. Second, as in the course of the century, making regular monetary gifts became a duty, the church relied on this income both in making up the salaries of the clerics and in providing for the local poor. Before the Reformation, wills characteristically enumerated payments of alms. Afterward, they did not entirely cease to do so, but this feature became less regular, less pronounced. But demographic expansion meant that the need for philanthropy was greater than ever. Many people stayed away from funerals in order to avoid putting their groat in the poorbox (*Armenkasten*). The result was that writers of ordinances and preachers harangued the people to attend funerals.[174] We should also accept at face value the reasons for going to burial services given in the ordinance of Count of the Rhenish Palatinate Ottheinrich in 1556: "in order to demonstrate the love that we bore them while they were alive and to confess the faith that we have in Christ..." It admonishes all to refrain from every superstitious and heathen practice on behalf of the dead.[175] Pastors could not be the first to throw or shovel dirt onto the body in the grave. Mourners could kneel in the church but not at the grave, in which setting it smacked of "papist superstition." Nor could people usually continue their local funeral observances. The visitors in the Württemberg countryside quickly concluded that the people's practice of kneeling by the grave and loudly (*mit lautter stimme*) reciting, after the Creed and the Our Father, the following "grave speech" (*Krufft spruch*) could not be tolerated, even though its content was not unorthodox:

Behold, all you brothers, how do you like this refuge?
Poor, rich, knight, and servant—it is deserved by all.
Death will bring all living people to this place.
Now you should get together and prepare,
For we all belong in this band. Do not spare good word and deed
While you're alive, for the world will pass like snow and ice;
Stay away from worldly pleasures, for what you sow you there will reap.
You can take nothing to the grave, not even your loveliest things,

No silver, gold, nor precious stone; nothing comes here but barest
bone.
The worms will eat the flesh, your kin keep all your goods
And let them lie around. The body sleeps till the Final Day,
When God will transfigure it and grant eternal joy.[176]

The recitation of grave speeches appears to have been customary
throughout this region. The visitors always eliminated them regardless
of their content. For one thing, they originated with the people
themselves, or if not with them, then in the shadowy Catholic past.
For either reason they were tainted. The people had to be told what to do,
sing, and say by evangelical experts. The sixteenth century was hardly an
age that invited suggestions from the laity.

Other ordinances mention that human beings would be "like
unreasoning animals" if they did not celebrate funerals but merely
deposited their dead in the earth.[177] And, indeed, when unregenerate
sinners were buried outside of consecrated ground, the princely court
used the same image, that of the unreasoning beasts ("*alß die
vnuornunftigen thier*"), in describing them.[178] Ceremony was a sign of
being human, provided it was the *correct* ceremony.

What was correct by Lutheran lights was still profoundly papist in
Calvinist eyes. The Reformed visitors of the county of Nassau-
Dillenburg, senior line (probably in 1582), castigated and ended
Lutheran practice, some of which was still left over from before the
Reformation. They ordered to be stopped: the burning of candles either
upon the biers of the dead or in any other place at funerals; kneeling and
praying before corpses; putting crosses on new graves; ringing bells
while carrying the dead to the cemetery; including such things in the
liturgy as, "May God be gracious to this soul"; and "the superstitious
ringing of all the bells at once."[179]

Whatever the nature of the observances in Lutheran or Calvinist
Germany, the funeral being over, those left behind were not to pray for
the dead, to decorate the graves, to mourn overlong or extremely, to
observe the anniversaries of their demise.[180] All of these either smacked
of Catholicism or suggested that the person who did such things did
not trust sufficiently in God. Andreas Musculus found it necessary to
write in 1565:

Here among us we have to report and consider, namely about the
poltergeists, about which some are of the opinion that the dead souls
move around and let themselves be seen in houses, gardens, in the
field, and wherever else. And how some people see such spirits and
from their form can tell that they were people known to them when
they were alive. How under the pope many things were done by such
spirits, and such ghosts really took care of the monks' and priests'
kitchen. But we want to respond to this briefly and with few words,

and say that we properly stand and stay by our opinion, namely, that the dead souls, once they come to the place to which God has ordered them...remain there until the Last Day and do not come again, let themselves be seen, and have anything more to do with people...For that reason you should regard such wandering spirits as nothing other than the ghosts and treachery of the Devil, indeed as the Devil himself...[181]

The dear departed were sleeping and could not hear; every communication with them had to wait until the trumpet should sound and the dead should be raised incorruptible. The living were thrown back, not upon their own resources—far from it—but upon the concentrated godhead. They could take no self-helpful action other than to contain their sinful impulses and to pray—for themselves and not for the dead. This was the theory. The visitation protocols reveal, of course, how few uneducated people were able to accept this despirited, streamlined world. And even the educated continued to believe that the Devil and his minions swirled about the external and internal interstices. For perhaps another century, nearly all the people affirmed the existence of Satan. They were also inclined to think that their conformity to Christian standards of behavior did help them get to heaven.

As a consolation for depriving the living of contact with the dead, and as an incentive to prepare during life for death, Lutheran preachers held the glorious rewards of heaven out to their congregations. They spoke to their congregations of the transfigured bodies of the saved, of their unspeakable joy at being lifted into the brilliantly luminous presence of God, of their joyous reunion with the earlier dear departed.[182] For the community of saints, even those who had not led entirely saintly lives—but who had deeply repented at the end—bliss was assured, and beyond mortal description.

CONTEXTS AND CONCLUSIONS

In the last twenty years, anthropologists have experienced a revived interest in death; their theories have been helpfully summarized and evaluated by Peter Metcalf and Richard Huntington.[183] The array of interpretation from the time of Émile Durkheim onward need not preoccupy us here. The most useful approaches for my purposes are, chronologically arranged, those of Arnold van Gennep, Robert Hertz, A. R. Radcliffe-Brown, and M. Bloch and J. Parry.

As we have seen, van Gennep, a student of Durkheim, looked upon funerary rituals as one of several categories of virtually universal rites of passage. For the survivors, funerals are at the same time ceremonies of separation and of transition.[184] The meaning of *separation* here requires no definition, but *transition* is not as clear. Van Gennep means that the living must reintegrate themselves into a new whole, which is to say that, having been bereaved, they must mend the rent in their social fabric and enter upon an altered collectivity. This is true for both Catholics and Lutherans (and Reformed) in our study. However, more needs to be said about the concept of separation. The Catholic practice was based upon the belief that the dead had departed bodily but not spiritually. Catholic theology was not uniform—and Protestants would elaborate one strand of it—but the conviction of the multitudes, including many parish priests, was that the dead continued to interact with the living. The interaction could be dangerous, but it could also be beneficial to both the quick and the dead. Thus, the spheres of this world and the other intersected. Rituals had as part of their purpose ensuring that the dead did not afflict those left behind.[185]

Lutheran and Calvinist divines, their parishioners' preferences notwithstanding, took a different view. They made the separation of the dead from the living quite complete. The souls of the dead were truly departed and beyond approach. Officially, not even those of criminals and marginal people could wander. All slept, awaiting the final call to their heavenly or hellish destinations. The dead were rendered harmless by the new creeds, and so were the living, who could no longer invoke the power of unseen worlds in negotiating the tangible scene. Once again Protestant authorities divested the populace of influence over its earthly condition and its fate. This represents a thoroughgoing separation between living and dead, and the removal of cemeteries is symbolic of the spiritual shift. It was also disciplinary. Early modern divines were intent on *preventing* superstitious indulgence wherever possible. Certainly population was expanding and inner-city burial grounds were overloaded. Certainly they feared that noisome odors from disintegrating corpses could cause disease. They also welcomed an opportunity to thwart superstitious behaviors by putting graves at greater distance from the living. And they had the contents of the ossuaries removed to these new sites and interred. Nonetheless, the dead remained in a liminal state within Protestantism as within Catholicism. We have to resist the temptation to say that Lutheran and Reformed authorities extended the period of liminality till the Last Judgment, for in fact during the sixteenth century they thought its occurrence imminent, perhaps even before the flesh of the newly buried had fallen off the bones.

To put this in the terms of Robert Hertz, the Protestant ecclesiastical establishment abolished secondary burial—along with the beliefs that had sustained it.[186] Under Catholicism, depositing the dead in the earth constituted for many a primary or provisional burial. As soon as the flesh had decayed and fallen off the bones, the skeletal remains could be carted away to the local *Beinhaus*. Although this second deposition did not include ceremony, it was nonetheless significant, for late medieval people saw in bare bones little or no danger; the souls of their earlier possessors had loosed their hold on them.[187] Lutheran and Calvinist superintendents banned both bones and buildings, nonetheless, in keeping with their general relegation of the dead from human settlement. Catholic priests had taught that the presence of the skeletons, like artistic and literary depictions of the *danse macabre*, served to focus Christians' attention on the nearness of death and their need to prepare for it. But Protestants were apparently confident that the regularity with which members of the community died served as sufficient reminder. In addition, Lutheran funeral sermons concentrated on this theme.

A. R. Radcliffe-Brown sought to understand the place of emotion in the society of the Andaman Islanders whom he studied.[188] According to Metcalf and Huntington, Radcliffe-Brown "based his entire theory of society on the ritual expression of sentiments."[189] The anthropologist was correct concerning the societal determination of emotion. We may infer that an innovation in the official norms regulating the display of emotion signals a shift within society, or at least within the circles from which the pronouncements come. One of the changes that Lutheranism and Calvinism attempted to introduce was in the display of emotion in association with the death of a family member. Although the Catholic Church seems not to have fostered displays of grief, it was tolerant of the widespread dramatic mourning. In the dying chamber, both before and after the Reformation, spouses, children, and even long-term servants wept at impending separation. In some parts of Germany, *Klageweiber* wailed as the body of the deceased lay waiting for burial, and they cried as it was borne to the grave. Post-Reformation authorities forbade these activities by hired women. In their sermons, they urged relatives not to give way to immoderate grieving but rather to think about the infinite joys that awaited their loved ones in paradise. Until then, the saintly dead were simply sleeping undisturbed, in itself an enviable condition. It is impossible to say how successful such exhortations were. They represent more a shift in elite expectation than either elite or ordinary practice, no doubt. Still, as an ideal of greater self-control, they are significant. And they are consistent with the overall campaign for restraint and self-discipline in early modern Europe. The stereotype of the Puritan has sometimes included the idea that one ought not to be too attached to earthly figures, even one's spouse, but should reserve the deepest fervor for God alone. Lutheran sermons on the Fall often mention Adam's immoderate love of Eve, which led him to accept the fateful apple. A study of precisely the control of emotional display in the Reformation ought to be done. Hans Medick and David Sabean have written that a growing burgher culture in early modern Germany encouraged familial sentimentality as a means of fostering social stability.[190] I would add that, in some settings, emotion may be a *destabilizing* force, particularly "excessive" emotion. It may be that the growing tendency of the bereft to decorate their persons with all manner of black apparel—with whole outfits if they were rich, with mere borrowed armbands if they were poor—reflects more than urban affluence and the imitation of elites. It may be that these silent accoutrements of mourning are an alternative way of showing grief when the openly, or "excessively," emotive is discouraged. The demonstration of feeling is, of course, not the same as feeling itself. But if bourgeois society looked with favor on emotional bonds among family members, and succeeded in strengthening them, the corollary of this achievement—if achievement it was, for Medick and Sabean regard it as often a foil for material interests—would be the danger that feelings would occasionally, as on the death of close relatives, get out of hand.

Finally, there is the question of ritual as social control. Catherine Bell has expressed skepticism toward those Left-leaning theorists who have wanted to see in ritual a formalized behavior imposed upon the participants by its perpetrators for the latter's political advantage.[191] Following Michel Foucault, she prefers an interpretation of power that is founded upon an interaction between those who dominate and those who generally submit—in short, upon a dynamic interaction between those at the top and underlings. Foucault did not concentrate upon ritual per se, but used the word as one of several "to indicate formalized, routinized, and often supervised practices that mold the body."[192] I find attractive Bell's insistence upon the contribution that the apparently ritually controlled actually make to the hegemony of one group over others—in this case the domination of lay society by ecclesiastical leaders in concert with the not yet entirely secularized state. Bell implicitly lends us an explanation of the persistence of folk practice despite the efforts of those in authority to discipline, regulate, and purify Lutheran society. Clearly, one of their favored instruments toward this end was the revival of Catholic *ars moriendi* rituals after Luther's death. As before the Reformation—though now regularly focused on in sermons—Christians must prepare for death all their lives. Theological controversy about good works notwithstanding, people needed to show through their cultic observances and moral uprightness that they were worthy of salvation. As their time approached, they were expected to perform ritual acts of repentance and submission that implicitly, symbolically, acknowledged the clergy as the doorkeepers of heaven. The heavy emphasis upon preparation for death was (at the spiritual level) a form of continuity with the late Middle Ages. At the palpable, mundane level, however, it was a mechanism used by church and state for achieving that intensely sought *order* within the body politic. Rulers espoused the art of dying for reasons more immediate than the eventual repose of soul.

6 Ritual change
Conclusions

AUTHORITY AND RITUAL

On the face of it, ritual change in the transition from Roman Catholicism to Protestantism in Germany was about returning to the "pristine" practice of the early church. The elite men who directed the Reformation thought carefully about the alterations that they introduced, and they were convinced that they were restoring biblically condoned observance to the sixteenth century. They saw themselves as purging from the agenda "papist" invention, much of which, in Lutheran and Calvinist teaching, was not harmless embroidery but rather a falsifying, injurious departure from the will of God. For God did not, in these divines' opinion, give mortals, including priests, license to arrogate to themselves power over supernatural domains. When they condemned "super-stition," as they repeatedly did, they included ritual practices within the church as well as ritualized folk measures that purported to render less noxious the teeming unseen elements that beset people's equilibrium and made them vulnerable to a bleak hereafter. Probably few late medieval clergy perceived the complementarity between official cere-monial assumptions and those adhered to by many ordinary people who, imitating the language, artifacts, and gestures of the church, confronted life's problems well fortified. Popular healers and the throngs who gave their custom to them tapped the magical powers of the church and applied them, as they thought, between Eucharistic Masses (strictly the ordained priests' domain) to a larger sphere. The incantations of cunning people and midwives were filled with the language of saintly invocation and Trinitarian blessing. Whenever possible, they employed sacramentals such as blessed candles, baptismal water, and bits of the Host that someone had managed to bring out of the church unswal-lowed. They meant to serve God aright, and the simple versions of righteousness that their unlettered priests shared with them and conveyed to them very likely reinforced their practice. The priests gave them blessed bread, pronounced their own protective formulae over their candles, fields, crops, beehives, and hovels, and lived similarly among them. If such men of the cloth objected to folkish measures, it was on the grounds that they alone within their respective parishes ought to wield the sword against Satan; they may have been jealous of their oft-resorted-to rivals. Nonetheless, their view of the universe was much the same as those of their charges.

The Reformers, in contrast, condemned the entire field of manipulators of the unseen: both priests and folk practitioners. Scripture did not validate their purported powers. Above all, only God himself could control. Even as the leaders of the new churches insisted that they directed their cleansing fires at that which was unsubstantiated in the Bible, we readers of ritual cannot help but observe that they simultaneously disenfranchized the priesthood and every other category of ether-penetrating operative. They would doubtless agree with me, for these all functioned without celestial approval. Within the Lutheran sphere, the process of desacralizing the pastorate was not complete until clerical exorcism ceased in most places by the end of the sixteenth century. It remained in Brandenburg even then.

But even in Lutheran churches the underlying message came across in the ritual innovations that mortals' hands were tied, and properly so. Human fate lay entirely in the disposal of the heavenly Father, whose plans Satan tirelessly attempted to frustrate. Mortals by their choices could effect little. Their mundane duty was to recognize and foil the Devil while trying to conform to God's wishes. But, in Lutheran thought, human beings remained *simul justi et peccatores*, unable to fulfill the Law, solely reliant for their salvation on Christ's atonement.

If we turn again to ritual change, we find that more than the personnel who approached the divine had undergone transformation. Even inside the churches, God was not present in the same way as before. The few images still in place were not to be objects of devotion. No candles burned before them. Altar paintings depicted scenes from the life of Christ, and their purpose was to indoctrinate. Not paintings, statuary vestments, or the much-depleted equipment of the Eucharist any longer possessed God's genius. It did no good to see them, touch them, or be in their presence. The single and singular exception to this was the Savior's physical presence in the Lutheran Eucharist. On those occasions when the confessed and absolved partook of Communion, they did come in contact with the divine. Luther and Calvin correctly saw that this issue set them far apart. To ingest the very Lord gave the creature a degree of access to the Creator that was denied to those who were spiritually nourished. Candles, increasingly elaborate clerical vestments, and reverberant organ music symbolically bore out the immediacy of the divine. By contrast, in Reformed Germany, whitewashed, unlighted sanctuaries bespoke the abstractness, even the remoteness, of God. Perhaps this is why the women of one Hessian village, on being ordered to adopt Calvinism in 1590, moved back to their parents' homes. They said that they did not want to accept a new religion.[1] A person had to look inward to find evidence of Him, and the untrained might miss Him altogether. Calvinist authorities strove especially hard to provide the necessary discipline.

Protestant leaders did not say to themselves, "We shall use ritual change as a means of impressing on Christians that they are powerless." Nevertheless, these leaders, these reworkers of the liturgy were part of their day. In those years, rulers at every level sought to expand and consolidate their hegemony, and they used every instrument at their disposal. Ritual was hardly a negligible tool, for with unabating regularity it inculcated upon its participant-observers those values of which both God and the state particularly approved: inner devotion to God and to governors, a subdued personal will, and an ordered domestic life in which high morality was both lived out and taught to the next generation. Every ritual we have examined incorporated these messages. While these ideals permeated the liturgy, now in subtle, now in explicit ways, the principal vehicles of these teachings were the carefully scripted hymns, prayers, admonitions, commentaries on the catechism, and sermons. Worship services in their entirety ceased with the Reformation to be the replication of a miracle and became instead a means of shaping the individual faithful.

If the potential for sanctity lay within human beings and not in churches or other places, objects, sacrificial replications, or magical formulae, then it was incumbent upon every Christian to bear religious conviction into the world and to sanctify the mundane. By their theology, ritual decisions, and social discipline, authorities of church and state indicated their determination to evangelize homes and workshops, marketplaces, fields, and the staterooms of politicians. They sincerely wished to reform society. The formal transactions of the sanctuary were an essential means of carrying out this reform.

Whether parish visitors, superintendents, consistories, public officials (including urban magistrates), and princes succeeded in becalming the members of the Body of Christ is another question entirely. I am convinced that they often did not.[2] While I appreciate the position of Maurice Bloch that ritual is a political weapon that intends to subdue the masses for the authorities' ends, I must finally agree with Catherine Bell. In the setting I have studied, at least, rulers failed to attain their goal of popular docility and submission.[3] As Bell points out, participants in ritual not only make their own contributions to ceremony, but they also interpret for their own purposes what has transpired.[4] Congregations may well have misunderstood the thoroughness of the ritual effort to mold them, and they may well have appropriated official ritual and modified it in practice, too. Certainly this was not hard to do in Lutheranism, where enough of the traditional, the Catholic-derived, remained, to make every observance familiar. It was doubtless more difficult in the Reformed setting, where changes were dramatic and unmistakable. In both contexts, however, the visitation protocols are plentiful evidence of an ongoing boisterous self-assertion. While I cannot see into the souls of the range of lesser-educated peoples of town and countryside in order to determine how they inwardly responded to ecclesiastical ritual, what is clear is that all levels of society, from nobles down to servants and day laborers, sustained a lively spectrum of what I shall call pararitual, and resolutely refused to abandon it. I mean by *pararituals* all those ritualized social practices that were sometimes, as in the case of marriage, only tenuously and initially perforce linked to ecclesiastical practice.[5] They took their primary significance from life events rather than theological dictates. The visitors regularly insisted that the forms they took were ungodly and had to stop, or at least had to accept drastic foreshortening. But the people never relinquished them, for they were deeply etched upon their communal life and dramatized their cultural inheritance. Engagement and wedding celebrations, highly prescriptive, are but the best examples, in that they took peripheral cognizance of what in popular eyes were little more than ecclesiastical ritual appendages. But every ritual except those of confession and the Eucharist had their parallel mundane observances: baptismal feasts that sometimes lasted for days, the prenatal and pre-churching rites of the becoming-mother's sodality and the post-churching women's gatherings, the neighborhood collection at the bedside of the dying and the sometimes elaborate wakes. We are probably arrogant to look upon these either as underscorings of official, ecclesiastical rites of passage or as unstructured ebullience, for each one, including its legitimate spontaneity, was in itself a prominent part of communal life and was carefully regulated by societal expectation. The Eucharist itself, which had earlier been a preeminent if indirect source of the potency of many extra-ecclesiastical rituals, was now confined to the sanctuary and the bedsides of the dying. Catholic ritual was embedded in the world of its devotees, but Protestant ritual was less so, or not at all. It attempted to be what ritual in fact cannot become—exclusively a means of making a populace over into an image envisioned by those in positions of power. In order to succeed, it must be rooted, too, in the worldviews of its participants, even if those worldviews may be seen on closer scrutiny, as in the case of churching, not to be identical. Further research into popular responses to the introduction of Calvinism may yield greater insight into the ways in which a ritual agenda not generated by, nor compromising with, the populace can ultimately gain acceptance. The ongoing prohibitions in both Lutheran and Calvinist visitation protocols on removing the Host and baptismal water from the churches suggests that the people widely continued to attribute to both the miraculous qualities of the late medieval Mass.

Ritual change also reveals more definable continuities. The retention, especially in Lutheran lands, of considerable historic Catholic elements is a technical aspect of that continuity. Beyond that we see in the presiding, admonishing, judgmental role played by the pastorate that, while theology had changed, clergymen aspired as much as ever to a special status in the universe. They no longer mediated between humans and God or had it in their capacity to alter anyone's eternal destination. They could not bring the historic Jesus into the presence of their congregations. Nevertheless, the ritual scripts insisted that they acted on earth "in God's stead." As preachers of the Word, they interpreted the divine will to the populace. They were God's mouthpieces in the post-Reformation world, preaching not their own but God's Word. They had lost their sacral potency, but their objective position among men and women rose. This does not mean that their congregations loved or respected them better. It means that, as their level of education improved and as they more often came of urban provenance, greater social distance set them farther apart from the people they led. Throughout the mature sixteenth and early seventeenth centuries, visitors insisted that pastors dress in scholarly attire, stay away from commoners' entertainments, read the Bible and other edifying books, provide a model of father of the household (*Hausvater*), and rigorously discipline straying parishioners. As the chief ritual practitioners, they no longer wrought miracles but they occupied a higher plane in a hierarchical community. They were separate and above. In town pastorates, those prize posts reserved for the brightest and best, they socialized with city councillors, physicians, and lawyers. Theirs was a new social class that a celibate and undereducated priesthood could not readily have constituted. The Protestant clergy formed a nexus between the upper ecclesiastical echelons and the people, and between the secular state and the people, but they did not always meld smoothly with worldly officialdom.

Nevertheless, they shared with local mayors and judges the obligation of disciplining the populace. Whether temperamentally disposed or not, in as well as out of the confessional they had to scrutinize their neighbors' deportment and punish major infractions.[6] The rituals of confession and the Eucharist came to be centerpieces in administering that discipline; as (to a lesser extent) were confirmation, the churching of women, and ministrations to the dying and over the dead. In each of these contexts, a ceremonial punishment meted out to individual transgressors was simultaneously a lesson to the innocent observer and to the bystander whose misdeed was as yet undetected.

COMMUNITY AND RITUAL

There is always the danger that one will interpret ecclesiastical ritual as a binding force within communities, for it took place at a gathering place prominently situated and solidly constructed. It included as onlookers, where not as participants, a sizable representation of all those who lived in proximity to one another. In the late Middle Ages, except for the tendency of all to fulfill their paschal Eucharistic duty at Eastertime, this was not so. Baptism and marriage were family matters, their churchly aspects carried out in a small, private circle. The midwife carried the infant to baptism along with one or several other godparents. The bridal couple with their witnesses appeared at the church door, and a priest summarily blessed their union. Rites for the dying both before and after the Reformation took place in the home, with, to be sure, neighbors and servants present. These constituted a domestic community but hardly one that included the entire local citizenry. Funerals too varied greatly in the numbers who came, with high attendances reserved to the dead of high rank.

The Reformation strove to place most of these rituals in a communal context, and it did this the more concertedly in the German southwest. There, fathers first had to be present at their infants' christenings, and this Christian initiation occurred before the congregation, which was told to pray for the children. By baptism, members of the new generation were engrafted onto the Body of Christ and were also introduced into the Christian polity.

We can detect similar impulses throughout Germany even if they are not as intense beyond the southwest. Visitors insisted that people attend weddings and funerals, and they repeated this order with such vehemence throughout the period under study that it would seem that parishioners were reluctant to comply. The Reformers desired to bring Christians together, but often they could not. Does this indicate a lack of social cohesion? I think that it rather reflects a highly stratified society, one in which people identified with, and lent their support to, those in their own stratum. In the name of godliness, Reformers and magistrates had eliminated many of the corporations, the confraternities, that had brought people together for recreation and mutual aid. They also attacked other settings within which people met their own, such as journeymen's associations. They removed from the calendar the festive observances—the processions, feasts, and plays—that had reinforced the identity of brotherhoods and guilds.

At one level, then, we could interpret ritual change in its sociopolitical context as part of an effort to forge out of disparate elements a communal whole, a unitary corporation that stood entire before God. But at another level we must observe that if this was the authorities' goal, they impeded their progress by adhering to the contradictory principle of hierarchy. The fluid atmosphere inside the late medieval sanctuary, in which people milled about and set up portable seats at the foot of the pulpit or pressed forward to witness transubstantiation, gave way during and after the Reformation to a far more rigorously striated and controlled ritual environment. Informal and flexible ways of looking and listening now gave way to an orderliness that was soon engraved in the ecclesiastical ordinances. To the earlier pews of princes, magistrates, and canons were added others, first for women (*frauenstuhle*) and then for men as well. But one had to be able to afford them. Acrimonious disputes arose everywhere over the positioning, height, and ownership of pews. The well-to-do wanted theirs placed to give them a clear view of the Communion table and the pulpit, and this often made it impossible for the lesser folk who knelt or stood behind them to see at all. This in turn undermined congregational discipline.

By the middle of the sixteenth century, the pew problem was widely solved, at least in urban parishes, by furnishing the entire nave with pews so that all might sit. In many parts of Germany, females sat on the left and males on the right, in their strict echelons according to local formulae that balanced wealth, prestige, marital status, and age. Pews held each individual's body in place, aiming the head (as the center of attention) toward the focal points of Communion table and pulpit. Congregations blended into what seems to us like an undifferentiated mass, perhaps to be equated with community; but in truth they incorporated rigid hierarchical values, which is to say, values that emphasized the differences among people. Congregations did not feel themselves in this setting to be a community, and their quiescent participation in church ritual did not make them such. Thus, they were reluctant to accord ritual honor, as at weddings and funerals, to those outside their group. Perhaps they were more inclined to do so as the authorities actively eroded many of the organizations, such as confraternities and guilds, that had served as the nuclei of identity. People had quite literally to regroup.

In theory, the unison singing of hymns in Lutheran congregations (strictly Psalms in Reformed churches) may have lent a sense of community, at least for the duration of the song.[7] Yet one of the constant visitorial complaints and points of inquiry has to do with parishioners' refusal to sing. Were they merely self-conscious at displaying themselves to those who sat near by? Did they worry that their voices were unattractive? While individuals might have had these feelings, the widespread unwillingness to sing contains a message of resistance to official ritual, with all its disciplinary signals. To sing was to submit to this tool of indoctrination, which adults did not like to do; they avoided catechism classes, for to learn and to recite was the role of a child. Similarly, to sing was to proclaim the values in the lyrics.[8] To sing was to accept the ritual command of an increasingly supervisory, directive, and judgmental clergyman. Not to sing was a way of affirming the integrity of one's unregenerated traditions—which included such activities as dancing, sexual display, and excessive drinking—that were central to the extra-ecclesiastical partner-rituals of baptism, churching, engagement and marriage, and funerals.

The Lord's Supper itself was not only administered within this ranked milieu but it also set apart, usually as a small group, those who communed. In Lutheran congregations, which, as we have seen, kept auricular confession, the few who gained admission to the Lord's Table sat in the choir and remained there until the end of the service. They were singled out and visible to their nonparticipatory acquaintances. In Reformed churches, all partook, for the state of one's soul was between that individual and God. Such heightened emphasis upon the individual also counters communal ideals.

Ecclesiastical rituals neither forged nor cemented congregational communities unless other factors caused people of different stations to cohere. And such factors were likely to be emergencies, like the threat of war or disease.

PEASANT LAUGHTER AND THE REFORM OF RITUAL

Ritual change was not confined to the cities. To be sure, the leading Reformers were invariably linked with towns. But many of these were small—Wittenberg at mid-century had fewer than 3000 inhabitants[9]—and maintained close ties to the rustic enclaves around them. Urban preachers first broadcast reformed perspectives into the countryside.[10] As the new creeds took hold, their leaders and urban magistrates undertook to disseminate more formally the newly favored beliefs into the villages under their dominion. Because of the ongoing process of establishing and maintaining Protestant churches in rural areas, and because so many visitation protocols have survived, these records provide us with a generally underutilized body of material from which to reconstruct peasant society—in conjunction with taxation and other sources. These records are more often qualitative than quantitative in nature, though some visitation records give minute detail on the numbers of souls and the financial worth of heads of households. It is certainly true that visitorial proceedings do not present a complete picture, for they are strongly biased toward elite, urban values, the values of the scribes. Indeed, visitation committees tended to disapprove of the rustic lifestyle and often made disparaging remarks about whole villages. During the Saxon visitation of 1529, in which Philipp Melanchthon played a prominent part, the scribe commented,

> And in both these parishes, namely Holtzendorf and Dubro, there is a very bad, mischievous [*mutwillig*] people who will not take advice except with the help of executioner and caning-master, or by driving them out of the land and planting other pious people in their stead.[11]

Nevertheless, the historian who has accumulated information from a multitude of sources can cautiously extract from these summaries valuable descriptions of peasant culture. At the same time, these descriptions are seriously flawed, by their failure to differentiate among the levels and types of peasants. The visitors essentially regarded rich and poor, farmers, cotters, and day laborers as one and the same.

The German peasantry, however variegated, resisted disciplining more effectively than any other group. To thoroughly citified folk, it appeared in the sixteenth century (as it continues to appear in non-anthropological circles today) as if peasants knew no moral boundaries but lived purely to indulge themselves in physical ways, by eating and drinking excessively and having opportunistic sex. They were raw and unmannered.[12] The great Russian literary scholar Mikhail Bakhtin in his way has reinforced this point of view through his presentation of the late medieval French peasants' "culture of laughter."[13] For Bakhtin, who intended to glorify the peasantry, the workers of the soil were Carnivalesque in a laudatory sense. They generated social parody, reducing the high and the mighty to their own lowly level, which is to say that in undoing hierarchy they generated democracy. They were irrepressibly scatological. These, to the Russian scholar, were the true revolutionaries, the advocates of change, a wellspring of bold creativity. Those who opposed them were the bearers of Lenten austerity, the upholders of privilege and the status quo. In seeking to suppress Carnival, they acted strictly in their own interest.

Robert Scribner has analyzed the meanings of Carnival as a particular season with characteristic types of play in early modern Germany, including a critical treatment of the applicability of Bakhtin's concept.[14] Among German scholars, Norbert Schindler is the most favorably inclined toward Bakhtin's peasant "culture of laughter," while literary scholars are generally skeptical.[15] I want to address not Carnival itself—which the Reformation quickly did away with—but the broader assertion that peasant culture year-round was one of laughter, writ large to include mockery and bitter derogation. Bakhtin, in any case, was willing to include what Gábor Klaniczay has termed "carnival-type folk festivities."[16] A considerable flaw in Bakhtin's perspective, one perhaps natural to a person writing in the Russian environment of the 1920s and 1930s, is that he divides the world into two camps: the spontaneous, ebullient peasantry and the dour, oppression-bent wielders of power. Carnival itself achieved its greatest creative flowering in the urban setting, where its enthusiastic participants included men (and some women) of several classes, if not of the entire social spectrum. It was not a peasant phenomenon, and within Germany it needs to be studied within the urban matrix, as Scribner has done. More serious, however, is the "two-tiered model of culture," as Lee Palmer Wandel has called it.[17] This obliterates the gradations, the overlapping, the multiple hues and nuances that in fact made up early modern society. This was true of interpersonal relations within the town, between town and country dwellers, and also among the peasants themselves. Parish visitors were guilty of the same oversimplification.

Having declared these misgivings, I nonetheless want to discuss the kinds of popular rituals, whether of city or hamlet, to which authorities of church and state objected so violently. These included every convivial gathering not presided over by a representative of the state, from silver miners' July breakfasts to women's post-parturition ales. In town and country they strove to eliminate spinning bees and engagement dances, the ritual drunkenness of wedding festivities and sexual license. From our perspective, they failed to understand the profound underlying meaning, indeed the relational necessity of each of these seemingly exuberant, indulgent activities. Engagement drinking sealed contracts between families, and demonstrated generosity and trust. Wedding parties and dances celebrated sexuality and the continuance of family bloodlines. The postponement of baptism allowed relatives from other regions to come and express their common identity as a family, and in the subsequent eating and drinking together to mark the continuity of kinship. The post-churching cake or meal thanked the women of the birthing chamber and brought an end to the feminine reproductive circle. Funerary meals resealed in a new configuration bonds cut open by death. These were hardly "laughing" matters. They stressed stability, not revolution. The leaders who condemned these and attempted to end or curtail them were the proponents of change. They obviously had no possibility of taking an anthropological view of the celebrations of the common person. Parish visitors perceived only an absence of restraint among the people, which produced unchristian excesses. They found the common people around them to be too ready to vent emotion in violent, drunken, and sexual acts. In short, they found what I have called pararituals, along with nearly all the ritualized popular observances not connected to ecclesiastical rites, to be impediments to the achievement of a godly order grounded in the sacred Writ. Some might see in these festivities a Carnivalesque turning of the world upside down, but such a label does not seem apt inasmuch as they were not designed to overturn or even to be the mirror reversal of an established order. For, in truth, the kind of order that the heads of church and state sought had never been established. The structures of peasant society were as yet the prevailing order: derived from another kind of organization of immemorial standing, designed in their symbolism as in their attainments to support kinship, reproductive, and agrarian values from which urban dwellers— that is, their ancestors—had originally departed for their economic betterment. If we could adopt the perspective of peasant communities whose recreation and morality visitation committees and consistories attempted to alter, we might think of the structures being imposed as "antistructures." Inevitably, however, the side with enforcing power is made the standard by which all else is judged, the venerability of "all else" notwithstanding, and my use of "pararitual" bespeaks this same reality. One could hardly think of the Mass, whether Catholic or Lutheran, as a rite existing "at the side" of, let us say, incantations by country healers, but such folk ritual prevailed long before the acceptance of the Mass among the populace.[18] The authorities, urban or urbanized men, regarded themselves as God's instruments in rectifying the disorder that Catholicism had tolerated. Yet, because many of the popular traditions, however gratifying to the bodily senses, were also rooted in socioeconomic necessity, the people would not give them up. They resisted furiously, and often successfully. When Protestant leaders outlawed St. John's Day festivities, the people transferred their customs to Pentecost; they practiced ritual substitution. In regions close to Catholic lands, nominal Protestants went to dances, weddings, and church fairs across the border. They continued to consult cunningwomen and -men, healers and fortune tellers of every passing description. They were inventive, they were resolute. Their admitted laughter contained great seriousness—even cosmic depth.

All the same, they made their concessions to officialdom. They had no choice, and they may have found some of the new ways attractive. They made their confessions, they allowed their children to be confirmed, they received the Eucharist occasionally and, as I have opined above, often still considered its elements to have supernatural power. Despite intense indoctrination, they doubtless interpreted these events in ways that differed from those of the clergy and other highly educated residents. Much work on the processes of internalization remains to be done. In the meantime, I agree with Eva Labouvie when she writes that the populace

> chose from the religious spectrum offered to them by the confessions primarily those elements that exhibited a concrete reference to everyday experience and to coping with life, and favored forms of belief and piety that took worldly and material aspects into account or that could be related to profane enjoyment of the fruits of their labor [*Nutznießung*].[19]

Ritual changes contain the signs of theological and social shifts. They must not, in the end, be dismissed as efforts by elites of church and state solely to grow in power at the masses' expense. The religious Reformations of the sixteenth century, and the generations that most immediately felt their weight, were also characterized by utopian fervor. Their pessimistic, neomonastic strands notwithstanding, taken together they constitute one of the most concerted efforts in Western history to make human beings the very best that they could be. In the ways Reformers behaved, we see their confidence that earthly society could be transformed. They used ritual as one among several means of elevating humankind. Their differences with humanism were not as great as is sometimes claimed: the ones relied on the Word of God, earthly discipline, and *bonae litterae*; the others on *bonae litterae*, the Word of God, and earthly discipline. Reformers and humanists disagreed only on the order of priority among these elements. These fellow nestlings met their disillusionment in the wars of words and weapons that rent their age. In attempting to apply sacral principles to all aspects of creaturely existence, they ran the risk of rendering the sacred so diffuse that it could easily dissipate in the emerging capitalist and rationalist atmosphere.

Notes

Abbreviations used (full titles are given when first mentioned in each chapter)

BLHAPot
Brandenburgisches Landeshauptarchiv Potsdam
B-WHSAS
Baden-Württembergisches Hauptstaatsarchiv Stuttgart
ELKAS
Evangelisches Landeskirchliches Archiv Stuttgart
HSADres
Sächsisches Hauptstaatsarchiv Dresden
HSAWei
Thüringisches Hauptstaatsarchiv Weimar
HSAWies
Hessisches Hauptstaatsarchiv Wiesbaden
KOO
Die evangelischen Kirchenordnungen des 16. Jahrhunderts
LHAMag
Sachsen-Anhalt Landeshauptarchiv Magdeburg
ELKABr
Evangelisches Landeskirchlichesarchiv Braunschweig
NSLHAW
Niedersächsisches Landeshauptarchiv Wolfenbüttel
WA
Dr. Martin Luthers Werke (Weimar: Böhlau, 1883–)

INTRODUCTION

1 One thinks of such influential and/or recent works as Natalie Zemon Davis, "The Rites of Violence," in idem, *Society and Culture in Early Modern France* (Stanford, Calif.: Stanford University Press, 1975), 152–88, originally published in *Past and Present* 59 (1973); Jacques Le Goff, "The Symbolic Ritual of Vassalage," in idem, *Time, Work, and Culture in the Middle Ages*, trans. Arthur Goldhammer (Chicago: University of Chicago Press, 1980),

237–87; M. E. James, "Ritual, Drama and Social Body in the Late Mediaeval English Town," *Past and Present* 98 (1983), 3–29; Charles Phythian-Adams, "Ceremony and the Citizen: The Communal Year at Coventry, 1450–1550," in Peter Clark, ed., *The Early Modern Town: A Reader* (New York: Longman, 1976), 106–28; Janos M. Bak, ed., *Coronations: Medieval and Early Modern Monarchic Ritual* (Berkeley, Calif.: University of California Press, 1990); Sara Hanley, *The lit de justice of the Kings of France: Constitutional Ideology in Legend, Ritual, and Discourse* (Princeton, N.J.: Princeton University Press, 1983), esp. chap. 2, 48–85; Edward Muir, *Civic Ritual in Renaissance Venice* (Princeton, N.J.: Princeton University Press, 1981); R. W. Scribner, "Ritual and Popular Religion in Catholic Germany at the Time of the Reformation," in idem, *Popular Culture and Popular Movements*, 104–22; Nicole Belmont, "The Symbolic Function of the Wedding Procession in the Popular Rituals of Marriage," trans. Elborg Forster, in Robert Forster and Orest Ranum, eds., *Ritual, Religion, and the Sacred: Selections from the Annales: Economies, Sociétés, Civilisations* (Baltimore: Johns Hopkins University Press, 1982), 1–7; André Burguière, "The Marriage Ritual in France: Ecclesiastical Practices and Popular Practices (Sixteenth to Eighteenth Centuries)," trans. Elborg Forster, in *Ritual, Religion, and the Sacred*, 8–23; Christiane Klapisch-Zuber, "Zacharias; Or the Ousting of the Father: The Rites of Marriage in Tuscany from Giotto to the Council of Trent," trans. Elborg Forster, in *Ritual, Religion, and the Sacred*, 24–56.

I greatly look forward to Edward Muir's forthcoming book, *Ritual in Early Modern Europe*, which will look across Europe and include secular as well as religious ritual. I am beholden to him for allowing me to read drafts of the two chaps. related to the Reformation.

2 For worthy shorter treatments, see Norbert Schindler, " 'Heiratsmüdigkeit' und Ehezwang: Zur populären Rügesitte des Pflug- und Blochziehens," in idem, *Widerspenstige Leute: Studien zur Volkskultur in der frühen Neuzeit* (Frankfurt/Main: Fischer, 1992), 175–214; Eva Labouvie, "Wider Wahrsagerei, Segnerei und Zauberei: Kirchliche Versuche zur Ausgrenzung von Aberglaube und Volksmagie seit dem 16. Jahrhundert," in Richard van Dülmen, ed., *Verbrechen, Strafen und soziale Kontrolle: Studien zur historischen Kulturforschung* (Frankfurt/Main: Fischer, 1990), 15–55; Robert Scribner, an Australian historian working in the United States, has been *the* pathbreaker in the area of German ritual. See especially his essays in *Popular Culture and Popular Movements*: "Ritual and Popular Religion in Catholic Germany at the Time of the Reformation," 17–47, which discusses, among others, the relationship between official liturgical and folk ritual; "Ritual and Reformation," 103–22; and "Reformation, Carnival and the World Turned Upside-Down," 71–101, which is about Carnival, but which in its rich theoretical dimensions has implications for other ritual.

3 Roger Chickering, *Karl Lamprecht: A German Academic Life (1856–1915)* (Atlantic Highlands, N.J.: Humanities Press, 1993); Luise Schorn-Schütte, *Karl Lamprecht: Kulturgeschichtsschreibung zwischen Wissenschaft und Politik* (Gütersloh: Gerd Mohn, 1984).

4 See Peter Burke's essay, "Theorists and Historians," in idem, *History and Social Theory* (Ithaca: Cornell University Press, 1992), 1–21.

5 Appleby, Hunt, and Jacob, *Telling the Truth About History* (New York: W. W. Norton, 1995), 248–50, here at 250.

6 Robert Finlay, "The Refashioning of Martin Guerre," *American Historical Review* 93, 3 (June 1988), 553–71, here at 571.

7 Natalie Zemon Davis, " 'On the Lame'," *American Historical Review* 93, 3 (June 1988), 572–603, here at 573.

8 Bourdieu, *Outline of a Theory of Practice*, trans. Richard Nice (Cambridge, England: Cambridge University Press, 1977), 114–15.

9 Van Gennep, *The Rites of Passage*, trans. Monika B. Vizedom and Gabrielle L. Caffee (Chicago: University of Chicago Press, 1960; French original, 1908).

10 Turner, *The Ritual Process: Structure and Anti-Structure* (Ithaca: Cornell University Press, 1969), 127.

11 For example, "Social Dramas and Ritual Metaphors," in idem, *Dramas, Fields, and Metaphors: Symbolic Action in Human Society* (Ithaca: Cornell University Press, 1974), 23–59.

12 "Religion as a Cultural System," in idem, *The Interpretation of Cultures: Selected Essays* (New York: Basic Books, 1973), 87–125.

13 "Thick Description: Toward an Interpretive Theory of Culture," in idem, *The Interpretation of Cultures*, 3–32.

14 "Ritual and Social Change: A Javanese Example," in idem, *The Interpretation of Cultures*, 142–69.

15 Bloch, "The Ritual of the Royal Bath in Madagascar," in David Cannadine and Simon Price, eds., *Rituals of Royalty: Power and Ceremonial in Traditional Societies* (Cambridge, England: Cambridge University Press, 1987), 271–97.

16 Fernandez, "Symbolic Consensus in a Fang Reformative Cult," *American Anthropologist* 67 (1965), 902–29.

17 Especially chap. 9, "The Power of Ritualization," in her *Ritual Theory, Ritual Practice* (New York and Oxford: Oxford University Press, 1992), 197–223. I also found helpful Ronald L. Grimes, *Beginnings in Ritual Studies* (Lanham, Md.: University Press of America, 1982).

18 See Natalie Zemon Davis's essay, "Toward Mixtures and Margins," *American Historical Review* 97, 5 (December 1992), 1400–09. Cf. Peter Burke, "Hegemony and Resistance," in idem, *History and Social Theory* (Ithaca: Cornell University Press, 1992), 84–88, in which he expresses misgivings about "simple" social divisions and raises several salutary questions about hegemony; Gábor Klaniczay, *The Uses of Supernatural Power* (Princeton, N.J.: Princeton University Press, 1990), 2–4, 46–47; Lee Palmer Wandel, *Voracious Idols and Violent Hands: Iconoclasm in Reformation Zurich, Strasbourg, and Basel* (Cambridge, England: Cambridge University Press, 1995), 1–8; Richard van Dülmen, "Volksfrömmigkeit und konfessionelles Christentum im 16. und 17. Jahrhundert," in Wolfgang Schieder, ed., *Volksreligiosität in der modernen Sozialgeschichte* (Göttingen: Vandenhoeck & Ruprecht, 1986), 14–30; and Schieder's own introduction, 7–13. Robert Whiting takes up relevant matters in England in *The Blind Devotion of the People: Popular Religion and the English Reformation*, Cambridge Studies in Early Modern British History (Cambridge, England: Cambridge University Press, 1989).

19 Ernst Walter Zeeden probably launched the idea of confessionalization in modern scholarship, except that he generally meant by it the process simply of delineating separate confessional identities. Nonetheless, his work has been seminal: *Die Entstehung der Konfessionen: Grundlagen und Formen der Konfessionsbildung im Zeitalter der Glaubenskämpfe* (Munich: Oldenbourg, 1965); *Konfessionsbildung: Studien zur Reformation, Gegenreformation und katholischen Reform* (Stuttgart: Klett-Cotta, 1985). The subsequent shapers of the term are, among others, Heinz Schilling, *Konfessionskonflikt und Staatsbildung: Eine Fallstudie über das Verhältnis von religiösem und sozialem Wandel in der Frühneuzeit am Beispiel der Grafschaft Lippe* (Gütersloh: Gerd Mohn, 1981), which is summarized, updated, and translated in his *Religion, Political Culture, and the Emergence of Early Modern Society: Essays in German and Dutch History* (Leiden: Brill, 1992); Wolfgang Reinhard,

"Gegenreformation als Modernisierung? Prolegomena zu einer Theorie des konfessionellen Zeitalters," *Archive for Reformation History* 68 (1977), 226–52; "Konfession und Konfessionalisierung in Deutschland," in idem, ed., *Bekenntnis und Geschichte: Schriften der Philosophischen Fakultäten der Universität Augsburg* (Munich: Vogel, 1981), 165–89; Wolfgang Reinhard, "Zwang zur Konfessionalisierung? Prologomena zu einer Theorie des konfessionellen Zeitalters," *Zeitschrift für historische Forschung* 10 (1983), 157–77. Some of Schilling's ideas concerning the special amenability of Calvinist regimes to confessionalization have been evaluated in Schilling, ed., *Die reformierte Konfessionalisierung in Deutschland—Das Problem der "2. Reformation"* (Gütersloh: Gerd Mohn, 1986).

The pioneer in developing the notion of social disciplining is Gerhard Oestreich, whose essays were published as *Geist und Gestalt des frühmodernen Staates* (Berlin: Duncker & Humblot, 1969), a somewhat modified version of which was translated posthumously as *Neostoicism and the Early Modern State*, ed. Brigitte Oestreich and Helmut G. Koenigsberger, trans. David McLintock (Cambridge, England: Cambridge University Press, 1982). See Winfried Schulze, "Gerhard Oestreichs Begriff 'Sozialdisziplinierung' in der frühen Neuzeit," *Zeitschrift für historische Forschung* 14 (1987), 265–302.

R. Po-chia Hsia has provided a useful compendium of the literature in *Social Discipline in the Reformation: Central Europe 1550–1750* (London and New York: Routledge, 1989). See also Heinrich Richard Schmidt, *Konfessionalisierung im 16. Jahrhundert* (Munich: Oldenbourg, 1992); Hans-Christoph Rublack, ed., *Die lutherische Konfessionalisierung*, Schriften des Vereins für Reformationsgeschichter 197 (Gütersloh: Gerd Mohn, 1992); and Harm Klueting, *Das konfessionelle Zeitalter 1525–1648* (Stuttgart: Eugen Ulmer, 1989), esp. 14–18, 108–12. The most recent overview is Ralf Georg Bogner, "Arbeiten zur Sozialdisziplinierung in der Frühen Neuzeit: Ein Forschungsbericht für die Jahre 1980–94, Erster Teil," *Frühneuzeit-Info* 7, 1 (1996), 127–42, with a second installment promised.

1 ENGAGEMENT AND MARRIAGE CEREMONIES: TAMING THE BEAST WITHIN

1 There is disagreement among French scholars as to whether pairing in France was at the whim of parents or whether young people could follow their inclinations. The former position is taken by Louis Roussel, *Le mariage dans la société française* (Paris: PUF, Cahiers de l'INED, 1975), 26; and the latter by Jean-Louis Flandrin, *Les amours paysannes* (Paris: Gallimard-Julliard, 1975), 243. Jeffrey R. Watt tidily summarizes scholarly debate on the selection of mates and emotion within familial ties in *The Making of Modern Marriage: Matrimonial Control and the Rise of Sentiment in Neuchâtel, 1550–1800* (Ithaca, New York: Cornell University Press, 1992), 1–23. Only a small part of the discussion to date has focused on Germany, especially (though for a later period) David Warren Sabean, *Property, Production, and Family in Neckarhausen, 1700–1870*, Cambridge Studies in Social and Cultural Anthropology 73 (Cambridge, England: Cambridge University Press, 1990), 36–37. The most recent work on the subject is Joel F. Harrington, *Reordering Marriage and Society in Reformation Germany* (Cambridge, England, and New York: Cambridge University Press, 1995).

For a survey of medieval marriage from an anthropologist's point of view, I recommend Jack Goody, *The Development of the Family and Marriage in Europe* (Cambridge, England: Cambridge University Press, 1983). Useful books that deal with medieval theology of marriage and with some examples of elite practice are Georges Duby, *Medieval Marriage, Two Models from Twelfth-century France* (Baltimore: Johns Hopkins University Press, 1978) and Christopher N. L. Brooke, *The Medieval Idea of Marriage* (Oxford: Oxford University Press, 1989).

2 *Here I Stand: A Life of Martin Luther* (New York, 1950), 298. Representative of this position are also Olavi Lähteenmäki, *Sexus und Ehe bei Luther,* Schriften der Luther-Agricola-Gesellschaft 10 (Turku, Finland, 1955); William H. Lazareth, *Luther on the Christian Home: An Application of the Social Ethics of the Reformation* (Philadelphia: Muhlenberg Press, 1960); and Ewald M. Plass, ed. and comp., *What Luther Says: An Anthology,* vol. 3 (St. Louis, 1959), 1456. Certain recent works continue in this confessional strain, notably Steven Ozment, *When Fathers Ruled: Family Life in Reformation Europe* (Cambridge, Mass.: Harvard University Press, 1983). Cf. Robert C. Gregg, "Die Ehe: Patristische und reformatorische Fragen," *Zeitschrift für Kirchengeschichte* 96 (1985), 1–12, in which the author finds marked parallels between the thought of Jovinian and Luther but concludes that the latter came to his ideas independently.

3 Ludwig Schmugge shows this clearly in *Kirche, Kinder, Karrieren: Päpstliche Dispense von der unehelichen Geburt im Spätmittelalter* (Zurich: Artemis & Winkler, 1995), pertinent to this work above all chap. 6, "Kirche und Illegitime im Deutschen Reich," 247–318.

4 On the obligation of every female to marry, even if she could remain a virgin and be much purer than every angel in heaven, Luther's sermon, "Am tag Johannis des heiligen Apostels und Euangelistens Euangelion Johannis xxi," *Dr. Martin Luthers Werke* (Weimar: Böhlau, 1883–   ), Weimarer Ausgabe (WA) 17/2: 347.

Luther wrote a great deal on the subjects of women and marriage. The main pertinent parts of his opus are "Ein sermon von dem ehelichen stand. 1519," WA 2: 166–71, in which (168) he still considers marriage a sacrament; "Themata de Votis. 1521," WA 8: 323–35; "De votis monasticis Martini Lutheri iudicium. 1521," WA 8: 573–669; "Welche Personen verboten sind zu ehelichen. 1522," WA 10/2: 263–66; "Vom ehelichen Leben. 1522," WA 10/2: 275–304; "An die Herren deutschs Ordens, daß sie falsche Keuschheit meiden und zur rechten ehelichen Keuschheit greifen, Ermahnung. 1523," WA 12: 232–44; "Das siebente Kapitel S. Pauli zu den Corinthern. 1523," WA 12: 92–142; a portion of "Predigten über das erste Buch Mose gehalten 1523 und 1524," WA 14: esp. 111–58; "Eine Geschichte, wie Gott einer Klosterjungfrau ausgeholfen hat. Mit einem Sendbrief M. Luthers. 1524," WA 15: 89–94; "Daß Eltern die Kinder zur Ehe nicht zwingen noch hindern, und die Kinder ohne der Eltern Willen, sich nicht verloben sollen. 1524," WA 15: 163–69; parts of "Auslegung der zehn Gebote. 1528," WA 16: esp. 500–12; "Euangelion am Sontage Sexagesime," 17/2: esp. 157–59; "Ein ander Sermon Doctor Martin Luthers, an dem andern Sontage nach der erscheinung Christi, Von dem ehelichen Stande," WA 21: 66–74; the parts on the first two chaps. of Genesis in "In Genesin Mosi librum sanctissimum Declamationes. 1527," WA 24: 24–103 passim; "Ein traubüchlein für die einfältigen Pfarrherr. 1529," WA 30/3: 74–80; "Von Ehesachen. 1530," WA 30/3: 205–48; "Ein Hochzeit predigt über den spruch zun [sic] Hebreern am dreizehenden Capitel," Jan. 8 (?[sic]), 1531, WA: 34/2: 50–75; parts of "In Primum Librum Mose Enarrationes," 1544,

WA 42: esp. 51–53, 87–163; "Predigt bei der Hochzeit Sigmunds von Lindenau in Merseburg gehalten," August 4, 1545, WA 49: 797–805; "Ein Trost den Weibern, welchen es ungerade gegangen ist mit Kindergebären. 1542," WA 53: 205–208; "Vorrede zu Joh. Freder, Dialogus dem Ehestand zu Ehren. 1545," WA 54: 171–75; "Grund und Ursach, daß Klosterleben unchristlich sei. 1528/31," WA 59: 100–103; plus numerous brief excerpts from other sermons and from the *Tischreden* and *Briefwechsel.*

5 Merry E. Wiesner, "Luther and Women: The Death of Two Marys," in Jim Obelkevich, Raphael Samuel, and Lyndal Roper, eds., *Disciplines of Faith: Studies in Religion, Politics, and Patriarchy* (London and New York: Routledge & Kegan Paul, 1987), 295–308; reprinted in Ann Loades, ed., *Feminist Theology: A Reader* (London: SPCK, 1990), 123–37; Thomas Fischer Miller, "Mirror for Marriage: Lutheran Views of Marriage and the Family, 1520–1600," unpublished Ph.D. dissertation, University of Virginia, 1981, in which (9) Miller remarks, "More than his coreligionists, writing sometimes only a few years later, Luther was truly on the leading edge of a change in the conception of marriage . . ." Sigrid Brauner's "Martin Luther on Witchcraft: A True Reformer?," in Jean R. Brink, Allison P. Coudert, and Maryanne C. Horowitz, eds., *The Politics of Gender in Early Modern Europe,* Sixteenth Century Essays & Studies 12 (Kirksville, Mo.: Sixteenth Century Journal Publishers, 1989), 29–42, places Luther's witchcraft views, as the Reformer himself did, in a context of opinion about the weakness and vulnerability of women.

6 In her book on late medieval French preaching, Larissa Taylor has shown how varied, and often positive toward women and marriage, sermons were (*Soldiers of Christ: Preaching in Late Medieval and Reformation France* [New York: Oxford University Press, 1992]). Her chapter, "The Preachers and Women," 156–78, surveys the wide variety of opinion without concealing the clergy's somewhat more negative estimation of the nature of women. The sermons were, however, mainly given to lay rather than celibate audiences. Taylor acknowledges that "attitudes hardened during the sixteenth century" (175).

7 Respectively: Merry E. Wiesner, *Working Women in Renaissance Germany* (New Brunswick, N.J.: Rutgers University Press, 1986); idem, "Frail, Weak, and Helpless: Women's Legal Position in Theory and Reality," in Jerome Friedman, ed., *Regnum, Religio et Ratio: Essays Presented to Robert M. Kingdon,* Sixteenth Century Essays & Studies 8 (Kirksville, Mo.: Sixteenth Century Journal Publishers, 1987), 161–69; Lyndal Roper, *The Holy Household: Women and Morals in Reformation Augsburg* (Oxford: Clarendon Press, 1989), esp. 132–205. Heide Wunder, however, is of the opinion that Reformation or no Reformation, the position of women did not appreciably deteriorate in the sixteenth and seventeenth centuries: '*Er ist die Sonn', sie ist der Mond: Frauen in der frühen Neuzeit* (Munich: C. H. Beck, 1992). She is, in my opinion, correct that the religious Reform did not, at any rate, *cause* a worsening of women's status; it would seem that, for a complex of reasons, an attitude shift was underway, and that the Reformation both participates in and reflects this.

8 Wiesner, "Luther and Women: The Death of Two Marys," in Jim Obelkevich, Lyndal Roper, and Raphael Samuel, eds., *Disciplines of Faith* (London and New York: Routledge & Kegan Paul, 1987), 295–308.

9 Norbert Schindler draws the dichotomy between untamed nature (*Wildheit*) and civilization, but confines his discussion to Carnival (*Widerspenstige Leute: Studien zur Volkskultur in der frühen Neuzeit* [Frankfurt/Main: Fischer, 1992], 133–34).

10 I am not invariably Freudian, but the concepts of repression and projection have, in my view, firmly entrenched themselves in our vocabulary; we are inevitably post-Freudians!

11 "Holy household" is obviously Lyndal Roper's designation of the post-Reformation domestic ideal: *The Holy Household: Women and Morals in Reformation Augsburg* (Oxford, England: Clarendon Press, 1989).

12 Luther used this phrase in "Ein Sermon von dem ehelichen stand. 1519," WA 2: 168–69.

13 Alison Futrell has pointed out that some early Christian writers saw sexual desire (rather than pride) as the cause of the Fall, not a consequence of it. "The Construction of Mary Magdalene as a Prostitute," paper presented August 7, 1995, at the Pacific Coast Branch meetings of the American Historical Association, Maui, Hawaii. According to this view, Adam accepted the apple from Eve because of what Futrell terms "fatal uxoriousness," which possessed erotic elements. On the notion of the Fall as caused by Eve's sexual allure, see H. Diane Russell, *Eve/Ave: Women in Renaissance and Baroque Prints* (Washington, D.C.: National Gallery of Art and New York: Feminist Press at the City University of New York, 1980); Larry Silver, "Jan Gossaert and the Renaissance Nude in the Netherlands," *Nederlands Kunsthistorisch Jaarboek* 37 (1986), 1–40, esp. 3–6; and Bridget Heal, "Adam, Eve and the Fall of Man: A Study of Sixteenth-Century Northern European Paintings," unpublished B.A. thesis, University of Cambridge, 1995.

14 Luther thought that fewer than one in 100,000 people could remain unmarried and be chaste: "Das siebente Kapitel S. Pauli zu den Corinthern. 1523," WA 12: 115.

15 Cf. Augustine of Hippo, "On the Good of Marriage," in Philip Schaff, ed., *St. Augustine: On the Holy Trinity, Doctrinal Treatises, Moral Treatises*, A Select Library of the Nicene and Post-Nicene Fathers of the Christian Church 3 (Grand Rapids, Michigan, 1956), 402. Luther's concept of marriage as *remedium ad peccatum* was, thus, not original, but somewhat more forgiving than Augustine's.

16 By way of comparison, see, for instance, the excerpt from Albrecht von Eyb's 1472 *Ehebüchlein* in Michael Dallapiazza, comp., *Wie ein Mann ein fromm Weib soll machen: Mittelalterliche Lehren über Ehe und Haushalt* (Frankfurt/Main: Insel Verlag, 1984), 80–93. Pertinent, in this same collection, is article 177 from Berthold von Freiburg's *Summa confessorum*, dating from the late thirteenth century (*Wie ein Mann*, 43–46); Luther would have agreed in general with the humane and realistic principles enunciated there.

17 For example, "Vom ehelichen Leben. 1522," WA 10/2: 303.

18 "Ein Sermon von dem ehelichen Stand. 1519," WA 2: 168–69.

19 Nor ought the woman to be on top during the sex act, for this symbolized the overturning of the proper social order in which the woman was "under" the man.

20 Esther Cohen and Elliott Horowitz, "In Search of the Sacred: Jews, Christians, and Rituals of Marriage in the Later Middle Ages," *Journal of Medieval and Renaissance Studies* 20, 2 (1990), 225–49.

21 Johannes C. Stracke, "Verlobung und Trauung—Gebräuche und Ordnungen," *Jahrbuch der Gesellschaft für bildende Kunst und vaterländische Altertümer zu Emden* 58 (1978), 7. In and around Emden, Adam and Eve were "almost always" shown; normally in entering the church, the women used the north door and the men the south. See p. 76 on women entering the north door, associated with the Devil, to be churched, and also

people's preference to be buried on the south side of the church: Friedberg, *Ehe und Eheschliessung im deutschen Mittelalter* (Berlin, 1864), 35. Dieckhoff, *Die kirchliche Trauung* (Rostock, 1878), 69–71.

22 George Elliott Howard, *A History of Matrimonial Institutions* (New York: Humanities Press, 1964), especially chap. 8, "Rise of Ecclesiastical Marriage: The Church Develops and Administers Matrimonial Law," 321–63, summarizes the legal aspects. His bibliography, 364–70, lists the classic works on German marriage law, such as Richter, *Lehrbuch*, 8th ed. (Leipzig, 1886); Adolf Scheurl, *Das gemeine deutsche Eherecht* (Erlangen, 1882) and idem, *Die Entwicklung des kirchlichen Eheschliessungsrechts* (Erlangen, 1877); Hofmann, *Handbuch des teutschen Eherechts* (Jena, 1789); Loy, *Das protestantische Eherecht* (Nuremberg and Altdorf, 1793); Hans Schubert, *Die evangelische Trauung* (Berlin, 1890); Dieckhoff, *Die kirchliche Trauung*; Rudolph Sohm, *Trauung und Verlobung* (Weimar, 1876).

Adolph Franz has pointed out that in the non-German lands, couples were typically brought inside the church before the end of the Middle Ages. It became customary in these places for bride and groom to receive consecrated bread and wine during the wedding ceremony. However, in Germany the pair received the so-called St. John's wine after their nuptials as a token of love, a custom Franz says that is still often observed. *Die kirchlichen Benediktionen im Mittelalter*, 2 vols. (Graz: Akademische Druck- und Verlagsanstalt, 1960, reprint of Freiburg/Breisgau: Herder, 1909), 1: 281–84.

23 I have found more variability than Arthur E. Imhof does in *Die verlorenen Welten: Alltagsbewältigung durch unsere Vorfahren—und weshalb wir uns heute so schwer damit tun* (Munich: C. H. Beck, 1984), 21; 156, fig. 24. However, Imhof's tabulated data are drawn from a later period.

24 Gerold Tietz has gained the same impression: "Verlobung, Trauung und Hochzeit in den evangelischen Kirchenordnungen des 16. Jahrhunderts," Ph.D. dissertation, Eberhard-Karls-Universität-Tübingen, 1969, 80–83.

25 Adolph Franz, ed., *Das Rituale des Bischofs Heinrich I. von Breslau* (Freiburg/Breisgau: Herder, 1912), 21–23, here at 21. Although the text refers to only one ring, two rings were widely in use in Germany in the early sixteenth century.

26 *The New English Bible with the Apocrypha* (Oxford and Cambridge, England: Oxford University Press and Cambridge University Press, 1970), used throughout this work, includes in parentheses a phrase omitted in the Breslau manual. I have omitted it.

27 Franz, *Das Rituale*, 23.

28 Lutheran orders of matrimony always refer to two rings, but they also occasionally allude to the possibility that a couple will not have been able to afford them. Spangenberg mentions rings (in the plural) as part of an old tradition. In short, I do not think that Protestantism introduced the use of two wedding rings.

29 In pre-Reformation Germany, couples who could not get along lived separately even though still married. Society accepted this form of separation. Scholarship has generally focused on divorce per se, yet the populace had remedies of its own. Lutheran authorities may have begun to allow divorce marginally more often than their predecessors, but among the people they sought to root out separation. Under Protestantism, then, effective divorce was much less available than before. In Württemberg in 1586, for instance, the parish visitors of a rural village found that a 70-year-old woman was living with her daughter and apart from her husband. The daughter supported her mother. Both women were imprisoned. Not even

the pastor and the local magistrates thought the aged woman should be compelled to cohabit with her husband, but the visitors insisted, "weyl man einen [*sic*] ie absonderung nit gestatten khunde" (Evangelisches Landeskirchliches Archiv Stuttgart [ELKAS], A1 Nr. 1 1586, vol. 1, fol. 66). On formal divorce, see Thomas Max Safley, *Let No Man Put Asunder* (Kirksville, Mo.: Sixteenth Century Journal Publishers, 1984); Robert M. Kingdom, *Adultery and Divorce in Calvin's Geneva* (Cambridge, Mass.: Harvard University Press, 1995).

30 Franz, *Das Rituale*, 23.

31 Franz, *Die kirchlichen Benediktionen*, 2: 177–84.

32 Eberhard Winkler agrees that Luther did not mean to make marriage simply profane, but he takes this position evidently under confessional inspiration: " 'Weltlich Ding' oder 'Göttlicher Stand'? Die Ehe als Bewährungsfeld evangelischer Frömmigkeit," *Luther* 3 (1991), 126–40. On changes in the legal status of marriage, see Joel F. Harrington, "Reformation, Statebuilding and the 'Secularization' of Marriage: Jurisdiction in the Palatinate, 1450–1619," *Fides et Historia* 22, 3 (Fall 1990), 53–63, and idem *Reordering Marriage and Society in Reformation Germany* (Cambridge, England: Cambridge University Press, 1995).

33 WA dates it to 1529: "Ein Traubüchlein für die einfältigen Pfarrherr. 1529," 30/3: 74–80.

34 Also reprinted in Emil Sehling, ed., *Die evangelischen Kirchenordnungen des 16. Jahrhunderts* (KOO), 15 vols. to date (vols. 1–5, Leipzig: O. R. Reisland, 1902–1913; vols. 6–15 Tübingen: J. C. Mohr [Paul Siebeck (*sic*)], 1955–1977], 1: 23–24.

35 This phrase could actually mean that the wedding took place at the front of the sanctuary. I cannot be sure. But usually one would have said *vor der Gemeinde* or *vorn in der Kirche* to indicate this location. Even today, *vor* (in the sixteenth century often *für*) *der Kirche* suggests outside, in front of the building. Sehling states that this phrase meant outside the church door (KOO, 6/2: 805, n. 12).

36 Here I am having to combine *The New English Bible* with my own translation from *Die Bibel, nach der deutschen Übersetzung D. Martin Luthers* (Altenburg: Evangelische Haupt-Bibelgesellschaft, 1968), because the former does not contain the essential word *helper*.

37 Genesis 2: 18, 21–24.

38 Ephesians 5: 22–29.

39 Genesis 3: 16.

40 Genesis 3: 17–19.

41 Genesis 1: 27–28, 31.

42 Proverbs 18: 22.

43 Susan C. Karant-Nunn, "Female Sexuality in the Thought of Martin Luther," unpublished paper presented August 1988 to seminar on Luther and women, Seventh International Congress for Luther Research, Oslo, Norway.

44 It is nonetheless significant that, with the coming of Protestantism, the laity no longer had to confess to and describe specific sinful acts.

45 Tietz, "Verlobung, Trauung und Hochzeit," 84–87. Niedersächsisches Landeskirchliches Archiv Braunschweig (LKABr), V 1938, "Verordnungen des Herzog Julius in Kirchensachen 1569–1575," fol. 7.

46 Tietz, "Verlobung, Trauung und Hochzeit, 83–84. In 1581 the pastor in Lüstnau/ Pfrondorf just outside Tübingen complained to the synod that his parishioners were disorderly about weddings, for "some of them married on Monday and others on Tuesday or Wednesday," and having to prepare so many wedding sermons interfered with his studies. The lords of the

synod saw through this complaint: Lüstnau and Pfrondorf were so small that there were not many weddings in any given year. ELKAS, A1 Nr. 1 1581, fol. 10.

47 Sachsen-Anhalt Landeshauptarchiv Magdeburg (LHAMag), Rep. 12A Gen. 2438, "Kirchenvisitation 1583/4, Städte im Holzkreis", fol. 193.

48 For example, in Pegau in 1574: Sächsisches Hauptstaatsarchiv Dresden (HSADres), Loc. 1986, "Registratur der Visitation, so uff empfangenen Churfürstlichen Sächsischen beuehlich...in der Superintendentz Pegau gehalten...anno 1574," fol. 5. But, contradicting this, in the city's largest church, St. Lorentz, the sexton received more for ringing the bells at an "early wedding" (fol. 41). The word *abent* was not the equivalent of our modern usage, however, for in the sixteenth century, evening began in the waning afternoon, perhaps as early as 3:00 or 4:00 p.m., depending on the season. Cf. Thüringisches Hauptstaatsarchiv Weimar (HSAWei), B. 4930, "Sächsische Weimarische Neue Verlöbnüs- Hochzeit- Kinttauff- vnd Begräbnüs Ordnung...1622," fol. 5, stating that *"Abendhochzeiten"* take place either at 3:00 or 4:00 p.m.

49 Hessisches Hauptstaatsarchiv Wiesbaden (HSAWies), Abt. 131 Nr. Xa, 1, fol. 47 (ca. 1618).

50 There were variations, of course. In the lands pertaining to the Stift of Halberstadt, ruled in 1589 by Duke Heinrich Julius of Braunschweig-Lüneburg, no-one could get married during Advent through New Year's Day, from the Sunday before Ash Wednesday through Trinity Sunday, or from St. Margaret's Day (July 13) through St. Bartholomew's Day (August 24). Both sexual and reveling connotations were seen to be at odds with the religious solemnity of the first two periods, and the third was a season of intense agricultural labor. LHAMag, Rep. A12 Gen. 2486, fols. 43^v–44^r. Cyriakus Spangenberg insisted that these prohibitions had nothing to do with marriage somehow tainting these holy seasons (*Ehespiegel, das ist Alles was vom heyligen Ehestande nützliches, nötiges, vnd tröstliches mag gesagt werden. In Sibentzig Braut predigten zusammen verfasset* [Strasbourg: Samuel Emmel, 1561], sermon 42, "Von anstellunge der Hochzeyt, vnd vom Auffbieten, Geste Laden, vnd anderer vorbereytunge," fol. clvii), but, he said, it was merely a matter of tradition. Obviously, I don't believe this.

51 Sehling, KOO, 1: 319. The parish visitors in Sachsen-Weimar in 1586 discovered a village pastor who was marrying couples "in the meadow or in houses," and he resisted correction. We do not learn his fate, but he was assuredly not allowed to continue this practice (HSAWei, Reg. Ji 67, "Kirchen- vnd Schul-Visitations-Acta. 1586," fol. 102).

52 There are several pertinent essays in Kathleen Ashley and Pamela Sheingorn, eds., *Interpreting Cultural Symbols: Saint Anne in Late Medieval Society* (Athens, Ga., and London: University of Georgia Press, 1990), among them, the editors' introduction (1–68); Francesca Sautman, "Saint Anne in Folk Tradition: Late Medieval France" (69–94); Gail McMurray Gibson, "Saint Anne and the Religion of Childbed: Some East Anglian Texts and Talismans" (95–110); and Kathleen Ashley, "Image and Ideology: Saint Anne in Late Medieval Drama and Narrative" (111–30).

53 Sehling, KOO, 1: 273–74; 1: 366–68. On the so-called *Heinrichsagenda*, see Günther Wartenberg, *Landesherrschaft und Reformation: Moritz von Sachsen und die albertinische Kirchenpolitik bis 1546* (Weimar: Hermann Böhlaus Nachfolger, 1988), 94–102.

54 Sehling, KOO, 1: 319 (1557).

55 LHAMag, Rep. 12A Gen. 2434, *Kirchenvisitation 1562/64, Städte im Holzkreis*, fol. 199.

56 An example of this may be seen in the 1552 church ordinance for Mecklenburg, in which the authorities first of all prescribe the abbreviated traditional wedding rite and then add, "If they want to hold their public going-to-church, one [the officiating cleric] may adhere in the church to the following ceremonies" (Sehling, KOO, 4: 210). On the two parts, see R. Sohm, *Das Recht der Eheschließung aus dem deutschen und canonischen Recht geschichtlich entwickelt* (Weimar, 1875), 159, 172–73. In 1589, Duke Heinrich Julius of Braunschweig-Lüneburg, acting in his capacity as bishop of the Halberstadt chapter, ordered the two pieces put together. Without explanation, he also abolished the wedding sermon LHA Magdeburg 12A Gen. 2486, fol. 43. Cf. HSAWeimar, Reg. Ji 68, "Kirchen- vnd Schul-Visitations-Acta 1587 bis 1632," fol. 168, village of Ernstroda.

57 Sehling, KOO, 2: 223. Michael Mitterauer and Reinhard Sieder have found that magistrates attempted in some parts of Germany and Austria to prevent impoverished people from marrying at all (*Vom Patriarchat zur Partnerschaft: Zum Strukturwandel der Familie* [Munich: C. H. Beck, 1991], 152–53). I would guess that this occurred only under Catholic regimes, for Protestantism regarded marriage as the indispensable safeguard for society against the ravages of unrestrained lust. If poor people were not married, society would be in danger. Catholics used a similar argument, however, in defense of condoned prostitution.

58 Sehling, KOO, 2: 224.

59 Sehling, KOO, 2: 224.

60 Admonitions in keeping with these to bride and groom may be found virtually through the church ordinances. Such an example is Sehling, KOO, 3: 173 (Mark Brandenburg, 1561); see also notes 61–64 below.

61 Sehling, KOO, 2: 225.

62 Sehling, KOO, 3: 173–74.

63 Sehling, KOO, 3: 175.

64 Sehling, KOO, 6/2: 808–809.

65 See chapter 5, on dying and death rituals, for an account of Lenz's work on funeral sermons.

66 But see Thomas Fischer Miller, "Mirror for Marriage: Lutheran Views of Marriage and the Family, 1520–1600," unpublished Ph.D. dissertation, University of Virginia, 1981, which concentrates on the sermons of Cyriakus Spangenberg, but also includes the sermons of Josua Opitz and Conrad Wolfgang Platz; Susan C. Karant-Nunn, *"Kinder, Küche, Kirche*: Social Ideology in the Sermons of Johannes Mathesius," in Andrew C. Fix, and Susan C. Karant-Nunn, eds., *Germania Illustrata: Essays on Early Modern Germany Presented to Gerald Strauss* (Kirksville, Mo.: Sixteenth Century Journal Publishers, 1992), 121–40; Scott H. Hendrix, "Christianizing Domestic Relations: Women and Marriage in Johann Freder's *Dialogus dem Ehestand zu Ehren*," *Sixteenth Century Journal* 23, 2 (1992), 251–66; Hans-Christoph Rublack, "Lutherische Predigt und soziale Wirklichkeiten," in idem, ed., *Die lutherische Konfessionalisierung in Deutschland*, Schriften des Vereins für Reformationsgeschichte 197 (Gütersloh: Gerd Mohn, 1992), 344–95.

During the late Middle Ages, preachers preached about women even though there were no wedding sermons as such. Two recent summaries of their messages have come to my attention: Larissa Taylor, *Soldiers of Christ*, chap. 9, "The Preachers and Women," 156–78; and Helga Schüppert, "Frauenbild und Frauenalltag in der Predigtliteratur," in *Frau und spätmittelalterlicher Alltag: Internationaler Kongress Krems an der Donau 2. bis 5. Oktober 1984* (Vienna: Verlag der Österreichischen Akademie der Wissenschaften, 1986), 103–56. Cf. such older works as Adolph Franz, *Drei deutsche Minoritenprediger aus dem XIII. und XIV Jahrhundert* (Freiburg/ Breisgau: Herder, 1907), for example, 93–94, 100–101.

67 Indicative of this is, for example, the 1585 ordinance of the Duchy of Lauenburg, according to which the church inspectors are supposed to inquire, among other things, "whether on the following day the groom and bride, along with a goodly number of their relatives and guests diligently come to the bridal mass and sermon" (Sehling, KOO, 5: 429).

68 Johannes Mathesius, *Vom Ehestand vnd Haußwesen, Fünfftzehen Hochzeytpredigten* (Nuremberg: Johann vom Berg and Vlrich Newber, 1563 [the editors of *Verzeichnis der im deutschen Sprachbereich erschienenen Drucke des XVI. Jahrhunderts* (VD 16), vol. 13, item M 1420, have a question mark by this date]); *Ehespiegel Mathesij, das ist: Christliche vnd Tröstliche Erklerung etlicher vornehmer Sprüche altes vnd Newes Testaments vom heiligen Ehestande* (Leipzig: Johan Beyer, 1592), seventy-six sermons evidently compiled posthumously by his admiring successors; Cyriakus Spangenberg, *Ehespiegel*.

69 Sehling, KOO, 13/3: 197 (Pfalz-Neuburg, 1576).

70 A brief study of the spread of Lutheran doctrines on marriage is Susan C. Karant-Nunn, "The Transmission of Luther's Teachings on Women and Matrimony: The Case of Zwickau," *Archive for Reformation History* 77 (1986), 31–46.

71 This retention is especially apparent in the visitation records of Saxony, many of which I have used in the Saxon Hauptstaatsarchiv in Dresden, and a number of which may be consulted in printed form in Karl Pallas, *Die Registraturen der Kirchenvisitationen im ehemals sächsischen Kurkreise* (Halle, 1906–1918), vols. 2–7.

72 " 'Going to Church and Street': Weddings in Reformation Augsburg," *Past and Present* 106 (February 1985), 62–101. See also, by Richard van Dülmen, "Fest der Liebe: Heirat und Ehe in der frühen Neuzeit," in idem, ed., *Armut, Liebe, Ehre: Studien zur historischen Kulturforschung* (Frankfurt: Fischer, 1988), 67–106; and "Heirat und Eheleben in der Frühen Neuzeit: Autobiographische Zeugnisse," *Archiv für Kulturgeschichte* 72 (1990), 153–72.

73 Johann Adolfi, genannt Neocorus, *Chronik des Landes Dithmarschen*, 2 vols., ed. F. C. Dahlmann (Kiel: Königliche Schulbuchdruckerei, 1827). Among other sources acknowledged by Adolfi are the *Sachsenspiegel* and "*Olt Ditmersch Lantrecht*." Adolfi probably died about 1630, for his handwriting disappears, according to the editor (unpaginated introduction), from the *Gildenbuche*. The material I am using comes from a section entitled "Van Friewervinge, Uthschuven unde hochtidlichen Frowden der Ditmerschen," 1: 100–23. Cf. the chronologically more inclusive and thus less useful Hans Dunker, *Werbungs-, Verlobungs- und Hochzeitsgebräuche in Schleswig-Holstein* (Neumünster: n.p., 1930).

74 Cyriakus Spangenberg, *Ehespiegel, das ist Alles was vom heyligen Ehestande, nützliches, nötiges, vnd tröstliches mag gesagt werden. In Sibentzig Braut predigten zusammen verfasset* (Strasbourg: Samuel Emmel, 1561). See T. F. Miller, "Mirror for Marriage," for a general assessment of Spangenberg's attitude toward women and wedlock. The descriptions I am drawing on are found chiefly in sermons 40–46, pp. biiii to gv. Spangenberg readily admits that his ideas are not novel. He lists as his sources, besides the Bible and the Church Fathers, among others, Martin Luther, Johannes Brentz, the author's own father Johannes Spangenberg, Erasmus Sarcerius, and Michael Celius (fol. ii).

75 See, for example, Wilhelm Rauls, "Eheschließung in der Geschichte der evangelisch-lutherischen Landeskirche in Braunschweig," *Jahrbuch der Gesellschaft für niedersächsische Kirchengeschichte* 77 (1979), 97–125, here at 118–21. Such sumptuary laws were in effect, with or without teeth, long before the sixteenth century. Friedrich III, Landgraf of Thuringia and Markgraf of Meissen, issued a detailed *Polizeiordnung* covering a range of issues including weddings in 1379: Hans Patze, ed., *Die Rechtsquellen der Städte im ehemaligen Herzogtum Sachsen Altenburg* (Cologne and Vienna: Böhlau, 1976), 11. This book includes numerous later examples, too, and during the sixteenth century these became increasingly detailed and rigorous.

    The visitors of the Holzkreis near Magdeburg in 1583–1584, in their prescriptions for a proper wedding, noted that the poor always imitated the rich—and consequently ruined themselves financially (LHAMag, Rep. 12A Gen. 2438, "Kirchenvisitation 1583/4, Städte im Holzkreis," fol. 260).

76 Adolfi specifically condemns as "a great disgrace" the wooing of a man by a woman (*Chronik* 1: 104).

77 Of interest is Christiane Klapisch-Zuber, "Une ethnologie du mariage au temps de l'humanisme," *Annales: Economies, Sociétés, Civilisations* 36 (1981), 1016–27.

78 Lyndal Roper, "Will and Honour: Sex, Words, and Power in Reformation Augsburg," *Radical History Review* 43 (1989), 45–71, reprinted as "Will and Honour: Sex, Words and Power in Augsburg Criminal Trials," in idem, *Oedipus and the Devil: Witchcraft, Sexuality and Religion in Early Modern Europe* (London and New York: Routledge, 1994), 53–78, esp. 64–66.

79 Germans took grave exception to unequal pairings, whether that inequality was in wealth and station, age, or health. Throughout the early modern period, wedding sermons decried ill matches. Artistic condemnations of differences in age are rife; and it was taken for granted that the only motive for entering into such a marriage was economic. See Alison G. Stewart, *Unequal Lovers: A Study of Unequal Couples in Northern Art* (New York: Abaris Books, 1978).

80 The word *Freund* could mean *friend* as we know it, but it usually referred to relatives. *Freundschaft* virtually always referred to relations, both of blood and of marriage.

81 Adolfi, *Chronik*, 1: 105.

82 Adolfi, *Chronik*, 1: 105.

83 Adolfi, *Chronik*, 1: 106–107.

84 In parts of Thuringia in the second half of the century, the groom-to-be gave the bride-to-be one Thaler as the coin of honor (for example, HSAWei, Reg. Ii 67, fol. 215).

85 A silver wedding goblet is depicted in Johannes C. Stracke, "Verlobung und Trauung," 17. There is a photograph of specially minted silver wedding pennies (*trouwpenninge*) on 18.

86 Adolfi, *Chronik*, 1: 107. Adolfi notes that as recently as the early sixteenth century, the people of this region did not give dowries with their daughters, but rather the groom has to pay a sum agreed upon in advance. Still, he says, the sons have always enjoyed the advantage in inheritance in that only in the complete absence of male heirs could women inherit real property. For that reason, marriages were contracted on the basis not of material advantage but the honor and virtue of the prospective bride (109). As for the meal that went with the *lövelbier*, in some places it was only customary to drink. See, for instance, Sehling, KOO, 7/1: 23, the ordinance of 1580 for the lands of the archchapter of Bremen: "Und wo an etlichen

örtern biß hieher gepreuchlich gewesen, das kein malzeit gegeben, sondern allein ein tonne bier aufgelegt und geschenkt worden, oder das sie gar keine geste gehapt hetten, so solte es an denselbigen ortern auch hinfurder dabei pleiben."

87 Spangenberg, *Ehespiegel*, sermon 40, "Von der Werbung," bvi.

88 Spangenberg, *Ehespiegel*, sermon 43, "Vom Kirchgang," ci.

89 Spangenberg, *Ehespiegel*, fol. cl. Spangenberg continues that the groom's wreath is a token of victory and of honor—which is true, but not entirely in the sense that the preacher would have it seem.

90 Bridal wreaths ranged from a circlet of leaves to elaborate gilded and bejeweled headdresses. Authorities deplored and forbade the latter.

91 Spangenberg, *Ehespiegel*, sermon 41, "Vom Wolleben zur verlöbnuß," fol. cliiii. According to Ann Tlusty, drinking was an essential part of sealing every sort of contract in early modern Germany ("The Contract Drink Ritual in Early Modern Germany," paper presented at Sixteenth Century Studies Conference, 1995, San Francisco). Her University of Maryland Ph.D. dissertation (1995) is on alcohol consumption in early modern Augsburg.

92 Spangenberg, *Ehespiegel*, sermon 42, "Von anstellung der Hochzeyt, vnd vom Auffbieten, Geste laden, vnd anderer vorbereytunge," di.

93 See, for example, the description of this process for Prussia, which in one form or another obtained in the lands that are German today (Sehling, KOO, 4: 193). Here the bride was not to be one of the bidders herself, unless she were too poor to have someone else perform this task.

94 Spangenberg, *Ehespiegel*, sermon 42, "Von anstellunge," clxi.

95 HSAWei, B. 7361, "Verlöbnüs- Hochzeit- Kindtauff- vnd Traur-Ord-nung...1614," fol. 7. Neither of these accounts refers even condemningly to the bridal bath (*braudtbadt*) that in Saxony at least was fairly widespread, judging by the extent to which it was condemned. Princes lent their muscle to the eradication of this practice, which was a licentious occasion.

96 Spangenberg, *Ehespiegel*, sermon 43, "Vom Kirchgang," eii.

97 Spangenberg gives a detailed explanation of the meaning of the wedding ring in *Ehespiegel*, sermon 43, clxv.

98 Spangenberg, *Ehespiegel*, sermon 43, "Vom Kirchgang," clxiii–clxvi.

99 Adolfi, *Chronik*, 1: 111.

100 Cf. Ottheinrich's use of the word *furtantz* in his Polizeimandat 1558, Sehling, KOO, 14: 263; see for Hohenlohe, Eheordnung, 1572, Sehling, KOO, 15/1: 193, *verdenntz*. In view of the usages in other places, the precise meaning in the case of Dithmarschen has to be constructed from Adolfi's text.

101 Adolfi, *Chronik*, 1: 112.

102 Adolfi, *Chronik*, 1: 113–14.

103 On the ritual of setting up the marriage bed, Johannes C. Stracke, "Verlobung und Trauung—Gebräuche und Ordnungen," *Jahrbuch der Gesellschaft für bildende Kunst und vaterländische Altertümer zu Emden* 58 (1978), 5–21, here at 12–13.

104 These could be, and originally probably always were, coins. Set in between 160–61 of Adolfi's *Chronik* are drawings of the married woman's clothing.

105 "[S]indt de alleß in der Hochtidt schaffen, regeren unde bestellen..." (Adolfi, *Chronik*, 1: 117).

106 We might see this swordplay as conveying the same meaning as the pistol shots that were sometimes fired even between the legs of the bride. See Nicole Belmont, "La fonction symbolique du cortège dans les rituels

populaires du mariage," *Annales* 33, 3 (1978), 650–55, here at 652. The charivari seems to have been unknown in this part of Germany, though, as John Cashmere reminds us, this collective violence was not necessarily associated with weddings: "The Social Uses of Violence in Ritual: *Charivari or Religious Persecution?*" *European History Quarterly* 21 (1991), 291–319. See also André Burguière, "The Charivari and Religious Repression in France During the Ancien Régime," in Robert Wheaton and Tamara K. Hareven, eds., *Family and Sexuality in French History*, 84–110, esp. 94–96, on the varied targets of the charivari.

107 There was a veritable campaign throughout Germany during the late sixteenth and seventeenth centuries to make couples wait until after the church ceremony, and women who bore babies too soon after their nuptials were punished. In one village near Braunschweig, the peasants acted surprised by the visitors' attitude and retorted that one had to count the months from the engagement and not the wedding: LKABr, V 1937, "Berichte über Pfarrer und Kirchengemeinden auf die Umfragen von 1638 und 1648," Lebenstedt, fol. 3ʳ.

In addition, princes were determined to lessen the scale and lack of inhibition that characterized the holding of *lövelbieren*. A good example of an effort at strict curtailment is that of 1596 in Emden (Sehling, KOO, 7/1: 530–31).

108 The 1614 Saxony-Weimar wedding ordinance mentions, and forbids, the giving of these gifts and much larger ones from the groom to the bride's relations, such as "dresses, caps, slippers, [and] shoes" (HSAWei, B. 7361, "Verlöbniß- Hochzeit- Kindtauff- vnd Traur-Ordnung . . . 1614," fol. 12).

109 The people ordinarily wore black, or sometimes grey or brown, so this red constituted a stark departure from the norm. See Ruth-Elisabeth Mohrmann, *Volksleben in Wilster im 16. und 17. Jahrhundert* (Neumünster: Karl Wachholtz Verlag, 1977), 254. On the matter of visiting the dead, E. Hoffmann-Krayer, *Handwörterbuch des deutschen Aberglaubens* (usually referred to as Hanns Bächtold-Stäubli, *Handwörterbuch*, etc.), vol. 4 (Berlin and Leipzig: Walter de Gruyter, 1931/1932), col. 148.

110 "Ehr unde Döget, Geluck unnd Heil, Ehr unnd Döget schall ehr ock wedderfahren" (Adolfi, *Chronik*, 1: 118).

111 Adolfi, *Chronik*, 1: 117–19.

112 Adolfi, *Chronik*, 1: 120–21.

113 None of the usual folkloric encyclopedias provided an explanation of this reference to the Holy Ghost. I am finally inclined to accept Friso Melzer's characterization of the spirit (ghost) as the opposite of the flesh: *Der christliche Wortschatz der deutschen Sprache: Eine evangelische Darstellung* ([Lahr/Baden: Ernst Kaufmann, 1951], 259–60). In the present context, the Holy Ghost would represent the end of material and sensual indulgence, but whether this meant because of death or hardship is not clear.

114 Adolfi, *Chronik*, 1: 121–22.

115 Spangenberg, *Ehespiegel*, sermon 44, ev–evi. These items were probably part of the "show meal" referred to disparagingly in Saxony-Weimar in 1614, prepared by the cook in order to garner admiration and especially tips (HSAWei, B. 7361, "Verlöbniß- Hochzeit- Kindtauff- vnd Traur-Ordnung . . . 1614," fol. 11). In addition, the wedding guests gave the bride and groom presents. In general, the women made gifts for the household, while the men gave money, either toward defraying the wedding costs—it was sometimes called "beer money"—or (if there was any left over) toward the expenses of setting up housekeeping. The visitors in and around Borna (Saxony) in 1574 specified in detail what the pastor and his wife and the

deacon and his wife were and were not obligated to give (HSADres, Loc. 1992, fol. 85).

116 Spangenberg, *Ehespiegel*, sermon 45, "Vom Tantz," fv–gi.

117 Spangenberg, *Ehespiegel*, sermon 46, "Vom Nachtessen, vnd Nacht täntzen," gii.

118 See the attempt in the district of Meissen, which the visitors reported to Elector August in 1574 (HSADres, Loc. 2050, "Visitation Acta 1574," fols. 158–59).

119 For example, in Sachsen-Weimar, where the wedding ordinance specified which officials and how many had to be present at such dances in order to detect and punish infractions (HSAWei, B. 4930, "Sächsische Weimarische Neue Verlöbnüs- Hochzeit- Kinttauff- vnd Begräbnüs Ordnung...1622," fol. 11). For a third offense, an individual could be imprisoned or exiled (fol. 12).

120 Spangenberg, *Ehespiegel*, sermon 46, "Vom Nachtessen, vnd Nacht täntzen," gii–gv.

121 Roper, " 'Going to Church and Street'," 66–67, inc. on 66, n. 12. Protestant legal authorities did not deal consistently with the matter of sexual consummation. The increasingly absolute prohibition of secret engagements and princes' insistence that these would simply be nullified when they came to light (for example, Sehling, KOO, 6/2: 805 [Calenberg-Göttingen, 1542]) was hard to reconcile with the persistent attitude that, barring rape and incest, a woman became the wife of the man with whom she lost her virginity; promises of marriage were frequently made in order to gain consent for intercourse. But in the age of confessionalization, when promiscuity was criminalized more than before, families, unwilling to abandon the collective socioeconomic strategy, pressed governments of church and state to lessen the weight allocated to their children's sexual experimentation. These two opposing principles made German authorities inconsistent in their rulings.

122 Jack Goody comments about the importance of virginity in southern Europe, and on first intercourse as the event that makes a true marriage, in *The Development of the Family and Marriage in Europe* (Cambridge, England: Cambridge University Press, 1983), 212–13.

123 That the sixteenth-century mind made this association may be supported by the 1529 visitorial instruction in the village of Untertriebel (Ernestine Thuringia) that the pastor should receive a cheese and a loaf (*laib*, homonymous with *Leib*: body) of bread from each pregnant woman for whom he invoked God's help in church (HSAWei, Reg. Ji 2, "Visitations Acta im Amte Voigtsberg, Plauen, Weida und Ronneburg im Jahre 1529," fol. 23).

124 I am convinced that Carolyn Merchant's fundamental thesis that the early modern centuries were a period of growing objectivication and exploitation of nature is correct (*The Death of Nature: Women, Ecology and the Scientific Revolution* [New York: Harper and Row, 1983]). As she amply demonstrates, nature was seen as disorderly, and this attitude held implications not just for those women and men accused of witchcraft but for such lowly transactions as getting engaged and married.

125 Johannes Mathesius uses the image of the horse in describing the rebellious nature of women. See *Ehespiegel*, sermon 16, 39, which I analyze in "*Kinder, Küche, Kirche*," 128–29. I am writing separately on the image of the bridle, which figures prominently in early sixteenth-century depictions of the troubled relationship between the sexes, as for example, the many portrayals of Phyllis riding Aristotle. The most skillfully executed,

sensuous, and amusing of these is Hans Baldung Grien's woodcut of 1513. I presented an initial treatment in a paper, "Bits, Whips, and Padlocks: The Metaphorical Discipline of Women in Early Modern Germany," Taft Lecture, University of Cincinnati, March 1996.

126 For an especially detailed wedding ordinance, setting exact limits on numbers of tables, guests, dishes, values of meals, and so on, see HSAMag, Rep. 12A Gen. 2486, *Kirchen-Visitationen von 1564 und 1589*, fols. 37–62, pertaining in this case to Halberstadt (1564), but no doubt applied elsewhere.

127 LHAMag, Rep. A12 Gen. 1332, "Qvedlinburgische Kirchen-Ordnung 15. April 1627," fol. 5.

128 Sehling, KOO, 7/1: 530–32. This "Emder Eheordnung" (529–36) is an all-around excellent example of the regulation and detail that govern weddings by late-century. Under pain of a five-gulden fine, the bridal dinner, for instance, must open and close with a prayer (534). In 1629 Duke Christian of Braunschweig-Lüneburg gave orders to his officials that "no pastor is to marry a person before you or your successor in office has sent them [the pastor] a certificate [*schein*]" (LHAMag, Rep. A12 Gen. 1687, no pagination).

129 For example, Sehling, KOO, 7/2^1: 1257 (County of Jever, 1582).

130 LHAMag, Rep. 12A Gen. 2348, fol. 260 (1580, city of Staffurt).

131 *Leibeigenschaft*, a particularly onerous form of personal servitude, which persisted into the sixteenth century, posed a particularly knotty problem inasmuch as people with this status could not marry without their lords' permission, which was sometimes withheld. Visitors occasionally encountered couples living together as wife and husband without benefit of marriage, yet they could not compel the hindering overlords to relent. See, for example, the visitors' complaint in HSAWies, Abt. 171 Nr. D245, "Protocollum Generalis Visitationis Aller Pastoreÿenn Vnnd darin gehörender Capellen in der Graueschafft Dietzs gehaltenn Anno 1590," fol. 112: "Sonsten seÿen ihrer viel, die lang als eheleut bey ein ander geseßen, aber wegen der leibeigenschafft wollen sie die herren nicht zusamen laßen."

132 In some peasant communities, women were expected to prove their fecundity *before* marriage. See Reinhard Sieder, "Ehe, Fortpflanzung und Sexualität," in Michael Mitterauer and Reinhard Sieder, eds., *Vom Patriarchat zur Partnerschaft: Zum Strukturwandel der Familie* (Munich: C. H. Beck, 1991), 149–69, here at 153–54.

133 Spangenberg, *Ehespiegel*, sermon 42, "Von anstellunge der Hochzeyt, vnd vom Auffbieten, geste laden, vnd anderer vorbereytunge," fols. clvi–clvii.

134 Heinz Schilling describes this phenomenon in " 'History of Crime' or 'History of Sin'?—Some Reflections on the Social History of Early Modern Church Discipline," in E. I. Kouri and Tom Scott, eds., *Politics and Society in Reformation Europe: Essays for Sir Geoffrey Elton on His Sixty-fifth Birthday* (New York: St. Martin's Press, 1987), 289–310. In Dutch cities, according to Schilling, sin and crime remained separate, but in parts of Germany the distinction blurred.

135 LKABr, V. 1937, "Berichte über Pfarrer und Kirchengemeinden auf die Umfragen von 1638 und 1648," fol. 3. In the early years of the Thirty Years' War in the villages of Calenberg and Göttingen, engaged couples ignored the pastors' admonitions not to have sex: LKABr, V. 1924, "Die kirchlichen und sittlichen Verhältnisse vornehmlich in den Fürstentümern Calenberg und Göttingen (1543) 1625–1630," fol. 255.

136 Baden-Württembergisches Hauptstaatsarchiv Stuttgart (B-WHSAS), A63, Büschel 10, "Eheordnung und Kirchenordnung 1553," unpaginated printed

document. This order includes couples who were engaged and intended to marry and those who were simply promiscuous. Duke Ludwig, Christoph's successor, was concerned in 1589 that couples in Tübingen who engaged in sex before marriage were not actually being imprisoned (B-WHSAS, A38, Büschel 9, fol. 29). Christoph's predecessor Ulrich declared in his visitation instructions of 1545 that visitors were to inquire about marital discord and about irregular (*unordentliche*) housekeeping, the latter referring mainly to cohabitation by unmarried women and men. This was, he noted, very damaging to society (B-WHSAS, A38, Büschel 8, no pagination).

137 LHAMag, Rep. 12A Gen. 2442, "Visitationsordnung 1585," fol. 105. On the symbolism of the bride's hair and wreath, see Roper, " 'Going to Church and Street'," 88–89.

138 "Forma copulandi copula carnali conjunctos," Sehling, KOO, 13/3: 551–52.

139 Sehling, KOO, 13/3: 551.

140 See Jean-Louis Flandrin, "Repression and Change in the Sexual Life of Young People in Medieval and Early Modern Times," *Journal of Family History* 2 (1977), 196–210, reprinted in Robert Wheaton and Tamara K. Hareven, eds., *Family and Sexuality in French History* (Philadelphia: University of Pennsylvania Press, 1980), 27–48. With regard especially to France, Flandrin opines elsewhere that sixteenth-century writers were "obsessed with the struggle against heresy and immorality" (*Families in Former Times: Kinship, Household and Sexuality*, trans. Richard Southern [Cambridge, England: Cambridge University Press, 1979], 143). He adds that the fight against immorality was considered more important than that against heresy, however.

141 Robert Muchembled, *Popular Culture and Elite Culture in France 1400–1750*, trans. Lydia Cochrane (Baton Rouge, La.: Louisiana State University Press, 1985), 195–96. See the entire chapter, "The Constraint of Bodies and the Submission of Soul: New Mechanisms of Power," 187–234.

142 Muchembled, *Popular Culture*, 196.

143 Muchembled, *Popular Culture*, 32; Jean Delumeau, *Catholicism between Luther and Voltaire: A New View of the Counter-Reformation* (Philadelphia: Westminster Press, 1977); Philippe Ariès, "Religion populaire et rèformes religieuses," in Jacques Duquesne et al., eds., *Religion populaire et réforme liturgique: Rites et symboles* (Paris: Cerf, 1975), 86; Natalie Zemon Davis, "Some Tasks and Themes in the Study of Popular Religion," in Charles Trinkaus and Heiko A. Oberman, eds., *The Pursuit of Holiness in Late Medieval and Renaissance Religion* (Leiden: E. J. Brill, 1974, 307–36), in which she at least implicitly argues that we should not accept a dichotomy between popular "pagan" religiosity and elite "true" Christianity.

144 LKABr V. 448, "Visitatio Anno Christj 1568 jn Ducatu Wolferbÿtano [and added later:] und Visitatio der Pfarren im Gerichte Asseburgk 1570," fol. 133.

145 Here again, R. Po-chia Hsia's survey is particularly valuable in providing an initial overview of the early modern period: *Social Discipline in the Reformation: Central Europe 1550–1750* (London and New York: Routledge, 1989).

146 It is curious that, while Norbert Elias has seen the royal court as the "source" of civilization in western Europe, that very court, in the personal practices of its members, regarded faithful monogamy as bourgeois: *The History of Manners*, trans. Edmund Jephcott, The Civilizing Process 1 (New York: Pantheon Books, 1978), 183–86. Whatever their private standards, they lent the full weight of their religious and bureaucratic power to the

enforcement of "bourgeois" morality in the sixteenth and seventeenth centuries.

147 HSAWei, B. 4930, "Sächsische Weimarische Neue Verlöbnüs- Hochzeit-Kinttauff- vnd Begräbnüs Ordnung...1622," fol. 5.

148 For instance, *The Elementary Forms of the Religious Life*, trans. J. W. Swain (New York: Free Press, 1965), originally published 1915.

149 Victor Turner, *The Ritual Process: Structure and Anti-Structure* (Ithaca: Cornell University Press, 1969), 132.

150 See Natalie Zemon Davis, "The Reasons of Misrule," in idem, *Society and Culture in Early Modern France* (Stanford: Stanford University Press, 1975), 100, 107.

151 *Natural Symbols: Explorations in Cosmology* (New York: Random House, 1973), 93–112.

152 Of interest is Roy Porter's essay, "History of the Body," in Peter Burke, ed., *New Perspectives on Historical Writing* (University Park, Pa.: Pennsylvania State University Press, 1992), 206–32.

153 While I personally am convinced of this, see Elias, *The History of Manners*.

154 Zwickau Stadtarchiv, A AII 11 Nr. 28b, fol. 1, reprinted by Reiner Gross, "Eine Denkschrift des Pfarrers Nikolaus Hausmann an den Rat zu Zwickau von Ende 1529," *Regionalgeschichtliche Beiträge aus dem Bezirk Karl-Marx-Stadt* 4 (1982), 60.

155 *Sin and Fear: The Emergence of a Western Guilt Culture 13th–18th Centuries*, trans. Eric Nicholson (New York: St. Martin's Press, 1990), esp. 505–57; also by Delumeau, *La Peur en Occident: Une cité assiégée* (Paris: Fayard, 1978).

156 *Des Ehelichen ordens Spiegel und Regel* (Wittenberg: Georg Rhaw, 1553).

157 Good examples are the statues of Elector August of Saxony (d. 1586) and Electress Anna (d. 1585) in the so-called cathedral (*Dom*) in Freiberg. Pictures of these are found in Heinrich Magirius, *Der Dom zu Freiberg* (Leipzig: Koehler and Amelang, 1986), figs. 184, 185, 189. The effigies of other members of the dynasty take the same general positions.

158 James W. Fernandez, "Symbolic Consensus in a Fang Reformative Cult," *American Anthropologist* 67 (1965), 902–29.

159 Antonio Gramsci, *The Modern Prince and Other Writings*, trans. Louis Marks (New York: International Publishers, 1957).

160 Catherine Bell, *Ritual Theory, Ritual Practice* (New York and Oxford: Oxford University Press, 1992), esp. chap. 8, "Ritual, Belief, Ideology," 182–96.

161 Foucault, *Power/Knowledge: Selected Interviews and Other Writings 1972–77*, ed. Colin Gordon (New York: Pantheon Books, 1980), esp. 187–201; "The Subject and Power," in Hubert L. Dreyfus and Paul Rabinow, eds., *Michel Foucault: Beyond Structuralism and Hermeneutics*, 2nd ed. (Chicago: University of Chicago Press, 1983), 208–26.

162 Foucault notes government uses of ritual that impinge upon the body at various points in *Discipline and Punish: The Birth of the Prison*, trans. Alan Sheridan (New York: Pantheon Books, 1977); Roper, *Holy Household*; Karant-Nunn, "Neoclericalism and Anticlericalism, 1555–1675" *Journal of Interdisciplinary History* 24, 4 (Spring 1994), 615–37, a subsidiary theme; but on the body politic, also much of the literature on confessionalization cited earlier.

163 Bell, *Ritual Theory*, 222.

2 TO BEAT THE DEVIL: BAPTISM AND THE CONQUEST OF SIN

1 Peter Cramer notices this in *Baptism and Change in the Early Middle Ages, c. 100–c. 1150* (Cambridge, England: Cambridge University Press, 1993):

> Thus one of the great questions raised by the history of baptism is how it was that even after the habit of infant baptism had become widespread in the churches of Latin Christendom, the *form* of adult baptism—of a rite of conversion celebrated either at Easter or Pentecost, and not just of passive or magical exorcism—continued largely to prevail (3).

2 Christiane Brusselmans, "Les Fonctions de parrainage des enfants aux premiers siècles de l'église (100–550)," unpublished Ph.D. dissertation, The Catholic University of America, Washington, D.C., 1964, 66–67, and Part 3, "Les Fonctions de parrainage des enfants en occident de 300 à 450," 123–77.

3 Alois Stenzel provides a general history of Latin baptism in *Die Taufe: Eine genetische Erklärung der Taufliturgie*, Forschungen zur Geschichte der Theologie und des innerkirchlichen Lebens 7/8 (Innsbruck: Felizian Rauch, 1957). The ecclesiastical ordinance of the Lutheran County of Hohenlohe, 1553, went so far as to forbid baptism on Easter!: Emil Sehling, ed., *Die evangelischen Kirchenordnungen des 16. Jahrhunderts* (KOO), 15 vols. to date (vols 1–5, Leipzig: O. R. Reisland, 1902–1913; vols. 6–15, Tübingen: J. C. Mohr [Paul Siebeck (*sic*)], 1955–1977, 15/1: 76.

4 For the details here I am quite reliant on Hermann Josef Spital, *Der Taufritus in den deutschen Ritualien von den ersten Drucken bis zur Einführung des Rituale Romanum*, Liturgiewissenschaftliche Quellen und Forschungen 47 (Münster/Westphalia: Aschendorff, 1968). Spital treats only the ritual handbooks (about 240) that were printed. As he acknowledges, many manuscript versions "still slumber in the libraries" (4).

5 I have consulted the sample provided in Adolph Franz, ed., *Das Rituale des Bischofs Heinrich I. von Breslau* (Freiburg/Breisgau: Herder, 1912), esp. "Ordo ad cathecuminum faciendum," 15–19. Spital remarks about this handbook that it is a model (*Musterexemplar*) made available by a bishop for the priests of his diocese to copy and use; it is, he says, the oldest "official" diocesan ritual, though one that evidently has not survived was available in Cologne (7–8).

6 Liturgists are concerned with the exact form that this inquiry took. See, for example, Spital, *Der Taufritus*, 43–45, discussing the variations of *Quis vocaris?* versus *Quo nomine vocaris?* or *Quomodo est iste infants nominandus?* or *Nominetis puerum* or *Wie soll das Kind heißen?* or *Nennet das Kind*. But I am interested in the pattern of identifying and simultaneously of naming the child. See "Baptism and the Giving of the Name," Appendix 2, Fisher, *Christian Initiation: Baptism in the Medieval West, a Study in the Disintegration of the Primitive Rite of Initiation*, Alcuin Club Collections 47 (London: SPCK, 1965), 149–57.

7 The problem of emergency baptism by midwives (*Nottaufe* or *Jähtaufe*) is very important. For lack of space, I shall largely neglect it here and take it up in a separate article. In short, the Lutheran authorities severely limited the conditions under which it could be administered, while Calvinist leaders eliminated it entirely.

8 Spital, *Der Taufritus*, 36–38; Franz, ed., *Das Rituale*, 15: "Primo sacerdos, in foribus ecclesie stans, masculos statuat ad dexteram, feminas ad sinistram." Cf. Joan Cadden, *Meanings of Sex Difference in the Middle Ages*:

Medicine, Science, and Culture (Cambridge, England: Cambridge University Press, 1993), esp. the many references to right–left opposition, passim.

9 In the wedding ceremony, the bride always stood on the groom's left.

10 The 1487 handbook of Augsburg gave particularly detailed instructions. Spital, *Der Taufritus*, 49.

11 For the early history of exorcism in the baptismal rite, see Franz Josef Dölger, *Der Exorzismus im altchristlichen Taufritual: Eine religionsgeschichtliche Studie*, Studien zur Geschichte und Kultur des Altertums 3/1–2 (Paderborn: Ferdinand Schöningh, 1909).

12 The texts of all five are in Spital, *Der Taufritus*, 59–61.

13 Fisher, *Christian Initiation*, 159.

14 Franz, ed., *Das Rituale*, 16.

15 Again, I have chiefly used the English translation in the Sarum manual (Fisher, *Christian Initiation*, 160), up through the word *bowels*, after which the Breslau manual departs slightly, though without change of meaning (Franz, ed., *Das Rituale*, 16).

16 Franz, ed., *Das Rituale*, 16; Fisher, *Christian Initiation*, 160; Spital, *Der Taufritus*, 64–69, "Die Salzzeremonie."

17 Spital provides a chart showing which exorcisms were used for males and females in the Gelasian Sacramentary and other rubrics, including the Rituale Romanum (*Der Taufritus*, 83). The Gelasian Sacramentary derived from Gaul in the first half of the eighth century; many of its formulae survive even to the twentieth century in Catholic ritual. A translation of this sacramentary is available in E. C. Whitaker, *Documents of the Baptismal Liturgy*, 2nd ed. (London: SPCK, 1974), 166–96, the gender-specific prayers at 170–72.

18 Fisher, *Christian Initiation*, 160–61; Franz, ed., *Das Rituale*, 17; Spital, *Der Taufritus*, 70–71.

19 Fisher, *Christian Initiation*, 162; Franz, ed., *Das Rituale*, 18; Spital, *Der Taufritus*, 70–71.

20 Fisher, *Christian Initiation*, 161; Franz, ed., *Das Rituale*, 17; Spital finds that this formula was sometimes used with both boys and girls (*Der Taufritus*, 76).

21 Fisher, *Christian Initiation*, 163; Franz, ed., *Das Rituale*, 18; Spital, *Der Taufritus*, 78.

22 Fisher, *Christian Initiation*, 164; Franz, ed., *Das Rituale*, 18–19; Spital, *Der Taufritus*, 95–97.

23 Spital, *Der Taufritus*, 96.

24 Fisher, *Christian Initiation*, 164; Franz, ed., *Das Rituale*, 19; Spital, *Der Taufritus*, 97–100.

25 Spital, "Die Einführung in die Kirche," *Der Taufritus*, 100–103. The Sarum manual has the priest making a cross on the infant's right hand and then holding that hand as he leads the party into the church (Fisher, *Christian Initiation*, 165).

26 Spital, *Der Taufritus*, 106.

27 On the early Christian meaning of the font, see Walter M. Bedard, *The Symbolism of the Baptismal Font in Early Christian Thought*, Studies in Sacred Theology, 2nd series (Washington, D.C.: The Catholic University of America Press, 1951), 45. The blessing in turn of the font and the water are in the Gelasian Sacramentary, Whitaker, *Documents*, 186–88. The conversion of the natural elements into sacramentals is visible in the language: "May the power of thy Holy Spirit descend into all the water of this font and make the whole substance of this water fruitful with

regenerating power" (187). The basic exorcism of water, by means of which it became holy, may be read in Franz, ed., *Das Rituale*, 3–4.

28 For the German variations, see Spital, *Der Taufritus*, 106–10.

29 Spital says that the baby's face was to be toward the water (*Der Taufritus*, 114); but the Sarum manual instructs the priest to take the baby's body on its side and to dip it so that the first time its face is toward the north and its head toward the east; the second time with its face toward the south; and the third time with its face toward the water (Fisher, *Christian Initiation*, 174).

30 Spital, *Der Taufritus*, 113–14, for example, in the Augsburg manual of 1512.

31 Spital, *Der Taufritus*, 118–23; Franz, ed., *Das Rituale*, 19.

32 Spital, *Der Taufritus*, 118; Franz, ed., *Das Rituale*, 19; Fisher, *Christian Initiation*, 174.

33 Spital, *Der Taufritus*, 123.

34 Spital, *Der Taufritus*, 124–25; Franz, ed., *Das Rituale*, 19; Fisher, *Christian Initiation*, 174.

35 Fisher, *Christian Initiation*, 86, 101–05, 120–40; Spital, *Der Taufritus*, 125–28.

36 In addition to the two "Taufbüchlein" described below, the other major sources of Luther's teachings on baptism may be consulted in "The Holy and Blessed Sacrament of Baptism. 1519," *Dr. Martin Luthers Werke* (Weimar: Böhlau, 1883–), Weimare Ausgabe (WA) 2: 727–37; *The Babylonian Captivity of the Church. 1520*, WA 6: 497–573; the shorter catechism, WA 30/1: 308–13; the longer catechism, WA 30/1: 212–22; "Von der heiligen Taufe Predigten," WA 37: 627–72.

37 For a brief treatment of Luther's liturgical changes, see Frieder Schulz, "Luthers liturgische Reformen: Kontinuität und Innovation," *Archiv für Liturgiewissenschaft* 25 (1983), 149–75, on baptism, esp. 250–56 and the tables, 268–71.

38 Editor's introduction to "Das Taufbüchlein," WA 12: 38. Luther's translation of 1523 was largely based on the Magdeburg ritual book of 1497. See J. D. C. Fisher's detailed comparison of the Lutheran text with the Magdeburger Agenda in *Christian Initiation, the Reformation Period: Some Early Reformed Rites of Baptism and Confirmation and Other Contemporary Documents*, Alcuin Club Collections 51 (London: SPCK, 1970), 8–16. Both of Luther's "Taufbüchlein" are reprinted in Sehling, KOO, 1: 18–21, 21–23.

39 "Das Taufbüchlein verdeutscht. 1523," WA 12: 42–48. Werner Jetter, *Die Taufe beim jungen Luther. Eine Untersuchung über das Werden der reformatorischen Sakraments- und Taufanschauung*, Beiträge zur historischen Theologie 18 (Tübingen: J. C. B. Mohr [Siebeck], 1954).

40 "Das Taufbüchlein," WA 12: 48.

41 Spital, *Der Taufritus*, especially 150–71, "Deutsche Ritualien und deutsche Ansprachen."

42 "Das Taufbüchlein," WA 12: 47–48.

43 "Das Taufbüchlein," WA 12: 43–44. For a discussion of the analogy between baptism, the Great Flood, and the Jews' passage through the Red Sea, see J. Daniélou, *Bible et Liturgie* (Paris, 1958), 104–44; also Heimo Reinitzer, "Wasser des Todes und Wasser des Lebens: Über den geistigen Sinn des Wassers im Mittelalter," in Hartmut Böhme, ed., *Kulturgeschichte des Wassers* (Frankfurt/Main: Suhrkamp, 1988), 99–144, on Luther and the Great Flood, 109–14.

44 "Ob man gemach faren, vnd des ergernüssen der schwachen verschonen soll, in sachen so gottis willen angehn" (1524), reprinted in Erich Hertzsch, ed., *Karlstadts Schriften aus den Jahren 1523–24*, vol. 1 (Halle: Max Niemeyer, 1956).

45 "Das Taufbüchlein aufs Neue zugerichtet. 1526," WA 19: 537–41, here in the introduction, 531.

46 WA 19: 539–41.

47 For a masterful yet simply presented discussion of Luther's theology concerning infant baptism and its several sources, see Jaroslav Pelikan, *Spirit Versus Structure: Luther and the Institutions of the Church* (London: Collins, 1968), chap. 4, "The Problem of Infant Baptism," 77–97. Cf. Karl Brinkel, *Die Lehre Luthers von der fides infantum bei der Kindertaufe* (Berlin: Evangelische Verlagsanstalt, 1958); and Paul Althaus, *The Theology of Martin Luther*, trans. Robert C. Schulz (Philadelphia: Fortress Press, 1966), chap. 26, "Baptism," 353–74.

48 This translation is from the "Large Catechism," *The J. N. Lenker Edition of Luther's Works*, 14 vols. (Minneapolis: Luther Press, 1903–1910), 14: 165.

49 WA 19: 541.

50 Osiander, "Ordnung wie man tauffet, bisher im latein gehalten verteütscht," Sehling, KOO, 11: 33–38.

51 Lau, "Reformationsgeschichte bis 1532," in Franz Lau and Ernst Bizer, *Reformationsgeschichte Deutschlands: Ein Handbuch* (Göttingen: Vandenhoeck & Ruprecht, 1964), 3–66, esp. 32–33. For discussion of Lau's point, see Bernd Moeller, "Was wurde in der Frühzeit der Reformation in den deutschen Städten gepredigt?" *Archive for Reformation History* 75 (1984), 176–93; and Susan C. Karant-Nunn, "What Was Preached in German Cities in the Early Years of the Reformation? *Wildwuchs* versus Lutheran Unity," in Phillip N. Bebb and Sherrin Marshall, eds., *The Process of Change in Early Modern Europe: Essays in Honor of Miriam Usher Chrisman* (Athens, Ohio: Ohio University Press, 1988), 81–96.

52 Osiander adopted the 1526 "Taufbüchlein" in 1533, as did, for example, Göttingen in 1530, Northeim in 1539, Duke Heinrich of Albertine Saxony in 1539, Halle in 1541, Schleswig-Holstein in 1542, Pomerania in 1542, Schweinfurt in 1543, Ritzebüttel in 1544, and Mecklenburg in 1552 (see Sehling, KOO, 1/1: 21). Sometimes the path of transmission was indirect, as from Mecklenburg to Lüneburg (1564) and from Lüneburg to Wolfenbüttel (1569): Wilhelm Rauls, "Die Taufe in der Geschichte der evangelisch-lutherischen Landeskirche in Braunschweig," *Jahrbuch der Gesellschaft für niedersächsische Kirchengeschichte* 73 (1975), 55–81, here at 55. It would be oversimplistic to maintain that initially, before any of the great territories turned toward Calvinism after mid-century, lands lying more or less in between the northeast and the southwest tended to find a theological and a ritual middle ground. It is interesting to see that Veit Dietrich, in his *Agendbüchlein* of 1545 for Nuremberg, says that the exorcism can either be left in or taken out (Sehling, KOO, 11: 506).

53 Johann Martin Usteri, "Die Stellung der Strassburger Reformatoren Bucer und Capito zur Tauffrage," *Theologische Studien und Kritiken* 57 (1884), 456–525.

54 Bucer wrote this, even though it went out under the names of nine men: *Grund und ursach auss gotlicher schrifft der neüwerungen an dem nachtmal des herren, so man die Mess nennet, Tauff, Feyrtagen, bildern und gesang in der gemein Christi, wann die zusamenkompt, durch und auff das wort gottes zu Strassburg fürgenomen*, reprinted in Robert Stupperich, ed., *Martin Bucers deutsche Schriften* (Gütersloh: Mohn, 1960), 1: 194–278.

55 See the fascinating account of Hughes Oliphant Old, *The Shaping of the Reformed Baptismal Rite in the Sixteenth Century* (Grand Rapids, Mich.: William B. Eerdmans, 1992), 51–62.

56 I have adopted the translation of Fisher, *Christian Initiation, the Reformation Period*, 34.

57 Fisher reprints the ritual used in Strasbourg between 1525 and 1530 in *Christian Initiation, the Reformation Period*, 35–37.

58 This outlook—that baptism was, at least in theory, not essential to salvation—quickly came to be reflected in the practice of burying in consecrated ground infants who had died without baptism. Calvinism insisted on this change, and before century's end it had penetrated Lutheran Germany as well. I am writing separately on this subject.

59 Characteristic for all of Protestant Germany from at least mid-century on is Duke Julius of Braunschweig-Wolfenbüttel's ordinance in 1572 that all babies must be baptized within the first three days of their lives (Landeskirchliches Archiv Braunschweig [LKABr], V. 1938, "Verordnungen des Herzog Julius in Kirchensachen 1569–1575," fol. 33).

60 Fisher, *Christian Initiation, the Reformation Period*, 35. David Wright confirms this communal principle in "Infant Baptism and the Christian Community in Bucer," in D. F. Wright (idem, but forms of name different on title page and on essay), ed., *Martin Bucer: Reforming Church and Community* (Cambridge, England: Cambridge University Press, 1994), 95–106. In the same volume, cf. Martin Greschat, "The Relation Between Church and Civil Community in Bucer's Reforming Work," esp. 24–27, 29–31.

61 In its detail and explanations, the Hessian ecclesiastical ordinance of 1566 provides an excellent example of the intended communal nature of the sacrament (Sehling, KOO, 8/1: 275–82, here at 281).

62 Sehling, KOO, 8/1: 175–76; 12: 63 (Augsburg 1537):

> sollen die prediger das volk vermanen, das si ire kinder auf die sonntäg, so die ganze gemain Gottes bei ainander ist, wo sie des sontags erwarten mögen, zum tauf bringen, auf das, so des kind der ganzen gemain eingeleibt werden solle, das auch die ganze gemain fur das kind bete und dise mittailung gottlicher kindschaft und des himelischen burgerrechts den kindern vor allen kindern Gottes und burgeren des himelreichs mitgetailt und ubergeben werde.

The analogy between the heavenly and earthly citizenry could hardly be clearer. Cf. the script of the rite that follows (12: 72–79).

63 Blickle is a prolific scholar. His basic theory is presented in English in *Communal Reformation: The Quest for Salvation in Sixteenth-century Germany*, trans. Thomas Dunlap (Atlantic Highlands, N.J.: Humanities Press, 1992).

64 Fisher, *Christian Initiation, the Reformation Period*, 35–37.

65 For example, Hessisches Hauptstaatsarchiv Wiesbaden (HSAWies), Abt. 171 Nr. D226, ca. 1572 for newly Calvinist county of Nassau-Dillenburg, the elder line, fol. 17.

66 Old, *Reformed Baptismal Rite*, esp. chap. 6, "Further Development and Revision of the Reformed Baptismal Rite, 1526–42," 145–78. Besides Strasbourg and Zurich, this chapter contains sections on Berne, Neuchâtel, Augsburg, and Geneva. On Anabaptist baptism, consult Rollin Stely Armour, *Anabaptist Baptism: A Representative Study*, Studies in Anabaptist and Mennonite History 11 (Scottdale, Pa.: Herald Press, 1966).

67 My women students often ask what happened to the girls, yet they are grateful not to live in a society that has adopted female circumcision! Girl children were subsumed under boy children.

68 Fisher, *Christian Initiation, the Reformation Period*, "The Strasbourg Order of Baptism after 1537," 38–42, here at 40.

69 Old, *Reformed Baptismal Rite*, 69 and also passim, as in connection with parents' duty to pray and to provide religious instruction at home and to insist that their children go to catechism classes. References to parents are numerous in the Hessian baptismal rubric of 1566 (Sehling, KOO, 8/1: 272–82), for example.

70 Sehling, KOO, 8/1: 272–74; also HSAWies, Abt. 131 Nr. Xa, 1, fols. 48–49, dating from 1610, which reflects Count Ludwig's deep concern that fathers be present when their children are baptised, that the godparents behave properly, and that the ritual is carried out absolutely correctly.

71 Sehling, KOO, 8/1: 279.

72 Sehling, KOO, 8/1: 279.

73 For example, in Regensburg (?1567), Sehling, KOO, 13/3: 482–83.

74 HSAWies, Abt. 131 Nr. Xa, 1, "Betr. Einführung, Erneuerung und Verbesserung von Kirchenordnungen in den nassau-saabrückischen Landen und Gemeinschaften 1559–1765," fol. 47.

75 For an illuminating treatment of the discussions among the Rhenish Reformers, including their theological justifications of one practice or another, see Old, *Reformed Baptismal Rite*, esp. chap. 10, "The Washing and the Word," 249–82.

76 Spital, *Der Taufritus*, 112–13.

77 Stenzel, *Die Taufe*, 279.

78 Luther wrote in "The Babylonian Captivity of the Church" (in John Dillenberger, ed., *Martin Luther, Selections from His Writings* [New York: Doubleday, 1962], 302),

> I would that those who are to be baptized were wholly submerged in the water, as the term implies and the mystery signifies; not that I consider it necessary to do so, but that I consider it to be a beautiful act to give the sign of baptism as fully and completely as possible.

79 Sehling, KOO, 1: 202.

80 Bugenhagen writes about the diversity in christening procedures in the ordinance he wrote for Hamburg, and his preference is clear. Nevertheless, he concedes that the Hamburg custom constitutes a valid baptism (WA 5: 510–12).

81 Photographs of this famous altar are available in various places. Three of them are Carl C. Christensen, *Art and the Reformation in Germany* (Athens, Ohio and Detroit, Mich.: Ohio University Press and Wayne State University Press, 1979), 117; Helmar Junghans, *Wittenberg als Lutherstadt* (Berlin: Union Verlag, 1979), 132, plate 68; and, especially valuable for its enlarged detail of this baptismal act, Karlheinz Blaschke, *Wittenberg die Lutherstadt* (Berlin: Evangelische Verlagsanstalt, 1977), plate 28.

82 Rauls, "Die Taufe...Braunschweig," 59.

83 Sehling, KOO, 14: 120. He added that if a child were to weak to tolerate the cold, it could be left swaddled during its baptism—presumably having water poured on its head alone.

84 Baden-Württembergisches Hauptstaatsarchiv Stuttgart (B-WHSAS), A281, Büschel 1020, "Neuffen 1601," passim.

85 Sehling, KOO, 15/1: 18 (Waldenburg, 1595). Indeed, Count Wolfgang did incline toward Calvinism. Many rural churches throughout Germany had never been able to afford stone fonts in any case and made do with basins; for example, Sachsen-Anhalt Landeshauptarchiv Magdeburg (LHAMag), Rep. A12, Gen 2440, "Kirchenvisitation 1583/84, Jerichow'scher Kreis," which lists brass baptismal basins in the inventories of most churches.

86 Paul Graff, *Geschichte der Auflösung der alten gottesdienstlichen Formen in der evangelischen Kirche Deutschlands*, 2 vols., 2nd ed. (Göttingen: Vandenhoeck & Ruprecht, 1937–1939), 1: 294–98. The authoritative treatment of this subject is Bodo Nischan, "The Exorcism Controversy and Baptism in the Late Reformation," *Sixteenth Century Journal* 18, 1 (1987), 31–51; summarized in respect to Brandenburg in idem, *Prince, People, and Confession: The Second Reformation in Brandenburg* (Philadelphia: University of Pennsylvania Press, 1994), 141–43.

87 On Württemberg, see Martin Brecht and Hermann Ehmer, *Südwestdeutsche Reformationsgeschichte* (Stuttgart: Calwer Verlag, 1984), 223–28; in general, see Graff, *Geschichte*, 1: 295.

88 Sehling, KOO, 3: 56–59. He also retained salt, chrism, and candle. See Nischan's discussion of Joachim II's ecclesiastical politics, including ritual, in *Prince, People*, 11–24.

89 Ernst Koch, "Ausbau, Gefährdung und Festigung der lutherischen Landeskirche von 1553 bis 1601," in Helmar Junghans, ed., *Das Jahrhundert der Reformation in Sachsen* (Berlin: Evangelische Verlagsanstalt, 1989), 212–15.

90 Karl Czok, "Der 'Calvinistensturm' 1592/93 in Leipzig—seine Hintergründe und bildliche Darstellung," *Jahrbuch zur Geschichte der Stadt Leipzig* (1977), 123–44.

91 Karl Pallas, *Die Registraturen der Kirchenvisitationen im ehemals sächsischen Kurkreise* (Halle: Otto Hendel, 1914), 5: 40–41.

92 Sächsisches Hauptstaatsarchiv Dresden (HSADres), Loc. 9477, "Visitation Acta Wegen Abschaffung des Exorcismi (1592)," fols. 8, 46. Issues other than exorcism also come into debate here, such as whether the true body and blood of Christ are present in the Lord's Supper. The theologians debated whether exorcism should be left out simply as an *adiaphoron*, a non-essential that did not make a valid baptism; or whether it had to be abolished because it was a "devilish, idolatrous thing." See, for example, Pallas, *Die Registraturen* (Halle: Otto Hendel, 1908), 3: 233–34 (parish of Jessen).

93 Brecht and Ehmer, *Südwestdeutsche Reformationsgeschichte*, 344–45.

94 Nischan, "The Exorcism Controversy," 39–46; idem, *Prince, People*, 142–43. Two contemporary treatises that defended their respective sides in the controversy are Philipp Arnoldi, *Caeremoniae Lutheranae. Das ist, Ein Christlicher Gründlicher Unterricht von allen fürnembsten Caeremonien, so in den Lutherischen Preussischen Kirchen … adhibirt werden … Den Calvinischen Caeremonienstürmern entgegen gesetzt* (Königsberg, 1616); and Martin Füssel, *Ceremoniae Christianae. Das ist, Kurtzer Bericht Von Lehr und Ceremonien Der Reformirten Kirchen der Chur Brandenburg Entgegen gesetzt, denen Ceremoniis Lutheranis …* (Frankfurt/Oder: Eichorn, 1616), and Füssel's specific response to Arnoldi's diatribe, *Brutum Fulmen, Excommunicationis Apologiae Füsselianae, Das ist, Gründlicher Bericht und Antwort auff … M. Philippus Arnoldi …* (Berlin: Runge, 1617).

95 The great ecclesiastical ordinance of Elector August of Saxony in 1580 tells the pastors "not to dispute long with those who seek baptism concerning the father of the [illegitimate] child, but when requested, to baptize the infant immediately and report such to the authorities …" (Sehling, KOO, 1: 426).

96 HSADres, Loc. 10601, "Erster Theill Der im Churfurstenthumb Sachssen im 1592 gehaltenen Visitation," fols. 103–04. Nobles, their treasurers (*collatores*), city councillors, electoral officials, and teachers also had to sign, as did any citizens who were suspected of being pro-Calvinist. Ironically, this visitation retained one feature of Calvinist baptism: the

elimination of exorcism. See also Loc. 10601, "Zweiter theil Der in Churfurstenthum Sachßen Ano 1592 gehaltenen christlichen Visitation," passim; and "Dritter theil zur Visitation Anno 1593 gehalten gehorigen Sachen," esp. fols. 46–47, the articles on baptism in greater detail, including "daß doch nicht die Eusserliche ceremonia der tauffe, sondern der glaube ahn Christum, der durch daß Wortt der verheissung, vnd diß daran gehste zeichen, erwecket vnd gestercket wirdt, auch in solchem wort vnd zeichen die angebotene genade gottes ergreiffet vnd fasset seelig mache, vnd also nicht alle getauffte, sonder die allein die solche glauben haben, daß ende irer tauffe nemlich die ewige seeligkeit dauon bringe." This clearly adds conditions that bring the Lutheran position closer to the Calvinist one, without, however, the explicit stress upon election as the means of acquiring faith.

During the local visitations of 1598 and 1599, all the pastors had to sign the articles again (HSADres, "Local Visitation des Gebirgischen Kreißes 1598. 99," passim).

97 Wolfgang Harms, ed., *Deutsche illustrierte Flugblätter des 16. und 17. Jahrhunderts* (Munich: Kraus International Publications, 1980), fig. 52; I saw it in Harry Oelke, *Die Konfessionsbildung des 16. Jahrhunderts im Spiegel illustrierter Flugblätter* (Berlin and New York: Walter de Gruyter, 1992), fig. 39.

98 See, for instance, the wording in the baptismal ceremony ordered in the Merseburg Synodalunterricht of 1544, including changes made in 1545 (Sehling, KOO, 2: 17, n. 3, righthand column):

> Das dis kindlein in sunden empfangen und geboren an sel und leib vorterbet, das ihme selbst noch kein creatur daraus kan helfen, ihr bringet es aber izo unserm lieben hern Christo ... derhalben zu bitten das durch das heilige sacrament der taufe und glauben, dem reich Christi Jesu eingeleibet, aller seiner guter und vordinst theilhaftig werde und bleibe ...

The language was similar in the Hessian ordinance of 1566: "Weil es aber in der erbsünd entpfangen und geborn und von natur ein kind des zorns sei ..." (Sehling, KOO, 8/1: 272). Cf. the ritual agenda for the county of Hohenlohe, 1553 (Sehling, KOO, 15: 60–61):

> Dieweyl die heylige tauf der gnadenbund Gottes ist, darinnen Gott der Vatter uns uf- und annympt zu gnaden, kindern gottes und erben des ewigen lebens und solchs vonwegen seines lieben Sons, der uns durch die tauf ufnympt in sein gnadenreych und uns also schenket in unsere hertzen seinen Heyligen Geyst, der uns in der tauf new gebirt und glaubig macht, das wir vehig und tuchtig werden des ewigen lebens ...

99 See Jan Rohls, *Theologie reformierter Bekenntnisschriften: Von Zürich bis Barmen* (Göttingen and Zürich: Vandenhoeck & Ruprecht, 1987), 245–60.

100 "Kirchen- vnd Schul-Visitations-Acta 1587 bis 1632," Thüringisches Hauptstaatsarchiv Weimar (HSAWei), Reg. Ii 68, fols. 166–67.

101 The entire text of one is recorded in Evangelisches Landeskirchliches Archiv Stuttgart (ELKAS), A1 Nr. 1, 1585, Württemberger village of Eningen, fol. 223.

102 R. W. Scribner, "Ritual and Popular Religion in Catholic Germany at the Time of the Reformation," in idem, *Popular Culture and Popular Movements in Reformation Germany* (London and Ronceverte: Hambledon Press, 1987), 33–34.

103 LHAMag, Rep. A12 Gen. 2442, "Des durchlauchtigsten...Fursten...herren Joachim Friderichen des Primatß vnd Ertzstifftß Magdeburgk Administratorn...General articül, Wie eß in den Kirchen dieses Ertzstiffts...gehalten werdenn soll," 1585, fol. 30.

104 This is one of the gifts prohibited (as a pagan remnant?) in "Sächsische Weimarische Neue verlöbnüs- Hochzeit- Kinttauff- vnd Begräbnüs Ordnung...1622," HSAWei, B. 4930, fols. 15–16.

105 ELKAS, A1 Nr. 1, 1585, untitled, fol. 132, village of Tapffer.

106 Peter Zschuncke, *Konfession und Alltag in Oppenheim*, Veröffentlichen des Instituts für Europäische geschichte Mainz 115 (Wiesbaden: Steiner, 1984), 160. For a summary of the European evidence, see Robert Jütte, *Poverty and Deviance in Early Modern Europe*, New Approaches to European History 4 (Cambridge, England: Cambridge University Press, 1994), 90–92.

107 "Sächsische Weimarische Neue verlöbnüs- Hochzeit- Kinttauff- vnd Begräbnüs Ordnung...1622," HSAWei, B. 4930, fol. 14. It is hard to say whether the requirement that fathers attend first appeared with the pro-Calvinist regime of Saxon elector Christian I (r. 1586–1591). To be sure, it is mentioned in the "Kirchen- vnd Schul-Visitations-Acta. 1586," HSAWei, Reg. Ii 67, fol. 369, where we learn that "the children's fathers don't want to be there, [and] allege that this is a new ordinance of the pastor." If the insistence did originate in a Calvinist setting, then it supports the more strongly my perception that strains from the southwestern part of the Empire broke more completely with Catholic precedent and emphasized community. Also HSAWies, Abt. 131 Nr. Xa, 1, fol. 48 (1610, for all the lands of Count Ludwig).

108 Authorities perpetually tried to prevent this. "Kirchen- vnd Schul-Visitations-Acta. 1641 bis 1647," HSAWei, B. 2891, fol. 17.

109 "Kirchen- vnd Schul-Visitations-Acta. 1586," HSAWei, Reg. Ii 67, fol. 45, village of Magdel. This is a typical complaint.

110 "Verlöbniß- Hochzeit- Kindtauff- vnd Traur-Ordnung...1614," HSAWei, B. 7361, fol. 22.

111 W. G. Naphy, "Baptism, Church Riots, and Social Unrest in Calvin's Geneva," *Sixteenth Century Journal* 26, 1 (1995), 87–97.

112 For example, HSAWies, Abt. 171 Nr. D 245, "Protocollum Generalis Visitationis Aller Pastoreÿenn Vnnd darin gehörender Capellen in der Graueschafft Dietzs gehaltenn Anno 1590," fol. 38, for a prohibition on inviting Catholics; HSAWies, Abt. 150 Nr. 3829, fol. 45, county of Nassau-Weilburg, elder line, 1586, in which case a Lutheran father invited a Calvinist woman, but her own ruler forbade her to serve.

113 For a Catholic view, see Burkhard Neunheuser, *Taufe und Firmung* (Freiburg: Herder, 1956), esp. 19–23, 47–59, 79–96; for a Lutheran assessment, Bjarne Hareide, *Die Konfirmation in der Reformationszeit: Eine Untersuchung der lutherischen Konfirmation in Deutschland 1520–1585*, Arbeiten zur Pastoraltheologie 8 (Göttingen: Vandenhoeck & Ruprecht, 1971); for a brief summary, Wilhelm Rauls, "Die Konfirmation in der Geschichte der evangelisch-lutherischen Landeskirche in Braunschweig," *Jahrbuch der Gesellschaft für niedersächsische Kirchengeschichte* 75 (1977), 145–63, here 145–46.

114 Thomas N. Tentler, *Sin and Confession on the Eve of the Reformation* (Princeton, N.J.: Princeton University Press, 1977), 84, briefly mentions the confessor's role as teacher, which reflects the decline of this function.

115 Erasmus had suggested in 1522, in an appendix to *Paraphrasis in evangelius Matthaei*, that pastors preach catechetical sermons every year during Lent, which young people be obligated to attend. There would follow an

examination. If they passed, they would renew their baptismal vows in the presence of the entire congregation. He denied that he was proposing a new sacrament, insisting that he wished only to revive the practice of early Christianity: John B. Payne, *Erasmus, His Theology of the Sacraments* (Richmond, Va.: John Knox Press, 1970), 172–74. Part of this proposal is available in English in Fisher, *Christian Initiation, the Reformation Period*, 169. I suspect that the translator has mistranslated *pueri* as "boys," when in fact Erasmus meant both boys and girls, subsumed under the masculine form of the noun. Fisher's collection contains other late medieval critiques of Catholic practice.

116 I have used Fisher's version in *Christian Initiation, the Reformation Period*, 172–73. See A. C. Repp, *Confirmation in the Lutheran Church* (St. Louis, Mo.: Concordia, 1964), 15–20, for a summary of Luther's opinions on confirmation.

117 WA 30/1: 266–67. For a somewhat longer discussion of conditions in the parishes, see my *Luther's Pastors: The Reformation in the Ernestine Countryside* (Philadelphia: The American Philosophical Society, 1979), 21–31.

118 WA 10/2: 282.

119 "Unterricht der Visitatoren an die Pfarrherrn im Kurfürstentum zu Sachsen," WA 16: 175–240. Expectations grew inexorably higher, so it is difficult to tell whether the performance that authorities decried in the seventeenth century would not have been satisfactory in the mid-sixteenth.

120 On confirmands' age, see Hareide, *Die Konfirmation*, 290.

121 On Erasmus's recommendations, see Hareide, *Die Konfirmation*, 62–71.

122 Aemilius Ludwig Richter, *Die evangelischen Kirchenordnungen des sechzehnten Jahrhunderts*, 2 vols. (Weimar, 1871), 1: 302–304. Rauls asserts that this is the first formal confirmation ordinance: "Die Konfirmation," 146; but Hareide looks for additional influences on Lutheran confirmation, from the directions of the Bohemian Brethren, the Waldensians, and the followers of Zwingli (*Die Konfirmation*, 13–15). Cf. Wright, "Infant Baptism," 101–06:

> Bucer's answer was to detach from baptism when given to infants much of its significance as the point of demarcation between the church and the world, and to reassign this to subsequent education and discipline and in due course to confirmation (101).

On the theological and political debates about confirmation in Germany in which Bucer was involved, see Hareide, *Die Konfirmation*, 110–27.

123 Described in Rauls, "Die Konfirmation," 147–48. According to Rauls, Chemnitz's program was popular in many Lutheran churches in the seventeenth century, for Pietism promoted confirmation as a renewal of the baptismal covenant and as an inner conversion (149). Hareide notes, "Zwar wurde die Konfirmation erst durch den Pietismus lutherisches Allgemeingut..." (*Die Konfirmation*, 9).

124 Hareide, *Die Konfirmation*, 250–73; for a bibliography of the primary sources, 302–306. See also Johann Friedrich Bachmann, *Die Geschichte der Einführung der Confirmation innerhalb der evangelischen Kirchen* (Berlin, 1852).

125 Fernandez, *Persuasions and Performances: The Play of Tropes in Culture* (Bloomington, Ind.: Indiana University Press, 1986), 6.

3 CHURCHING, A WOMEN'S RITE

1 An earlier version of this chapter appeared as "Churching, a Women's Rite: Ritual Modification in Reformation Germany," in R. W. Scribner and R.

Po-chia Hsia, eds., *Problems in the Historical Anthropology of Early Modern Europe*, Wolfenbütteler Forschungen (Wiesbaden: Harrassowitz).

2 Peter Rushton, "Purification or Social Control? Ideologies of Reproduction and the Churching of Women after Childbirth," in Eva Garamarnikow, ed., *The Public and the Private* (London: Heinemann, 1983), 118–31; Adrian Wilson, "The Ceremony of Childbirth and Its Interpretation," in Valerie Fildes, ed., *Women as Mothers in Pre-Industrial England: Essays in Memory of Dorothy McLaren* (London and New York: Routledge, 1990), 68–107; and David Cressy, "Purification, Thanksgiving, and the Churching of Women in Post-Reformation England," *Past and Present* 141 (1993), 106–46. I wish to thank Merry E. Wiesner-Hanks, Ann Weikel, and David Cressy for their advice. The latter was kind enough to allow me to read his essay in manuscript. Lyndal Roper is informed that Ludmila Jordanova is doing research on churching in the modern period. Other scholars have mentioned English churching in passing, notably Keith Thomas in *Religion and the Decline of Magic* (New York: Charles Scribner's Sons, 1971), esp. 38–39, 59–61. Thomas notes the disagreement within the Church of England between Puritans and non-Puritans, the former regarding churching as a superstitious remnant of popery. Jacques Gelis, *L'arbre et le fruit* (Paris: Fayard, 1984), translated into English under the title *History of Childbirth: Fertility, Pregnancy and Birth in Early Modern Europe* (Boston: Northeastern University Press, 1991), does not discuss churching, despite the fact that the author tries to place human reproduction in its socio-psychological setting. Nor does Clarissa W. Atkinson in *The Oldest Vocation: Christian Motherhood in the Middle Ages* (Ithaca: Cornell University Press, 1991).

3 Scribner, "The Impact of the Reformation on Daily Life," in *Mensch und Objekt im Mittelalter und in der frühen Neuzeit: Leben–Alltag–Kultur* (Vienna: Österreichische Akademie der Wissenschaften, 1990), 315–43, here at 331–34.

4 Ernst Walter Zeeden noticed the survival of churching in "Katholische Überlieferungen in den lutherischen Kirchenordnungen des 16. Jahrhunderts," *Konfessionsbildung: Studien zur Reformation, Gegenreformation und katholischen Reform* (Stuttgart: Klett-Cotta, 1985), 142–43. However, my research indicates that the new mother did not invariably circle the altar.

5 Ronald L. Grimes's "Ritual Criticism of a Catholic Liturgical Evaluation," in idem, *Ritual Criticism: Case Studies in its Practice, Essays on its Theory* (Columbia, S.C.: University of South Carolina Press, 1990), 28–62, esp. 40–50, is an amusing example of the variety of observers' experiences of a Catholic Mass.

6 Luke 2: 22–39. The Old Testament prescription is found in Leviticus 12: 1–8. References are to *The New English Bible with the Apocrypha* (Oxford and Cambridge, England: Oxford University Press and Cambridge University Press, 1970). In contrast to the King James translation, this edition renders Luke 2: 22 as "Then, after *their* [my emphasis] purification had been completed...," noting implicitly that Jesus, too, had been ritually impure. On concepts of impurity in the early church, see Dorothea Wendebourg, "Die alttestamentlichen Reinheitsgesetze in der frühen Kirche," *Zeitschrift für Kirchengeschichte* 95 (4th series 33), 2 (1982), 149–70.

7 In 1601, an Augustinian canon in Würzburg, Christophor [sic] Marianus, explained the several meanings of the occasion in a series of meditations on Mary's confinement: *Pverperium Marianum, Vnser lieben Frawen Kindelbeth...* (Constance: Nicolas Kalt), 317.

8 Gertrud Schiller, *Iconography of Christian Art*, trans. Janet Seligman (Greenwich, Conn.: New York Graphic Society, 1971), 1: 90–94. I am indebted to Sylvia Gray Kaplan and John Patrick Donnelly, S. J., for their assistance in compiling medieval and early modern depictions of the Presentation—for this is what all the renderings were called, which is in itself significant. The definitive survey is Dorothy C. Shorr, "The Iconographic Development of the Presentation in the Temple," *Art Bulletin* 28 (1946), 17–32.

9 Shorr discusses the appearance of Joseph and Anna in "Iconographic Development," 26.

10 Marcelle Auclair, *Christ's Image*, trans. Lionel Izod (New York: Tudor Publishing Company, n.d.), 19.

11 Erwin Panofsky, *Early Netherlandish Painting: Its Origins and Character* (Cambridge, Mass.: Harvard University Press, 1958), plate 108, no. 235.

12 *Encyclopedia of World Art* (New York: McGraw-Hill, 1959), 9: 316, plate 180. The painting is at the Landesmuseum in Darmstadt. Frank Günter Zehnder, ed., *Stefan Lochner Meister zu Köln: Herkunft–Werke–Wirkung* (Cologne: Locher, 1993), 51, plate 4.

13 Shorr, "Iconographic Development," 17–18; Francis X. Weiser, *The Holyday Book* (New York: Harcourt, Brace and Co., 1956), 86–87.

14 Shorr, "Iconographic Development," 18. She presents much fascinating detail. Cf. Weiser, *Holyday Book*, 88.

15 Venerable Bede, "De temporum ratione," in Jacques-Paul Migne, *Patrologiae cursus completus. Series Latina*, 221 vols. (Paris 1844–1902), 90: 351.

16 Adolph Franz, *Die kirchlichen Benediktionen im Mittelalter*, 2 vols. (Graz: Akademische Druck- und Verlagsanstalt, 1960, reprint of Freiburg/Breisgau: Herder, 1909), 1: 209.

17 On the first, historians of women and the family have documented this deterioration. See David Herlihy, *Medieval Households* (Cambridge, Mass.: Harvard University Press, 1985), 7–111.

18 Franz, *Die kirchlichen Benediktionen*, 1: 210–12.

19 The anthropological literature is so replete with examples, it seems hardly necessary to document this point. Nevertheless, see James George Frazer, *The Golden Bough: A Study in Magic and Religion*, 12 vols., 3rd ed. (London: Macmillan, 1955), 3: 145–57. Modern anthropologists are often critical of Frazer, but I do not see that they dispute the kind of citation to be found here. For ancient Judaism, see Leonard Swidler, *Women in Judaism: The Status of Women in Formative Judaism* (Metuchen, N.J.: Scarecrow Press, 1976), esp. 1–21, chap. 6, "Women and Sex," 126–66. In preparing this paper, I have confined myself to studying Indo-European instances, among others Ruth S. Freed and Stanley A. Freed, *Rites of Passage in Shanti Nagar*, Anthropological Papers of the American Museum of Natural History 56, part 3 (New York, 1980), esp. 329–95; and Jamsheed K. Choksy, *Purity and Pollution in Zoroastrianism* (Austin, Tex.: University of Texas Press, 1989), esp. 69–100. A particularly extreme instance of pollution belief may be found in Richard A. Schweder's study of the Oriya Brahmans, "Menstrual Pollution, Soul Loss, and the Comparative Study of Emotions," in idem, *Thinking Through Cultures: Expeditions in Cultural Psychology* (Cambridge, Mass.: Harvard University Press, 1991), 241–67. Schweder's informant told him (262),

> If the wife touches her husband on the first day of her period, it is an offense equal to that of killing a guru. If she touches him on the second day, it is an offense equal to killing a Brahman. On the third day to touch

him is like cutting off his penis. If she touches him on the fourth day, it is like killing a child.

20 Franz, *Die kirchlichen Benediktionen*, 1: 211–12.
21 Psalm 81: 8–12.
22 Franz, *Die kirchlichen Benediktionen*, 1: 212, 220–23; 214.
23 Franz, *Die kirchlichen Benediktionen*, 1: 216.
24 Franz, *Die kirchlichen Benediktionen*, 1: 218.
25 Franz, *Die kirchlichen Benediktionen*, 1: 218.
26 Franz, *Die kirchlichen Benediktionen*, 1: 229.
27 Franz, *Die kirchlichen Benediktionen*, 1: 220.
28 I have found no instance of a mother attempting to postpone her infant's baptism to coincide with her own churching. Wilson did find such cases in England ("The Ceremony of Childbirth," 80).
29 Sint-Janskerk in Gouda is an example of a church having such a door. See I. T. Sterenborg, ed., *De Restauratie van de Sint-Janskerk te Gouda 1964–1980* (Gouda: Stichting fonds Goudse Glazen, 1980), 29, 33, 79. I am grateful to Professor Carol Janson, an art historian at Western Washington University, for bringing this to my attention. On the association between the north and the Devil, see Jeffrey Burton Russell, *Lucifer: The Devil in the Middle Ages* (Ithaca: Cornell University Press, 1984), 69, 71, 138–39.
30 Johannes Mathesius, *Ehespiegel Mathesij, das ist: Christliche vnd Tröstliche Erklerung etlicher vornehmer Sprüche Altes vnd Newes Testament vom heiligen Ehestande* (Leipzig: Johan Beyer, 1592), sermon 16, 39; Cyriakus Spangenberg, *Ehespiegel, das ist Alles was vom heyligen Ehestande, nützliches, nötiges, vnd tröstliches mag gesagt werden. In Sibentzig Braut predigten zusammen verfasset* (Strasbourg: Samuel Emmel, 1561), sermon 12, Fii. Married women also wore small veils, often just on their foreheads rather than over their eyes. The magistrates of Zwickau ordained that a 5-year-old tot who had been sexually abused by a man had thenceforward to wear such a veil. This was clearly a token of sexual initiation. Cressy, "Purification, Thanksgiving," contains a fascinating account of the English debate over the veiling of women and its significance (132–39).
31 Adolph Franz, ed., *Das Rituale des Bischofs Heinrich I. von Breslau* (Freiburg/ Breisgau: Herder, 1912), 20–21. Franz notes that under an interdict women could not be led into the church or be aspersed with holy water; new mothers could enter the church in the company of a priest, make their offering, and kiss a reliquary or a Gospel (67).
32 Franz, *Die kirchlichen Benediktionen*, 1: 228.
33 Franz, *Die kirchlichen Benediktionen*, 1: 227.
34 In the late medieval English mystery play, "The Nativity," the impurity of new mothers is explicit (Peter Happé, ed., *English Mystery Plays* [Baltimore: Penguin, 1975], 242):

> His [Christ's] modyr a mayde as sche was beforn,
> Natt fowle polutyd as other women be...

35 Franz, *Die kirchlichen Benediktionen*, 1: 233–34.
36 Franz, *Die kirchlichen Benediktionen*, 1: 233. The pre-Vatican II modern Catholic ritual of churching was astonishingly like the medieval, down to the priest extending the lefthand end of his stole to the woman (*The Old Catholic Missal and Ritual* [New York: AMS Press, 1901], 273–75). Cf. the post-Vatican II ritual set forth in *Collectio Rituum pro dioecesibus civitatum foederatarum americae septentrionalis* (Collegeville, Minn.: Liturgical Press,

1964), 396–405. In the latter, the priest wears a white stole and surplice but does not offer the stole to the woman being churched.

37 Franz, *Die kirchlichen Benediktionen*, 1: 240.

38 Franz, *Die kirchlichen Benediktionen*, 1: 244.

39 Emil Sehling, ed., *Die evangelischen Kirchenordnungen des 16. Jahrhunderts* (KOO), 15 vols. to date (vols. 1–5, Leipzig: O. R. Reisland, 1902–1913; vols. 6–15 Tübingen: J. C. Mohr [Paul Siebeck (sic)], 1955–1977), 3: 399 (Breslau, 1528), for example. R. W. Scribner refers to the dangers posed by such mothers' souls in "The Impact of the Reformation," 337.

40 *Dr. Martin Luthers Werke* (Weimar: Böhlau, 1883–   ), Weimarer Ausgabe (WA) 9: 565–71, here at 569.

41 WA 12: 420–26, here at 422.

42 Anyone who has read Luther's works will hardly require documentation of this point. Rainer Alsheimer has compiled Luther's sayings about the Devil that are contained in his *Table Talk*: "Katalog protestantischer Teufelserzählungen des 16. Jahrhunderts," in Wolfgang Brückner, ed., *Volkserzählung und Reformation: Ein Handbuch zur Tradierung und Funktion von Erzählstoffen und Erzählliteratur im Protestantismus* (Berlin: Erich Schmidt, 1974), 431–36.

43 WA 26: 175–240; Sehling, KOO, 1: 149–74, here at 170. Haug Marschalck, the Augsburg pamphleteer, complained that women were not being churched; men joked, he said, that they were just as good to sleep with, blessed or unblessed (Miriam U. Chrisman, "Haug Marschalck, Lay Supporter of the Reform," in Andrew D. Fix and Susan C. Karant-Nunn, eds., *Germania Illustrata: Essays on Early Modern Germany Presented to Gerald Strauss*, Sixteenth Century Essays and Studies 16 [Kirksville, Mo.: Sixteenth Century Journal Publishers, 1992], 66).

44 Niedersächsisches Landeskirchliches Archiv Braunschweig (LKABr), V. 443, "Protokolle der Kirchen- und Schulvisitationen im Stifte Halberstadt 1589," n.p., village of Wolfferstet. In truth, the prince had ordered in 1569 or 1570 that churching was to be performed in every parish (V. 1634, "Helmstedt die ander Visitation...Anno 1570 Mense aprili," fol. 2).

45 Franziska Conrad, *Reformation in der bäuerlichen Gesellschaft: Zur Rezeption reformatorischer Theologie im Elsass* (Stuttgart: Franz Steiner, 1984), 170.

46 Sehling, KOO, 1/2: 223.

47 Sehling, KOO, 1: 63 (Saalfeld, 1554–1555), 285 (Saxony, 1540), 625 (Oschatz), 654 (Salza/Thuringia); 1/2: 156 (Reuss lands), 460 (Querfurt); 5: 96 (Kurland); 6/1: 163 (Wolfenbüttel); 7/2: 731 (Harlingerland); 11: 739–40 (Thüngen), for example. The abolition of the leading in by the priest could mean, however, that the women might arrive at church whenever they chose. The visitors in Nassau-Saarbrücken in about 1618 inquired specifically whether the women were arriving "in starcken comitatu" in the middle of the sermon, which caused disruption. Hessisches Hauptstaatsarchiv Wiesbaden (HSAWies), Abt. 131 Nr. Xa, 1, "Betr. Einführung, Erneuerung u. Verbesserung von Kirchenordnungen in den nassau-saarbrückischen Landen u. Gemeinschaften 1559–1765," fol. 48.

48 Sehling, KOO, 1: 460 (Lodersleben and Obhausen, 1583); 3: 447 (Brieg in Schleswig, 1592), as examples.

49 Sehling, KOO, 6/1: 163.

50 Cf. Sachsen-Anhalt Landeshauptarchiv Magdeburg (LHAMag), Rep. 12A Gen. 2438, "Kirchenvisitation 1583/4, Städte im Holzkreis," fols. 257–58: "Vom Kirchgang der SechsWöchrinn."

51 Sehling, KOO, 13: 56. For an early seventeenth-century view, see Philipp Hahn, *Kirchenbuch D. Philip. Hanen, Dom Predigers zu Magdeburg...* (Magdeburg: Ambrosius Kirchner, 1615), 82–88.

52 Karl Pallas, *Die Registraturen der Kirchenvisitationen im ehemals sächsischen Kurkreise*, 7 vols. (Halle: Otto Hendel, 1906–1918), 4: 208 (Kobershain near Torgau, 1671).

53 Pallas, *Registraturen*, 4: 225 (Langenreichenbach near Torgau, 1671), for example.

54 Pallas, *Registraturen*, 5: 80 (Cröbeln near Liebenwerda, 1672).

55 Pallas, *Registraturen*, 5: 276 (Boragk near Liebenwerda, 1675).

56 Pallas, *Registraturen*, 6: 139.

57 One thinks of the prostitutes of Leipzig, who annually processed around the city outside the walls and were given a meal by the city fathers (von Posern-Klett [sic], "Frauenhäuser und freie Frauen in Sachsen," *Archiv für sächsische Geschichte* 12 [1874], 81). The visitors of Schlieben in 1602 told of a custom there that, when a person had died, his corpse was laid down next to the grave, and then his closest relatives (*die nächsten Freunde*) walked around the church and returned to the cemetery. Only then could the burial take place. They were capturing the sanctity of the church for the benefit of the dead. The visitors forbade the continuance of this "superstitious" ritual (Pallas, *Registraturen*, 6: 34). On the protective type of circling (rather than that designed to tap the sacred power at the center), see Charles Zika, "Hosts, Processions, and Pilgrimages in Fifteenth-century Germany," *Past and Present* 118 (1988), 39–40. See Scribner, "The Impact of the Reformation," 334; Zeeden, *Konfessionsbildung*, 142–43.

58 Thüringisches Hauptstaatsarchiv Weimar (HSAWei), B. 7361, "Verlöbniß-Hochzeit- Kindtauff- vnd Traur-Ordnung...1614," fols. 22–23.

59 Reprinted in idem, *The Interpretation of Cultures: Selected Essays* (New York: Basic Books, 1973), 3–30. For his own purposes Geertz defines "thick description" as "setting down the meaning particular social actions have for the actors whose actions they are..." (27). Geertz continues his reflections on the difficulties of ethnographic interpretation in *Works and Lives: The Anthropologist as Author* (Stanford, Calif.: Stanford University Press, 1988).

60 Wilson, "The Ceremony of Childbirth," esp. 83–93.

61 *The Rites of Passage*, trans. Monika B. Vizedom and Gabrielle L. Caffee (Chicago: University of Chicago Press, 1960; French original, 1908). Wilson states that he originally so regarded the ceremony of childbirth but then abandoned the position ("The Ceremony of Childbirth," 84).

62 Wilson, "The Ceremony of Childbirth," 84–85. See Thomas's views in *Religion and the Decline of Magic*, 59–61.

63 Wilson, "The Ceremony of Childbirth," 85–88, 94–97. Davis's thought is derived from her essay, "Women on Top," in idem, *Society and Culture in Early Modern France* (Stanford, Calif.: Stanford University Press, 1975), 125–51, esp. 145, 313.

64 R. W. Scribner, "Ritual and Popular Religion in Catholic Germany at the Time of the Reformation," in idem, *Popular Culture and Popular Movements in Reformation Germany* (London and Ronceverte: Hambledon Press, 1987), esp. 41, 43, 45, fig. 6, concerning what the author calls magical and folklorized ritual.

65 In the discussion that followed my presentation of the original version of this paper at the Herzog August Bibliothek in Wolfenbüttel, Lyndal Roper drew attention to the matter of the uneven distribution of power among the members of the birthing group. Clearly, most power was concentrated in

the hands of the midwife. Ordinarily she alone could perform an emergency baptism, and it is very likely that she alone touched the genitals of the becoming-mother. She also bore the infant to its baptism.

66 On pollution, see Mary Douglas's classic study, *Purity and Danger: An Analysis of the Concepts of Pollution and Taboo* (New York: Routledge & Kegan Paul, 1966, paperback edition, 1984).

67 Hanns Bächtold-Stäubli, comp., and E. Hoffmann-Krayer, ed. *Handwörterbuch des deutschen Aberglaubens*, 12 vols. (Berlin and Leipzig: Walter de Gruyter, 1927–1942), 12: 107–22. On the water as a symbol of spiritual cleansing, Heimo Reinitzer, "Wasser des Todes and Wasser des Lebens: Über den geistigen Sinn des Wassers im Mittelalter," in Hartmut Böhme, ed., *Kulturgeschichte des Wassers* (Frankfurt/Main: Suhrkamp, 1988), 99–144; on sexual and reproductive associations, Horst Bredekamp, "Wasserangst und Wasserfreude in Renaissance und Manierismus," in Böhme, *Kulturgeschichte des Wassers*, 145–88, esp. 155–59.

68 As I stated in the preceding chapter, people were incensed by the elimination of exorcism from baptism, which is related to the attitude toward churching. The visitors in Saxony were told that people were now reluctant to have their babies christened at all. In one case, a certain mother had undergone churching "several days before her child's baptism"; other parishioners were so enraged that they refused to receive the Eucharist (Pallas, *Registraturen*, 5: 40–41).

69 For example, Johannes Mathesius, *Sarepta* [alias *Bergpostille*], *Darinn von allerley Bergwerck vnnd Metallen...guter bericht gegeben* (Nuremberg: Dietrich Gerlatz, 1571), 2: 7. This was originally published in 1562. The serpent approached Eve and not Adam because of her already established ambition and pride.

70 Within a burgeoning literature, the indispensable works are still Merry E. Wiesner, *Working Women in Renaissance Germany* (New Brunswick, N.J.: Rutgers University Press, 1986), for economic manifestations of women's declining position; and Lyndal Roper, *The Holy Household: Women and Morals in Reformation Augsburg* (Oxford, England: Clarendon Press, 1989) for the Reformation sense of the need to impose better discipline on women and the family. For Wiesner's more recent thoughts on these subjects, and on women in general, see *Women and Gender in Early Modern Europe* (Cambridge, England: Cambridge University Press, 1993), esp. 82–114, 179–217.

71 Susan C. Karant-Nunn, "*Kinder, Küche, Kirche*: Social Ideology in the Sermons of Johannes Mathesius," in Fix and Karant-Nunn, *Germania Illustrata*, 121–40. This essay shows the harshness with which one well-known and revered preacher depicted women's nature and proper roles. Not all preachers were equally hostile. Scott Hendrix has found that Johann Freder (Irenaeus) was more generous toward women than Mathesius ("Christianizing Domestic Relation: Women and Marriage in Johann Freder's *Dialogus dem Ehestand zu ehren*," *Sixteenth Century Journal* 23, 2 (1992), 151–66.

72 New series (Marburg: N. G. Elwert, 1977), "Glaube und Brauch bei der Wöchnerin," maps 65–68d (information gathered in 1933).

73 Ortner, "Is Female to Male as Nature is to Culture?" in Michell Zimbalist Rosaldo and Louise Lamphere, eds., *Woman, Culture, and Society* (Stanford, Calif.: Stanford University Press, 1974), 67–88, esp. 84–86.

74 Unfortunately, at the time I did not anticipate wishing to cite this paper, and I made no note on it. I inquired of Mary Winkler, but it turns out not to have been her paper. I thank her for her help, nevertheless. The early

modern debate—partly satirical and very active in Germany even into the eighteenth century—about whether women were human beings, typically compares women to such animals as hyenas, cats, dogs, wolves, and swine.

75 Ortner, "Female to Male," 84–86.

76 Ardener, "Belief and the Problem of Women," in J. S. La Fontaine, ed., *The Interpretation of Ritual* (London: Tavistock Publications, 1972), 135–58, here 151–52, also 154, fig. 2.

77 Merchant, *The Death of Nature: Women, Ecology and the Scientific Revolution* (San Francisco: Harper and Row, 1980, new introduction 1989).

78 Most reviewers have detected major flaws in Merchant's book. Yet even a highly critical reviewer like medievalist Marcia L. Colish has found salvageable elements in it (*Journal of Modern History* 54 [March 1982], 66–70).

79 Merchant, *Death of Nature*, chap. 6, "Production, Reproduction, and the Female," 149–63.

80 HSAWies, Abt. 171 Nr. D 245, "Protocollum Generalis Visitationis Aller Pastoreÿenn Vnnd darin gehörender Capellen in der Graueschafft Dietzs gehaltenn Anno 1590," fol. 5, inquires pointedly if any women should still be having themselves churched, for this is not allowed. This Calvinist alteration may be one of the reasons why "Die Weiber ziehen sich vf ihre Eltern, beschweren sich einen nawen glauben anzunehmen"/"The [married] women are moving back to their parents' [homes because] they complain about accepting a new religion" (fol. 107). Also Abt. 171 Nr. D 226, no general title but various documents pertaining to the county of Nassau-Dillenburg (Calvinist; fol. 19), insisting that churching not be carried out.

81 J. Max Patrick, ed., *The Complete Poetry of Robert Herrick* (New York: New York University Press, 1963), H-898, 377.

82 Sächsisches Hauptstaatsarchiv Dresden (HSADres), Rep. A 28 II, no. 314, "Acta, Die in Helldrungen und dasiger Dioeces gewöhnliche Einsecgnung derer ihren Kirchgang haltenden sechswöchnerinnen und ihrer ehelichen Kinder... Ober-Consistorium Anno 1788," fols. 1–3.

83 HSADres, Rep. A 28 II, no. 314, fols. 4–6, here fol. 6.

84 HSADres, Rep. A 28 II, no. 314, fol. 7.

4 REPENTANCE, CONFESSION, AND THE LORD'S TABLE: SEPARATING THE DIVINE FROM THE HUMAN

1 Jacques Le Goff, *The Birth of Purgatory*, trans. Arthur Goldhammer (Chicago: University of Chicago Press, 1981); Nicole Bériou, "Autour de Latran IV (1215): La Naissance de la confession moderne et sa diffusion," in Groupe de la Bussière, *Pratiques de la confession: des pères du désert à Vatican II, quinze études d'histoire* (Paris: Cerf, 1983), 73–93; Bernhard Poschmann, "The Theology of Penance from the Early Scholastic Period to the Council of Trent," in idem, *Penance and the Anointing of the Sick*, trans. and rev. Francis Courtney (New York: Herder and Herder, 1964), 155–93; Joseph A. Spitzig, *Sacramental Penance in the Twelfth and Thirteenth Centuries*, Studies in Sacred Theology 2nd series, 6 (Washington, D.C.: Catholic University of America Press, 1947).

2 The Catholic liturgist's view seems to be that, by and large, the ritual of the Mass was fully developed at a much earlier date. See, for example, Fernand Cabrol, *The Mass of the Western Rites*, trans. C. M. Antony (St. Louis: Herder, 1934), much of which is devoted to the period prior to the sixteenth

century. The modern historian, however, observes the substantial changes that occurred in the period under discussion: Miri Rubin, *Corpus Christi: The Eucharist in Late Medieval Culture* (Cambridge, England: Cambridge University Press, 1991), concentrates on English and French evidence, but her findings are equally true of Germany. For Germany itself, see Charles Zika, "Hosts, Processions and Pilgrimages in Fifteenth-century Germany," *Past and Present* 118 (1988), 25–64; Peter Browe, *Die Verehrung der Eucharistie im Mittelalter* (Munich: M. Hueber, 1933); and idem, *Die eucharistischen Wunder des Mittelalters* (Munich: M. Hueber, 1938). The reader should note Browe's anecdote of some people's fear at seeing the Host in the hands of the priesthood, equating the officiant with the Devil (*Verehrung der Eucharistie*, 68, cited by Zika, "Hosts, Processions," 31). My position in this book is that, while from the twelfth century anticlericalism was growing, at least in rural settings many people had a great deal in common with their parish priest and would not have equated him with the Devil.

3 No-one could enumerate all their venial sins, and these were ultimately relieved by means of private regret, Christ's atonement, and God's mercy, as well as some period of time in purgatory.

4 Rubin, *Corpus Christi*, 84–85.

5 Poschmann, *Penance of the Anointing*, esp. chap. 1, "Early Christian Penance," 5–121; Bruno Judic, "Pénitence publique et pénitence privée et aveu chez Grégoire le Grand (590–604)," in Groupe de la Bussière, *Pratiques de la confession*, 41–51; Michel Rubellin, "Vision de la société chrétienne à travers la confession et la pénitence au IXe siècle," in Groupe de la Bussière, *Pratiques de la confession*, 53–70; Bériou, "Autour de Latran IV (1215)," in Groupe de la Bussière, *Pratiques de la confession*, 73–93; Jacques Berlioz and Colette Ribaucourt, "Images de la confession," in Groupe de la Bussière, *Pratiques de la confession*, 95–115.

6 Arthur Mirgeler, *Mutations of Western Christianity*, trans. Edward Quinn (Notre Dame, Ind.: University of Notre Dame Press, 1968), 66–81.

7 For a very brief summation of the early history, Thomas N. Tentler, *Sin and Confession on the Eve of the Reformtion* (Princeton, N.J.: Princeton University Press, 1977), 3–27, including, for further bibliography, 3–4, n. 1. In addition, for a long, anti-Catholic (yet heavily documented) account, Henry Charles Lea, *A History of Auricular Confession and Indulgences in the Latin Church*, 3 vols. (New York: Greenwood Press, 1968; reprint of the 1896 original ed.), 1 and 2 (on confession and absolution).

8 Lea, *History of Auricular Confession*; Poschmann, *Penance and the Anointing*; Spitzig, *Sacramental Penance*; Henriette Danet, *La Confession et son histoire* (Paris: Mame, 1983); Bonaventure A. Brown, *The Numerical Distinction of Sins According to the Franciscan School of the Seventeenth and Eighteenth Centuries*, Studies in Sacred Theology 2nd series, 10 (Washington, D.C.: The Catholic University of America Press, 1948), the background, 1–36, including Thomas Aquinas and John Duns Scotus; Bertrand Kurtscheid, *Das Beichtsiegel in seiner geschichtlichen Entwicklung* (Freiburg/Breisgau: Herder, 1912), esp. 1–103, up to the Council of Trent; on attrition and contrition, Tentler, *Sin and Confession*, 263–73.

9 My translation from the French of R. Foreville, *Latran I, II, III et Latran IV: Histoire des conciles oecuméniques*, vol. 4 (Paris: L'Orante, 1965), 357–58.

10 In reality, the authors of confessors' manuals were not unanimous on this and a number of other points. For a nuanced differentiation, see Tentler, *Sin and Confession*, 82–133. Tentler is evaluating the manuals and not descriptions of actual instances of confession, the latter being rarely available.

11 The classic mnemonic device for confessors was: *Quis, quid, ubi, quibus auxiliis, cur, quomodo, quando* (Bériou, "Autour de Latran IV," 88). On confessors' manuals, see the excellent survey in Tentler, *Sin and Confession,* 28–53. That these were very widespread is attested to by the large number of extant copies.

12 Tentler, *Sin and Confession,* 286–94.

13 Christians could also purchase indulgences that freed them from deserved temporal punishment, including after death in purgatory, for sins duly repented of, confessed, and absolved at the time they bought their certificate. Indulgences also represented some surety against the penalties due all but the most saintly for their incessant commission of venial, or petty, sins, with which (surely on practical grounds) one was not to burden one's confessor. In addition, the Church had adopted a theology of vicarious satisfaction, whereby one could indeed gain remission of some purgatorial suffering for Christians already dead and in the cleansing fires. The Church did indeed accept the maxim contained in the famous couplet, "Sobald die Munz' im Kasten klingt, die Seel' vom Fegefeuer springt." I want to confine my discussion, however, to the transactions associated with the Eucharistic Mass.

  Many people of humble means did go on pilgrimages to nearby shrines: Jonathan Sumption, *Pilgrimage: An Image of Medieval Devotion* (Totowa, N.J.: Rowman and Littlefield, 1975), 268–88; Philip M. Soergel, *Wondrous in His Saints: Counter-Reformation Propaganda in Bavaria* (Berkeley, Calif.: University of California Press, 1993). Whenever a "prophet" arose, the population from the surrounding countryside traveled to see and consult him or her. For example, the servingmaid Anna Hillig—see my unpublished paper, "Forbidden Visions: Why Were There No Lutheran Beatas?" presented at the meetings of the Society for Reformation Research, Kalamazoo, Michigan, May 1993, based on Sächsisches Landeskirchenarchiv Dresden, no sig., "Matrikel Freiberg 1617 II," fols. 664–67. See also William A. Christian, Jr., *Apparitions in Late Medieval and Renaissance Spain* (Princeton: Princeton University Press, 1981), esp. 150–87. To the twentieth-century mind, it is amusing to read in the archives of people from Catholic territories trying to visit shrines in lands that have been Reformed. Protestant authorities had to raze these shrines in order to discourage this "idolatrous" practice.

14 St. John's Church in Halberstadt had a "confession chapel" (*Beicht Capelle*), probably a particular altar (Sachsen-Anhalt Landeshauptarchiv Magdeburg [LHAMag], Rep. A12 Gen. 2486, "Kirchen-visitationen von 1564 und 1589," fol. 68).

15 Tentler (*Sin and Confession,* 82) found that the first confessional boxes dated to the second half of the sixteenth century. This, of course, would have been in Catholic Europe and owing to the continuation of a celibate clergy and the need to enumerate and describe every sin, including the sexual. But in the Lutheran milieu—sins not being described and the clergy being married—no one seems to have thought it necessary to protect the modesty of the confessee or to shield the clergy unduly from the temptation presented by, let us say, young women describing their lustful thoughts. Reinle, *Die Ausstattung deutscher Kirchen im Mittelalter: Eine Einführung* (Darmstadt: Wissenschaftliche Buchgesellschaft, 1988), 66–67, speculates concerning very rare enclosed confessionals in the early sixteenth century.

16 Musée Royal des Beaux-Arts, Antwerp.

17 For a longer treatment of this subject, see Erich Roth, *Die Privatbeichte und Schlüsselgewalt in der Theologie der Reformatoren* (Gütersloh: Bertelsmann,

1952); Emil F. Fischer, *Zur Geschichte der evangelischen Beichte*, 2 vols. (Leipzig: Dieterich, 1902–1903), 1: *Die katholische Beichtpraxis bei Beginn der Reformation und Luthers Stellung dazu in den Anfängen seiner Wirksamkeit*, and 2: *Niedergang und Neubelebung des Beichtinstituts in Wittenberg in den Anfängen der Reformation*; Richard Franke, "Geschichte der evangelischen Privatbeichte in Sachsen," *Beiträge zur Sächsischen Kirchengeschichte* 19 (1905), 41–142; Laurentius Klein, *Evangelisch-lutherische Beichte: Lehre und Praxis*, Konfessionskundliche und kontroverstheologische Studien 5 (Paderborn: Bonifacius Druckerei, 1961); Kurt Aland, "Die Privatbeichte im Luthertum von ihren Anfängen bis zu ihrer Auflösung" in idem, *Kirchengeschichtliche Entwürfe* (Gütersloh: Gütersloher Verlagshaus, 1960), 452–519; Ernst Bezzel, *Frei zum Eingeständnis: Geschichte und Praxis der evangelischen Einzelbeichte*, Calwer Theologische Monographien 10 (Stuttgart: Calwer, 1982), 11–25. Cf. Tentler, *Sin and Confession*, 349–50.

18 For a brief discussion of Luther's definition of sacrament, see Paul Althaus, *The Theology of Martin Luther*, trans. Robert C. Schulz (Philadelphia: Fortress Press, 1966), 345–52. Not everyone agreed with Luther in confining the sacraments to two: the Hohenlohe ecclesiastical ordinance of 1553 still insisted that there were three, including absolution (penance): Emil Sehling, ed., *Die evangelischen Kirchenordnungen des 16. Jahrhunderts* (KOO), 15 vols. to date (vols. 1–5, Leipzig: O. R. Reisland, 1902–1913; vols. 6–15 Tübingen: J. C. Mohr [Paul Siebeck (*sic*)], 1955–1977), 14: 57, 60.

19 Reproduced in English translation in John Dillenberger, ed., *Martin Luther: Selections from His Writings* (New York: Doubleday, 1962), 490–500.

20 Dillenberger, *Martin Luther: Selections*, 320. Cf. Luther's intermediate writings: "Sermo de poenitencia. 1518," *Dr. Martin Luthers Werke* (Weimar: Böhlau, 1883–   ), Weimarer Ausgabe (WA) 1: 319–24; "Eine Freiheit des Sermons päpstlichen Ablaß und Gnade belangend. 1518," WA 1: 383–93; and "Eine kurze Unterweisung, wie man beichten soll. 1519," WA 2: 59–65.

21 "Von der Beicht, ob die der Bapst macht habe zu gepieten. 1521," WA 8: 138–204. Luther addressed this treatise to Franz von Sickingen.

22 Luther also was initially reluctant to see a new form of priestly ordination adopted. But Johann Friedrich, stunned by events in Münster, insisted on ordination as a form of examination and licensing (Susan C. Karant-Nunn, *Luther's Pastors: The Reformation in the Ernestine Countryside* [Philadelphia: The American Philosophical Society, 1979], 56–60).

23 I basically agree with Tentler's analysis, *Sin and Confession*, 351–62. His conclusion is summed up with "The correct word is forgive, not purify" (361). Confession and absolution convey God's loving pardon; they do not purge or relieve of guilt.

24 WA 12: 215–16.

25 *Ain Sendtbrieff herrn Joh. Bugenhagen Pomern, Pfarrern zu Wittemberg, über ain frag vom Sacrament. Item ain underricht von der Beycht und Christlicher Absolution* (Wittenberg, 1525).

26 "Von der Beichte," WA 10/3: 61.

27 Reflecting his earlier preference for the collective confession and absolution, Bugenhagen's first three church ordinances contained such a ritual (Johannes H. Bergsma, *Die Reform der Messliturgie durch Johannes Bugenhagen [1485–1558]* [Kevelaer: Butzon and Bercker; Hildesheim: Bernward Verlag, 1966], 179).

28 Joachim Friedrich, Margrave of Brandenburg and primate of the archchapter of Magdeburg, ordered in his visitation instructions of 1585 that those making their confession did not have to recount the details, "darmitt nichtt wiederumb eine solche greuliche Carnificina conscientia

dardurch angerichtet...": Sachsen-Anhalt Landeshauptarchiv Magdeburg (LHAMag), Rep. A12 Gen. 2442, "Visitationsordnung 1585," fol. 30. He concluded, "Dann dieße beichtt nichtt zur Inquisition der heimlichenn vnnd verborgenenn Sunndenn, Sonndern furnemlich zur Lehr vnnd vnntterweißung der vnuerßtenndiegenn, vnnd zum troßt der betrubten angefohtenen gewißen verordenet ißt...", fol. 38. Hessisches Hauptstaat-sarchiv Wiesbaden (HSAWies), Abt. 171 Nr. S 303, "Ein bedenckens von heÿligentrachten, Walfarthen, Kirchweyhungen etc. Vnd andern Ceremonien vor alten Ze[iten?]," probably before 1530, provides that priests are to ask no untoward questions in the confessional, fols. 4–5. There is always a certain sexual threat associated with the confessional, it seems. A century later in Thuringia, parish visitors thought that they had to inquire in every community whether those who were confessing stood too close to the clergyman: Thüringisches Hauptstaatsarchiv Weimar (HSA-Wei), B. 2891, "Kirchen- vnd Schul-Visitations-Acta, 1641 bis 1647," fol. 17.

29 Translated by me from the German contained in Leif Grane, *Die Confessio Augustana: Einführung in die Hauptgedanken der lutherischen Reformation*, 4th. ed. (Göttingen: Vandenhoeck & Ruprecht, 1990), 175–76.

30 We must bear in mind that this was not a new use of the confessional: Catholic confessors were to make sure that those to whom they ministered knew the rudimentary articles of the faith (for example, Tentler, *Sin and Confession*, 84). But Lutherans were faced with the need to *alter* the beliefs of nearly everyone they encountered, and so the confessor's role as teacher became more prominent than before.

31 Sächsisches Hauptstaatsarchiv Dresden (HSADres), Loc. 10598, "Registration der Visitation etliccher Sächsischen und Meißnischen Kreise, Ämter, Städte, Klöster u. [*sic*] Dörfer 1529 [documents actually end 1531]," fol. 12.

32 In central Saxony in 1617, the pastors were uncertain whether they themselves could take Communion if they had not first confessed to a neighboring cleric. Some thought they could only receive Communion from another clergyman, and some just went ahead and took it themselves. The visitors did not record their decision: HSADres, Loc. 1999, "Local-Visitation der Superintendentzen Leipzigk, Grimma, Penigk, Eulenburgk, Borna, Rochlitz, Pegau 1618–20 [contains much from 1617 too]," fol. 393. Rural pastors were also in doubt as to whether they had the power to speak public absolution in urban parishes during the ritual of the Mass in cases where they were standing in for city clergy (fol. 394)!

33 Friedrich Wilhelm Oediger, *Über die Bildung der Geistlichen im späten Mittelalter* (Leiden: Brill, 1953), esp. "Das notwendige Wissen," 46–57; Susan Karant-Nunn, *Luther's Pastors*, 13–21; Adolph Franz, *Die Messe im deutschen Mittelalter: Beiträge zur Geschichte der Liturgie und des religiösen Volkslebens* (Darmstadt: Wissenschaftliche Buchgesellschaft, 1963), 639–40, in which he notes that in the thirteenth century at least two bishops were unseated for being illiterate.

34 Evangelisches Landeskirchliches Archiv Stuttgart (ELKAS), A1 Nr. 1, fol. 134.

35 "...und was im der geistlichen güter oder habe mangel, in gemein, oder besondern verhören lassen..." I take this in this context to refer to a general summation versus an enumeration of sins.

36 Sehling, KOO, 1: 202.

37 For example, in the 1605 instructions to the visitors in the Württemberg superintendency of Marbach (Baden-Württembergisches

Hauptstaatsarchiv Stuttgart [B-WHSAS], A281 Bü 827, "Superintender [*sic*] Marbach. Kirchenvisitationen 1605," fol. 1.

38 Melanchthon told the story of a rural pastor who, when asked if he taught the Ten Commandments, replied, "I don't have that book yet" (Paul Drews, *Der evangelische Geistliche in der deutschen Vergangenheit* [Jena: E. Diederich, 1905], 15). In 1562 in a village governed by Magdeburg, priest Thomas Kruger told the visitors that God the Holy Ghost had been created by God the Father, and that God the Father and the Mother of God were the first person in the Godhead (LHAMag, Rep. A12 Gen. 2435, "Kirchenvisitation 1462/64 Städte im Holzkreis," Brumbÿ). Kruger had been pastor there for twenty years. Similar anecdotes are, of course, many.

39 Sehling, KOO, 1: 268–69, "Albertinisches Sachsen, 1539." For other examples, see also 1, 318; 3: 460, "Kirchenordnung für Teschen von 1584"; 4: 445, "Das Herzogthum Pommern"; 5: 207, "Mecklenburg, Kirchenordnung von 1552," which adopts the language of Heinrich of Saxony's Agenda; 6/1: 560, "Lüneburg, Kirchenordnung 1564"; 13/3: 56–57, "Herzogtum Pfalz-Neuburg, Kirchenordnung von 1543"; 13/3: 395–97, "Reichsstadt Regensburg, 1542," a long admonition to be used in before collective confession and absolution; 15: 64, "Grafschaft Hohenlohe, Kirchenordnung 1553."

40 Fischer, *Zur Geschichte der evangelischen Beichte.*

41 The Albertine Saxon ordinance of 1539 approved by Duke Heinrich, Sehling, KOO, 1: 269.

42 For example, the case of Sundhausen, a village in Württemberg, in 1584, where, the pastor reported to the visitors, the women didn't come often to the sermon. The head visitor told the clergyman that during the next Easter confession he should examine each one of them in particular concerning their faith (ELKAS, A1 Nr. 1, 1584, fol. 46; Cannstadt near Stuttgart, 1563). So many people come to Communion during the week before Easter (and only then) that it is impossible to hold *priuatam explorationem* with each one, and even when times for confession are announced, no-one comes (B-WHSAS, A281 310a, "Das Nachtmal," no pagination).

43 Some village pastors must have been tempted to wait in the warmth of their parsonages, for the minutes of visitations sometimes prohibit this or note that a particular pastor does not do so; for example, the Saxon village of Großpetschau in 1617 (HSADres, Loc. 1999, "Local-Visitation der Superintendentzen Leipzigk, Grimma, Penigk, Eulenburgk, Borna, Rochlitz, Pegau 1618–20 [contains much from 1617 too]," fol. 57).

44 Shortly after that holiday in 1627, Abbess Dorothea Sophia of Quedlinburg sternly admonished her subjects (LHAMag, Rep. A12 Gen. 1332, "Qvedlinburgische Kirchen-Ordnung 15. April 1627," fol. 4):

> At confession and Communion an improper situation exists such that often young and other thoughtless people forcefully press themselves forward [in line], driving old people and also pregnant women back, which is to be avoided. In the future, these weaker people are to be allowed to go to the front of the line.

45 HSAWies, Abt. 171 Nr. S 303, fol. 28.

46 For example, HSAWei, Reg. Ji 67, "Kirchen- vnd Schul-Visitations-Acta. 1586," fol. 281; B-WHSAS, A281 310a, 1563, Cannstadt, no pagination

47 Pertinent background on the Swiss perspective is Johannes Oecolampadius, *Quod non sit onerosa christianis confessio* (Basel, 1521), an attack on auricular confession to priests. On the Duchy of Württemberg

and its retention of a common absolution in the service of worship, see Martin Brecht and Hermann Ehmer, *Südwestdeutsche Reformationsgeschichte* (Stuttgart: Calwer, 1984), 226. See the Nassau-Saarbrücken ecclesiastical ordinance of shortly after 1618, HSAWies, Abt. 131 Nr. Xa, 1, "Betr. Einführung, Erneuerung u. Verbesserung von Kirchenordnungen in den nassau-saarbrückischen Landen u. Gemeinschaften 1559–1765," fols. 50, 93. For a theological discussion of Reformed teachings on penance, see Jan Rohls, *Theologie reformierter Bekenntnisschriften* (Göttingen: Vandenhoeck & Ruprecht, 1987), 166–73.

48 Burnett, *The Yoke of Christ: Martin Bucer and Christian Discipline*, Sixteenth Century Essays and Studies 26 (Kirksville, Mo.: Sixteenth Century Journal Publishers, 1994), passim; also her earlier article, "Church Discipline and Moral Reformation in the Thought of Martin Bucer," *Sixteenth Century Journal* 22 (1991), 439–56.

49 Sehling, KOO, 13: 397–400. In 1567, a new emphasis on the reform of behavior after confession and Communion was added (13: 400–402).

50 In 1586, the visitors in the Württemberg countryside discovered a pastor who used the collective confession and absolution because individual confession "was not in use before and many people were frightened away from communion by it" (ELKAS, A1 Nr. 1, 1586), fols. 176–77. The visitors insisted that he abandon his idiosyncratic practice and conform to the rules. On Calvin's estimation of confession, see Roth, *Privatbeichte*, 133–61; Tentler, *Sin and Confession*, 349–50, 365–66.

51 Otto Weber, ed. *Der Heidelberger Katechismus* (Gütersloh: Gerd Mohn, 1990); Volkmar Joestel, "Kurfürst Friedrich III. von der Pfalz (1515–1576)," in Rolf Straubel and Ulman Weiss, eds., *Kaiser, König, Kardinal: Deutsche Fürsten 1500–1800* (Leipzig: Urania, 1991), 124–30; Brecht and Ehmer, *Südwestdeutsche Reformationsgeschichte*, 375–77.

52 Hans R. Guggisberg, "Das lutheranisierende Basel," in Hans-Christoph Rublack, ed., *Die lutherische Konfessionalisierung in Deutschland*, Schriften des Vereins für Reformationsgeschichte 197 (Gütersloh: Gerd Mohn, 1992), 200.

53 HSAWies, Abt. 171 Nr. D226, no title, no date but clearly the 1570s, fol. 19. See the concise account of Paul Münch in Anton Schindler and Walter Ziegler, eds., *Die Territorien des Reichs im Zeitalter der Reformation und Konfessionalisierung: Land und Konfession 1500–1650*, vol. 4, *Mittleres Deutschland* (Münster: Aschendorff, 1992), 243–48 and the bibliography 249–52. Newly published is Johannes Wolfart, "Why Was Confession so Contentious in Early Modern Lindau?" in Bob Scribner and Trevor Johnson, eds., *Popular Religion in Germany and Central Europe 1400–1800* (London: Macmillan, 1996), 140–65.

54 Augsburg's ecclesiastical ordinance of 1537 includes a collective confession and absolution before the Eucharist, with the warning that "kain buoler, kain geiziger, kain götzendiener, kain lösterer, kain trunkner, kain rauber und, was desgleichen ist" should come to the table unless they felt regret ("reu und laid") for their sins (Sehling, KOO, 12/2: 80). This indicates that at this time Lutherans in Augsburg did not undergo auricular confession. The collective form was still in use in 1555 (KOO, 12/2: 102).

55 Nischan, *Prince, People, and Confession: The Second Reformation in Brandenburg* (Philadelphia: University of Pennsylvania Press, 1994), 144–45.

56 Vogler, "Die Gebetbücher in der lutherischen Orthodoxie (1550–1700)," in Rublack, *Die lutherische Konfessionalisierung*, 424–34, here at 426.

57 John Bossy, "The Social History of Confession in the Age of the Reformation," *Transactions of the Royal Historical Society* 25 (1975), 21–38;

Hervé Martin, "Confession et contrôle social a la fin du Moyen Age," in Groupe de la Bussière, *Pratiques de la confession*, 117–36; Nicole Bériou, "Autour de Latran IV," 80; R. Rusconi, "De la prédication à la confession: transmission et contrôle de modèles de comportement au XIIIe siècle," in *Faire croire* (Rome: École française de Rome, 1981), 67–85.

58 Martin, "Confession et contrôle social," esp. 132–33. See, too, Thomas N. Tentler, "The *Summa* for Confessors as an Instrument of Social Control," in Charles Trinkaus and Heiko A. Oberman, eds., *The Pursuit of Holiness in Late Medieval and Renaissance Religion* (Leiden: Brill, 1974), 103–26, in which, despite the title, Tentler regards confession as multidimensional, and having the purpose of relieving the human conscience as well as to control behavior. Leonard E. Boyle, of the Pontifical Institute of Mediaeval Studies, responds with the Catholic view that the confessors' manuals were designed exclusively to assist and teach the Christian (*The Pursuit of Holiness*, 126–30), in answer to which Tentler tends somewhat more to the social-control side of the argument. To these positions ought to be added the Protestant one, represented by Steven Ozment, who referred to the great psychological burden of late medieval Catholicism (*The Reformation in the Cities: The Appeal of Protestantism to Sixteenth-century Germany and Switzerland* [New Haven: Yale University Press, 1975], 9, 50, and the section entitled "The Burden of Late Medieval Religion," 22–33).

59 Tentler, *Sin and Confession*, 363–70. I have the impression that confession gradually became optional during the eighteenth century. For example, Niedersächsisches Staatsarchiv Wolfenbüttel (NSAW), Findbuch, describing Act. no. 2 Alt 15010–11, "Die Beichte und das Abendmahl, Beichtdispense, die Änderung der Beichtvorschriften, Abschaffung des Beichtstuhls und Erlaß der VO[?] betr. die in Ansehung der Privatbeichte verstattete Gewissensfreiheit, 1745–1783." For a favorable assessment of Catholic confession, see Lawrence G. Duggan, "Fear and Confession on the Eve of the Reformation," *Archive for Reformation Germany* 75 (1984), 153–75.

60 See the abbreviated bibliography on confessionalization and social disciplining in the Introduction, n. 19.

61 See, for instance, Philippe Denis, "Remplacer la confession: absolutions collectives et discipline ecclésiastique dans les églises de la réforme au XVIe siècle," in Groupe de la Bussière, *Pratiques de la confession*, 165–76.

62 For the case of Saxony, see my "Neoclericalism and Anticlericalism in Saxony, 1555–1675," *Journal of Interdisciplinary History* 24, 4 (Spring 1994), 615–37, esp. 624–26. Other evidence is plentiful. Johann Wilhelm of Ernestine Saxony commanded all his *Schosser* in 1557 "with serious diligence" to detect and punish moral transgressors and people who did not receive the sacrament. They should report such people to higher tribunals at any time: HSAWei, Reg. Ii 2667, "1557. Schriften betr. die von dem Pfarrer, Schosser und Rath zu Altenburg erstattete allgemeine Anzeige der verschiedenen Mangel und Gebrechen . . . ," fol. 19. A particularly harsh instance of the involvement of secular authorities is provided by the visitation ordinances of 1533–1534 in Saxony, in which it is ordered that, if a child should swear by God's name, "he shall be brought before the authorities, and either the father or the mother or the next closest relation shall be called in and in the presence of the authorities shall give the child twelve strokes of the rod." If they did not wish so to punish their child, they were to be imprisoned for four days and nights or put in the stock: HSAWei, Reg. Ii 6, "Visitation zu Altenburg, Remsen, Born, Colditz,

Nimpschen, Grim, Eilenburg, Torgau, Dieben vnndt Gräffenhänichen 1533, 34," fol. 296.

63 ELKAS, A1 Nr. 1, 1585, fols. 64–65.

64 ELKAS, A1 Nr. 1, 1586, fol. 169.

65 ELKAS, A1 Nr. 1, 1586, fol. 47.

66 HSAWei, Reg. Ii 2775, "1560. Schriften betr. die Beschwerde der Fraw des Mullers Clemens König und deren Sohn gegen den Pfarrer zu Graizschen wegen verweigerter Absolution," fols. 1–3.

67 LHAMag, Rep. A12 Gen. 1332, "Qvedlinburgische Kirchen-Ordnung 15. April 1627," fol. 3. Cf. Brandenburgisches Landeshauptarchiv Potsdam (BLHAPot), Pr. Br. Rep. 40A 549, "Osterburgischer Kirchenvisitations Abschied wegen Osterburg von 1581," fol. 8; BLHAPot, Pr. Br. Rep. 40A 648, "Neustadt Salzwedel," 1579, fol. 62; HSAWies, Abt. 131 Nr. Xa, 1, "Betr. Einführungen, Erneuerung u. Verbesserung von Kirchenordnungen in den nassau-saarbrückischen Landen u. gemeinschaften 1559–1765," shortly after 1618, fol. 46.

68 ELKAS, A1 Nr. 1, 1584, fol. 63.

69 HSAWies, Abt. 171 Nr. Z1975, fol. 29, no date, and it is not clear who is making this complaint or exactly to whom. The writer continues that no one can see into another's heart, and the ministers of the word, in his opinion, should not try to do so. Public ecclesiastical penance is designed as an additional punishment and infamy.

70 HSAWei, Reg. Ii 2667, "1557. Schriften betr. die von dem Pfarrer, Schosser, und Rath zu Altenburg erstattete allgemeine Anzeige der verschiedenen Mangel und Gebrechen...," fols. 1–2. He sent the same instructions to every superintendent and every city council in his lands (internal evidence, fol. 16), and he threatened every unregenerate sinner with exile (fol. 16).

71 Niedersächsisches Landeskirchliches Archiv Braunschweig (LKABr), V1938, "Verordnungen des Herzog Julius in Kirchensachen 1569–1575," fol. 24. In or with the visitation protocols, one can sometimes find lists of the names of sacrament-avoiders, for example, NSLHAW, 14 Alt Fb. 1 Nr. I 37I (the preceding digit is a Roman numeral one), no title but from the county of Eberstein, no firm date but apparently 1571, no pagination, separate lists of seventeen and thirty-three such individuals, mostly men. A separate document in this miscellaneous mass—again, without pagination—contains the complaint that the men rarely come to the sacrament, usually only at Eastertime. On the relations among prince, clergy (including theologians), nobility, and cities in Braunschweig-Wolfenbüttel, and their differences in motivation, see Luise Schorn-Schütte, "Lutherische Konfessionalisierung? Das Beispiel Braunschweig-Wolfenbüttel (1589–1613)," in Rublack, ed., *Die lutherische Konfessionalisierung*, 163–94.

72 Ozment, *Reformation in the Cities*, 9, 50, and the section entitled, "The Burden of Late Medieval Religion," 22–32. Ozment's problem, in my opinion, is the result of his purporting to study common people using exclusively the treatises of learned men—Ozment remains a historian of ideas.

73 Ozment, *Reformation in the Cities*, 47–54.

74 Ozment, *Reformation in the Cities*, 44.

75 We should not forget Bernd Moeller's insightful article on the intensity of Germany piety at the end of the Middle Ages, published in English as "Piety in Germany around 1500," trans. Joyce Irwin, in Steven E. Ozment, ed., *The Reformation in Medieval Perspective* (Chicago: Quadrangle Books, 1971), 50–75.

76 Heinrich Gerlach, "Kleine Chronik von Freiberg," *Mittheilungen von dem Freiberger Alterthumsvereins* 12 (1875), 7. Gustav Hermann Ulbricht, *Geschichte der Reformation in Freiberg* (Leipzig: Carl Heinrich Reclam, 1837), 13, says that Tetzel was simply mocked.

77 Miriam Usher Chrisman, *Conflicting Visions of Reform: German Lay Propaganda Pamphlets, 1519–1530* (Atlantic Highlands, N. J.: Humanities Press, 1996), 93–98.

78 Chrisman, *Conflicting Visions of Reform*, 168–71. Among others, Rysschner, *Ain gesprech buchlin/von ainem Weber und ainem Kramer uber das buchlin Doctoris Mathie Kretz von der haimlichen Beycht...* (n.p., 1524). On Rysschner and the setting in which he wrote, see Paul A. Russell, *Lay Theology in the Reformation; Popular Pamphleteers in Southwest Germany 1521–1525* (Cambridge, England: Cambridge University Press, 1986), 112–27; and for the views of Sebastian Lotzer of Memmingen, see 99.

79 The clergy, however, debated this issue among others. Johann Sommer, pastor in Wiesbaden, wrote in approximately 1560 to his prince about his inclination to make ecclesiastical reforms modeled on those of Palatine Count Wolfgang, which is to say Calvinist reforms. He urged the ruler to restore private confession and absolution "previously done away with and stopped," because it was, in his view, "nottig von wegen der Jugent vnd sonderlichem trost der gewißen" (HSAWies, Abt. 131 Nr. Xa, 1, "Betr. Einführung, Erneuerung u. Verbesserung von Kirchenordnungen in den nassau-saarbrückischen Landen u. Gemeinschaften 1559–1765," fol. 6.

80 "Lutherische Beichte und Sozialdisziplinierung," *Archiv für Reformationsgeschichte* 84 (1993), 127–55. Rublack's footnotes point the way to the larger body of literature on local confession.

81 WA, *Tischreden* 4: 693–94, nos. 5174, 5175.

82 The pastor in Borna (Saxony) still receives *Beichtpfennige* in 1574: HSADres, Loc. 1992, "Visitation der Superintendentur Borna 1574," fol. 3.

83 Rublack, "Lutherische Beichte," 143–44.

84 Luther, in thinking about writing a German Mass, proposed informally to Nicolaus Hausmann a vernacular admonition to those who were about to commune, that included the following (WA 19: 47):

> Welche aber noch in offentlichen Sunden stecken, als Geiz, Haß, Zorn, Neid, Wucher, Unkeuscheit und dergleichen, und nicht abzulassen gedenken, den sei hiemit abgesagt, und warnen sie treulich, daß sie nicht erzu gehen...

85 ELKAS, A1 Nr. 1, 1582, fols. 55–56, 118; cf. A1 Nr. 1 1586, fols. 93, 236.

86 Sabean, "Communion and Community: The Refusal to Attend the Lord's Supper in the Sixteenth Century," in idem, *Power in the Blood: Popular Culture and Village Discourse in Early Modern Germany* (Cambridge, England: Cambridge University Press, 1984), 37–60. He addresses the attitude that sin often drew upon itself the punishment of illness, and also the relationship between individual transgression and social unity.

87 [No first name given] Wolters, "Die Kirchenvisitationen der Aufbauzeit (1570–1600) im vormaligen Herzogtum Braunschweig-Wolfenbüttel," *Zeitschrift der Gesellschaft für niedersächsische Kirchengeschichte* 43 (1938), 204–37, here at 227.

88 ELKAS, A1 Nr. 1 1581, fol. 62; A1 Nr. 1 1585, 104; A1 Nr. 1 1586, fols. 197, 224.

89 For an introduction to medieval church interiors, see Reinle, *Die Ausstattung deutscher Kirchen*.

90 On differences of opinion among medieval theologians as to what exactly transubstantiation was, see Gary Macy, "The Dogma of Transubstantiation in the Middle Ages," *The Journal of Ecclesiastical History* 45, 1 (1994), 11–41.

91 I am taking the position that many people did witness the elevation. Many rood screens were at least modestly transparent, and others had peep holes. In addition, monstrances presented the consecrated Host to the popular view. On the liturgical colors, see the recent Rudolf Suntrup, "Liturgische Farbenbedeutung im Mittelalter und in der frühen Neuzeit," in Gertrud Blaschitz, Helmut Hundsbichler, Gerhard Jaritz, and Elisabeth Vavra, *Symbole des Alltags, Alltag der Symbole* (Graz: Akademische Druck- und Verlagsanstalt, 1992), 445–67, the footnotes of which will lead back to a sizable older secondary literature.

92 For a thorough investigation of bourgeois patronage that resulted in the rich decoration of church interiors in late medieval Cologne, see Wolfgang Schmid, *Stifter und Auftraggeber im spätmittelalterlichen Köln*, (Cologne: Kölnisches Stadtmuseum, 1994).

93 Michael Baxandall, *The Limewood Sculptors of Renaissance Germany* (New Haven, Conn.: Yale University Press, 1980).

94 For a brief list of such "annoying, damaging, and unnecessary…spectacles and theater," see the ecclesiastical ordinance of Hohenlohe for 1553, Sehling, KOO, 14: 76–77. Surviving *Palmesel* can still be seen in museums all over Germany. One dating from about 1200 is in the collection of the Staatliche Museen Preußischer Kulturbesitz in Berlin, in the gallery of medieval sculpture. The best collection I know of is across the Swiss border at the Historisches Museum Basel, in the Barfüsserkirche.

95 Erwin Panofsky's controversial essay, *Gothic Architecture and Scholasticism* (London, 1957), on the Gothic cathedral's embodiment of key mental habits of scholastic theology, presents a thesis that, even if true, can hardly have been perceived by the laity. Of considerable interest is Umberto Eco, *Art and Beauty in the Middle Ages*, trans. Hugh Bredin (New Haven: Yale University Press, 1986), but it, too, deals only with the esthetic perceptions of the great intellectuals of the era.

96 On the development of the altar, its structure and materials, its meanings, and its accoutrements, see Joseph Braun, *Der christliche Altar in seiner geschichtlichen Entwicklung*, 2 vols. (Munich: Alte Meister Günther Koch, 1924). Adolph Franz's *Die Messe im deutschen Mittelalter* takes up popular attitudes toward the altar and all its accessories, 87–114; also Reinle, *Die Ausstattung deutscher Kirchen*, 3–23.

97 Braun, *Der christliche Altar*, 1: 525–660, on the altar as a grave. One of the most popular Eucharistic depictions of the fifteenth century was of Gregory the Great (590–604) elevating the Host and the living Christ appearing on the altar. See Uwe Westfeling, ed., *Die Messe Gregors des Grossen. Vision, Kunst, Realität. Katalog und Führer zu einer Ausstellung im Schnütgen-Museum der Stadt Köln* (Cologne, 1982).

98 Bernard Vogler understands the significance of the church bell in *Vie religieuse en Pays Rhenan dans la second moitié du XVIe siècle (1556–1619)*, 3 vols. (Lille: Université de Lille III Service de reproduction des thèses, 1974), 1: 586–94.

99 As more and more pews were installed in Lutheran churches during the sixteenth century, much conflict arose, in part because they obstructed other people's view of the altar (for example, Sehling, KOO, 4: 421 [Lauenburg, 1585]). On the strange phenomenon of iconoclasts ripping pews out of Zurich churches, see Peter Jezler, "Etappen des Zürcher Bildersturms: Ein Beitrag zur soziologischen Differenzierung

ikonoklastischer Vorgänge in der Reformation," in Bob Scribner, ed., *Bilder und Bildersturm im Spätmittelalter und in der frühen Neuzeit*, Wolfenbütteler Forschungen 46 (Wiesbaden: Otto Harrassowitz, 1990), 143–74, here at 156–63.

100 See, for instance, the illustrated flier by Georg Pencz (ca. 1500–1550), "Inhalt zweierley predig, yede in gemein in einer kurtzen summ begriffen," reproduced in Friedrich W. H. Hollstein, *German Engravings, Etchings and Woodcuts ca. 1400–1700*, vol. 31, ed. Tilman Falk (Roosendaal, The Netherlands: Koninklijke van Poll, 1991), 247. Often they simply sat down on the floor, as shown in Urs Graf's (ca. 1485–1527/1528) illustration of the title page of Michael Lochmayer's *Parachiale Curatorum*, reproduced in Hollstein, *German Engravings*, vol. 11, ed. Fedja Anzelewsky and Robert Zijlma (Amsterdam: Van Gendt, 1977), 150.

101 Franz states that the Church demanded that people attend Mass on Sundays and holidays, but they did not strictly enforce this rule. One difficulty was that the churches of the mendicants gave people a choice of places to hear Mass: *Die Messe im deutschen Mittelalter*, 15–16.

102 On the *missa sicca* and its history, see Franz, *Die Messe im deutschen Mittelalter*, 79–84.

103 Emmanuel Le Roy Ladurie, *Montaillou: The Promised Land of Error*, trans. Barbara Bray (New York: Vintage Books, 1979), 303–05, 322–26.

104 Rubin, *Corpus Christi*, especially the sections entitled "Teaching the Laity" and "Teaching the Eucharist with Miracles," 98–129. I do disagree with Rubin's categorical statement that "a political end motivated the whole exercise of teaching..." (115). See also Edward Muir's forthcoming *Ritual in Early Modern Europe* (Cambridge, England: Cambridge University Press, 1997), esp. chap. 5, "The Reformation as a Revolution in Ritual Theory," 4–15 of draft 2. I am most grateful to Professor Muir for allowing me to see this in advance of publication.

105 On the late medieval liturgical engagement of people's senses, see Bob Scribner, "Das Visuelle in der Volksfrömmigkeit," in idem, ed., *Bilder und Bildersturm im Spätmittelalter und in der frühen Neuzeit*, Wolfenbütteler Forschungen 46 (Wiesbaden: Otto Harrassowitz, 1990), 9–20.

106 For the history of the Mass before the fifteenth century, as well as after the Council of Trent, see Josef Andreas Jungmann, *Missarum Sollemnia: Eine genetische Erklärung der römischen Messe*, 2 vols., 2nd ed. (Vienna: Herder, 1949); trans. Francis A. Brunner as *The Mass of the Roman Rite: Its Origins and Development (Missarum Sollemnia)*, 2 vols. (New York: Benziger Brothers, 1951, 1955). A popular modern treatment of the pre-Vatican II Latin Mass is John Coventry, *The Breaking of Bread: A Short History of the Mass* (London and New York: Sheed and Ward, 1950).

107 Terence Bailey, *The Processions of Sarum and the Western Church* (Toronto: Pontifical Institute of Mediaeval Studies, 1971). Bailey's charts of rogation antiphons used in major dioceses in France, Italy, German-speaking Switzerland, and Mainz shows a shared body of liturgical material, from which, however, Mainz (though not as often Einsiedeln and St. Gall) departed (122–27). See particularly the drawings from the Sarum processional of 1502 of the vestments, sacramental objects, and order of march to be employed in various processions (180–92).

108 Franz, *Die Messe im deutschen Mittelalter*, 622–37, concerning the priestly desire to keep aspects of the Mass secret from the people. Virginia Reinburg has pointed out that even the Gospel was read in Latin, for its purpose in the ceremony was not to edify the people, nor, certainly, to give them access to the scriptural message ("Liturgy and the Laity in Late

Medieval and Reformation France," *Sixteenth Century Journal* 23, 3 (1992), 526–47, here at 531.

109 Eva Labouvie, *Zauberei und Hexenwerk: Ländlicher Hexenglaube in der frühen Neuzeit* (Frankfurt/Main: Fischer, 1991), 233–34.

110 Franz, *Die Messe in deutschen Mittelalter*, 54–55, and in general on the fruits of the Mass, 36–72. There were numerous versions other than Nider's.

111 Otto Nußbaum, *Kloster, Priestermönch und Privatmesse*, Beiträge zur Religions- und Kirchengeschichte des Altertums 14 (Bonn: Peter Hanstein, 1961), esp. 152–58; A. L. Mayer, "Die Liturgie und der Geist der Gotik," *Jahrbuch für Liturgiewissenschaft* 6 (1926), 86, 93.

112 Fernand Cabrol, *Mass of the Western Rite*, 175.

113 Franz, *Die Messe im deutschen Mittelalter*, surveys votive Masses, Masses designed to relieve tribulation, Masses for the dead, Masses in times of extreme distress, 178–291.

114 Nußbaum, *Privatmesse*, 209–11.

115 François Amiot, *History of the Mass*, trans. Lancelot C. Sheppard (New York: Hawthorn Books, 1959), 63–64.

116 Johannes Bergsma reproduces the text of an early sixteenth-century Catholic Mass, one that was printed in Paris in 1530, in *Die Reform der Messliturgie*, 39–48.

117 For a modern priest's explanation of the secret prayers, see Coventry, *The Breaking of Bread*, 104.

118 Wandel, "Envisioning God: Image and Liturgy in Reformation Zurich," *Sixteenth Century Journal* 24, 1 (1993), 21–40, here at 29–31.

119 Nevertheless, the manuscript illumination reproduced in Rubin, *Corpus Christi*, 41, shows the kneeling Christian holding the cloth under his own chin with both hands, which would have compelled the priest to place the Host in his mouth.

120 HSAWies, Abt. 171 Nr. D245, "Protocollum Generalis Visitationis Aller Pastoreÿenn Vnnd darin gehörender Capellen in der Graueschafft Dietzs gehaltenn Anno 1590," fol. 5. Among practices to be abolished were "porrectio sacrorum symbolorum in ora communicantium."

121 Johann P. B. Kreuser, *Heilige Meßopfer, geschichtlich erklärt*, 2nd ed. (Paderborn: Ferdinand Schöningh, 1854), unpaginated schematic plan at back of volume. For a broader context, see Joan Cadden, *Meanings of Sex Difference in the Middle Ages: Medicine, Science, and Culture* (Cambridge, England: Cambridge University Press, 1993), esp. the references to right–left opposition, passim.

122 Bugenhagen observes to the Danish superintendents that he has seen disorder in the mixing of men and women at the sacrament in Copenhagen and anticipates that the order will eventually prevail that exists in Wittenberg (Otto Vogt, *Dr. Johannes Bugenhagens Briefwechsel* [Stettin: Leon Saunier, 1888], 185, no. 6, April 28, 1539).

123 For example, LHAMag, Reg. 12A Gen. 2434, "Kirchenvisitation 1562/64, Städte im Holzkreis," fol. 198: "Ds in emtpfahung des hochwirdigen sacraments das volck ordentlich vmb denn altar gehen soll, vnd nicht vnder ein ander wie vor geschehen, lauffen, vnordnung vnd gefher zu verhueten."

124 For an abbreviated treatment of Luther's liturgical alterations, see Frieder Schulz, "Luthers liturgische Reformen: Kontinuität und Innovation," *Archiv für Liturgiewissenschaft* 25 (1983), 249–75, on the Mass (256–63) and the tables (272–74).

125 "Ein Sermon von dem hochwürdigen Sakrament des heiligen wahren Leichnams Christi und von den Brüderschaften. 1519," WA 2: 738–58;

"Ein Sermon von dem Neuen Testament das ist von der heyligen Messe. 1520," WA 6: 353–78; "De abroganda missa privata. 1521," WA 8: 398–466; its reworking in German, "Vom miszbrauch der Messe. 1522)," WA 8: 477–563; "Von beider Gestalt des Sakraments zu nehmen. 1522," WA 10/2: 1–41; "Von Anbeten des Sakraments des heiligen Leichnams Christi," WA 11: 417–56; "Vom Greuel der Stillmesse. 1525," WA 18: 8–36; "Wider die himmlischen Propheten, von dene Bildern und Sakrament. 1525," WA 18: 37–125; "Vom Abendmahl Christi, Bekenntnis. 1528," WA 26: 241–509; "Von der Winkelmesse und Pfaffenweihe. 1533," WA 38: 171–256. See also "Die Disputation contra missam privatam. 29. Januar 1536," WA 39/1: 139–73, which also records the individual views of Luther's Wittenberg colleagues. In addition, especially around Easter, Luther preached not only on Christ's passion but on the sacrament of the altar, so that the student wishing to pursue this subject should search all the Reformer's sermons, for example, those from the year 1524, WA 15: 490–506.

126 "Sermon von dem Neuen Testament," WA 6: 375. Franz, *Die Messe im deutschen Mittelalter*, has surveyed the numerous commentaries on the Mass produced by medieval authors. Luther could, of course, have seen various of them, but probably available to him were those of Egeling Becker and Gabriel Biel, both of whom studied (Biel taught in the arts faculty there too) at the University of Erfurt and continued their friendship and professional association in Mainz (537–55); Balthasar von Pforta, who taught in Leipzig (584–90); and Johans Bechofen, like Luther an Augustinian eremite (592–96).

127 For example, Luther's attack on silent Masses, "Vom Greuel der Stillmesse. 1525," WA 18: 8–36. For a typical attack on the "abominable" Catholic Mass, see the Wolfenbüttel ecclesiastical ordinance of 1569, Sehling, KOO, 6/1: 126–28; or that of Hohenlohe in 1553, KOO, 14: 67–68.

128 Ottfried Jordahn, "Martin Luthers Kritik an der Messliturgie seiner Zeit," *Archiv für Liturgiewissenschaft* 26 (1984), 1–17, esp. 2–8.

129 WA 12: 206. In his remarks immediately following this (207–208), Luther indicates how he thinks the Mass in its early sixteenth-century form has evolved.

130 "Von Anbeten des Sakraments," WA 11: 432–33.

131 "Von Anbeten des Sakraments," WA 11: 434.

132 "Von Anbeten des Sakraments," WA 11: 436–38.

133 "Von Anbeten des Sakraments," WA 11: 438–39.

134 "Von Anbeten des Sakraments," WA 11: 443–49.

135 "Von Anbeten des Sakraments," WA 11: 450. Readily available treatments of Luther's theology of the sacrament are Paul Althaus, *Theology of Martin Luther*, 375–403; Basil Hall, "*Hoc est corpus meum*: The Centrality of the Real Presence for Luther," in Gregory Yule, ed., *Luther: Theologian for Catholics and Protestants* (Edinburgh: T. and T. Clark, 1985), 112–44. An older study is E. Sommerlath, *Der Sinn des Abendmahls nach Luthers Gedanken über das Abendmahl, 1527–29* (Leipzig, 1930).

136 For a schematic summary of Luther's changes in the Mass, see Bergsma, *Die Reform der Messliturgie*, 57–58.

137 "Formula missae et communionis," WA 12: 205.

138 "Formula missae et communionis," WA 12: 208.

139 "Formula missae et communionis," WA 12: 206–207.

140 "Formula missae et communionis," WA 12: 208–10. I am not including in this discussion Luther's remarks on special seasonal Masses, for I am

attempting to summarize his recommendations for the general pattern of the service.

141 In the end, it appears to have been rather more lords and magistrates than pastors who decided what vestments and objects were to be retained. Brandenburg was the most conservative ritually and kept not only gestures, such as elevation, long after it had been abolished in Wittenberg, but also the full traditional regalia of the Mass, with the exception of some biblically unsubstantiated art. In the lands governed by the cathedral chapter in Madgeburg, the ritual equipment even in some, but not all, villages remained colorful and complex. See, for example, LHAMag, Rep. A12 Gen. 2439, "Kirchenvisitation 1583/4 Dörfer im Holzkreis," *passim*. The use of such artifacts gave rise to intense discussion during the century. See pamphlet by Flacius, "Der vnschuldigen Adiaphoristen Chorrock, darüber sich die vnrugige vnd Störrische Stoici mit ihnen zancken" (Magdeburg: Pankratz Kempf, 1548–1550). Even late in the century, a village church could include in its inventory "1 gebluembdte leinwandts Kasell" (LHAMag, Rep. A12 Gen. 2440, "Kirchenvisitation 1583/84, Jerichow'scher Kreis," fol. 140).

142 Nearly a century later, the count of Nassau-Saarbrücken was still ordering his visitors to inquire (HSAWies, Abt. 131 Nr. Xa, 1, fol. 50):

> ob irgentwo noch vf den hohen altarn wie mannß von alters genent im Chor den Abentmahl verrichtet werde, so von den Volck etwaß weit abgesondert zu sein pfleget, also dz sie die vorgehend vermahnung etwan nicht wohl verstendtlich hören können?

143 *Formula missae*, 211–13.
144 *Formula missae*, 212–15.
145 Thomas Müntzer's was the first. Thomas Müntzer, *Deutsche Evangelische Messe 1524*, ed. Siegfried Bräuer (Berlin: Evangelische Verlagsanstalt, 1988).
146 WA 19: 45.
147 WA 19: 50–51.
148 For a sense of this, see the 1555 ecclesiastical ordinance for Nördlingen (Sehling, KOO, 12: 317–29).
149 This is a very technical aspect of the Mass. Interested parties should begin with WA 19: 53–60.
150 See, for example, the Calenberg-Göttingen church ordinance of 1542, according to which all of the service but three prayers and the sermon was sung (Sehling, KOO, 6/2: 811–17).
151 WA 19: 72–73.
152 WA 19: 112.
153 WA 19: 88–96.
154 This act aroused even more controversy than had the previous retention of elevation. Luther had to reassure Prince Georg von Anhalt, among others (WA, *Briefwechsel*, 10: 85–86, no. 3762, June 26, 1542). The extensive footnotes (86–88) to the letter just cited constitute a veritable summation of this debate.
155 WA 26: 241–509.
156 HSADres, Loc. 10601, "Dritter theil zur Visitation Anno 1593 gehalten gehorig sachen," fols. 47–48; further at fols. 110–11.
157 In the village of Sindelfingen near Stuttgart in 1583, one peasant was so bold as to tell the visitors, who found great fault with him for attending church services in nearby Catholic lands, "Men predige alda eben so wol gottes wort, als zu Sindelfingen." He was reported to the superintendent for disciplinary action ELKAS, A1 Nr. 1 1583, fol. 178).

158 In this section, I am heavily reliant upon Bergsma, *Die Reform der Messliturgie*.

159 In Bugenhagen's 1528 church ordinance for Braunschweig, see the long admonition before Communion (Bergsma, *Die Reform der Messliturgie*, 73–74). For Hamburg (80), Lübeck (87), Bremen (99), Schleswig-Holstein (123), Hildesheim (134), and Wolfenbüttel (139); however, he does not provide a precise text, specifying only that an exhortation should be made. By the 1540s, he clearly has specific texts in mind. For Bremen, he ordains that Martin Luther's commentary and admonition on the Lord's Prayer should be read (99). This must have been readily available to the clergy there as elsewhere. For Pomerania (112), he gives the first line of an admonition to be used before the sacrament. Melanchthon wrote an admonition as part of the Leipzig Interim (1549) that specifically contained "nothing objectionable" (150).

   In his influential instructions to pastors in 1539, Heinrich of Saxony ordered that an admonition be read aloud to the people before the words of institution (Sehling, KOO, 1: 271). These are subsequently found throughout Germany.

160 Sehling, KOO, 1: 202. Elector August of Saxony was even stricter (Sehling, KOO, 1: 430–31).

161 The ecclesiastical ordinances offer many other examples. See, for instance, the decree of Joachim II of Brandenburg in 1540 (Sehling, KOO, 3: 53), in which the dangers of pastoral freedom are noted.

162 Depictions of the Lutheran practice of having women commune on the left and men on the right are many. Examples are Cranach the Younger, "Unterscheid zwischen der waren Religion Christi vnd falschen Abgöttischen lehr des Antichrists," in Friedrich W. H. Hollstein, *German Engravings*, vol. 6, ed. K. G. Boon and R. W. Scheller (Amsterdam: Menno Hertzgberger, 1959), 128; either by or after Lukas Cranach the Elder, illustration of flier, "Der Christlich gebrauch des hochwirdigen Sacraments...," reproduced in Harry Oelke, *Die Konfessionsbildung des 16. Jahrhunderts im Spiegel illustrierter Flugblätter* (Berlin: De Gruyter, 1992), fig. 27. Everywhere church leaders were very concerned to ensure that women not go to the Communion table or altar before or along with the men, at least not on the same side of the altar; lay*men* were concerned to keep women from going before them (for example, B-WHSAS, 310a–312, miscellaneous documents, unpaginated but pertaining to Cannstadt, 1601, where the women go forward first, and the town is ordered to change its practice). In Weida in 1533, Elector Johann Friedrich's visitors ordered a barrier to be erected that would prevent the sexes from mingling as they received the sacrament (HSAWei, Reg. Ii 7, "Visitation in Voitlande vnnd Obermeißen...1533/34," fol. 196). One church elder in Saxony at the beginning of the seventeenth century tattled to the visitors because he had had to wait to commune until the women had finished. The pastor insisted that this was an error—possibly a procedural one, inasmuch as the elders held the sacramental napkins under people's chins! (HSADres, Loc. 1999, "Local-Visitation der Superintendentzen Leipzigk, Grimna, Penigk, Eulenburgk, Borna, Rochlitz, Pegau 1618–20 [also includes 1617]," fol. 456).

163 This separation is especially apparent in HSAWei, Reg. Ii 7, "Visitation in Voitlande vnnd Obermeißen...1533/34," fol. 81, city of Plauen.

164 HSAWei, Reg. Ii 2487, "1555. Bericht der Visitatoren über die in der abgehaltenen Visitation gemachten Wahrnehmungen," fol. 6.

165 Ernst Bizer, *Studien zur Geschichte des Abendmahlsstreits im 16. Jahrhundert*, Beiträge zur Förderung christlicher Theologie, 2nd series, 46 (Gütersloh: Gerd Mohn, 1940, reprinted Darmstadt: Wissenschaftliche Buchgesellschaft, 1972), 23. This book is nonetheless a valuable survey of the struggle among divines. For the ongoing debate in the seventeenth century, see John A. Farren, "The Lutheran Krypsis–Kenosis Controversy: The Presence of Christ 1619–1627," unpublished Sac. Theol. Dr. dissertation, Pontifical Faculty of the Immaculate Conception, Dominican House of Studies, Washington, D.C., 1974.

166 Ian Hazlett, "Eucharistic Communion: Impulses and Directions in Martin Bucer's Thought," in D. F. Wright, ed., *Martin Bucer: Reforming Church and Community* (Cambridge, England: Cambridge University Press, 1994), 72–82. In the same collection, see Irena Backus, "Church, Communion, and Community in Bucer's Commentary on the Gospel of John," 61–71.

167 See Thomas A. Brady, Jr.'s superb analysis of the relationship between politics and religion in *Protestant Politics: Jacob Sturm (1489–1553) and the German Reformation* (Atlantic Highlands, N.J.: Humanities Press, 1995), for my purposes esp. chap. 3, "The Formation of German Protestantism," 53–102, and on the Wittenberg Concord, 89.

168 We shall see what conclusions come out of the scholarly conferences that in 1997 will mark the five hundredth anniversary of Melanchthon's birth!

169 Toward the south and west of Germany it was generally disapproved of, along with all other artifacts that smacked of popish doctrines of the Eucharist; in Brandenburg and Saxony, it remained. In the hamlets of Saxony, the (lay) church elders (*kirchenvetter*) held the napkin.

170 HSAWies, Abt. 131 Nr. Xa, 1, "Betr. Einführung, Erneuerung u. Verbesserung von Kirchenordnungen in den nassau-saarbrückischen Landen u. Gemeinschaften 1559–1765," fols. 45–54, ca. 1618.

171 In order for this arrangement to be possible, churches had to have essentially two altars: the older "high" altar and one at the front of the altar dais that was used for the distribution of Communion. This latter is the one that the pastor could be either behind or in front of; this is the one that communicants could walk behind when they were finished.

172 For example, B-WHSAS, A281 Büschel 1020–26, no general title, no pagination, 1601.

173 Zeeden, *Katholische Überlieferungen in den lutherischen Kir-chen-ord-nung-en des 16. Jahrhunderts*, Vereinsschriften der Gesellschaft zur Herausgabe des Corpus Catholicorum 17 (Münster/Wain: Aschendorff, 1959), esp. 11–46.

174 The portion of the ecclesiastical ordinance of Geneva that is devoted to the sacrament is reprinted in Wilhelm Niesel, *Bekenntnisschriften und Kirchenordnungen der nach Gottes Wort reformierten Kirche* (Zollikon-Zürich [*sic*]: Evangelischer Verlag, n.d., but probably 1938), 51; and of the 1563 catechism of the Rhenish Palatinate, 166–70.

175 Vogler, *Vie religieuse*, 1: 627.

176 Sehling, KOO, 13: 266. The document itself has not survived. See also the terms of the Calvinization of the county of Nassau-Dillenburg, Ältere Linie, around 1572, HSAWies, Abt. 171 Nr. D226, "Wasserleÿ Ceremonien vndt ordnungen In dero kirchen nacherheischenden notturfft vndt gelegenheitt dieser landes wegen geendert vndt verbessertt worden," fols. 16–20: no candles could be burned by daylight, no altars but only tables, the words of institution and admonition to be spoken facing the people, small round Hosts to be supplanted by ordinary table bread, and for the Chalice and everyday cup, the people must take these in their own hands,

and the people were not to bow or kneel or clasp their hands in prayer as they received the sacrament.

177 BLHAPot, Pr. Br. Rep. 23A B562, "Acta betref. wegen der zu Haltenden Kirchenvisitationen und Religions Sachen 1599, 1667, 1698," fol. 52, March 28, 1614. Also Bodo Nischan's invaluable treatment of the politics of liturgy in his *Prince, People*, esp. 111–60. A treatise, written in the midst of the Brandenburg struggle, that is designed to show the liturgical differences between Lutheranism and Calvinism is Philipp Arnoldi, *Caeremoniae Lutheranae. Das ist, Ein Christlicher, Gründlicher Unterricht von allen fürnembsten Caeremonien, so in den Lutherischen Preussischen Kirchen ... adhibirt werden ... Den Calvinischen Caeremonienstürmern entgegen gesetzt* (Königsberg: Schmidt, 1616).

178 Artists, especially in the early modern Low Countries, have left us a visual record of the stark, white, often cavernous Gothic interiors, as, for instance, Pieter Saenredam (1597–1665), *Grote Kerk, Haarlem*, in the National Gallery, London. On the "cleansed" nature of the Reformed service, see Vogler, *Vie religieuse*, 1: 604–605.

179 See Vogler's treatment, including his (?) sketches of church interiors, *Vie religieuse*, 1: 572–75. Artistic renderings also bear out this shift in interior architecture. Christopher S. Wood has questioned whether the removal of all images could really alter the "period eye" of the sixteenth century, that is, the way in which people perceived ("The Defense of Images: Two Local Rejoinders to the Zwinglian Iconoclasm," *Sixteenth Century Journal* 19, 1 [1988], 26–44, here at 44). Robert Scribner asks what might be a related question, whether pro-Reformation popular propaganda did not itself have to tap those ways of seeing in order to be effective; however, in Zurich (the object of Wood's study), the church leaders' bias against images militated against their using this form of propaganda at all (*For the Sake of Simple Folk: Popular Propaganda for the German Reformation*, Cambridge Studies in Oral and Literate Culture 2 [Cambridge, England: Cambridge University Press, 1981], 249).

180 Of course, they did not always submit. For possible ways of resisting, and clues to underlying attitudes, see (for example) Jeffrey R. Watt, "Women and the Consistory in Calvin's Geneva," *Sixteenth Century Journal* 24, 2 (1993), 429–39.

181 James Thomas Ford, one of Robert Kingdon's doctoral students at the University of Wisconsin, gave a pertinent paper, "Between Wittenberg and Zurich: Wolfgang Musculus and the Struggle for Confessional Hegemony in Reformation Augsburg, 1531–1548," at the meetings of the Sixteenth Century Studies Conference, San Francisco, October 1995. His dissertation will doubtless shed more light on Augsburg's idiosyncratic path.

182 Sehling, KOO, 13: 481. Joseph Koerner, "Quotes in Images and Images in Quotes: Pictures for Luther's Reformation," a paper on word paintings presented at the first international conference of Frühe Neuzeit Interdisziplinär, April 1995, Duke University. I would like to hear more from Professor Koerner about the specific cities in which these paintings were found, for I suspect that they represent a compromise with Calvinist views of images, even if technically in Lutheran churches.

183 HSADres, Loc. 10610, "Erster Theill Der im Churfurstenthumb Sachssen ... in 1592 gehaltenen ... Visitation," fol. 2.

184 The three sons of Johann Friedrich of Saxony ordained for all their lands "das die Casel, Albe, Mesgewant, vnd abgottische bilder, so sich mit biblischer historien nit vorgleichen, aus der kirchen weg gethan werden ..." (HSAWei, Reg. Ii 23–26, "Registration der visitation welche

Anno 1554 gehalden," fols. 186–87). In one village, a picture of St. George was specificially labeled as idolatrous (fol. 155). Despite Carl C. Christensen's presentation of Lutheran examples of the retention of medieval images, and the fundamental truth that fewer (that is, not all) images were removed in Lutheran Germany (*Art and the Reformation in Germany* [Athens, Ohio, and Detroit, Mich.: Ohio University Press and Wayne State University Press, 1979], 108–09), I would have to insist that, on the basis of archival documents pertaining to the countryside and to smaller cities, a very high percentage of late medieval religious art had disappeared by the end of the century, a longer period than Christensen takes into account.

185 On the iconoclasm of the early Reformation, see Carlos M. N. Eire, *War against the Idols: The Reformation of Worship from Erasmus to Calvin* (Cambridge, England: Cambridge University Press, 1986); Sergiusz Michalski, *The Reformation and the Visual Arts: The Protestant Image Question in Western Europe* (London and New York: Routledge, 1993), esp. 43–98; Bob Scribner, ed., *Bilder und Bildersturm*, containing a number of valuable essays; and most recently Lee Palmer Wandel, *Voracious Idols and Violent Hands: Iconoclasm in Reformation Zurich, Strasbourg, and Basel* (Cambridge, England: Cambridge University Press, 1995) and Norbert Schnitzler, "Bilderstürmer—Aufrührer oder Blasphemiker?" in Marie Theres Fögen, ed., *Ordnung und Aufruhr im Mittelalter: Historische und juristische Studien zur Rebellion* (Frankfurt/Main: Vittorio Klostermann, 1995), 195–215.

While I am searching for general patterns, I must not overlook the acts of iconoclasm that were directed against all the equipage of the Mass as the Reformation began. While these fascinating episodes rivet our attention and did indeed help to usher in the Reformation in such cities as Basel, Zurich, and Strasbourg, they were by no means typical of the early Reformation. We possess no statistics as to the numbers of participants, but they were usually small even though the acts of these people were violent and destructive. Lee Palmer Wandel has made a most nuanced effort to analyze three different iconoclastic settings, and, in my judgment, with much success. But I personally doubt whether the rebels' attitude was characteristic, and I regard both acts and mentality as manifestations, albeit harsh ones, of late medieval affective piety, in which laity and artifacts "interacted." Iconoclasm was part not of a Protestant, but of a Catholic, milieu. Such affective and physical demonstrativeness was promptly brought to an end with the official adoption of evangelism. I have written separately about the suppression of emotive religiosity in "Die semiotische Unterdrückung des Gefühls: Ritualveränderung in der deutschen Reformation," forthcoming in an as-yet-unnamed volume being edited by Bernhard Jussen and Craig Koslofsky.

186 HSAWei, Reg. Ii 2771, "1560. Schriften betr. die vom Amtmann zu Tenneberg Asmus v. Gleichen gelieferten Nachwiese [*sic*] über die Veranderung [*sic*] der Altäre und das Vorhandensein kirchlicher Gegenstände in den Kirchen des Amtes Tenneberg," is a unique survival in my experience, for it describes parish by parish what paintings were still present and where they now stood in the churches, even if they had been removed to the sacristy. Useful, but not as valuable, are Reg. Ii 2770, "1560. Schriften betr. die auf ergangenen Befehl von dem Schosser zu Volkenrode gelieferten Bericht über die Veranderung [*sic*] der Altäre und die vorhandenen Kleinodien"; and Reg. Ii 2769, "1560. Schriften betr. den ... Bericht über die Veränderungen der Altare [*sic*], Ceremonien und noch vorhandenen Kirchen ornate, Bucher [*sic*] ... " In the latter, it comes

out that old Catholic Latin songbooks were still being used for Communion services (fol. 3).

187 In affected regions, towns and princes gathered and sold off *cleinodien* in order to raise money for waging war against the peasants in 1525, and again in 1546 as the Schmalkaldic War loomed. Betwixt and between, they found other good causes to justify the sale of costly objects. A good example of both of these motives is HSAWei, Reg. Ii 3, "Visitation in Lande zue Döringen an der Salla, Jehna, Naustadt an deer Orla, Peßneck vnndt Saalfeldt 1529," fols. 121, 128, 144, 358, 391, 501–502. Nobles and patricians who had donated costly objects to churches strove mightily to take them back, and they often succeeded.

188 See the rainbow array of vestments in the holdings of St. Lorenz's Church in Pegau, HSADres, Loc. 1986, "Registratur der Visitation, so uff empfangenen Churfürstlichen Sächsischen beuehlich... in der Superintendentz Pegau gehalten...anno 1574," fols. 42–44; HSADres, Loc. 1999, "Local-Visitation der Superintendentzen Leipzigk, Grimna, Penigk, Eulenburgk, Borna, Rochlitz, Pegau 1618–20 [and 1617]", passim on evaluation of vestments and their use in the countryside. The visitors (fol. 371) order the parish of Hartmannsdorf (and doubtless other parishes) to get new ones, for theirs were "zürißen vnd zerlumpt." The best treatment of sixteenth-century Lutheran vestments is Arthur Carl Piepkorn, *The Survival of the Historic Vestments in the Lutheran Church after 1555* (St. Louis: School for Graduate Studies, 1956; 2nd ed. 1958), in German, *Die liturgischen Gewänder in der lutherischen Kirche seit 1555*, ed. and trans. Jobst Schöne and Ernst Seybold (Marburg an der Lahn: Oekumenischer Verlag Dr. R. F. Edel, 1965; 2nd printing Lüdenscheid/ Lobetal: Oekumenischer Verlag Dr. R. F. Edel, 1987), on the sixteenth and seventeenth centuries, chaps. 3 and 4, 14–58. I am grateful to Pastor Rolf Sieber of Zwickau for bringing this to my attention.

Vogler (*Vie religieuse*, 1: 577, 585) has compiled tables of cultic objects that remained in the parishes of Sponheim in 1560 and 1591.

189 Nischan, *Prince, People*.

190 Vogler, *Vie religieuse*, 2: 710. See Vogler's entire chapter, "Le respect de la cène, valeur sacrale," 705–60. The author favors the view that people were concerned with ritual correctness, and I don't doubt this. However, I would add that ordinary Protestants still regarded the consecrated Host as the flesh of Christ, with all the weight that that entails.

191 LKABr, V443, "Protokolle der Kirchen- und Schulvisitationen im Stifte Halberstadt 1589," no pagination, but the village of "Sistedt."

192 Wandel, "Envisioning God," 33–34.

193 LHAMag, Rep. A12 Gen. 2435, fol. 79.

194 B-WHSAS, A281 310a, passim.

195 Sehling, KOO, 4: 199.

196 See the detailed description of weekly religious services in Plauen, HSAWei, Reg. Ii 2, "Visitations Acta im Amte Voigtsberg, Plauen, Weida und Ronneburg im Jahre 1529," fols. 149–50. The history of the evangelical hymn is a research topic of its own, one of much complexity and interest. See Patrice Veit, *Das Kirchenlied in der Reformation Martin Luthers: Eine thematische und semantische Untersuchung* (Stuttgart: Franz Stein Verlag Wiesbaden [sic], 1986).

197 See, for example, the schedule of services for St. Wenzel Church in Naumburg of 1537/1538 (Sehling, KOO, 2: 71–73), where no sermon was preached on Monday, Wednesday, Friday, and Saturday. This is (71–84) a particularly detailed and specific order of worship. Another long and

meticulous one is that for Nördlingen in 1555 (Sehling, KOO, 12: 317–29), approved by the superintendent, Melchior Runtzler, but extensively based on Caspar Löhner's plan of 1544. This plan states exactly which songs should be sung on which days of the church calendar. By mid-century this was possible inasmuch as many Protestant songs had been now composed or collected.

198 Sehling, KOO, 1: 273, n. 1 for the whole text. Other examples are also given here (274–80). These are part of Elector Heinrich of Saxony's very detailed (1539) instructions.

199 Sehling, KOO, 4: 202 (Mecklenburg). The catechism had a prominent position in every church service in the villages pertaining to Braunschweig, if they conformed to the ordinance (Sehling, KOO, 6/1: 473–74). See also the land (*Herrschaft*) of Rothenberg (1618), Sehling, KOO, 13: 547–48.

200 LKABr, V470 and V471, "Predigten verschiedener Pastoren von Januar und Februar 1573, z. T. nur in Konzepten." Mary Jane Haemig of Pacific Lutheran University has begun to work on these sermons. In the same archive, I found two folders (V1765 and V1942) containing thirty-eight funeral sermons given by rural pastors in 1666 in memory of Duke August the Younger. Although in one sense equally revealing of the tendency toward uniformity even in sermons, in another way these are different. Their authors were compelled to prepare them, and the text was assigned (though evidently misunderstood). Memorial Masses for dead family members were evidently a holdover from Catholic *seelenmessen* that the ruling house could not shake (V1760, "Des Herzogs Heinrich des Jüngern Gedächtniß Feier, so den 12. Dez. 1569 gehalten worden").

201 Sehling, KOO, 14: 327–52.

202 LKABr, V1924, "Die kirchlichen und sittlichen Verhältnisse vornehmlich in den Fürstentümern Calenberg und Göttingen (1543) 1625–1630," fol. 255.

203 Boës, "Die reformatorischen Gottesdienste in der Wittenberger Pfarrkirche von 1523 an," *Jahrbuch für liturgische Geschichte* 4 (1958/59), 9.

204 Sehling, KOO, 14: 520. Wolfgang was not merely serving his busy self, but applied this principle to all the churches in the district (*Amt*) of Döttingen.

205 Sehling, KOO, 14: 639–40.

206 In St. John's Church of Halberstadt, the visitors ordered in 1564 that during each of three Sunday services, the pastor should preach for one hour, but on Friday at 5:00 a.m. the sermon should only be three-quarters of an hour long (LHAMag, Rep. A12 Gen. 2486, "Kirchen-Visitationen von 1564 und 1589," fol. 67). Similarly, HSAWies, Abt. 131 Nr. Xa, 1, "Betr. Einführung, Erneuerung und Verbesserung von Kirchenordnungen in den nassau-saarbrückischen Landen und Gemeinschaften 1559–1765," fol. 46, ca. 1618.

207 Sehling, KOO, 14: 130.

208 HSAWies, Abt. 171 Nr. S. 303, no unified title but numerous documents, fol. 67.

209 Sehling, KOO, 1: 319.

210 HSAWei, Reg. Ii 2667, "1557 Schriften betr. die von dem Pfarrer, Schosser und Rath zu Altenburg erstattete allgemeine Anzeige der verschiedenen Mangel und Gebrechen," fols. 15–16. This entire register displays this principle prominently.

211 As I have already shown for Saxony, "Neoclericalism and Anticlericalism in Saxony". See also Robert W. Scribner, "Anticlericalism and the Reformation in Germany," in idem, *Popular Culture and Popular Movements in Reformation Germany* (London and Ronceverte: Hambledon Press, 1987), 243–56, on this point, esp. 255–56. Certain other visitation records display especially clearly this cooperative method of detection and enforcement

between pastors and secular officials, for example HSAWei, Reg. Ii 56, "Registranda vber die Visitations vnnd Religions hendel, 1573 vnd 1574," passim.

212 Schilling, " 'History of Crime' or 'History of Sin'?—Some Reflections on the Social History of Early Modern Church Discipline," in E. I. Kouri and Tom Scott, eds., *Politics and Society in Reformation Europe: Essays for Sir Geoffrey Elton on His Sixty-Fifth Birthday* (New York: St. Martin's Press, 1987), 289–310.

213 *Todtschlag.* In early modern Germany, murder would have incurred the death penalty. However, accidentally killing someone or doing so in a fit of rage or out of ignorance, which I have translated as *manslaughter*, was dealt with less harshly. The civil penalties under Germanic law were usually fines (*wergeld*) or exile, while the spreading Roman law encouraged corporal punishment or imprisonment.

214 Sehling, KOO, 2: 39–42. This ceremony from beginning to end is astonishingly long and, whenever used, would have taken a good deal of time out of two church services.

215 Sehling, KOO, 2: 40–42.

216 Sehling, KOO, 2: 41.

217 Other examples are: Sehling, KOO, 5: 452–58 (Lauenburg, 1585, one of the lengthiest instructions I have found); 6/2: 1056–58 (Grubenhagen, 1581), where to manslaughter and adultery are added the categories of *lesterer, wucherer,* and *trunkenbolz*); 12: 215–17 (Lindau, 1573), 248–52 (Memmingen, 1532); 13: 185–87 (Duchy of Pfalz-Neuburg, 1576), where the named offenses are "gotteslesterung vel trunkenhait [*vel: alterius generis*]"; 14: 296–301 (Hohenlohe, 1578).

218 Sehling, KOO, 13: 185.

219 HSAWei, Findbücher to Reg. B, vol. 2, fol. 609, n.d., "Das ein treuer Pfarrer vndt Sehlsorger vmb daß ansehens willen einiger Persohn, midt der Kirchenbuße nicht könne dispensiren vnd sie fallen Laßenn, Anthonius Bobus der heyligen Schrifft Doctor vndt Superintendens Generalis zun [*sic*] Weÿmar."

220 On the surface, Luther seems to have become less concerned with predestination as time went on. Toward the end of his life, however, he revealed that he continued to worry about it. He resorted once again to the theological distinction between God's secret will and that will that He chose to make known through the Word to His children. People had no alternative but to rely completely on that version of His will to which they had access, even while acknowledging that there was another divine will (WA, *Tischreden*, 4: 641–42, no. 5070).

221 See especially Keith Thomas's conclusions to *Religion and the Decline of Magic* (New York: Charles Scribner's Sons, 1971), 631–68.

222 Eire, *War Against the Idols:*, 3.

223 On secularization and Reformation, see Hans-Christoph Rublack, "Reformation und Moderne: Soziologische, theologische und historische Ansichten," *Archive for Reformation History*, Sonderband Washington (Gütersloh: Gerd Mohn, 1992), 31–34.

224 Bossy, "The Mass as a Social Institution 1200–1700," *Past and Present* 100 (August 1983), 29–61, on sacrifice 52–53.

225 Bossy, "Mass as a Social Institution, 53.

226 Bossy, "Mass as a Social Institution, 57. Cf. Willem Frijhoff, "The Kiss Sacred and Profane: Reflections on a Cross-cultural Confrontation," in Jan Bremmer and Herman Roodenburg, eds., *A Cultural History of Gesture*

(Ithaca: Cornell University Press, 1992), 210–36, which ignores the kiss of the Mass and comes to very different conclusions than Bossy.

227 Reinburg,"Liturgy and the Laity," 542.

228 See Hans-Werner Goetz, "Der 'rechte' Sitz: Die Symbolik von Rang und Herrschaft im Hohen Mittelalter im Spiegel der Sitzordnung," in Gertrud Blaschitz, Helmut Hundsbichler, Gerhard Jaritz, and Elisabeth Vavra, eds., *Symbole des Alltags*, 22–48.

229 Reinle, *Die Ausstattung deutscher Kirchen*, 67–69.

230 Reinle, *Die Ausstattung deutscher Kirchen*, 60–61.

231 The leaders of the Counter-Reformation quickly adopted this method too of molding the beliefs and behavior of those in their spiritual care: Dietz-Rüdiger Moser, *Verkündigung durch Volksgesang: Studien zur Liedpropaganda und -katechese der Gegenreformation* (Berlin: Erich Schmidt Verlag, 1981); Inge Mager, "Das lutherische Lehrlied im 16. und 17. Jahrhundert," *Jahrbuch der Gesellschaft für niedersächsische Kirchengeschichte* 82 (1984), 77–95; Veit, *Das Kirchenlied*.

232 Quoted by Robert Jütte, "Der anstößige Körper: Anmerkungen zu einer Semiotik der Nacktheit," in Klaus Schreiner and Norbert Schnitzler, eds., *Gepeinigt, begehrt, vergessen: Symbolik und Sozialbezug des Körpers im späten Mittelalter und in der frühen Neuzeit* (Munich: Wilhelm Fink, 1992), 121. Both Jütte and Dreitzel admire Norbert Elias's theories concerning the courtly origin of European civilization. I am inclined to look to Italian urban culture as a major model for German cities, particularly in the south and southwest. Nuremberg, for example, looked to Venice, and lesser urban centers such as Zwickau aped Nuremberg styles and manners. Dreitzel's conclusion, nevertheless, rings true.

5 THE BANNING OF THE DEAD AND THE ORDERING OF THE LIVING: THE SELECTIVE RETENTION OF CATHOLIC PRACTICE

1 Craig R. Thompson, ed. and trans., *The Colloquies of Erasmus* (Chicago and London: University of Chicago Press, 1965), 359–73. Thompson reports that Johannes Froben published the colloquies in 1518 without Erasmus's knowledge, and that the author was annoyed, and for several years had no interest in the book (xxi).

2 Alberto Tenenti has asserted that the Renaissance (as a period, stretching from 1450 to 1650) was dominated by a "religion of death" and that the genre of *ars moriendi* literature bears witness to this (*Il senso della morte e l'amore della vita nel Rinascimento [Francia e Italia]*, [Turin: Einaudi, 1957]). See Kuno Böse, "Das Thema 'Tod' in der neueren französischen Geschichtsschreibung: Ein Überblick," in Paul Richard Blum, ed., *Studien zur Thematik des Todes im 16. Jahrhundert*, Wolfenbütteler Forschungen 22 (Wolfenbüttel: Herzog August Bibliothek, 1983), 1–20, here 13. Cf. R. Rudolf, *Ars moriendi: Von der Kunst des heilsamen Lebens und Sterbens* (Cologne: Böhlau, 1957). The Council of Florence at the beginning of the fifteenth century produced *Speculum artis bene moriendi*, which served as the model of books on the art of dying for the remainder of the medieval period. See the bibliography on the medieval art of dying in Arno Borst, Gerhard von Graevenitz, Alexander Patschovsky, and Karlheinz Stierle, *Tod im Mittelalter* (Constance: Universitätsverlag Konstanz, 1992), 330–34.

3 Vovelle, *La mort et l'Occident de 1300 à nos jours* (Paris: Gallimard, 1983), 142; Franz Falk, *Die deutschen Sterbebüchlein von der ältesten Zeit des Buchdruckes bis zum Jahre 1520* (Cologne: Bachem, 1890).

4 In this frame, the artist does not show Christ's limbs as nailed to the cross, perhaps to allow contortion as evidence of suffering.

5 Imhof has returned to further analysis of the latter of this pair of illustrations in chap. l, "Ars moriendi: Die Kunst des Sterbens vor 500 Jahren," in his book, *Ars moriendi: Die Kunst des Sterbens einst und heute* (Vienna and Cologne: Böhlau, 1991), 32–51, here 35–40. Perhaps because this is a book written for the popular audience, Imhof feels free to expound at length on his personal lifestyle and attitudes toward death. See also his chatty *Im Bildersaal der Geschichte, oder Ein Historiker schaut Bilder an* (Munich: C. H. Beck, 1991).

6 Arthur E. Imhof, *Geschichte sehen: Fünf Erzählungen nach historischen Bildern* (Munich: C. H. Beck, 1990), 59–92. This booklet was in great demand and sold not just in Germany but also in the Low Countries, France, England, Italy, and Spain (85–86).

7 Imhof, *Geschichte sehen*, p. 83.

8 Adolph Franz, *Das Rituale des Bischofs Heinrich I. von Breslau* (Freiburg/ Breisgau: Herder, 1912), 33–35. This manual was widely used. It contains additional pre-death rites, including a prayer for the dying (*Obsequium circa morientes*, 35–37) that is made up substantially of invocations of a long list of saints. Franz notes (79) that the saints included on the list changed between the early fourteenth and the end of the fifteenth century, and that by the latter time the number of holy virgins, such as Barbara, Hedwig, Elisabeth, and Anne, had noticeably increased. Also included in this manual is a commendation of the spirit (*Commendatio anime*, 37–39). Both the *Obsequium* and the *Commendatio* are described as though intended for use in a community of canons or monks. No doubt, they were also used when a public person of high rank was about to die.

9 *The Old Catholic Missal and Ritual* (New York: AMS Press, 1901), 273–75. See Durandus's lengthy explication of the meanings of the stole, Buijssen, *Durandus' Rationale in spätmittelhochdeutscher Übersetzung*, 3 vols. (Assen, The Netherlands: Van Gorcum, 1974–1983), 1: 203–05.

10 The subject of holy water is so broad that Franz (*Die kirchlichen Benediktionen im Mittelalter*, 2 vols. [Freiburg/Breisgau: Herder, 1909]), devotes much space to it (1: 43–220).

11 See Miri Rubin, *Corpus Christi: The Eucharist in Late Medieval Culture* (Cambridge, England: Cambridge University Press, 1991), esp. 35–82.

12 Buijssen, *Durandus' Rationale*, 3: 309–10. I have used *The New English Bible with the Apocrypha* (Oxford and Cambridge, England: Oxford University Press and Cambridge University Press, 1970).

13 Buijssen, *Durandus' Rationale*, 3: 310–11. According to Adolph Franz, the blessing of oil for anointing the very aged goes back at least to Tertullian. In the early church, oil was regarded as a sure defense against demonic influences and as protection against physical and spiritual evils. It could heal sickness, too, which is hardly surprising in view of the close connection drawn throughout the Middle Ages between sin and physical ails. Stories of miraculous cures effected through the application of oil circulated in the ancient church (*Die kirchlichen benediktionen*, 1: 335–53).

14 Franz, *Die kirchlichen Benediktionen*, 1: 42–60. For non-ecclesiastical (but nonetheless overlapping) connotations of candles, consult Hanns Bächtold-Stäubli, comp., and E. Hoffmann-Krayer, ed., *Handwörterbuch des deutschen*

Aberglaubens (Berlin and Leipzig: Walter de Gruyter, 1927–1942), vol. 4, cols. 1243–55.

15 By Ariès, especially *L'Homme devant la mort* (Paris: Éditions du Seuil, 1977), the English translation by Helen Weaver appearing as *The Hour of Our Death* (New York: Alfred A. Knopf, 1981); his earlier lectures, *Western Attitudes toward Death from the Middle Ages to the Present*, trans. Patricia M. Ranum (London: Marion Boyars, 1976); Ariès, *Images de l'homme devant la mort* (n.p.: Seuil, 1983); "L'histoire de l'au-delà dans la chrétienté latine," in Philippe Ariès, Françoise Dolto, F. Marty, Ginette Raimbault, and Léon Schwartzenberg, *En face de la mort* (Toulouse: Éditions Privat, 1983), 11–45; Michel Vovelle, *La Mort et l'Occident*; Vovelle, comp., *Mourir Autrefois: Attitudes collectives devant la mort aux XVIIe et XVIIIe siècles* (Paris: Gallimard/Julliard, 1974).

Just as Ariès is heavily reliant on artistic evidence, cf. Alberto Tenenti, *La Vie et la mort à travers l'art du XVe siècle*, Cahiers des Annales, 8 (Paris: Armand Colin, 1952); Gaby and Michel Vovelle, *Vision de la mort et de l'au-delà en Provence d'aprés les autels des âmes du purgatoire, XVe–XXe siècles* (Paris: Armand Colin, 1970); Michel Vovelle, "Les attitudes devant la mort: Problèmes de méthode, approches et lectures différentes," *Annales: Economies, Sociétés, Civilisations (Annales)* 31 (1976), 120–32.

See also Lucien Febvre, "La mort dans l'histoire," *Annales* 7 (1952), 223–25; François Lebrun, *"Les hommes et la mort en Anjou au 17e et 18e siècles. Essai de démographie et de psychologie historique* (Paris and The Hague: Mouton, 1971); Pierre Chaunu, *La mort à Paris: XVIe, XVIIe, XVIIIe siècles* (Paris: Fayard, 1978). The publishers of *Annales* devoted an entire issue to the subject of death: *Autor de la mort*, vol. 31 (1976).

For a recent popular survey of death in late medieval Europe, see Norbert Ohler, *Sterben und Tod im Mittelalter* (Munich: Artemis, 1990). On the German evidence, Alois M. Haas, *Todesbilder im Mittelalter: Fakten und Hinweise in der deutschen Literatur* (Darmstadt: Wissenschaftliche Buchgesellschaft, 1989); Siegfried Wollgast, "Zum Tod im späten Mittelalter und in der Frühen Neuzeit," *Frühneuzeit-Info* 2, 2 (1991), 63–74.

16 In addition, as Eamon Duffy observes, "Astonishingly, for example, there is no real discussion of the Offices of the Visitation of the sick, anointing, burial, or 'Dirige' in the most important modern historical treatment of death and dying, Ariès's *The Hour of Our Death* (*The Stripping of the Altars: Traditional Religion in England 1400–1580* [New Haven: Yale University Press, 1992], 313).

17 Ariès, *Hour of Our Death*, 106–10.

18 Steven E. Ozment, *The Reformation in the Cities: The Appeal of Protestantism to Sixteenth-century Germany and Switzerland* (New Haven: Yale University Press, 1975), 22–32.

19 John Bossy levels mild criticism at Ariès's emphasis upon the radical individualism of death in the late Middle Ages. See *Christianity in the West 1400–1700* (Oxford and New York: Oxford University Press, 1985), 26–27. While I see what Bossy means, and although it is evident that both family and larger community played parts in the rites of dying, Ariès strikes me as correct in his qualitative judgment that during the late Middle Ages, the individual, including his or her personal demise, rises in importance. In my opinion, the condemnation of Siger of Brabant, and with him Averroist renditions of the future of souls, would need to be taken into account in tracing this development.

20 A Harris poll released on September 11, 1994 revealed that more than 62 percent of all Americans profess a belief in the Devil (reported in The *Oregonian*, September 12, 1994).

21 Jeffrey Burton Russell treats theologians' opinions on how much authority the Devil had in *Lucifer: The Devil in the Middle Ages* (Ithaca: Cornell University Press, 1984), 202, 206, 235, 260, 292. Thomas Aquinas, William Langland, and Johannes Tauler represented the prevalent late-medieval learned opinion that the Evil One could not mislead the faithful. It would be ill-advised to accept their views as widespread among the masses, however. See Ariès, *Western Attitudes toward Death*, 36–39.

22 Ariès notices this in *Western Attitudes toward Death*, 56–58, and he remarks further on the phenomenon in *Hour of Our Death*, 369–70, 392–95; see also Vovelle, *La mort et l'Occident*, 213–24.

23 Robert W. Scribner, "Vom Sakralbild zur sinnlichen Schau: Sinnliche Wahrnehmung und das Visuelle bei der Objektivierung des Frauenkörpers in Deutschland im 16. Jahrhundert," in Klaus Schreiner and Norbert Schnitzler, eds., *Gepeinigt, begehrt, vergessen: Symbolik und Sozialbezug des Körpers im späten Mittelalter und in der frühen Neuzeit* (Munich: Wilhelm Fink, 1992), 309–36, here esp. 323–29. See also Joseph Leo Koerner, *The Moment of Self-portraiture in German Renaissance Art* (Chicago: University of Chicago Press, 1993), on the moralizing nature of erotic images of death.

24 "Ein Sermon von der Bereitung zum Sterben," in *Dr. Martin Luthers Werke* (Weimar: Böhlau, 1883–   ), Weimarer Ausgabe (WA) 2: 685–97. See W. Goez, "Luthers 'Ein Sermon von der Bereitung zum Sterben' und die spätmittelalterliche ars moriendi," *Lutherjahrbuch* 48 (1981), 97–114. According to Hans-Martin Barth, following Goez, neither the Latin phrase *ars moriendi* nor its German translation *Kunst des Sterbens* occurs in Luther's writings: "Leben und Sterben können: Brechungen der spätmittelalterlichen 'ars moriendi' in der Theologie Martin Luthers," in Harald Wagner, ed., *Ars moriendi: Erwägungen zur Kunst des Sterbens* (Freiburg/Breisgau: Herder, 1989), 45–66, here 45, n. 1. This itself is not proof, Barth agrees, that Luther was not interested in death.

25 Rudolf Lenz, *De mortuis nil nisi bene? Leichenpredigten als multidisziplinäre Quelle unter besonderer Berücksichtigung der historischen Familienforschung, der bildungsgeschichte und der Literaturgeschichte*, Marburger Personalschriften-Forschungen, 10 (Sigmaringen: Jan Thorbecke, 1990), 9. Lenz would probably agree with this statement. The publication history of this sermon may be found in WA 2: 680–83.

26 "Death and Ritual in Reformation Germany," Ph.D. dissertation, University of Michigan, 1994, 47–55. Koslofsky compares Luther's evolving views with those of Wessel Gansfort and Andreas Bodenstein von Karlstadt (27–55). This work is forthcoming as a book; its title is not yet set.

27 WA 2: 685–86.

28 WA 2: 686.

29 WA 2: 686.

30 WA 2: 692.

31 WA 2: 692–93.

32 WA 2: 696–97.

33 WA 2: 696.

34 WA 17/1: 199–200 (Luther's comments), and 199, n. 1.

35 On the elimination of the oil, see WA 6: 567–69.

36 Barth, "Leben und Sterben," 58.

37 WA 17: 204. Ariès comments on the simultaneity in Protestant lands of the elimination of purgatory and the "reemergence" of repose as an intermediate stage ("L'histoire de l'au-delà dans la chrétienté latine," 31).

38 Koslofsky, "Death and Ritual," 52.

39 Roland H. Bainton, *Here I Stand: A Life of Martin Luther* (New York: New American Library, 1950), 237.

40 This translation is from Jaroslav Pelikan and Helmut T. Lehmann, eds., *Luther's Works*, 55 vols. (St. Louis: Concordia Publishing House, and Philadelphia: Fortress Press, 1955–1986), 51: 238–39. By convention, this abridgement of Luther's complete works is abbreviated SL (Saint Louis) for the original city of publication. The original texts of the two sermons may be found in WA 36: 237–70.

41 SL 51: 242.

42 SL 51: 248 (the second funeral sermon for Johann).

43 SL 51: 248.

44 For a treatment written from an anthropological perspective, see Mary Lindemann, "Armen- und Eselbegräbnis in der europäischen Frühneuzeit, eine Methode sozialer Kontrolle," in Blum, ed., *Studien zur Thematik des Todes*, 125–39. Rudolf Mohr has examined the few funeral sermons given (and afterward printed) for persons who had died in unusual ways: *Der unverhoffte Tod: Theologie- und kulturgeschichtliche Untersuchungen zu außergewöhnlichen Todesfällen in Leichenpredigten*, Marburger Personalschriften-Forschungen, 5 (Marburg: Schwarz, 1982).

45 "Bekenntnis der Artikel des Glaubens," WA 26: 509.

46 WA *Tischreden*, 5: 446, no. 6029. This translation is by Ewald Plass, comp., *What Luther Says: An Anthology* (St. Louis: Concordia Publishing House, 1959), 1: 381.

47 WA 48: 63–64, trans. Plass, *What Luther Says*, 1: 382.

48 In this chapter, as before, I have used Emil Sehling, ed., *Die evangelischen Kirchenordnungen des 16. Jahrhunderts* (KOO), 15 vols. to date (vols. 1–5, Leipzig: O. R. Reisland, 1902–1913; vols. 6–15, Tübingen: J. C. B. Mohr [Paul Siebeck (*sic*)], 1955–1977).

49 KOO, 1: 269–71.

50 For a verse as much a part of the English language as this one, I have used the King James version of the Bible instead of *The New English Bible*.

51 Actually, 27, n. 1 says the 116th Psalm, and the beginning text is given; but this corresponds in all the Bibles at my disposal to the 117th: "Praise the Lord, all nations ... "

52 Very occasionally, Psalm 130 ("Out of the depths have I cried unto Thee, O Lord") is given as a possible alternate, as in the Palatinate of the Rhine in 1556 and 1577 (Sehling, KOO, 14: 171). This is the most moderate of the penitential Psalms in that it turns from despair and sin immediately to forgiveness, hope, and God's love. Martin Luther incorporated this Psalm into the Lutheran liturgy for all time when he wrote the hymn, "Aus tieffer not schrey ich zu dir."

53 For example, Sehling, KOO, 5: 208–209 (Mecklenburg, 1552); 8/1: 326 (Hesse, 1566), followed on 327–28 by much additional detail; 12/2: 103–104 (Augsburg, 1555); 14: 170–71 (Palatinate of the Rhine, 1556) and again in the Palatinate, 1563, KOO, 14: 402–403.

54 Sehling, KOO, 8/1: 327 (the 1566 ordinance of Philipp of Hesse).

55 Sehling, KOO, 1: 279. Martin Luther provided the German translation of the traditional liturgical prayer, "Kyrie eleison, Christe eleison," in 1528, which includes the line, "Vor bösem schnellen Tod behüt uns, lieber Herre Gott."

56 Sehling, KOO, 7/2^1: 124.

57 Sehling, KOO, 12/2: 64; 14: 405.

58 Sehling, KOO, 11: 508–22, here esp. 508–10.

59 Sehling, KOO, 12/2: 104–107.

60 Thüringisches Hauptstaatsarchiv Weimar (HSAWei), Reg. Ji 68, "Kirchen-vnd Schul-Visitations-Acta 1587 bis 1632," fol. 246^r.

61 Sehling, KOO, 12/1: 216.

62 Sehling, KOO, 14: 169 (Palatinate of the Rhine, 1556; repeated 1577). Nonetheless, the pastors are instructed separately that if the moment of a soul's departure is truly at hand and haste is unavoidable, the instruction (*vermanung*) may be left out (172). The sacrament itself is the sine qua non. Sometimes it was the pastors' fault that the dying received the sacrament at the last moment. See Sachsen-Anhalt Landeshauptarchiv Magdeburg (LHAMag), Rep. A12 Gen. 1332, "Qvedlinburgische Kirchen-Ordnung 15. April 1627," fol. 4^v.

63 Hessisches Hauptstaatsarchiv Wiesbaden (HSAWies), Abt. 171 Nr. D245, fol. 137, for example, village of Oberweyer; fol. 140, village of Nieder Hadamer. At the same time, however, the people used the services of a wise woman named Elß [Elsa], who said a ritual blessing over the belt of the sick person—she insisted it cured sick animals, too:

> If God will, and the dear holy virgin Saint Christina [Christeni], and the holy virgin Saint Agnes, and the holy virgin Saint Dorothea, and the holy virgin Saint Margaret, the same holy virgins help me to exhort and ask God, whether this person has 72 evils, or 72 [nacht ruhn] [?wandering spirits of the night], if he were one of those who are not from God, that he is given a punishment from God the heavenly father. Through the Father, through the Son, through the Holy Spirit. Jesus Christ, Amen.

The belt gives a sign, indicating whether the person really is sick, and if so, he is to say five Our Fathers, five Hail Marys, five Creeds, and then he is made well (fols. 145–46).

64 Sehling, KOO, 14: 404, for example (Palatinate of the Rhine, 1562). Within three or four days of a person's taking to bed, the pastor must be notified.

65 LSAMag, Rep. 12A Gen. 2438, "Kirchenvisitation 1583/4, Städte im Holzkreis," fols. 251^v–252^r, where the fees are set specifically for Holy Communion. The nobles pay more than citizens, and the pastor receives more than the deacon. The people do not have to pay for a simple visit, instruction, and consolation from a clergyman. This sounds good, but it is to be remembered that the people generally continued to believe that the sacrament contained special potency, and most would not have been satisfied by a mere visit.

66 HSAWei, Reg. Ji 67, "Kirchen- vnd Schul-Visitations-Acta. 1586," fol. 104^r.

67 Baden-Württemberg Hauptstaatsarchiv Stuttgart (B-WHSAS), A281, Büschel 1020, n.p.

68 As, for example, during the general Ernestine (Saxon) visitation of 1573, as a result of which some rural pastors were dismissed for conveying the teachings of Flaccius Illyricus to their congregations. See HSAWei, Reg. Ji 57, "Visitation im Ernestinischen Gebiet 1573," passim. In the super-intendency of Weimar, 32 out of 107 pastors were dismissed. While some rural clergy may not have realized that their messages were "flawed," the superintendents definitely did. As a result of this particularly vicious visitation, nine superintendents were driven out of their posts: those of

Jena, Coburg, Weimar, Gotha, Eisenach, Römhild, Königsberg, Ronneburg, and Saalfeld.

69 Evangelisches Landeskirchliches Archiv Stuttgart (ELKAS), A1 Nr. 1, 1585, e.g. village of Klein Sachsenhaim, fol. 202; A1 Nr. 1 1582, fol. 117, Görlingen. Whenever the plague struck, however, the bell was not to be rung, for during those dire times it would have to be kept ringing all the time.

70 The practice of delivering funeral orations was very widespread in Italian humanist circles. No doubt they were an aspect of humanist rhetoric that spread northward during the fifteenth century—but, again, usually confined to the burial rites of famous people. See John McManamon, S.J., "Continuity and Change in the Ideals of Humanism: The Evidence from Florentine Funeral Oratory," in Marcel Tetel, Ronald G. Witt, and Rona Goffen, eds., *Life and Death in Fifteenth-century Florence* (Durham, N.C., and London: Duke University Press, 1989), 69–87. The debate over the desirability of funeral sermons, and especially over the extravagant praise of the dead included in them, went beyond the German borders: Frederic B. Tromly, " 'According to sounde religion': The Elizabethan Controversy over the Funeral Sermon," *Medieval and Renaissance Studies* 13, 1 (1983), 293–312.

71 Rudolf Mohr, *Der unverhoffte Tod*, Marburger Personalschriften-Forschungen 5 (Marburg: Schwarz, 1982), 53.

72 On humanist funeral oratory in Florence, see John McManamon, S.J., "Continuity and Change", 68–87.

73 Mary Lindemann, "Armen- und Eselbegräbnis," in Blum, ed., *Studien zur Thematik des Todes*, 125–39.

74 When a prince died, sometimes every pastor in the land was required to compose a funeral sermon for delivery to his congregation, as in 1666, when Duke August the Younger of Braunschweig-Wolfenbüttel died (Niedersächsisches Landeskirchliches Archiv Braunschweig [LKABr], V 1765 and V 1942). A text (Psalm 90: 14–16) was assigned them, but there must have been some confusion, for some of the sermons address other biblical passages. In order to verify that they had carried out the order, authorities collected all these sermons, thirty-eight of which lie in manuscript in the archive. They are, in any case, neither original nor startling.

75 Lenz, *De mortuis nil nisi bene?* 20–21.

76 Anyone interested in funeral sermons would be well advised to begin with several of the thousands of originals at the Herzog August Bibliothek in Wolfenbüttel, followed by a survey of Lenz's works, among others: *De mortuis nil nisi bene?*; "Die Forschungsstelle für Personalschriften an der Philipps-Universität Marburg," *Genealogie* 29 (1980), 225–33; "Gedruckte Leichenpredigten (1550–1750)," in idem, ed., *Leichenpredigten als Quelle historischer Wissenschaften* (Cologne and Vienna: Böhlau, 1975), 1: 36–51; idem, ed., *Katalog der Leichenpredigten im Stadtarchiv Rothenburg ob der Tauber*, Marburger Personalschriften-Forschungen 6 (Marburg: Schwarz, 1983); idem, ed., *Katalog der Leichenpredigten und sonstiger Trauerschriften im Hessischen Staatsarchiv Marburg* (Sigmaringen: Jan Thorbecke, 1992); idem, ed., *Katalog der Leichenpredigten und sonstiger Trauerschriften in der Hessischen Landes- und Hochschulbibliothek Darmstadt*, 2 vols. (Sigmaringen: Jan Thorbecke, 1990); idem, ed., *Katalog der Leichenpredigten und sonstiger Trauerschriften in der Universitätsbibliothek Marburg*, Marburger Personal-schriften-Forschungen 2/1, 2, 2 vols. (Marburg: Schwarz, 1980), and a long addendum to this, *Katalog der Leichenpredigten und sonstiger Trauerschriften in der Universitätsbibliothek Marburg. Nachtrag* (Sigmaringen: Jan Thorbecke, 1990); idem, ed., *Leichenpredigten als Quelle historischer Wissenschaften*, 3 vols.

(Cologne and Vienna: Böhlau, 1975; Marburg: Schwarz, 1979; Marburg: Schwarz, 1984); idem, ed., *Leichenpredigten: Eine Bestandsaufnahme: Bibliographie und Ergebnisse einer Umfrage*, Marburger Personalschriften-Forschungen 3 (Marburg: Schwarz, 1980); "Leichenpredigten: Eine bislang vernachlässigte Quellengattung: Geschichte, Forschungsstand, methodologische Probleme, Bibliographie," *Archiv für Kulturgeschichte* 56, 2 (1974), 296–312; "Leichenpredigten—eine Quellengattung," *Blätter für deutsche Landesgeschichte* 111 (1975), 15–30; "Leichenpredigten und die Methoden ihrer Erschließung," *Bibliothek: Forschung und Praxis* 3, 2 (1979), 112–21; idem, ed., *Studien zur deutschsprachigen Leichenpredigt der frühen Neuzeit*, Marburger Personalschriften-Forschungen 4 (Marburg: Schwarz, 1981); "Vorkommen, Aufkommen und Verteilung der Leichenpredigten: Untersuchungen zu ihrer regionalen Distribution, zur zeitlichen Häufigkeit und zu Geschlecht, Stand und Beruf der Verstorbenen," in idem, ed., *Studien zur deutschsprachigen Leichenpredigt der frühen Neuzeit*, Marburger Personalschriften-Forschungen 4 (Marburg: Schwarz, 1981), 223–48; "Zum Stand der Erschließung von Personalschriften," *Wolfenbütteler Barock-Nachrichten* 13, 3 (1986), 105–11; Lenz and G. Keil, "Johann Christoph Donauer (1669–1718): Untersuchungen zur Soziographie und Pathographie eines Nördlinger Ratskonsulenten aufgrund der Leichenpredigt," *Zeitschrift für bayerische Landesgeschichte* 38 (1975), 317–55; idem, *Katalog ausgewählter Leichenpredigten der ehemaligen Stadtbibliothek Breslau*, Marburger Personalschriften-Forschungen 8 (Marburg: Schwarz, 1986); Lenz et al., comp., *Katalog der Leichenpredigten und sonstiger Trauerschriften in Bibliotheken und Archiven der Vogelsbergregion*, Marburger Personalschriften-Forschungen 9 (Marburg: Schwarz, 1987); Lenz et al., comp., *Katalog der Leichenpredigten und sonstiger Trauerschriften in der Universitätsbibliothek Gießen*, Marburger Personalschriften-Forschungen 7/1, 2, 2 vols. (Marburg: Schwarz, 1985). See also Cornelia Niekus Moore, "Praeparatio ad Mortem: Das Buch bei Vorbereitung und Begleitung des Sterbens im protestantischen Deutschland des 16. und 17. Jahrhunderts," *Pietismus und Neuzeit* 19 (1993), 9–18. A complete bibliography of the literature on funeral sermons would require a book of its own. For that reason, I shall cite further only those works that were helpful for my purposes.

77 Klaus Schreiner, "Der Tod Marias als Inbegriff christlichen Sterbens," in Borst, von Graevenitz, Patschovsky, and Stierle, *Tod im Mittelalter*, 261–312.

78 Jacob Herbrandt ("der heiligen schrifft doctor"), *Warhafftige History vnd Bericht, welcher gestalt, weylandt der Durchleuchtige, Hochgeborne Fürst vnd Herr, Herr Albrecht der Jünger, Marggraff zu Brandenburgk...Aus diesem jamerthal Christlich verschieden, vnd sein end genommen habe* (Erfurt: Gervasius Stürmer, 1557).

79 Herbrandt, *Warhafftige History*, Aii^r–Biii^r.

80 Andreas Musculus, *Sepultur Des Durchleuchtigsten Hochgebornen Fürsten vnnd Herrn, Herrn Joachim, Marggraffen zu Brandenburgk, des heyligen Römischen Reichs Ertzkammerer, vnnd churfürst, etc. In Gott seligklich entschlaffen, den 2. Januarij in der nacht, zwischen vier vnd fünff vhr, jhrer Churfürst. G. alters im 66. friedlicher regierung aber im 36. jar begraben, den 26. Januarij, des 1571. Jars, mit Christlichen, ehrlichen vnd Fürstlichen Ceremonien, wie folgent ordentlich verzeichnet vnd erzehlet, etc.* (Frankfurt an der Oder: Johann Eichorn, 1571).

Musculus (1514–1581) early became a strong partisan of Luther, taught at the University of Frankfurt/Oder and then became the Hofprediger and advisor of Elector Joachim II and of his successor Johann Georg. He avidly engaged in theological controversy and fought categorically the belief that in any sense good works are necessary for salvation. He used nearly Catholic language in the Eucharist and supported the reintroduction of the elevation of the elements as a means of refuting sacramentarianism. He wrote and published a great deal on these and other matters. See *Allgemeine Deutsche Biographie* (Berlin: Duncker & Humblot, 1970, reprint of 1886 edition), 23: 93–94; Christian Wilhelm Spieker, *Lebensgeschichte des Andreas Musculus: Ein Beitrag zur Reformations- und Sittengeschichte des 16ten Jahrhunderts* (Nieuwkoop: B. de Graaf, 1964, reprint of original 1858 edition).

81 Musculus, *Sepultur,* Aiii^v–Aiv^r.

82 Musculus, *Sepultur,* Aiv^r–Aiv^v.

83 Werner Friedrich Kümmel, "Der sanfte und selige Tod—Verklärung und Wirklichkeit des Sterbens im Spiegel lutherischer Leichenpredigten des 16. bis 18. Jahrhunderts," in Lenz, ed., *Studien zur deutschsprachigen Leichenpredigt,* 199–226.

84 On Selnecker's dismissal, see Helmar Junghans, ed., *Das Jahrhundert der Reformation in Sachsen* (Berlin: Evangelische Verlagsanstalt, 1989), 213. D. Nicolaus Selnecker, *Christliche Leychpredigten, So vom Jar 1576 bis fast an das 1590. Jar zu Leipzig...geschehen* (Magdeburg: Paul Donat, 1590), sermons 1–82; *Ander Theil Christlicher Leychpredigten zu Leipzig gehalten, von Anno 1584 bis auff das 1589. Jar...* (Magdeburg: Paul Donat, n.d. [but presumably also 1590]), sermons 83 to 170.

Selnecker had also given a number of sermons at the funerals of members of ruling families, and he saw six of these bound together and printed in 1591, even though the earliest one, that for King Christian of Denmark, dated from 1559: *Sechs Wonderbare Leichpredigten vber Keyser, Kön. Chur vnd Fürsten, Todt vnd begengnis* (n.p.: 1591). Christian is described as having died while singing, along with all those in attendance in his chamber, "Mit fried vnd freud ich fahr dahin," a beloved Lutheran hymn (fol. 11^v).

85 Selnecker, *Christliche Leychpredigten,* fols. 122^r–124^v.

86 There are two fine articles specifically about the images of women in the funeral sermons. Heide Wunder concludes, on the basis of her extensive reading in the Marburg collections, that there is no such thing as specifically feminine religiosity: "Frauen in den Leichenpredigten des 16. und 17. Jahrhunderts," in Lenz, ed, *Studien zur deutschsprachigen Leichenpredigt,* 57–68. Jill Bepler sees in the funeral sermons prescribed traits and modes of behavior for women: "Women in German Funeral Sermons: Models of Virtue or Slice of Life?" *German Life and Letters* 44, 5 (October 1991), 392–403. See, also by Wunder, "Der gesellschaftliche Ort von Frauen der gehobener Stände im 17. Jahrhundert," in Karen Hausen and Heide Wunder, eds., *Frauengeschichte, Geschlechtergeschichte* (Frankfurt and New York: Campus Verlag, 1992), 50–56. In addition, Eileen T. Dugan has written about the image of the family conveyed in the sermons: "The Funeral Sermon as a Key to Familial Values in Early Modern Nördlingen," *Sixteenth Century Journal* 20 (1989), 631–44. For an English setting, see Mary Ellen Lamb, "The Countess of Pembroke and the Art of Dying" in Mary Beth Rose, ed., *Women in the Middle Ages and the Renaissance: Literary and Historical Perspectives* (Syracuse: Syracuse University Press, 1986), 207–26.

87 Both in the Middle Ages and in the post-Reformation era, this familiar scriptural metaphor was frequently used, and nuns and mystics thought of themselves as the brides of Christ. Protestant pastors explained to their congregations that the Christian church was the bride of Christ, and in many wedding sermons they drew the well-worn parallel between Christ's

marriage to his bride, the church, and a man being wed to a woman. See, for example, Martin Moller, *Mysterivm Magnvm. Fleissige vnd andächtige Betrachtung des grossen Geheimniß der Himlischen Geistlichen Hochzeit ... Jesu Christi mit der Christgleubigen Gemeine seiner Braut ...* (Görlitz: Johann Rhambaw, 1595.) What is unusual here is Frau Seeman's apparent reversion to the more medieval (or, at any rate, Catholic) image of the individual marriage to Christ.

88 *Soliloquia de passione Iesu Christi. Wie ein jeder Christen Mensch das allerheyligste Leyden vnd Sterben vnsers HERRN Iesu Christi in seinem Hertzen bey sich selbst betrachten Allerley schöne Lehren vnd heylsamen Trost daraus schöpffen vnd zu einem Christlichen Leben vnd seligen Sterben in teglichem Gebet vnd Seufftzen nützlich gebrauchen sol* (Görlitz: Ambrosio Fritsch, 1587).

89 *Verzeichnis der im Deutschen Sprachbereich Erschienen Drucke des XVI. Jahrhunderts 16*, vol. 14 (1989), cols. M 6053–M 6054.

90 *Manuale De praeparatione ad mortem. Heilsame vnd sehr nützliche betrachtung wie ein Christen Mensch aus Gottes Wort sol lernen Christlich leben vnd Seliglich sterben* (Görlitz: Ambrosius Fritsch, 1593), VD 16, vol. 14, cols. M 6035–M 6036. There being as yet no *Verzeichnis der im deutschen Siprachbereich erschienenen Drucke des XVII. Jahrhunderts*, I have no firm information on the work's appearance during the seventeenth century, but my citations come from the 1673 edition (Leipzig: Johann Heinrich Ellinger, 1673), which I came across in the Herzog August Bibliothek. The title has been somewhat modified: *Christliche Lebens- und Selige Sterbe-Kunst, Heilsame, und sehr nützliche Betrachtung, wie ein Christ sein gantzes Leben führen, in steter Busse zubringen, und sich allezeit zu einem seligen Sterb Stündlein bereit und gefast halten, auch dermahleins nach gottes Willen in kräfftigem Glaubens-Trost wider allerley Anfechtung und Schrecken durch einen sanfften und seligen Tod von dieser Welt frölich und freudig abscheiden könne und solle.*

91 Ernst Koch has written that (not counting Luther's tract of 1519) between 1522 and 1600 in Albertine Saxony, 120 works on the subject of dying by various authors were published: "Ausbau, Gefährdung und Festigung der lutherischen Landeskirche von 1553 by 1601," Helmar Junghans, ed., *Jahrhundert der Reformation*, 218.

92 Moller, *Sterbe-Kunst*, 3.

93 Moller, *Sterbe-Kunst*, 10.

94 Moller, *Sterbe-Kunst*, 13–14.

95 Moller, *Sterbe-Kunst*, 19–20.

96 Moller, *Sterbe-Kunst*, 28.

97 Moller, *Sterbe-Kunst*, 44–45.

98 Moller's elaboration on this point (106–107) is a pointed instruction to submit to those who wield power and to suppress ambition:

> Attend diligently to your calling which the Lord has ordained for you, so that you live it out properly, with complete patience and mildness ... Don't go after higher rank, and don't think about your wealth, but only about what God has ordained for you; always accept that ... Don't mix in matters that don't pertain to you, and don't press yourself in God's presence into offices. Don't let yourself think that you are sufficiently qualified for them, for such darkness has betrayed many .... For it is impious to gape after something that has not been ordained for you.

99 Moller, *Sterbe-Kunst*, 57–58.

100 Moller, *Sterbe-Kunst*, 120–21.

101 Moller, *Sterbe-Kunst*, 124–25.

102 Moller, *Sterbe-Kunst*, 128.
103 Moller, *Sterbe-Kunst*, 131–32.
104 Moller, *Sterbe-Kunst*, 132.
105 Moller, *Sterbe-Kunst*, 156.
106 Moller, *Sterbe-Kunst*, 191.
107 Moller, *Sterbe-Kunst*, 204.
108 Moller, *Sterbe-Kunst*, 217–18.
109 Moller, *Sterbe-Kunst*, 222–23.
110 Moller, *Sterbe-Kunst*, 269–72.
111 Moller, *Sterbe-Kunst*, 263–64. Moller may have written this poem himself. If not, he does not attribute it to another author.
112 Zachaeus Faber, Jr., *Coronae Funerale...Das ist...Christliche Leichpredigten* (Leipzig: Eliz. [*sic*] Rehefelds and Johann Großen Buchhändl. [*sic*], n.d. [but early seventeenth century]), 91–92. On the subject of the popular Catholic practice of using clothing associated with saints' statues to heal the sick and aid the dying, see Richard C. Trexler's fascinating essay, "Der Heiligen neue Kleider: Eine analytische Skizze zur Be- und Entkleidung von Statuen," in Klaus Schreiner and Norbert Schnitzler, eds., *Gepeinigt, begehrt, vergessen*, 365–402.
113 See Bob Scribner's seminal article, "Ritual and Popular Religion in Catholic Germany at the Time of the Reformation," in idem., *Popular Culture and Popular Movements in Reformation Germany* (London and Ronceverte: Hambledon Press, 1987), 17–47, including the diagrams on 28, 45. This essay originally appeared in *Journal of Ecclesiastical History* 35 (1984), 47–77.
114 This was in Martin Luther's hymnbook of 1524. It retains an honored place in German Lutheran hymnals today.
115 R. W. Scribner, "Anticlericalism and the Reformation in Germany," in idem, *Popular Culture and Popular Movements*, 243–56; Susan C. Karant-Nunn, "Neoclericalism and Anticlericalism in Saxony 1555–1675," *Journal of Interdisciplinary History* 24, 4 (Spring 1994), 615–37.
116 ELKAS, A1 Nr. 1 1585, vol. 1, fols. 64–65.
117 Sehling, KOO, 2: 135 (the earldom of Schwarzburg, 1574), for example.
118 Sehling, KOO, 8/1: 337 (Hesse, 1566).
119 ELKAS, A1 Nr. 1 1584, vol. 2, fol. 134.
120 Selnecker, *Christliche Leychpredigten*, no. 18, fol. 67^r. Selnecker is referring to the popular conception of the Devil as appearing often in the form of a black dog. He retells the dream of an 8-year-old boy who awoke from a nightmare screaming and crying. When asked what the matter was, he said he had seen a coffin with a black dog lying by it, but a little girl came quickly and threatened the dog. She told him that he was to leave the boy in peace or she would tie him up. Selnecker comments that even children can overcome death and the Devil if they come to catechism lessons regularly and commend themselves to God through Christ by means of the Lord's Prayer.
121 On the matter of loudness, see Kümmel, "Der sanfte und selige Tod," 211.
122 My findings fully coincide with those of Richard Wunderli and Gerald Broce in "The Final Moment before Death in Early Modern England," *Sixteenth Century Journal* 20, 2 (1989), 259–75, of which I was reminded after writing this chapter.
123 Peter Ulner, *Leichpredig uber* [*sic*] *der fürstlichen Leich und Begrebnuss des durchleuchtigen...Fürsten...Herrn Heinrichen des Jüngern...welcher dieses jetztlauffenden 1568 Jars am 11...Julii...in Gott entschlafen* (Wolfenbüttel: C. Horn, 1568), Aiii^v. On whether Heinrich was Lutheran at the end, see E. G. H. Lentz, *Geschichte der Einführung des evangelischen Bekenntnisses im*

Herzogthume Braunschweig (Wolfenbüttel: Albrechts Buchhandlung, 1830), 181–82. Before he died, Heinrich ordered all pastors to hold a memorial service for him one year after his death, but when Julius, his heir, carried out this wish and issued such a command on June 6, 1569, it met considerable resistance as a papist practice (LKABr, V 1923, fols. 3^r–5^v, about Nicolaus Budanus's refusal to comply; and V 1760, esp. fols. 2^r–20^r).

Somebody ought to have a doctoral student examine the demeanor of Christ on the cross in Lutheran Passion sermons. I suspect that in them Jesus is shown to be less agonized and more quiescent than in the Catholic versions.

124 I quite agree with Werner Kümmel that, at least as far as Lutheran Germany is concerned, Ariès was mistaken in thinking that in the sixteenth and seventeenth centuries people departed from the late medieval view of death as the moment of judgment for individual souls ("Der sanfte und selige Tod," 224). One might gain an opposite impression in reading learned Lutheran treatises on the fate of the body and the nature of the afterlife, but in fact these treatises deal mainly with what happens to the saved. The condemned have already met their eternal reward at the moment of death. Or if they have not and also sleep, we must assume that theirs is not a "sweet repose" until the Last Judgment. Whatever their condition—and it is hardly ever discussed—the damned cannot haunt the earth or return to human society in any way, according to Lutheran teaching. Lucas Lossius, for example, says nothing about the nature of the sleep of the condemned, but he retains the classic pattern of all humans being awakened on the Last Day and those who had led evil lives being cast down into eternal fire (*Ewiger Warhafftiger vnd Göttlicher Trost, Hülffe, Errettunge vnd Beystand, in allerley Verfolgung, Not, Angst, Anfechtung vnd erschreckung der Sünde, Todt, Teuffel, Helle, Welt, eigem Fleisch vnd Blut* [Frankfurt: Peter Braubach, 1556] 148, 150).

125 Arnold van Gennep, *The Rites of Passage*, trans. Monika B. Vizedom and Gabrielle L. Caffee (Chicago: University of Chicago Press, 1960; original French edition, 1908), 146–65. Cf. Klaus Guth, "Sitte, Ritus, Brauch: Bräuche um Tod und Begräbnis," *Archiv für Liturgiewissenschaft* 31 (1989), 100–18, here 100.

126 In this country, the work of Ralph E. Giesey, *The Royal Funeral Ceremony in Renaissance France* (Geneva: Librairie E. Droz, 1960) was a pioneer, and since its appearance the genre has grown apace. A recent example pertaining to German-speaking lands is Sebastian Roser and Armin Ruhland, "Trauerfeierlichkeiten," in Karl Möseneder, ed., *Feste in Regensburg: Von der Reformation bis in die Gegenwart* (Regensburg: Mittelbayerische Druckerei- und Verlags-Gesellschaft, 1986), 57–67, which deals with the funeral of Emperor Maximilian II in 1576.

127 Franz, ed., *Das Rituale*, 83. Ohler notes that in the warmer Mediterranean regions it was imperative that the body be buried within one day, for it began to decay perceptibly. He thinks that incense was intended in part to conceal the smell of the rotting corpse (*Sterben und Tod im Mittelalter*, 83).

128 Here again, Ariès's treatment of the dead body seems to have little or no relevance to sixteenth-century parish practices in Germany. Ariès draws his evidence from the sometimes spectacular, and in no case typical, testimony of the elite dead. See chap. 8, "The Dead Body," *Hour of Our Death*, 353–95, in which, besides, the discussion often has to do with the eighteenth century in (Catholic) France. On *Seelweiber*, see K.-S. Kramer, *Volksleben im Fürstentum Ansbach und seinen Nachbarstaaten (1500–1800): Eine Volkskunde auf Grund archivalischer Quellen* (Würzburg: F. Schoningh, 1961), 235; and

Richard van Dülmen, *Kultur und Alltag in der Frühen Neuzeit*, vol. 1, *Das Haus und seine Menschen 16.–18. Jahrhundert* (Munich: C. H. Beck, 1990), 217; Ohler, *Sterben und Tod*, 80. Van Dülmen's section on "Sterben und Begräbnis" (215–28) is of interest, but it attempts to span three centuries and is thus too general for my purposes.

129 Robert Muchembled writes ("Le corps, la culture populaire et la culture des élites en France [XVe–XVIIIe siècle]," in Arthur E. Imhof, ed., *Leib und Leben in der Geschichte der Neuzeit* [Berlin: Duncker & Humblot, 1983], 141–53, here 145):

> Les femmes se situent à la croisée des chemins, à l'intersection du visible—corps humain, monde extérieur—et de l'invisible—intérieur du corps, monde surnaturel. Elles acquièrent de ce fait une forte ambivalence, car elles peuvent à la fois guérir et nuire, en utilisant les secrets qu'elles connaissent et en déchaînant les forces qu'elles savent identifier. En d'autres termes, elles se placent à la charnière de la vie et de la mort, non seulement parce qu'elles interviennent seules dans le mystère de la naissance des êtres et qu'elles jouent un rôle fondamental au chevet des malades ou lors des cérémonies funèbres, mais aussi parce qu'elles sont un trait d'union permanent entre le macrocosme universel et le microcosme du corps humain, entre lesquels elles tissent ou détruisent à leur gré des liens et des correspondances.

130 Otto Döhner says that barber-surgeons were dishonorable until 1548, but he doesn't say what happened to change their condition in that year. It is true that other categories of "dishonorability" were fading during the sixteenth century. See *Krankheitsbegriff, Gesundheitsverhalten und Einstellung zum Tod im 16. bis 18. Jahrhundert*, Marburger Schriften zur Medizingeschichte 17 (Frankfurt/Main: Peter Lang, 1986), 58.

131 Bächtold-Stäubli and Hoffmann-Krayer, *Handwörterbuch des deutschen Aberglaubens* 8: col. 1074.

132 Franz, ed., *Das Rituale*, 40.

133 Franz, ed., *Das Rituale*, 41.

134 Franz, ed., *Das Rituale*, 42–43.

135 Franz, ed., *Das Rituale*, 44.

136 Claude Lecouteux, *Geschichte der Gespenster und Wiedergänger im Mittelalter* (Cologne and Vienna: Böhlau, 1987), 6–7; Carlo Ginsburg, *Ecstasies: Deciphering the Witches' Sabbath*, trans. Raymond Rosenthal (New York: Penguin Books, 1991), 102, 105; Jean-Claude Schmitt, *Les revenants: les vivants et les morts dans la société médiévale* (Paris: Gallimard, 1994).

137 On the ties between the living and the dead in the early Middle Ages, see Patrick J. Geary, "Exchange and Interaction Between the Living and the Dead in Early Medieval Society," in idem, *Living with the Dead in the Middle Ages* (Ithaca: Cornell University Press, 1995), 77–92.

138 Jean Delumeau, *Catholicism Between Luther and Voltaire: A New View of the Counter-Reformation* (Philadelphia: Westminster Press, 1977).

139 Jean Delumeau, *Sin and Fear: The Emergence of a Western Guilt Culture 13th–18th Centuries*, trans. Eric Nicholson (New York: St. Martin's Press, 1990), 302 and passim. The original French edition was entitled *Le péché et la peur* (Paris: Librairie Artheme Fayard, 1983).

140 Lecouteux, *Geschichte der Gespenster*, 33, reproduces a table from Delumeau, *Le péché et la peur*, 86, of the categories of walking dead seen by people in the nineteenth century. I cannot find this table in the English translation. The

highest percentages are of those who died unbaptized (90 cases, 18 percent of total) and those who drowned (101 cases, 20.2 percent of the total).

141 1: cols. 976–1001; 5: cols. 1024–1167; 7: cols. 942–51, 953–55, 1627–35; 8: 436–58, 970–1095; 9: cols. 570–78.

142 Theo Brown, *The Fate of the Dead: A Study in Folk-eschatology in the West Country after the Reformation* (Ipswich: D. S. Brewer, and Totowa, N.J.: Rowman and Littlefield, 1979), 36, on prejudice against burial on the north side in England. Also on England, see Robert Dinn, "'Monuments Answerable to Mens [*sic*] Worth': Burial Patterns, Social Status and Gender in Late Medieval Bury St Edmunds," *Journal of Ecclesiastical History* 46, 2 (1995), 237–55, here at 249–50.

143 On this point, thanks to Frederick M. Nunn for pointing out that the churches themselves are used as latrines in certain Central American countries, and that this use in the people's eyes seems not to be at odds with their fervent devotion. I have occasionally come across suggestive admonitions in the Lutheran visitation protocols, describing the foul condition of some churches and urging the sextons to clean them out at regular intervals. These had led me to wonder whether especially urban churches were sometimes so used in the early modern period.

144 For a spectacular arrangement of even the fine bones in a Roman example, see Ariès, *Bilder zur Geschichte des Todes*, trans. Hans-Horst Henschen (Munich: Carl Hanser, 1984), 100. This is the German translation of *Images de l'homme devant la mort*.

145 One of the unpaginated, unnumbered photographs in Ariès's *Hour of Our Death* shows of the catacombs of the Capuchin Convent in Palermo, where the skeletons of the individual brothers are not only intact but also labeled.

146 Ariès, *Hour of Our Death*, 54; Vovelle, *La mort et l'Occident*, 159.

147 Ariès, *Hour of Our Death*, 61.

148 For a very recent example, equally applicable to Germany, see Dinn, "Monuments Answerable to Mens [*sic*] Worth," 237–55.

149 On various groups of dishonorable people in Cologne—the categories pertain to the rest of Germany too—see Franz Irsigler and Arnold Lassotta, *Bettler und Gaukler, Dirnen und Henker: Außenseiter in einer mittelalterlichen Stadt* (Munich: Deutscher Taschenbuchverlag, 1989); and for all over Germany, see Bernd Roeck, *Außenseiter, Randgruppen, Minderheiten: Fremde im Deutschland der frühen Neuzeit* (Göttingen: Vandenhoeck & Ruprecht, 1993), esp. 106–18.

150 This separation of the dead from the living is a prominent theme in Craig M. Koslofsky's *Death and Ritual*. On the struggle over the creation of extramural cemeteries, see esp. chap. 3, "Bodies: Placing the Dead in the German Reformation," 56–134. Koslofsky presents here a close study of Leipzig.

151 In Salzwedel (Brandenburg) in 1600, Elector Joachim-Friedrich ordered that no more bodies be buried in the wall of the main church, for the placing of graves had destabilized the whole edifice.

152 LHAMag, Rep. 12 Gen. 1332, fol. 6^r.

153 LHAMag, Rep. 12A Gen. 2438, "Kirchenvisitation 1583/4, Städte im Holzkreis," fols. 259^r–260^r.

154 Jürgen Döring, "Geschichte der alten Göttinger Friedhöfe," *Göttinger Jahrbuch* 31 (1983), 95–142, here 96. Curiously—an exception proving the rule—this ossuary was renovated in 1533, 1565, and 1585, but Döring does not say that these renovations did not result in the concealment of the skeletons. I would guess that they did.

155 For example, in Salzwedel in 1600, gravediggers could still use a *Beinhaus* if necessary (Brandenburgisches Landeshauptarchiv Potsdam [BLHAPot], Pr. Br. Rep. 40A 639, fol. 256^v).

156 HSAWies, Abt. 171 Nr. D245, "Protocollum Generalis Visitationis Aller Pastoreÿenn Vnnd darin gehörender Capellen in der Graueschafft Dietzs gehaltenn Anno 1590," passim. Also Abt. 171 Nr. D535, "Protocollum Generalis Visitationis Aller Pfarrenn, Pastoreÿenn vnd darin gehörenden Capellen, in der Inspection Dillenberg [sic] gehalten Anno 1590," passim.

157 Wilhelm Rauls, "Das Begräbnis in der Geschichte der evangelisch-lutherischen Landeskirche in Braunschweig," *Jahrbuch der Gesellschaft für niedersächsische Kirchengeschichte* 78 (1980), 115–43, here 117.

158 Sehling, KOO, 1: 195. Cf. Sehling, KOO, 13: 196 (Duchy of Pfalz-Neuburg 1576): "Wo irgend zwaierlei gottsacker in und außerhalb der statt weren und etwa furnembste leut iren begrebnussen in der statt haben und begeren wurden, soll denselbigen ein solches unverbeten sein, doch daß si deswegen ein anzal gelts in gottskasten geben."

159 BLHAPot, Pr. Br. Rep. 40A 727, fol. 41ʳ, Seehausen 1541.

160 Luther's translation into German of this Latin prayer appeared in the hymnal of 1524.

161 Sehling, KOO, 1: 274–76.

162 A territorial ordinance for Saxony-Weimar in 1622 specifies that people may not wear these or other mourning insignia after the funeral. Each community was to acquire these so that they could be loaned out to people who needed them but couldn't afford to buy them (HSAWei, B. 4930, "Sächsische Weimarische Neue Verlöbnüs-Hochzeit-Kinttauff- vnd Begräbnüs Ordnung ... 1622" fol. 19ᵛ).

163 Elisabeth Blum, "Tod und Begräbnis in evangelischen Kirchenliedern aus dem 16. Jahrhundert," in Paul Richard Blum, ed., *Studien zur Thematik des Todes*, 97–110, here 104. For a more detailed history of this hymn, see WA 35: 306–07.

164 "Nun lassen wir ihn hie schlafen und gehn all heim unsre Straßen, schicken uns auch mit allem Fleiß, denn der Tod kommt uns gleicherweis" (Michael Weiße, 1531), *Evangelisches Kirchen-Gesangbuch* (Berlin: Evangelische Verlagsanstalt, 1968), 175, song no. 174.

165 Sehling, KOO, 1: 371–74. Cf., for example, KOO, 13: 197 (Pfalz-Neuburg, 1576): "Wann aber zu sterbenszeiten leichpredigen ze tuen, der pfarrer oder kirchendiener von jemand gebeten, soll er dieselbige, im fall er sonsten nicht uberlegt und ime möglich, verrichten, wo nit, aus ermelter kirchenordnung furlesen," or KOO, 13: 552–57 (Rothenberg in Bavaria, 1618), where "Vermahnungen" are given so that they may be read at ordinary people's funerals. Pastors were at liberty to compose original ones for high-ranking people who were able to pay them an honorarium for their work.

166 Sehling, KOO, 1: 393.

167 Sehling, KOO, 2: 481. This ordinance also abolishes funeral sermons (481). Such action was most unusual.

168 Sehling, KOO, 11: 739 (Thüngen, 1564).

169 Sehling, KOO, 12: 213 (Lindau, 1573).

170 LKABr, V443, n. p. This is attested again in LHAMag, Rep. A12 Gen. 2486, "Visitationbuch des Stiffts Halberstadt. Von dem Hockwurdigen, Durchlauchtigen Hochgebornen Fursten vnd Herrn, Herrn Heinrichen Julio, Postulirten Bischoffen des Stiffts Halberstadt vnd Hertzogen zu Braunschweig vndt Luneburgk angeordnet. Anno Domini 1589," for the village of Osterwiegk, fol. 386ᵛ.

171 Rauls, "Das Begräbnis," 117.

172 Sehling, KOO, 3: 399 (Breslau, 1528).

173 For example, in the superintendency of Grimma (Saxony) in 1574 (Sächsisches Hauptstaatsarchiv Dresden [HSADres], Loc. 1991, fol. 85ᵛ), where adults get all three bells rung for them, but children only two. The visitors on this occasion noted in every rural parish how many bells there were, and in fact how many of these villages had clocks hooked up to the small bell. The biggest bell was called the "great" (*grosse*) bell; the middle-sized bell the *Salveglocke* after the Latin prayer, "Salve regina"; the small bell, the "follow" bell (*Volgeglocke*); the little bell, the baptismal bell (*Tauffglocke*); and hand-held bells, signal bells (*signirglocklein*) (HSADres, Loc. 1992, fol. 12ʳ, Borna, 1574).

174 For example, Sehling, KOO, 5: 429 (Duchy of Lauenburg, 1585).

175 Sehling, KOO, 14: 173. To this relatively simple text were added in 1577 a selection of complete "admonitions" for the pastors to read, varying, as elsewhere, according to the sex and age of the dead (173–79).

176 ELKAS, A1 Nr. 1 1585, vol. 2, fol. 223. Visitors said that now that there were funeral sermons, such speeches at the grave were not necessary. Because there was nothing objectionable in the message itself, the pastor should gradually wean the people away from this tradition. Similar instances are at ELKAS, A1 Nr. 1 1586, vol. 2, fol. 165; fol. 176; fols. 180–81, where foodstuffs are placed upon the altar for the officiant.

177 Sehling, KOO, 15: 80 (County of Hohenlohe, 1553), for instance.

178 BLHAPot, Pr. Br. Rep. 40A 648, fol. 62 (Salzwedel-Neustadt, 1579).

179 HSAWies, Abt. 171 Nr. D226, fol. 20; Ursula Rohner-Baumberger von Rebstein, *Das Begräbniswesen im calvinistischen Genf* (Basel: Stehlin, 1975), which in general would apply to other Reformed territories. Rohner-Baumberger also summarizes early developments in Zurich and other Swiss lands besides Geneva (11–16).

180 I found only one mention of decorating recent graves with wooden crosses with wreaths hung over them—in the Württemberg village of Linsenhofen in 1601 (B-WHSAS, A281, Büschel 1020, n.p.). During the seventeenth century, this practice undoubtedly spread as death observances became more elaborate.

181 Andreas Musculus, *Gelegenheit, Thun vnd Wesen der Verstorbenen, von jrem Abschied an, aus diesem Leben, bis zum eingang nach gehaltenem Jüngsten Gericht, zum ewigen Leben* (Frankfurt/Oder: Johann Eichorn, 1565), Dⁱᵛ, Dᵛⁱ.

182 On the body's fate in medieval thought, see Caroline Walker Bynum's fine book, *The Resurrection of the Body in Western Christianity, 100–1336* (New York: Columbia University Press, 1995).

183 Peter Metcalf and Richard Huntington, *Celebrations of Death: The Anthropology of Mortuary Ritual*, 2nd ed. (Cambridge and New York: Cambridge University Press, 1991).

184 Arnold van Gennep, *The Rites of Passage*, 146–47.

185 See Paul Barber, *Vampires, Burial, and Death: Folklore and Reality* (New Haven: Yale University Press, 1988), especially the last four chaps., 154–97.

186 "A Contribution to the Study of the Collective Representation of Death," in Robert Hertz, *Death and the Right Hand*, trans. Rodney and Claudia Needham (Glencoe, Ill.: Free Press, 1960), 27–86. Originally published as "Contribution à une étude sur la représentation collective de la mort," *Année sociologique* 10 (1907), 48–137.

187 Hertz, "Collective Representation of Death," 46.

188 A. R. Radcliffe-Brown, *The Andaman Islanders* (New York: Free Press, 1964).

189 Metcalf and Huntington, *Celebrations of Death*, 44. Their entire chapter, "Emotional Reactions to Death, 43–61, is useful.

190 Hans Medick and David Sabean, "Emotionen und materielle Interessen in Familie und Verwandtschaft: Überlegungen zu neuen Wegen und Bereichen einer historischen und sozialanthropologischen Familienforschung," in Medick and Sabean, eds., *Emotionen und materielle Interessen: Sozialanthropologische und historische Beiträge zur Familienforschung* (Göttingen: Vandenhoeck & Ruprecht, 1984), 27–54, here at 30.

191 Metcalf and Huntington, for example, criticize Maurice Bloch and Jonathan Parry as adhering to a reductionist interpretation of ritual as social control (*Celebrations of Death*, 6–8).

192 Catherine Bell, *Ritual Theory, Ritual Practice* (New York and Oxford: Oxford University Press, 1992), 200–04, this quotation at 201. Michel Foucault, *Power/Knowledge: Selected Interviews and Other Writings 1972–77*, ed. Colin Gordon (New York: Pantheon, 1980); and "The Subject and Power," in Hubert L. Dreyfus and Paul Rabinow, eds., *Michel Foucault: Beyond Structuralism and Hermeneutics*, 2nd ed. (Chicago: University of Chicago Press, 1983), 208–26.

6 RITUAL CHANGE: CONCLUSIONS

1 Hessisches Hauptstaatsarchiv Wiesbaden (HSAWies), Abt. 171 Nr. D245, "Protocollum Generalis Visitationis Aller Pastoreÿenn Vnnd darin gehörender Capellen in der Graueschafft Dietzs gehaltenn Anno 1590," fol. 107. The Genevan consistory may rightly have been especially concerned to oversee women's religious beliefs and practice (Jeffrey R. Watt, "Women and the Consistory in Calvin's Geneva," *Sixteenth Century Journal* 24, 2 [1993], 429–39).

2 I do not intend to echo the conclusion of Gerald Strauss in *Luther's House of Learning: Indoctrination of the Young in the German Reformation* (Baltimore: Johns Hopkins University Press, 1978), which has given rise to much debate. Strauss takes his study to about mid-century, or the death of Martin Luther, noting that at that time leading Reformers perceived that they had not achieved their desired end of conversion. My own investigation takes in the period up to the outbreak of the Thirty Years' War, and within that expanse it appears wholly unrealistic of Luther and his followers to have expected to convert Germany to their way of thinking. Luther was discouraged that the Word of God had not worked the transformations he had hoped for. In the longer term, however, those in authority most assuredly won a good deal of outward conformity to their ordinances. I am speaking of failure with regard to *inward* acceptance of the values pressed upon them by the clergy and secular officials, and I am thinking of acceptance in anthropological as well as moral terms.

3 Bloch, "The Ritual of the Royal Bath in Madagascar," in David Cannadine and Simon Price, eds., *Rituals of Royalty: Power and Ceremonial in Traditional Societies* (Cambridge, England: Cambridge University Press, 1987), 271–97; "Symbols, Song, Dance and Features of Articulation: Is Religion an Extreme Form of Traditional Authority?" *Archives Européenes de Sociologie* 15 (1974), 55–81.

4 Bell, "The Power of Ritualization," in idem, *Ritual Theory, Ritual Practice* (New York and Oxford, England: Oxford University Press, 1992), 197–223.

5 Bob Scribner has used the phrase "paraliturgical ritual" with reference to nonessential elaboration of official liturgy ("Ritual and Popular Religion in Catholic Germany at the Time of the Reformation," in idem, *Popular Culture and Popular Movements in Reformation Germany* (London and Ronceverte:

Hambledon Press, 1987), 17–47, here at 22. This is a fascinating and useful essay, delineating several categories of popular ritual, but I do not find one that quite conveys my meaning: the celebration of life events that were worthy of societal notice before as after the advent of Christianity. Christianity attempted to incorporate and alter them but never entirely succeeded.

6 See Martin Brecht, "Lutherische Kirchenzucht bis in die Anfänge des 17. Jahrhunderts im Spannungsfeld von Pfarramt und Gesellschaft," in Hans-Christoph Rublack, ed., *Die lutherische Konfessionalisierung in Deutschland* Schriften des Vereins für Reformationsgeschichte 197 (Gütersloh: Gerd Mohn, 1992), 400–20.

7 John Bossy, "The Mass as a Social Institution, 1200–1700," *Past and Present* 100 (August 1983), 60–61. Cf. Richard van Dülmen, *Kultur und Alltag in der Frühen Neuzeit*, vol. 3, *Religion, Magie, Aufklärung* (Munich: C. H. Beck, 1994), 63–65.

8 For the perspective of one hymnbook author, see Elsie Anne McKee, *Reforming Popular Piety in Sixteenth-century Strasbourg: Katharina Schütz Zell and Her Hymnbook*, Studies in Reformed Theology and History 2, 4 (Princeton: Princeton Theological Seminary, 1994).

9 Karlheinz Blaschke, *Historisches Ortsverzeichnis von Sachsen* (Leipzig: Bibliographisches Institut, 1957); Helmar Junghans, *Wittenberg als Lutherstadt* (Berlin: Union Verlag, 1979), 74–75.

10 Manfred Hannemann, *The Diffusion of the Reformation in Southwestern Germany, 1518–1534* (Chicago: University of Chicago Department of Geography, 1975).

11 Sächsisches Hauptstaatsarchiv Dresden (HSADres), Loc. 10598, "Registration der Visitation etlicher Ssächsischen und Meißnischen Kreise, Ämter, Städte, Klöster u. Dörfer 1929 [actually goes to 1531]," fol. 34. I give additional examples in "Neoclericalism and Anticlericalism in Saxony, 1555–1675," *Journal of Interdisciplinary History* 24, 4 (Spring 1994), 628.

12 Keith Moxey, "Festive Peasants and the Social Order," in idem, *Peasants, Warriors, and Wives: Popular Imagery in the Reformation* (Chicago: University of Chicago Press, 1989), 67–100.

13 Bakhtin, *Rabelais and His World*, trans. Hélène Iswolsky (Bloomington, Ind.: Indiana University Press, 1984), esp. 59–144.

14 Scribner, "Reformation, Carnival and the World Turned Upside-down," *Social History* 3 (1978), 234–64; reprinted in idem, *Popular Culture and Popular Movements*, 71–101.

15 Schindler, "Karneval, Kirche und die verkehrte Welt: Zur Funktion der Lachkultur im 16. Jahrhundert," *Jahrbuch für Volkskunde* (1985), 9–57, reprinted in idem, *Widerspenstige Leute: Studien zur Volkskultur in der frühen Neuzeit* (Frankfurt/Main: Fischer, 1992), 121–74, esp. 151–74; Dietz-Rüdiger Moser, with whom Schindler has not been gentle, has taken a contrasting position in his ongoing work on *Fastnacht*, but he is gratuitously *ad hominem* in "Lachkultur des Mittelalters? Michael Bachtin und die Folgen seiner Theorie," *Euphorion: Zeitschrift für Literaturgeschichte* 84 (1990), 89–111, his attack on Schindler at 110; see also Heidy Greco-Kaufmann, "*Kampf des Karnevals gegen die Fasten*: Pieter Bruegels Gemälde und die Diskussion um Karneval und Lachkultur," *Euphorion: Zeitschrift für Literaturgeschichte* 86 (1992), 319–32; and Rainer Stollman, "Lachen, Freiheit, und Geschichte," *Jahrbuch für internationale Germanistik* 20, 2 (1988), 25–43.

16 Klaniczay, "The Carnival Spirit: Bakhtin's Theory on the Culture of Popular Laughter," in idem, *The Uses of Supernatural Power*, ed. Karen Margolis,

trans. Susan Singerman (Princeton, N.J.: Princeton University Press, 1990), 10–27, here at 13.
17 Wandel, *Voracious Idols and Violent Hands: Iconoclasm in Reformation Zurich, Strasbourg, and Basel* (Cambridge, England: Cambridge University Press, 1995), 1–9, including her summary of the recent literature. Wandel believes that this oversimplistic model robs the people of agency including the ability to shape the Reform movement (3).
18 Valerie J. Flint, *The Rise of Magic in Early Medieval Europe* (Princeton, N.J.: Princeton University Press, 1991). Needless to say, the earliest Christian presence decried such practices and hardly accorded them the status of religion.
19 Labouvie, "Wider Wahrsagerei, Segnerei und Zauberei: Kirchliche Versuche zur Ausgrenzung von Aberglaube und Volksmagie seit dem 16. Jahrhundert," in Richard van Dülmen, ed., *Verbrechen, Strafen und soziale Kontrolle: Studien zur historischen Kulturforschung* (Frankfurt/Main: Fischer, 1990), 15–55, here at 23.

Index